Secondary/
Middle School
Teaching

Secondary/ Middle School Teaching: a Handbook for Beginning Teachers and Teacher Self-Renewal

Kenneth H. Hoover
ARIZONA STATE UNIVERSITY

ALLYN AND BACON, INC.
Boston London Sydney

Copyright © 1977 by Allyn and Bacon, Inc.,
470 Atlantic Avenue, Boston, Massachusetts 02210.

LIBRARY OF CONGRESS CATALOGING IN PUBLICATION DATA

Hoover, Kenneth H
   Secondary/middle school teaching.

   Includes bibliographies and index.
   1. High school teaching. 2. Middle schools.
I. Title.
LB1607.H68   373.1'1'02   76-47027
ISBN 0-205-05588-5

To my teen-aged daughter, Rana, who inadvertently called my attention

to the need for structured learning experiences

Contents

Preface

The art of teaching is mastered slowly over a period of time. Thus a probationary period of about three years is common for beginning teachers. Until recently such teachers were all too often left to their own resources. By conferring with experienced teachers in the school the new teacher sometimes was helped over the "rough" spots. It is generally recognized, however, that what "works" for one teacher will not necessarily succeed for another.

Currently there is a decided trend toward the development of planned programs for new teachers. It is now recognized that even the best pre-service experiences often need supplementing with a field-based program. In many instances the colleges and universities are cooperating with local schools in developing such programs. Sometimes this entails classes or small groups; occasionally the approach may be wholly individualized. Whatever the system, there is a demand for competency-based experiences to help the beginning teacher become a truly professional teacher and educator. In accomplishing this task, some sort of delivery system is essential. Such is the basic function of this book.

The term *new or beginning teacher*, as used in this manual, applies to those who are about to move into the field of teaching (pre-service teachers), those who are still on probationary status, and those who are moving into new subject areas or into other new teaching situations. Thus this manual may also find a place in in-service workshops, teacher centers featuring instruction for both pre-service and in-service teachers, and general methods classes featuring performance activities. It should be especially useful when conventional classes have been combined with an on-site (field) approach to teacher education.

The manual consists of six modules, each divided into two or three *learning activity packages* (LAPs). The user may elect to proceed through each module in turn or to complete one or more of the modules independently. All are somewhat self-instructional. Their use can be immensely facilitated, however, if they are used in conjunction with the author's *The Professional Teacher's Handbook*, 2nd ed. (Allyn and Bacon, Inc., 1976), or with selected supplementary sources, listed at the end of each LAP.

The learning activities of each LAP culminate in practice in actual class situations or (as an option) in realistically contrived simulated situations. Such experiences usually call for small-group activities. Although committee groups are desirable, an individual working alone also can profit from the experiences. As an optional activity, direct observation of teachers in the field is planned. If conditions warrant, such observational experiences might well be advanced to the required level. An accuracy level of approximately 90 percent has been established. The instructor or workshop director will soon recognize, however, that considerable leeway must be provided for interpreting student responses. In most cases the idea is emphasized, rather than specific facts.

The task of reducing the complexities of instructional method to a series of LAPs has been a formidable one. Thus only the basics are emphasized. Moreover, the reader will readily note that not all methods and techniques have been treated. If such gaps can be bridged through conventional instruction, however, this manual for the first time essentially places instructional methods on a sound self-instructional basis. As in any initial adventure, systematic feedback is needed if improvement and refinement are to be effected. The writer or the publisher may be contacted for this purpose.

Kenneth H. Hoover

A Note to the Student

This manual is basically a self-instructional tool for treating broad instructional methods and techniques. Each LAP features a) a rationale or justification for studying the methods and techniques; b) an overview, consisting of basic concepts and new terms; c) specific competencies (expressed as behavioral objectives) which you should achieve and demonstrate; d) a preliminary reading section for background information; e) Preassessment items to help you gain an overall perspective and frame of reference for the experience; f) learning experiences and self-assessment items, to help you develop these needed competencies; g) optional experiences and self-assessment items, if needed; and h) a posttest to help you assess your final competency level. A minimum competency level of 85 to 90 percent has been established. The LAPs, organized into modules, can be used as a total package or independently. Their use can be facilitated if they are utilized in conjunction with the author's *The Professional Teacher's Handbook*, 2nd ed. (Allyn and Bacon, Inc., 1976), or with the selected supplementary references listed at the end of each LAP.

You will find answers to all Preassessment items, self-assessment items, and post-tests at the end of each LAP. In effect, all tests serve as essential learning experiences. It is imperative that you answer items fully *before* checking answers. Be sure to study supporting reasons for all selection-type items in the Preassessment items and posttests. It is recommended that you study each LAP through, including the preliminary reading section, take the Preassessment items, study the Preassessment answers provided at the end of the LAP, and then complete the LAP as directed.

You will note that each LAP culminates in some sort of actual practice. Flexibility is provided, however, for those who are working alone as well as for those who find themselves in workshop, class, or classlike groups. In addition, options are furnished for those who are teaching and also for those who are not teaching or who do not have immediate access to students. Each learning experience is usually followed by a critique in the small-group context. Individual (as opposed to group) performance is emphasized, however. In some cases you will not fully agree with the writer's answers to the self-assessment items. (In the area of instructional methodology, precise answers frequently are impossible.) This situation in itself may be a useful departure for further learning as members of your group interact. You will note that the optional items frequently call for direct observation or visitation of actual classes and teachers. You will find that, on occasion, not all of your group will agree with the writer's points of emphasis. Again, this should provide a basis for more in-depth analysis. The supplementary reading references should be useful in this connection.

Although the LAPs, of necessity, feature certain steps and sequences, in some cases the arrangement is somewhat arbitrary. What is essential is that a broad framework of reflective processes be employed. The materials in this manual are based on the assumption that learning is essentially a process of problem solving. Instructional methods and techniques are viewed as different approaches to this process. Some techniques do not complete the entire problem-solving process and thus in practice must be combined and supplemented with other techniques. This is just one of the gaps that is not readily apparent in this manual and partially accounts for the fact that teaching, ultimately, is to some extent a personal invention often involving considerable creativity.

As you work through these modules and LAPs, unforeseen problems and difficulties will emerge. By communicating fully with your principal, workshop director, instructor, or supervisor, the writer and the publisher can be provided much needed feedback for improving this self-instructional approach to instructional methodology.

Kenneth H. Hoover

Secondary/
Middle School
Teaching

module
I

PREINSTRUCTIONAL EXPERIENCES

Effective teaching represents the culmination of a series of preparatory activities. Long hours of careful preparation often go into one class period. In setting the stage for instruction, the teacher must be a skillful predictor of events. Knowledge of students and a thorough knowledge of the subject field are necessary prerequisites to instructional excellence. Yet, of themselves, they are inadequate. The professional competence of a teacher ultimately rests on his or her ability to anticipate student needs and behaviors *in advance* of the actual experience. Instructional preparation, then, involves applied imagination in planning for the experience. Such is the subject of the LAPs in this module.

Instructional methods and techniques are designed to facilitate the teaching of content. One may teach algebra, American history, biology, or a foreign language. What aspects of such courses should be emphasized? As facts are quickly forgotten they should be emphasized as means rather than as ends. The first LAP in this module provides a technique for organizing content around basic concepts or ideas. Since concepts transfer readily from one situation to another, they become the foundations of all instruction.

Once basic concepts have been identified, instructional aims or purposes can be developed. The teacher, in establishing educational direction, focuses upon unit and lesson aims or goals. When purpose has been determined, the rest of the instructional process begins to take shape. The key to effective planning and to effective teaching is the formulation of goals in behavioral terms. These techniques are treated in LAP 2.

Long- and short-range planning, discussed in LAP 3, remains a controversial

1

instructional issue. The issue is not whether or not one should plan; rather, it is the nature and the extent of planning necessary. There are effective teachers who prefer an unstructured classroom experience just as there are those who insist on a highly structured classroom experience. Both extremes can be beneficial in certain situations, depending upon the particular objectives involved. When lesson planning is viewed as a problem-solving experience, the dilemma becomes much less ambiguous. Each person must resolve his or her problems in his or her own way. Planning needs will vary with each instructor and with each learning experience. Aside from the lesson objective, some teachers will need the psychological security of thoroughly developed lesson plans; other teachers will feel limited or boxed in with detailed lesson plans.

In an effort to provide a basis for the extreme needs associated with lesson planning, detailed long- and short-range planning techniques are offered. Every teacher needs some experience in detailed unit and lesson planning. Just as a beginning lawyer relies heavily upon his debate brief, so does a beginning teacher need the benefit of elaborate planning. As the lawyer gains experience, he tends to carry an increasing amount of the debate brief in his head. The same holds true for experienced teachers. The precise amount of written planning necessary must be decided by each teacher *in each teaching situation.* In the final analysis, the essential function of planning is to set the stage for learning. In a sense it is a dress rehearsal for the real thing. Even the best-laid plans go awry. Nevertheless, the mere act of planning can prepare one for the unexpected.

lap
1

Formulating Concepts

RATIONALE. The mental images we carry around in our heads are known as concepts. A concept is a mental picture of an object, event, or relationship derived from experience. Concepts help us classify or analyze; they help us associate or combine as well. These mental images gain meaning from subsequent experiences. As meaning becomes fully established, we develop feelings about an idea or concept.

In the educative process, concepts are thought to form the basic structure of content areas. An understanding of the structural dimensions of a field of knowledge provides the learner with a frame of reference for thinking and for evaluating future experiences. Although facts traditionally have been emphasized in teaching, often they are quickly forgotten. Facts are most appropriately emphasized as a means of teaching concepts, the major residue of learning.

OVERVIEW

Key Concepts

1. Instructional concepts exist at different levels.
2. Course concepts (often known as unit titles) and unit concepts are derived by the teacher in preinstructional activities.
3. Unit concepts, usually phrased as simple, declarative statements, provide the basic structure of the teaching unit.
4. Lesson concepts (generalizations) are derived by students as a culmination of the learning experience.

3

5. Factual materials provide the necessary background data essential for derivation of concepts.

New Terms

1. Unit (LAP, module, mini-course) titles: Derived from broad course concepts, unit titles often consist of two dimensions: (1) An indication of content and (2) some indication of the major thrust or emphasis anticipated.

2. Unit concepts: Basic centralized ideas (structural properties) of a unit from which all other aspects of instruction evolve. Unit concepts suggest real-life applications.

3. Lesson generalizations: The culmination of each lesson. Derived by students, lesson generalizations collectively embody the unit concept upon which the lesson rests.

OBJECTIVES. After this experience you should be able to develop appropriate unit titles and their supporting (unit and lesson) concepts, as evidenced by your ability to:

1. List three essential characteristics of unit concepts.

2. Distinguish between a unit title, a unit concept, and a lesson generalization in eight of nine instances from a provided list.

3. Select eight out of nine appropriately stated unit concepts from a provided list of twenty assorted statements.

4. Construct three unit concepts when provided with broad topics.

PRELIMINARY READING. Since the elements of instructional methodology are somewhat variable, the following excerpts are provided to help you develop a frame of reference as a point of departure for this experience. If you prefer, you may proceed directly to the preassessment items.

Unit Titles

Once the broad content areas are identified, they will be developed into appropriate unit titles. A unit consists of a group of related concepts. Each unit (LAP, module, mini-course) title calls attention to the content area and *also to the major unit thrust or focus for the unit.* This thrust or focus serves as a constant reminder of the major reason for teaching a given unit. Thus it will suggest a real-life application. In deciding upon a major unit thrust or focus, the teacher must ask this question: "Why should this unit be taught? It is only after the teacher can provide some practical, real-life applications, *immediate to the lives of students,* that he or she is ready to proceed further with planning activities.

Each subject area has its own specific requirements. In American literature, for example, the content area involving the study of Julius Caesar might be focused on the unit theme (thrust or focus) of *Ambition*. Thus the unit title might be *Julius Caesar: Ambitious to a Fault*. Such a unit appropriately would begin with a study of contemporary issues of vital concern to young people. Stress would be placed upon development of concepts of ambition and the characteristics that compose it. Julius Caesar would provide a basic content reference; indeed the unit likely would culminate in an intensive study of Julius Caesar. Thus content emphasis is shifted from subject matter as an end in itself to its appropriate place as a means to attainment of more basic learnings. Other *thematic* unit thrusts might be *Frustration, Loneliness, Death*. Some unit titles in English, however, might be *topical* in nature, such as *Grammar: Efficient Written Communication*. In the latter illustration, the title serves as a reminder that the unit focus will be on the easy, practical conveying of one's thoughts in writing. Unit titles in several different subject areas will suggest a variety of unit functions.

History: The Roosevelt Era: A Socialistic Trend.

Home Economics: Clothing: Improving Your Personal Appearance.

Industrial Arts: Sketching: A Gateway to Good Design.

Art: Line: Capturing Movement.

Physical Education: Team Sports: Cooperative Relationships.

Chemistry: Carbon: The Chemistry of Life.

Mathematics: Set Theory: Understanding Relationships.

Business: Economic Losses: Protection through Insurance.

Humanities: The Arts in Ancient Greece: Idealism as a Guide to Behavior.

Biology: Body Systems: Interdependency Functions.

Foreign Language: The Spanish Alphabet: English Parallels.

Unit Concepts

Each unit, in turn, is broken into six or eight unit concepts. Based upon content, they provide the basic threads of a unit. Stating them specifically, *in advance of the instructional experience*, provides direction to the unit and insures that none of the important threads will be omitted. It is usually best to state each concept in a simple, declarative statement form. Again, a current-life application is essential. In many subject areas it is relatively easy to meet the criterion of current-life application. In a few subject areas, however, this is a rather complicated, but nevertheless essential task. In history (or any unit of a historical nature), for example, a two-step process seems necessary. First, one must identify the major content ideas of the unit, then expand into concepts that are viable today. Without the second step, history teaching is likely to remain the dry and generally useless process of memorizing names, dates, and places.

The following illustration is based upon a unit in United States history entitled *World War I: To Make the World Safe for Democracy.*

Content Ideas

1. Wilson's personal belief that democracy could save all mankind greatly affected the U.S. and its involvement in World War I.

2. The timing of America's entrance into World War I was related to its isolationist policy.

3. Wilson's idea of peace without victory was impractical.

Major Unit Concepts

1. The misleading notion (even today) that democracy can save all mankind was popularized by Woodrow Wilson.

2. Isolation and lack of communication, whether between nations or individuals, lead to inevitable conflict.

3. Peace without victory may set the stage for later conflict.

It is seen from the foregoing that major United States history concepts are derived from ideas that are specific to a given era of history. Some unit concepts will occur again and again as the student studies other history units. In this way the learner can become aware of the repetition of diplomatic errors, etc. New concepts, of course, will be emphasized in each subsequent unit.

In other subject fields the task of concept identification often is complicated by textbook organization. In American literature, for example, textbook content may be organized around broad topics of literary forms, historical themes, and the like. A historical theme on Colonial America, for example, offers the reader numerous selections, each with its own story theme. The teacher's task, again, is twofold in nature. First, he or she must identify major unit themes (e.g., major threads of thought that occur repeatedly), then identify the particular selections that can be used in teaching each given concept.

Unit concept illustrations in other subject fields follow.

Industrial Arts: Accuracy in measuring affects the work of those who must interpret meaning from a drawing.

American Literature: Realities of life are not always consistent with ideals.

Home Economics: Fabric content determines what can be made from a selected fabric.

Physical Education: One must be physically active to achieve a high level of physical fitness.

Chemistry: Sugars and starches are products of natural organic chemical processes.

Humanities: Idealism can result if a society believes that there is a rational order to the universe.

Health: Many aspects of health are personal; others are community problems.

Mathematics: Sets can unite, intersect, or have differences.

Art: Inspiration for design can be found in almost everything in our environment.

Lesson Generalizations

Each lesson is based upon a unit concept previously identified by the teacher. A lesson culminates in the derivation of a number of important generalizations (concepts). Lesson generalizations should be derived *by students* as an outgrowth of a given experience. Collectively they will embody the unit concept. Thus a lesson generalization is more specific than a unit concept. To illustrate from a lesson on health:

> *Unit concept:* Use of drugs may permanently damage an individual's health and well-being.
>
> *Lesson generalizations:*
>
> 1. LSD users may incur permanent brain damage.
>
> 2. While under the influence of LSD, a person loses his or her ability to distinguish between reality and fantasy.
>
> 3. Use of LSD may render an individual emotionally dependent upon the drug.

Although generalizations can be derived by students in a number of ways, some authorities insist that they be written out. In this manner the teacher is able to provide assistance to those who are experiencing difficulty. In many practical situations, teachers find it convenient to let students evolve generalizations through a culminating class discussion. Usually the more able students will quickly formulate key lesson generalizations. When they are placed on the chalkboard, the less able students may write them out in their notes and then later memorize for a test. Understanding may be partially or totally lacking. As a safeguard, considerable probing is necessary. Such experiences cannot be rushed.

PREASSESSMENT ITEMS (answers provided on pp. 15–16)

This experience is designed to help you gain an overall perspective of how concepts are used in teaching. After completing the items, turn to the end of this LAP and check your answers. Note that answers (both correct and incorrect) are generally provided with supporting reasons to guide your efforts as you work through the LAP.

> A. List three essential characteristics of an appropriate unit concept.
> (To illustrate: A unit concept suggests a real-life application.)
>
> 1.
>
> 2.
>
> 3.
>
> B. Place the following code letters before each of the following nine listed statements:
>
> C - Course concept (unit title)
>
> U - Unit concept
>
> L - Lesson generalization

1. Man's alienation from man.

2. Power often rests in the hands of a select few.

3. Love is a basic human emotion.

4. Competition is a driving force that may lead to unusual achievement.

5. The poor, uneducated individual often does not understand the extent of his rights.

6. An accused indigent (pauper) is entitled to a court-appointed public defender.

7. The law, protector of human rights.

8. Justice is blind, showing no preference for one's station in life.

9. Unbridled ambition leads to disgrace and destruction.

C. From the following list of "concepts," place a check (√) by nine of those that meet the criteria of an appropriately stated *unit* concept.

1. Is reward for courageous acts a true indication of courage?

2. One who admits his mistake and places himself at the mercy of the court is a courageous individual.

3. Tales of courage provide the basis for many myths and legends.

4. Standing up for your rights in a hostile group demands courage.

5. President Truman's decision to order the use of the atomic bomb was an act of courage.

6. Courage is displayed in many ways.

7. Courage essentially is the willingness to take a stand in the face of adversity.

8. Definitions of courage change from culture to culture.

9. Can a coward be courageous?

10. Determination of a courageous act is assessed in terms of one's motivation at the time the act was committed.

11. Young men who refused to fight in the Vietnam conflict had to exercise considerable courage.

12. Courage represents a basic characteristic of man's behavior.

13. The colonists who came to settle a harsh, new land were courageous.

14. Was the cave man as courageous as today's man in our complex society?

15. Courage is closely associated with the emotion of fear.

16. Risking one's life in time of war represents courage at its best.

17. Courage is closely associated with perceptions of the consequences of one's behavior.

18. Courage demands some overt act.

19. Courage is relative to the individual.

20. Self-defense is an act of courage.

D. Prepare one unit concept for each of the listed topics.

    1. Drug abuse.

    2. Revolutionary War.

    3. First aid.

If you were able to correctly provide twenty-two of the twenty-four requested responses, you are to be congratulated. In this case it is likely that you already possess the necessary competency in the area. Thus you should proceed directly to the LAP on Instructional Objectives. Even if you were able to provide only a few of the answers, you should not be dismayed, as the following learning activities are designed to help you quickly achieve mastery in the area.

LEARNING ACTIVITIES

Work through each learning activity, complete the self-assessment items, and check your answers before moving to the next one. Note that the last learning activity is optional, depending upon your needs and situation at that point. You should be able to complete this LAP in about three hours.

A: *Read.* Re-examine the overview and the preliminary reading sections of this LAP and examine the brief case that follows. You will broaden your understanding substantially by studying Chap. 1 of *The Professional Teacher's Handbook*, 2nd ed., and/or by studying the selected references for this module.* Note specifically the following points:

1. The difference between a fact and a concept.

2. How the thrust of a unit title sets the stage for development of unit concepts.

3. The two-step nature of developing appropriate unit concepts in history or units of a historical nature.

4. Differences between a unit concept and a lesson generalization.

CASE: CONTRASTING POINTS OF VIEW

Students in Mr. Tompkin's American Problems class were to do an investigation of the facts and events associated with some of our American heroes. They were instructed to determine, if possible, how these individuals differed from ordinary people in such a way as to contribute to greatness. Selection was left to the student so long as it was restricted to early American heroes. Considerable supporting data were expected. The project was to run for three weeks.

Mike Williams decided to write about General Custer. He entitled

In some cases The Professional Teacher's Handbook, 2nd ed., and the abridged edition of The Professional Teacher's Handbook are referred to merely as the Hoover texts.

his paper *George Armstrong Custer: An American Hero?* As he dug into the problem, Mike began to note certain fallacies associated with the Battle of the Little Bighorn. This spurred him to greater effort. In fact, he became totally involved in the task, going to great lengths to examine his hypothesis that Custer probably was not a hero at all. Mike wrote and rewrote his paper several times, being careful to document his points carefully. He was happy with the paper and rather looked forward to Mr. Tompkin's reactions.

Mr. Tompkin was more than a little disturbed by Mike's paper. Instead of supplying evidence that contributed to greatness, Mike had apparently attempted to discredit the man. Although he awarded Mike a "C" for his efforts, he carefully pointed out the things he saw wrong with the point of view developed.

When Mike saw his mark and comments (in red ink), he was extremely disappointed. He had really worked and gotten involved on this paper. "What does the teacher want?" he wondered. "Is it right or ethical to immortalize an individual as a hero who really had 'feet of clay'?" He wondered if he would bother to return to class.

Self-assessment Items (answers provided on p. 17)

1. Distinguish between a fact and a concept.

2. Using the recent American conflict in Vietnam as an example, develop three different thrusts for a unit title.

3. Using history (or a historical unit in your subject field) as a frame of reference, write out a major content idea and then follow with a statement of the concept.

4. Students occasionally may evolve the unit concept as one of their lesson generalizations. Defend or refute.

5. Based upon the above case, write a basic concept of a hero *from Mike's point of view.* Now write another concept of a hero *from Mr. Tompkin's point of view.*

At this point you may select either Option B_1 or Option B_2, depending upon your particular situation. Those who are presently teaching should select Option B_1. Those who are not teaching or who do not have immediate access to students should select Option B_2.

Option B_1: *Examination of concept models.* The objective of this experience is to provide you with an opportunity to observe correct models of concept development at different levels. The experiences may vary somewhat, depending upon prevailing local conditions.

First, the concept illustrations section in Chap. 1 of *The Professional Teacher's Handbook,* 2nd ed., may be examined.

From a number of teachers who base their instruction on concepts, it may be possible to obtain lists from different fields of specialization.

Your supervisor may be prepared to supply his/her own list of concepts, or it may

be that a film or videotaped presentation of concept development can be found.*
Sometimes curriculum guides may be useful in this respect.

It is important to note differences between the provided illustrations and the
model offered in this LAP.

Working in a committee of three, if possible, direct your attention to the following
points:

1. Problems associated with developing meaning from complex unit
   concepts.

2. The relative predominance of different concept types (classificational,
   correlational, theoretical) in different subject areas.

3. The recurring nature of concepts from unit to unit.

4. The characteristics of a vague unit concept as opposed to a specifically
   stated one.

Self-assessment Items (answers provided on p. 17)

1. Explain why complex statements of concepts should be avoided.

2. "The social science teacher normally would be expected to emphasize
   theoretical concepts, whereas the science teacher would likely stress
   classificational and correlational concepts." Defend or refute.

3. Certain concepts have been observed to come up again and again in
   certain courses. How should this be handled?

4. "Correct table-setting is important." Rework this concept to make it
   more meaningful.

Option B$_2$: *Preliminary application and comparison.* At this point you should test
your initial ability to prepare concepts at different levels. Then compare with supplied
models.
Use the theme *Ambition* for this experience.

1. Write out three unit concepts.

   a.

   b.

   c.

2. Construct two lesson generalizations for one of these.

   a.

   b.

---

*One such film entitled "Concept Formation: Intermediate Level" is available
from Addison-Wesley Publishing Co., Inc., Off South Street, Reading, Mass.
01867.

3. Now refer to the concept illustrations provided in the Hoover methods texts (Chap. 1) or other selected references.

   a. How do your unit concepts and lesson generalizations differ from the provided illustrations?

   b. Would you consider these differences basic or merely a matter of focus and style?

Prepare a short paragraph describing how unit and lesson concepts differ.

Self-assessment Items (answers provided on p. 17)

1. Using your lesson generalizations and unit concepts from the foregoing exercise, derive a unit thrust from the theme provided (Ambition).

2. "In some cases a unit concept may be identical to a lesson generalization." Defend or refute.

C: *Concept application.*   Using a course in your major field of specialization, construct concepts as follows:

1. For every unit develop a unit title (a unit normally ranges from three to six weeks in length).

2. Develop six to ten unit concepts for one of your selected units.

3. Evaluate your unit concepts based on the list of characteristics provided in problem A of the Preassessment items (see p. 7).

If possible, discuss your problems with other prospective teachers in different fields who have completed this task. (Sometimes such materials are made available through a resource center.) Focus attention on the following points:

1. Why the thrust of the unit title may be better interpreted as "purpose" in some fields.

2. The impact of using past tense in concept development.

3. The importance of including (or implying) a real-life application for each concept.

Self-assessment Items (answers provided on p. 17)

1. Why is the major thrust of a unit title often more critical in such classes as history, political science, and literature than it is in such classes as mathematics or art?

2. Why is the practice of phrasing concepts in past tense to be avoided?

3. What role does a "real-life application" play in the phraseology of the concept?

If, after reviewing your learning activities for this LAP, you feel that you can meet the stated objectives, proceed to the posttest. If not, you should complete the optional activity. Note that it provides for a number of optional situations, depending upon your own individual circumstances.

Optional Activity

D: *Class observation and visit with experienced teachers.* Visit an actual class or classes in your field of specialization. (If possible, also arrange to visit a teacher in some other field of specialization.*) Proceed as follows:

1. Compile a list of generalizations that seem evident from your observation. (In some cases these will be evolved orally by students; in other cases it will be necessary for you to construct your own generalizations, based on the experience.)

2. Now attempt to formulate the basic unit concept(s) upon which the lesson rests.

3. If possible, ask the teacher to identify for you the "major idea behind the lesson."

4. In a sentence or two, attempt to account for differences between the teacher's ideas and yours relative to the nature of the major (unit) concept of the lesson.

Self-assessment Items (answers provided on p. 18)

(1) "A unit concept (upon which the lesson rests) worded in the present tense promotes real-life applications of the lesson." Defend or refute.

(2) "Unit and lesson concepts are more practical in some subject areas than in others." Defend or refute.

(3) Why is it deemed important for students themselves to evolve generalizations from a lesson?

(4) "Vaguely conceived unit concepts contribute to vague lessons." Defend or refute.

POSTTEST (answers provided on pp. 18–19)

After you have completed the learning activities, complete the posttest and evaluate by checking your answers at the end of this LAP.

A. List three essential characteristics of an appropriate concept.

1.

2.

3.

---

*A *live or videotaped simulation of an actual class offers another alternative for completing this activity.*

B. Place the following code letters before each of the following nine listed statements:

C - Unit title (course concept)

U - Unit concept

L - Lesson generalization

1. Too much reform at once often leads to turmoil.

2. Organized labor: The working man speaks.

3. Spiraling inflation is especially damaging to those living on fixed incomes.

4. The Jacksonian Era: Rise of the common man.

5. The two-party political system is threatened by splinter parties with a common cause.

6. Economic stresses tend to work against the party in power.

7. The war to end all wars.

8. Unskilled service workers find it difficult to improve their lot through organized labor unions.

9. Colonial America: Birth of a new culture.

C. From the list of "concepts," place a check (√) by nine of those you feel meet the criteria of an appropriately stated *unit* concept.

1. Freedman schools were established by zealous Northerners in the South following the Civil War.

2. A substantial number of the Southern whites were disenfranchised following the Civil War.

3. Should a conqueror be permitted to force his will on the conquered?

4. Private schools that emphasize a given point of view are tolerated in our society.

5. The Republican Party in the 1860s was a sectional political party.

6. Our nation has consistently provided assistance to conquered nations in an effort to maintain future peaceful relations.

7. Certain basic principles cannot be compromised.

8. Compulsory arbitration means that the disputing parties must abide by the recommendations of a third party.

9. Basic human rights apply equally to all citizens of our society.

10. The Civil War Amendments to the Constitution extend basic human rights.

11. The state of West Virginia was created in violation of the Constitution.

12. Law represents the will of the people.

13. Should the Supreme Court, in effect, make law through its decisions?

14. The federal government is responsible for restoring order when efforts of the states fail.

15. Peaceful demonstrations are accepted in our nation as a form of communication.

16. Andrew Johnson, like some other Presidents, was unable to control his political opponents.

17. The poor seldom appreciate charitable contributions.

18. Splinter parties in this nation seldom wield much influence since they are usually based on local issues.

19. The South was at the mercy of her Northern conquerors.

20. The time tends to produce needed military leaders.

D. Develop one unit concept for each of the listed topics.

1. Triangles

2. Meal Planning

3. Détente between the Superpowers

Your successful completion of this LAP calls for definite congratulations. Translating facts and theory into practical, teachable concepts is a monumental task. Even if you failed to reach the recommended criterion of 85 to 90 percent accuracy (about twenty-one out of twenty-four requested responses), proceed to the LAP on Instructional Objectives. You probably will find that the close relationship between these two LAPs will further clarify any remaining misconceptions. Good luck!

ANSWERS TO PREASSESSMENT ITEMS

You can make the Preassessment items a most valuable learning experience by studying the provided reasons for both correct and incorrect responses. You will note also that since Part A has no specific number of correct responses, several additional points (characteristics) are provided. Since the last series of questions calls for your constructed answers, they are not expected to be identical to those supplied by the author. Such feedback, however, can considerably enhance your understanding.

A. 1. Suggests a real-life application.

2. Stated in present tense.

3. Restricted to one basic idea.

4. In statement form.

5. Ties into the major thrust or focus of the unit.

6. Is based upon the user's frame of reference.

7. Is part of a basic idea.

B. 1–C. This is a major theme.

2–U. Describes a major attribute of an idea (power).

3–C. Describes a basic idea.

4–U. Suggests one direction (of many) that the basic idea (competition) may take.

5–L. A specific idea.

6–L. Refers to one specific right (among many) of an accused indigent.

7–C. Contains a basic idea, along with a basic thrust.

8–U. Provides an attribute of the basic idea (justice).

9–U. Provides an idea (among several) that tie in with a more basic idea (ambition).

C. 3, 6, 8, 10, 12, 15, 17, 18, 19. (Each provides an attribute of a central idea that ties in with the present.)
Reasons for rejected "concepts" from the list.

1 (In question form.)

2 (Too specific; describes courage based upon a specific situation.)

4 (Based upon a specific situation.)

5 (Based upon a specific situation.)

7 (More of a definition than an attribute.)

9 (In question form.)

11 (Based upon a specific situation; thus more of a lesson generalization.)

13 (Too specific.)

14 (In question form; also based on a specific situation.)

16 (Too specific.)

20 (Deals with a specific situation.)

D. *Examples*

1. Hard drug use is damaging to one's health.

2. People resent the presence of an outside power if individual expression is denied.

3. An assessment of the nature of the injury is the rescuer's first task.

ANSWERS TO SELF-ASSESSMENT ITEMS

Self-assessment items are designed to assist you in gaining depth of understanding as you proceed through the various learning activities. Most of them do not have single correct answers. For feedback, however, you should compare your answers with the sample answers provided here.

Learning Activities

A. (1) A fact is a specific point of information; a concept is an idea or generalization.

    (2)   a. American Conflict in Vietnam: Power Struggle Between the Superpowers

        b. American Conflict in Vietnam: An Economic Disaster

        c. American Conflict in Vietnam: Exploitation of an Underdeveloped Nation

    (3) The Negro slave, having no individual rights, made little effort to improve his lot in life. *Concept:* Depriving one of his individual rights leads to apathy and dependency.

    (4) Refute. A unit concept is much broader than a lesson generalization. Indeed, several lesson generalizations collectively embody one unit concept.

    (5) Mike's view: A military leader who is responsible for unnecessary destruction of lives is incompetent.
Mr. Tompkin's point of view: A military leader who can rally his troops in the face of overwhelming odds is a hero.

Option B_1. (1) Complex statements can only lead to confusion since lessons are based upon concepts.

    (2) Defend. Since the social sciences are presently less exact than science courses, concepts in these areas would tend to be of a theoretical nature.

    (3) To a substantial degree this is desirable since it provides for greater depth of learning. Usually there is a wide variety of concept choices for emphasis; thus familiar concepts can be used as a basis for the development of more complex ones.

    (4) Correct table-setting contributes to ease and efficiency of eating. (The second concept tells why the idea is important.)

Option B_2. (1) If, for example, the unit concepts and generalizations tend to focus upon the dangers associated with excessive ambition, a likely title could be: *Greed, Key to Man's Downfall.*

    (2) Refute. Lesson generalizations are much more specific than unit concepts, several embodying one unit concept.

C. (1) In history or literature there are often several "directions" a unit may take. It is essential that the teacher clarify the alternative that he or she wishes to elect. In other classes, such as mathematics, there is usually a specific focus or direction to be taken.

    (2) This relegates instruction to textbook teaching. The history teacher, for example, who uses past tense may never relate concepts to today's world.

    (3) A concept which cannot be applied probably is hardly worth teaching. A real-life application, on the other hand, tends to make learning a meaningful experience.

Optional Activity

D.　(1)　Defend. This forces one to go beyond mere textbook materials.

　　(2)　Refute. Whatever is worth learning must be weighed on the basis of its usefulness to the individual.

　　(3)　If the instructor "gives" lesson generalizations to students, they may merely memorize them with little or no meaning. The process involves the reflective process that should culminate every lesson experience.

　　(4)　This is probably true. It is more likely, however, to contribute to textbook teaching. If a teacher is not certain of the concept or idea behind a lesson, students are likely to be equally confused.

ANSWERS TO POSTTEST

For most beneficial results you should work through the entire LAP before you check answers to the posttest. Failure to meet the provided minimum standards probably suggests certain weaknesses that need to be corrected. As with the Preassessment items, you will find supporting reasons for answers. It is hoped that this will serve as desirable feedback in your quest for mastery.

A.　1.　Suggests a real-life application.

　　2.　Stated in present tense.

　　3.　Restricted to one basic idea.

　　4.　In statement form.

　　5.　Ties into the major thrust or focus of the unit.

　　6.　Is based upon the user's frame of reference.

　　7.　Is part of a basic idea.

B.　1-U.　Describes a major attribute of an idea (reform).

　　2-C.　A basic idea with a definite thrust.

　　3-L.　The idea (spiraling inflation) treats a specific condition.

　　4-C.　Emphasizes a content dimension and suggests a general focus.

　　5-U.　Describes one attribute of the idea (two-party system).

　　6-L.　One of many possible specifics that deal with a basic idea (two-party system).

　　7-C.　A broad idea.

　　8-L.　Refers to a specific group (among many) that are subsumed under a basic idea.

　　9-C.　Identifies a basic content package and provides a major dimension of emphasis.

C. 4, 7, 9, 10, 12, 14, 15, 17, 20. (Each provides an attribute of a central idea that ties in with the present.)
Reasons for rejected "concepts" from the list.
1. (More of a statement of fact; deals with the past.)
2. (More of a statement of fact; deals with the past.)
3. (In question form.)
5. (More of a statement of fact; deals with the past.)
6. (What would be a unit concept is culminated with a specific reason, as might be expected for a lesson generalization.)
8. (Essentially a definition.)
11. (A fact; in the past.)
13. (In question form.)
16. (A specific (factual); past tense.)
18. (What would otherwise be an acceptable unit concept is culminated with a specific.)
19. (A fact and of the past.)

D. *Examples*
1. The angles of a triangle sum 180 degrees.
2. Meal planning is economical of time and energy.
3. The U.S. and the U.S.S.R. attempt to work together in certain specific areas.

SUPPLEMENTARY SOURCES

The following sources may be used in lieu of The Professional Teacher's Handbook, *2nd ed., or, preferably, as supplementary to it. Generally they are consistent with the models provided in the LAPs in this manual. As such, the references do not represent all of the most recent references in the area; rather, they constitute selective references designed to broaden or expand needed background information.*

Bruner, Jerome S., *The Process of Education* (Cambridge, Mass.: Harvard University Press, 1960).

Fryer, D. A., and others, "Levels of Concept Mastery: Implications for Instruction," *Educational Technology* 12: 23-29 (Dec., 1972).

Hoover, Kenneth H., *The Professional Teacher's Handbook*, 2nd ed. (Boston: Allyn and Bacon, Inc., 1976), Chap. 1.

Hoover, Kenneth H., and Paul M. Hollingsworth, *Learning and Teaching in the Elementary School*, 2nd ed. (Boston: Allyn and Bacon, Inc., 1975), Chap. 6.

Klausmeier, Herbart J., Elizabeth S. Ghalata, and Dorothy A. Fryer, *Conceptual Learning and Development: A Cognitive View* (New York: Academic Press, 1974).

Kuhn, D. J., "Science Teaching: Concept Formation and Learning Theory," *Science Education* 56: 189-196 (April, 1972).

Martorella, Peter H., et al., *Concept Learning: Designs for Instruction* (Scranton, Penn.: Intext Educational Publishers, 1972).

Novak, J. D., *Analysis of Concept Learning* (New York: Academic Press, 1966).

Pella, Milton O., "Concept Teaching in Science," *The Science Teacher* 33: 31-34 (Dec., 1966).

Ringness, Thomas A., *The Affective Domain in Education* (Boston: Little, Brown & Co., 1975).

Formulating Instructional Objectives

RATIONALE. The most fundamental aspect of teaching is the formulation of worthwhile aims or goals. Just as a list of educational purposes is useful in determining the nature of the curriculum, so do goals guide the teacher and student in selection, organization, and finally the evaluation of learning experiences. Actually, goals or purposes constitute the hub around which all other instructional activities revolve.

Unless goals are stated in meaningful terms, they do not serve a worthwhile purpose. Although most teachers acknowledge the importance of instructional goals, relatively few actually use them effectively as a guide for selecting appropriate learning activities. The almost inevitable consequence is an unimaginative, memory-type of experience, commonly known as textbook teaching. When this situation exists, there is a tendency to emphasize textbook facts as ends in themselves. Accordingly, relatively little transfer or application to related life problems can be expected.

OVERVIEW

Key Concepts

1. Instructional objectives are derived from basic unit concepts.

2. Although the three domains of instructional objectives (cognitive, affective, and psychomotor) are somewhat overlapping, individual emphasis is necessary to assure goal achievement.

3. Instructional objectives in the cognitive domain range from simple to complex. "Higher"-order outcomes incorporate "lower"-order outcomes.

4. Instructional objectives are culminated in terms of projected pupil behavioral outcomes.

5. Degree of specificity will vary, depending upon whether an outcome is minimum essential or developmental in nature.

6. Instructional objectives, with their projected behavioral outcomes, provide a sound basis for subsequent instructional and evaluational experiences.

New Terms

1. Cognitive domain: A hierarchical domain of objectives that involves basic reasoning (reflective) processes.

2. Affective domain: A continuum of objectives involving values and emotions.

3. Psychomotor domain: A continuum of objectives involving mental and motor skills.

4. Behavioral outcomes: Actual pupil behaviors that may be anticipated at the culmination of a given learning experience or sequence.

5. Minimum essentials outcomes: Most appropriate in the mental and motor skills area, such outcomes indicate the *specific conditions* and the *minimum level* of performance anticipated.

6. Developmental outcomes: Most appropriate in the "academic areas," this group of outcomes suggests a "class" or group of anticipated behaviors. Since *maximum* achievement is sought, anticipated conditions and minimum level of performance criteria are not needed.

OBJECTIVES. After this experience you should be able to develop instructional objectives and behavioral outcomes for teaching, as evidenced by your ability to:

1. List five of the essential characteristics of an appropriately stated instructional objective and its behavioral outcomes.

2. Distinguish between a minimum essentials and a developmental outcome in eight out of nine instances from a provided list.

3. Select eight out of nine appropriately stated behavioral outcomes (minimum essentials and developmental) from a provided list of twenty.

4. Construct developmental and minimum essentials outcomes from two selected topics.

PRELIMINARY READING. Since the elements of instructional methodology are somewhat variable, the following excerpts are provided to help you develop a frame of reference as a point of departure for this experience. If you prefer, you may proceed directly to the preassessment items.

The Cognitive Domain

For many years teachers have used the expressions "to know," "to understand," and "to comprehend" as a means of denoting cognitive or intellectual goals of learning. Such categories, however, do not denote sharp distinctions between cognitive levels. Fortunately a useful taxonomy of cognitive objectives has been developed.[1] The elements of the taxonomy range from the simple to the complex behaviors and from the concrete or tangible to the abstract or intangible. The six cognitive levels are as follows:

Knowledge. This involves the lowest level of learning, including recall and memory.

Comprehension. This represents the lowest level of understanding. The individual is able to make use of the materials or ideas without relating them to other materials. At the highest level of this category, the learner may be able to *extend* his or her thinking beyond the data by making simple inferences.

Application. This level entails the *use* of information in specific situations. The information may be in the form of general ideas, or concepts, principles, or theories that must be remembered and applied.

Analysis. This involves taking apart the information and creating relationships. The purpose is to clarify by discovering hidden meaning and basic structure.

Synthesis. At this level the learner is able to reassemble the component parts for new meaning. This recombining process permits the emergence of a new pattern or structure not previously apparent. Thus the learner may develop new or creative ideas from the process.

Evaluation. The highest level of cognition involves making judgments on the materials, information, or method for specific purposes. When conceived in relation to the problem-solving process, evaluation involves selecting one of the proposed alternatives over all the rest.

The Affective Domain

This domain is described in terms of relative degrees of *internalization*.[2] By internalization the authors mean a process through which there is first an incomplete and tentative adoption of the desired emotion, then a more complete adoption of the feeling in the latter stages of learning. The five levels of the affective domain follow:

---

[1] *Benjamin S. Bloom, ed.,* Taxonomy of Educational Objectives, Handbook I: Cognitive Domain *(New York: David McKay Co., Inc., 1956).*

[2] *David R. Krathwohl, Benjamin S. Bloom, and Bertram S. Masia,* Taxonomy of Educational Objectives, Handbook II: Affective Domain *(New York: David McKay Co., Inc., 1964).*

Receiving (attending). At this first level the learner merely becomes aware of an idea, process, or thing. Thus he or she is willing to listen or to attend to a given communication.

Responding. This level involves doing something with or about the phenomenon other than merely perceiving it. At this low level of commitment, the student does not yet hold the value. To use a common expression of teachers: "He displays *interest* in the phenomenon."

Valuing. As the term implies, at this level a thing, phenomenon, or behavior has worth. Behavior at this level reflects a belief or an attitude. Thus it might be said that one "holds the value." At the lower end of the continuum, the learner might be said to hold the belief somewhat tentatively; at the other end, his value becomes one of conviction—certainty "beyond a shadow of a doubt."

Organization. Here the individual has established a conscious basis for choice-making. He or she has organized values into a system—a set of criteria—for guiding behavior.

Characterization. At this level the internalization process is complete. Values are *integrated* into some kind of internally consistent system. Thus the person is described as having a recognized philosophy of life.

The Psychomotor Domain

Teachers have long recognized that as a result of certain instructional activities, students should be able to perform certain motor skills, as in playing tennis or basketball. Sometimes the skill will be primarily of a mental nature, as in spelling and writing sequences. Other skills will be neuromuscular, as in writing or operating a machine. Frequently the development of certain habits is emphasized, as in science laboratory techniques. This taxonomy has been extrapolated from established methodology, sometimes called "drill technique." The four psychomotor levels are as follows:

Observing. At this level the learner observes a more experienced person in performance of the activity. Observation of sequences and relationships and a close look at the finished product are usually emphasized.

Imitating. By the time the learner has advanced to this level, he has begun to acquire the basic rudiments of the desired behavior. He follows directions under close supervision. The total act is not important, nor is timing or coordination emphasized. Deliberate effort is made to imitate the model.

Practicing. The entire sequence is performed repeatedly at this level. All aspects of the act are performed in sequence. Conscious effort is no longer necessary as the performance becomes more or less habitual in nature.

Adopting. The terminal level is often referred to as "perfection of the skill." The process involves adapting "minor" details which, in turn, influence the total performance.

Minimum Essentials and Developmental Outcomes

Culminating instructional goals with specific behavioral outcomes is a relatively simple task. There are considerable controversy and confusion, however, concerning how specifically such outcomes should be stated. Some suggest that, along with specific behaviors, the teacher should also specify the *conditions* under which the behavior is exhibited and the minimum level of performance expected. To illustrate: "Given twenty sentences containing a variety of mistakes in capitalization, the student is able, with at least 90 percent accuracy, to identify and rewrite correctly each word that has a mistake in capitalization." Such an outcome might be considered one of several *minimum essentials* expected for mastery. They are relatively easily achieved and serve as prerequisites for further learning.

Others would have the teacher emphasize *developmental* outcomes. Here emphasis is on encouraging each student to progress as far as possible toward predetermined goals. Thus such outcomes are more general than those at the mastery level. At the developmental level, *maximum achievement* is sought, rendering levels of performance practically impossible to define. The developmental outcome ". . . ability to identify fallacies in arguments," for example, appropriately does not call for a minimum level of performance. This will depend upon each student's interpretation. Furthermore, the terminal activity, being *merely representative* of previous instructional experiences, would not necessarily elicit any minimum number of "fallacies."

Both minimum essentials and developmental outcomes are useful in most classes. In skill areas (e.g., typing, shorthand, physical education, and shop courses), more emphasis is usually placed upon the minimum essentials type of outcome. In the academic areas (e.g., English, biology, history, and general business courses), the developmental type of outcome should be more in evidence. Generally, outcomes should be stated as simply and concisely as possible. They are characterized by "action" words such as identify, name, construct, describe, order, and so on. These verbs are less ambiguous than other (more commonly used) verbs.

Constructing Instructional Objectives and Behavioral Outcomes

As a means of focusing attention upon the student, it is recommended that each instructional goal begin with the introductory clause, "After this unit (or lesson) the student should . . . ." In this way the emphasis tends to be shifted from what the teacher wants to what the student needs.

The next step is identification of the domain to be emphasized. The terms *understanding, attitudes and appreciations,* and *skills and habits* are commonly employed to denote the cognitive, affective, and psychomotor domains, respectively. For example, "After this lesson the student should have furthered his *understanding* of . . . ." Each goal should be restricted to a given domain and to a single idea.

A student's behavior offers the best clues to what is learned. These are referred to as behavioral outcomes. For each instructional goal, a number of pupil outcomes will suggest goal achievement or means to achievement. It is desirable to identify as many outcomes as possible and then to select those which seem most practical for use as a guide to instructional activities.

Behavioral outcomes are usually incorporated within the goal framework. For example, "After this unit in American literature the student should further appreciate the social inequalities resulting from a social class structure, as evidenced by (1) his realistic *responses* in a class discussion on the problem "What should be the United States' policy with respect to migrant workers?" (2) his willingness to examine feeling reactions resulting from a sociodrama designed to portray feelings in a specified social situation, and (3) his greater cooperation with underprivileged students in class and society." It should be noted that outcome (1) relates to level two of the affective domain (responding), while outcomes (2) and (3) suggest different levels of number three (valuing) of this domain. By becoming thoroughly familiar with the various levels of each domain, the teacher can select those outcomes which seem most appropriate for any given set of circumstances. It is seen that unit outcomes provide definite clues to desirable class activities.

PREASSESSMENT ITEMS (answers provided on pp. 34–35)

This experience is designed to help you gain an overall perspective of how goals and outcomes are used in teaching. After completing the pretest, turn to the end of this LAP and check your answers. Note that answers (both correct and incorrect) are generally provided with supporting reasons to guide your efforts as you work through the LAP.

A. List five essential features of an appropriately developed instructional objective and its behavioral outcomes. (To illustrate: An instructional objective embodies one unit concept.)

   1.

   2.

   3.

   4.

   5.

B. Place a check (√) before each of the listed minimum essentials behavioral outcomes and a plus (+) before those which you consider developmental in nature.

   1. Identifies hidden assumptions in an actual presentation entitled "Our Polluted Environment."

2. Selects the topic sentence in seven out of eight instances from an assorted list of fifteen paragraphs.

3. Completes the obstacle course in fifteen minutes with a maximum of two errors.

4. Identifies social trends from selected readings.

5. Identifies eighteen out of twenty-one misspelled words from a word list of fifty.

6. Selects eight out of nine basic democratic principles from an assorted list of twenty concepts.

7. Lists an ordered priority of safety precautions in eight of ten cases from a list of fifteen safety rules.

8. Provides a defensible rationale for his proposed solution to the problem of overpopulation in the United States.

9. Provides a reasonable defense of each major point of his debate.

C. From the list of "outcomes" place a check (√) by nine of those that meet the criteria for either developmental or minimum essentials outcomes.

1. Understands the prejudicial structure of the English language.

2. Shows interest in the variety of art forms in the special school display.

3. Checks out at least ten books from the library voluntarily over the past month.

4. Selects an appropriate color combination in eight of ten instances from twenty-five assorted ensembles.

5. Displays appropriate platform speech behavior and voice quality during a fifteen-minute presentation.

6. Identifies logical contradictions in the senator's speech on "honesty in politics."

7. Lists the grammatical errors in a provided theme on "our national forests."

8. Selects the most appropriate workshop tool in eight of ten instances from a sample of twenty-five woodworking tasks.

9. Appreciates home safety rules.

10. Responds during a class discussion on the "impact of mass transit systems on large cities."

11. Defends art media used in connection with the assigned project.

12. Demonstrates the ability to employ analysis level questions during the discussion.

13. Employs an appropriate genetic cross in eight of ten instances from provided problems.

14. Comprehends fallacies in the speaker's argument.

15. Types a perfect copy of a provided typing drill.

16. Interacts with those in his committee on the need for political reform.

17. Explains the merits of using pickets during a labor dispute.

18. Understands the basic essentials of first aid.

19. Displays interest in the merits of the extended family.

20. Is aware of grammatical errors in a provided three-page document on "our national debt."

D. Construct one developmental and one minimum essentials outcome for each of the listed topics.

   1. Use of drugs

      a.

      b.

   2. Typing business letters.

      a.

      b.

If you were able to correctly provide twenty-four of the twenty-seven requested responses, you are well ahead of most new teachers at this point and probably do not need the experiences provided in this LAP. In this event you should proceed directly to the LAP on Planning for Teaching. Even if you "struck out" on the Preassessment items (as expected), do not be discouraged. The writer has provided reasons for correct (and incorrect) answers, and also a series of practical learning experiences to help you quickly attain mastery in the area. Good luck!

LEARNING ACTIVITIES

Work through each learning activity, complete the self-assessment items, and check your answers before moving to the next one. Note that the last learning activity is optional, depending upon your needs and circumstances at that point. You should be able to complete this LAP in about four hours.

A: *Read.* Re-examine the overview and the preliminary reading sections for this LAP and for the preceding one (Formulating Concepts). You will broaden your understanding substantially by studying Chap. 2 in *The Professional Teacher's Handbook,* 2nd ed., and/or by studying the selected references listed at the end of this LAP. Note specifically the following points:

1. The overlap between the three domains.

2. Those levels of the affective and the psychomotor domains that are ordinarily beyond the scope of the individual classroom teacher.

3. How the unit concepts, instructional goals, and behavioral outcomes are integrated.

4. The rationale for beginning each goal with the introductory clause, "After this unit (lesson) the student should . . . ." and culminating the goal with the phrase, "As evidenced by."

Self-assessment Items (answers provided on p. 36)

(1) Why is the evaluational level of the cognitive domain in particular seen as overlapping with the affective domain?

(2) Identify the levels of the affective and the psychomotor domains that are generally beyond the scope of the *individual* classroom teacher.

(3) How are concepts tied in with instructional objectives?

(4) Why is it recommended that each goal begin with the clause, "After this unit (lesson) the student should . . . ," and culminate with the phrase, "As evidenced by"?

At this point you may select either Option B$_1$ or Option B$_2$, depending upon your particular situation. Those who are presently teaching should select Option B$_1$. Those who are not teaching or who do not have immediate access to students should select Option B$_2$.

Option B$_1$: *Examination of objectives models.* This experience can be acquired in several ways. First, a number of useful films and filmstrips have been developed for this purpose. Most of these, however, feature the writing of *minimum essentials* behavioral outcomes only. Such aids are readily accessible from a number of commercial suppliers.*

The illustrations section of Chap. 2 of the Hoover texts and a number of other books, listed in the module bibliography, provide a variety of objectives and outcomes in various fields. Some especially useful sources are Bloom, Krathwohl, and Harrow's books on the cognitive, the affective, and the psychomotor domains. In addition, Gronlund's book on behavioral objectives provides some useful developmental outcomes.

Another approach might include an analysis of goals and outcomes prepared by selected teachers in your school.

Whatever means are utilized, it is imperative that the examined materials be modeled as closely as possible after the approach offered in this LAP. Any existing discrepancies should be thoroughly understood by the user.

Working in a committee of three, if possible, direct your attention to the following:

1. The nature and role of action verbs in behavioral outcomes.

2. Identify the cognitive level of each outcome.

3. Note the differences between minimum essentials and developmental outcomes.

4. Identify possible learning activities that are foreshadowed in the behavioral outcomes.

5. Identify those outcomes that could be considered en route and those that could be considered terminal in nature.

One filmstrip series, entitled Developing and Writing Performance Objectives, *is available from Multi-Media Associates, 4901 E. 5th St., Tucson, Ariz. 85732.*

Self-assessment Items (answers provided on p. 36)

    (1) Illustrate the role of action verbs in determining cognitive level of outcomes.

    (2) Why are minimum essentials outcomes deemed more appropriate for the skills area whereas developmental outcomes often are preferred in "academic" areas?

    (3) In what way do behavioral outcomes foreshadow learning activities?

    (4) What is the difference between en route and terminal outcomes?

Option B$_2$: *Preliminary objectives application and comparison.* Develop one cognitive, one affective, and one psychomotor instructional objective with two accompanying outcomes for each. Make sure that both minimum essentials and developmental outcomes are represented. Use the area of "Woodworking" (industrial arts area) for this experience.*

Cognitive domain

1.

2.

Affective domain

1.

2.

Psychomotor domain

1.

2.

Using objectives and outcomes from selected books as models (noting especially the illustrations in the Hoover texts), compare with your own efforts. If you are working with other students, the formation of small groups is recommended. Proceed as follows:

    1. Differences in specificity of instructional goals when a concept is and is not embodied in the statement.

    2. Levels of specificity of the various behavioral outcomes.

    3. Degree to which the "higher" levels were represented in the various behavioral outcomes.

    4. Problems which were (or might be) evident when the phrase "as evidenced by" was omitted.

    5. Basic differences between minimum essentials and developmental outcomes.

---

*After you have completed this experience and discussed it with your committee members you may turn to p. 39 for sample answers provided by the author.

Self-assessment Items (answers provided on pp. 36–37)

(1) "Cognitive, affective, and psychomotor outcomes may appear under instructional goals that feature only one of the three objective domains." Defend or refute.

(2) Some authorities recommend emphasis on minimum essentials outcomes in the cognitive domain (as well as in the psychomotor domain). What is likely to be the effect of such a practice on learning?

(3) Why are some action verbs, such as interest, understand, and know, deemed inappropriate for use in behavioral outcomes?

C: *Instructional application.* Using three of your unit concepts as a basis (developed in connection with the LAP on gaining the concept), prepare an instructional objective (goal) and several behavioral outcomes for each of the selected unit concepts. Focus on one instructional objective in the cognitive domain (understands), another in the affective domain (appreciates, interests, or values), and the third in the psychomotor domain (skills and habits). Proceed as follows:

1. Prepare at least eight behavioral outcomes for *each* instructional objective. Then combine and delete until about half of the original outcomes remain.

2. Make sure that both "higher" and "lower" levels of the taxonomies are represented.

3. Be sure to construct minimum essentials outcomes for the psychomotor objective and developmental outcomes for the cognitive and affective objectives.

4. Now attempt to change your developmental outcomes into minimum essentials outcomes, noting difficulties.

After completing the foregoing tasks, discuss your experience with other new teachers, if possible. Focus on both the rationale and the difficulties encountered in each of the above.

Self-assessment Items (answers provided on p. 37)

(1) Why is it desirable to initially construct several behavioral outcomes for each instructional objective?

(2) Why is the valuing level of the affective domain so difficult to assess within the classroom setting?

(3) Why are the words "understand," "appreciate," "value," "skills," and the like considered appropriate in instructional goals but inappropriate in behavioral outcomes?

(4) Why does a minimum essentials outcome in the cognitive domain tend to be at a relatively "low" level of cognition?

(5) Why is a minimum essentials outcome at the valuing level of the affective domain meaningless?

If, after reviewing your learning activities for this LAP, you feel that you can meet the stated objectives, proceed to the posttest. If not, you should complete the optional activity. Note that it provides for a number of optional situations, depending upon your own individual circumstances.

Optional Activity

D: *Visit with experienced teachers.* Working in a committee of three, if possible, arrange to visit experienced teachers who work in areas that tend to emphasize the different domains of instructional objectives. (You may elect to invite such individuals to visit with your committee.) Proceed as follows:

1. Have one member of your committee visit a *social science* teacher for the purpose of obtaining the following information:

   a. A list of the objectives for the *unit* being studied.

   b. A list of the objectives for the *lesson* being studied.

   c. If the teacher's objectives are not written out, determine, if you can, how the teacher would phrase objectives. (Be sure to ascertain key verbs preferred, such as understand, learn, recall, apply, and the like.)

   d. Obtain the teacher's views relative to the importance of goals and behavioral outcomes as a basis for developing unit and lesson plans.

2. Have a second member of your committee visit a *literature* teacher. Obtain the same information as in the above.

3. Have a third member of your committee visit a teacher who deals with a *skills class* (e.g., physical education, home economics, industrial arts, foreign language, mathematics, speech, certain business courses). Obtain the same information as in the above.*

4. Following the visits, compare notes and discuss the following questions:

   a. What action verbs predominated (understand, learn, name, list, apply, etc.)?

   b. What level of behavioral outcomes predominated? What influence might this have on instructional activities?

   c. Logically, the social science teacher might be expected to emphasize cognitive, the literature teacher to emphasize affective, and the skills area teacher to emphasize psychomotor objectives. Did this pattern seem to apply? Speculate on any wide deviations from the foregoing emphasis.

   d. Discuss the probable impact of ill-defined (or inappropriate) goal domain emphasis on instruction in the subjects represented.

   e. What were the teachers' overall assessments of the role of objectives and outcomes in teaching?

---

*If working alone, you may be able to reduce the number of visits by visiting a teacher(s) who is emphasizing more than one type of instructional objective at the time of your visit.

Self-assessment Items (answers provided on p. 37)

(1) Why do ill-defined goals and behavioral outcomes increase the tendency for "textbook teaching"?

(2) You will recall that unit concepts deal with current applications. This necessitates a two-step process for the history teacher. First, the teacher must identify several major content ideas and then translate these into concepts (with current applications). What influence might a breakdown in this two-step process have upon the history teacher's goals and behavioral outcomes?

(3) Most professional educators consider goals and outcomes the "hub around which all other instructional activities evolve." Explain.

(4) Distinguish between unit and lesson outcomes.

POSTTEST (answers provided on pp. 37–39)

After you have completed the learning activities, complete the posttest and evaluate by checking the answers found at the end of this LAP. Note that supporting reasons are provided for both correct and incorrect responses.

A. List five essential features of an appropriately developed instructional objective and its behavioral outcomes.

1.

2.

3.

4.

5.

B. Place a check (√) before each of the listed behavioral outcomes you consider of the minimum essentials type and a plus (+) by those you consider developmental in nature.

1. States the concept in his own words.

2. Provides an illustration of the principle involved.

3. Selects eight out of nine compound sentences from an assorted list of twenty sentences.

4. Points out inconsistencies in a class debate.

5. Makes a legal tennis serve in eight out of nine attempts on a regulation tennis court.

6. Selects the appropriate chemical reagent in eight out of nine chemistry experiments.

7. Develops criteria for a solution to the problem.

8. Completes the obstacle course with a maximum of two mistakes.

9. Translates a 300-word selection into Spanish with a maximum of three errors over a time span of fifteen minutes.

C. From the list of "outcomes," place a check (√) by nine of those that meet the criteria for either developmental or minimum essentials outcomes.

1. Displays interest in the local art exhibit.

2. Voluntarily attends the science fair.

3. Appreciates the value of modern art forms.

4. Uses the principles of factoring in eight of nine provided sample problems.

5. Desires to return to school to complete the experiment.

6. Provides an acceptable rationale for his planned project.

7. Provides context meaning of twelve out of fifteen selected "problem words" in foreign language class.

8. Displays enthusiasm for the art display.

9. Writes an acceptable critique of a provided 500-word theme.

10. Displays a favorable attitude toward poetry based on ten selected poetic selections.

11. Ranks the issues in order of importance in eight of nine instances from a provided list.

12. Makes a collection of ten butterflies and is able to identify the anatomical structure of a butterfly.

13. Habitually completes class assignments.

14. Provides a critique of the issues in the forthcoming municipal election.

15. Displays a deep commitment to basic democratic ideals.

16. Realizes that all human beings are basically equal.

17. Identifies fossil remnants found in an actual field excavation.

18. Analyzes supporting social science data and classifies them according to criteria developed in class.

19. Takes perfect dictation at the normal rate of conversation.

20. Makes a list of ten banking principles following a visit to a nearby bank.

D. Construct a developmental *and* a minimum essentials outcome for each of the listed topics.

1. Playing table tennis (ping-pong)

   a.

   b.

2. Use of alcohol

   a.

   b.

Your successful completion of this LAP represents a significant step on your way to becoming an outstanding teacher. Indeed, instructional goals and behavioral outcomes set the stage for effective planning activities. Even if you failed to fully satisfy the recommended mastery level for this LAP, proceed to the next one on *Planning for Teaching*. Concept formation, instructional objectives, and planning are so closely related that clarification of one tends to contribute to understanding of the others.

ANSWERS TO PREASSESSMENT ITEMS

> *You can make the Preassessment items a most valuable learning device by studying the provided reasons for both correct and incorrect responses. You will note that since Part A has no specific number of correct responses, several additional points (characteristics) are provided. Since the last part calls for your constructed responses, your answers are not expected to be identical to those supplied by the writer. Such feedback, however, can enhance your understanding of the items.*

A. 1. An instructional objective embodies one unit concept.

2. By beginning with the clause, "After this unit the student should . . . ," emphasis is focused on *student* achievement at the culmination of the experience.

3. By culminating with the phrase, "as evidenced by," the instructional objective focuses upon actual student behaviors indicative of goal attainment.

4. Unit outcomes foreshadow instructional and evaluational activities.

5. Some outcomes (minimum essentials or those in basic skills areas) indicate the *specific conditions* and the *minimum level* of performance anticipated.

6. Other outcomes (in the "academic" areas) merely suggest a "class" or group of anticipated behaviors, rendering specific conditions and a minimum level of performance unnecessary.

7. Some behavioral outcomes are intermediate (en route) in nature; others are of the terminal variety.

8. The instructional objective indicates the domain; behavioral outcomes suggest the hierarchical level sought.

9. Each behavioral outcome is restricted to one specific behavior or class of behaviors.

B. 1 + (A flexible number of hidden assumptions may be identified, depending upon the learner's frame of reference.)

2 √ (Provides both the conditions and the minimum level of performance expected.)

3 √ (Provides both the conditions and the minimum level of performance expected.)

4 + Such points as "social trends" are usually inferred, thus flexibility must be accepted.)

5√ (Both the conditions and the minimum level of acceptability are provided.)

6√ (Contains specific conditions and minimum level of acceptability.)

7√ (Both specific conditions and minimum level of acceptability are included.)

8 + (A "defensible rationale" is individualistic in nature; there can be no clear-cut minimum level of acceptability.)

9 + (A "reasonable defense" depends upon many variables.)

C. 3, 4, 6, 8, 10, 11, 13, 15, 17. (Each of these describes some specific behavior.)

Reasons for rejected "outcomes" from the list.

1 (Understanding is internal; no behavior indicative of understanding is offered.)

2 (Does not call attention to any specific behavior that would suggest interest.)

5 (Includes two distinct aspects of delivery; a behavioral outcome should be restricted to one specific behavior.)

7 (In an area involving a definite skill, a minimum essentials objective should be used. No minimum level of acceptability is offered.)

9 (Appreciation is internal; an identified behavior is needed before this "appreciation" can be assessed.)

12 (This is vague; a number of specific behaviors might suggest this ability.)

14 (Comprehension is internal; necessary to specify evidence of this.)

16 (This is vague; the nature of this "interaction" should be specified.)

18 (Understanding is internal; a specific behavior indicative of this understanding is needed.)

19 (Interest is internal. What behavior would suggest this?)

20 (What would be evidence of this awareness?)

D. 1. Use of Drugs

Developmental outcome example: Analyzes the logical fallacies in a forum on use of drugs.

Minimum essentials outcome example: Is able to rank (in nine out of ten cases) ten selected drugs and stimulants in order of danger to the human body.

2. Typing a business letter

Developmental outcome example: Types business letters that make the receiver want to respond in a positive manner.

Minimum essentials outcome example: Types a dictated business letter with a maximum of two mistakes.

ANSWERS TO SELF-ASSESSMENT ITEMS

Self-assessment items are designed to assist you gain depth of understanding as you proceed through the various learning activities. Most of them do not have single correct answers. For feedback, however, you should compare your answers with the sample answers provided here.

Learning Activities

A. (1) Evaluation cannot be done in the absence of values.

(2) Affective: Organization; Characterization.

Psychomotor: Adapting level.

(3) The concept is embodied in the instructional objective. The instructional objective is then followed by specific behavioral outcomes.

(4) The introductory clause shifts the frame of reference from what the teacher wants to the student at the culmination of the experience.

Option B_1 (1) Such verbs as name, order, or identify usually require little more than mere recall of information (knowledge level). Other action verbs, such as illustrate, construct, classify, and apply, demand the manipulation and integration of ideas (application and analysis levels, for example).

(2) Skill development is readily identifiable and quantified. For example, if we wish to ascertain an individual's ability to complete effective serves in tennis, we can readily observe this.

In the case of cognition, however, the task is often more difficult since a class of behaviors is often present. For example, if we wish to ascertain an individual's ability to identify fallacies in an argument, it may be inappropriate to establish a minimum level of performance of approximately 90 percent. The identifiable fallacies of an argument would depend somewhat upon an individual's own frame of reference. Thus maximum, as opposed to minimum, level of performance is sought.

(3) Behavioral outcomes indicate what one who has reached the objective can do; learning activities provide experiences necessary for attaining these ends.

(4) An en route outcome must be reached before the terminal outcome is attainable.

Option B_2 (1) This is quite possible, as there is considerable overlapping of of the domains. A preferred procedure, however, is to keep the domains separate to facilitate preparation of appropriate learning activities and to minimize the risk of neglecting certain domains.

(2) The general emphasis will shift to relatively low levels of learning. For example, it would be relatively easy to expect the student to *name* ten of the twelve listed causes of the Revolutionary War. It would be extremely difficult, however, to set up a minimum

       level of performance for a student who is expected to draw parallels to today's world.

(3) Such learnings are internal with the person. Evidence of achievement is reflected in more specific behaviors.

C. (1) Provides the teacher with several instructional alternatives (foreshadowed in the different outcomes).

(2) Demands voluntary behavior; most class activities are assigned.

(3) In instructional goals such verbs merely serve to identify the domain, whereas in behavioral outcomes the focus is upon actual behavior.

(4) By specifying a minimum level of performance, facts provide about the only solid clue to agreement on performance standards.

(5) To set up a minimum level of performance for voluntary behavior within the class setting disregards social pressures. Minimum level of performance and voluntary behavior tend to be self-contradictory.

Optional Activity

D. (1) Without an adequate destination (goals) and anticipated behavioral outcomes, the textbook is about the only instructional guide left.

(2) Goals tend to remain at a "low" level of cognition. (Textbook teaching.)

(3) Goals and behavioral outcomes foreshadow means (class activities) of reaching these ends. The hierarchical structure of the goal domains suggests degree of complexity of learning activities.

(4) Unit outcomes foreshadow a given activity or group of activities. Lesson outcomes focus on specific activities of a given method or technique (activity).

ANSWERS TO POSTTEST

> *For most beneficial results you should work through the entire LAP before you check your answers to the posttest. Failure to meet the provided minimum standards probably suggests certain weaknesses that need to be corrected. As with the Preassessment items, you will find supporting reasons for answers. It is hoped that this will serve as desirable feedback in your quest for mastery.*

A. 1.   An instructional objective embodies one unit concept.

   2.   By beginning with the clause, "After this unit the student should . . . ," emphasis is focused on *student* achievement at the culmination of the experience.

3. By culminating with the phrase, "as evidenced by," the instructional objective focuses attention on actual student behaviors indicative of goal attainment.

4. Unit outcomes foreshadow instructional and evaluational activities.

5. Some outcomes (minimum essentials or those in basic skills areas) indicate *specific conditions* and the *minimum level* of performance anticipated.

6. Other outcomes (in the "academic" areas) merely suggest a "class" or group of anticipated behaviors, rendering specific conditions and a minimum level of performance unnecessary.

7. Some behavioral outcomes are intermediate (en route) in nature; others are of the terminal variety.

8. The instructional objective indicates the domain; behavioral outcomes suggest the hierarchical level sought.

9. Each behavioral outcome is restricted to one specific behavior or class of behaviors.

B.   1+ (Flexibility must be permitted; thus no minimum level of acceptability is possible.)

     2+ (Each illustration may be different, rendering specific conditions unnecessary.)

     3√ (A definite skill is involved.)

     4+ (A maximum, as opposed to a minimum, number of inconsistencies is sought.)

     5√ (Involves a definite skill that can be readily observed.)

     6√ (Involves a definite skill that can be readily observed.)

     7+ (A variable number of criteria could be developed; thus a maximum rather than a minimum number is in order.)

     8√ (A skill that can be observed.)

     9√ (A skill that can be observed.)

C.   2, 4, 6, 7, 9, 11, 17, 19, 20. (Each describes a specific behavior.) Reasons for "rejected" outcomes from the list.

     1 (Interest is internal.)

     3 (Appreciation is not a behavior.)

     5 (A desire comes from within; must see evidence of this through some definite behavior.)

     8 (Enthusiasm is vague. What special behavior would suggest this?)

     10 (No evidence of this "favorable attitude" is provided.)

     12 (Contains two different behaviors, e.g., collects and identifies.)

     13 (Too vague; how often is habitually?)

     14 (Too vague; the elements of the critique should be broken into specifics.)

     15 (What evidence suggests this "definite commitment"?)

16 (Realization is internal. What evidence suggests this?)

18 (Contains two definite behaviors, e.g., analysis and classification.)

D. 1. Playing table tennis (ping-pong)

Developmental outcome example: Views table tennis as a sport that can be enjoyed by both sexes at all ages.

Minimum essentials outcome example: Is able to perform, in nine out of ten instances, a backspin serve that bounces at least twice on the opponent's court.

2. Use of alcohol

Developmental outcome example: Identifies basic relationships associated with alcohol consumption and subsequent behavior.

Minimum essentials outcome example: From a provided list of fifteen symptoms of alcoholism, is able to select in four out of five instances those indicative of advanced alcoholism.

Sample responses for Learning Activity B_2

Cognitive domain

1. After this unit the student should have furthered his understanding of the importance of appropriate wood finishes, as evidenced by his ability to:

   a. classify eight out of ten different finishes from selected samples.

   b. prepare a finished product with high gloss.

Affective domain

2. After this unit the student should have increased his appreciation of different wood finishes, as evidenced by his voluntarily:

   a. attending an industrial arts fair, featuring a variety of wood finishes.

   b. offering to refinish any of his own work which does not meet provided standards.

Psychomotor domain

3. After this unit the student should have developed skill in the preparation of woodworking finishes, as evidenced by his ability to:

   a. prepare adequate finishes from a variety of selected wood products.

   b. provide an accurate description of finishing touches needed for a selected group of improperly finished wood products.

SUPPLEMENTARY SOURCES

The following sources may be used in lieu of the Hoover texts or, preferably, as supplementary to them. Generally they are consistent with the models provided in the LAPs of this book. As such, the references do not represent all of the most recent references in the area; rather, they constitute selective references designed to broaden or expand needed background information.

Bloom, Benjamin S., ed., *Taxonomy of Educational Objectives, Handbook I: Cognitive Domain* (New York: David McKay Company, Inc., 1956).

Gronlund, Norman E., *Stating Behavioral Objectives for Classroom Instruction* (New York: Macmillan Company, Inc., 1970).

Harrow, Anita J., *A Taxonomy of the Psychomotor Domain* (New York: David McKay Company, Inc., 1972).

Hoover, Kenneth H., *The Professional Teacher's Handbook*, 2nd ed. (Boston: Allyn and Bacon, Inc., 1976), Chap. 2.

Hoover, Kenneth H., and Paul M. Hollingsworth, *Learning and Teaching in the Elementary School*, 2nd ed. (Boston: Allyn and Bacon, Inc., 1975), Chap. 7.

Kibler, Robert J., and others, *Objectives for Instruction and Evaluation* (Boston: Allyn and Bacon, Inc., 1974).

Krathwohl, David R., Benjamin S. Bloom, and Bertram S. Masia, *Taxonomy of Educational Objectives, Handbook II: Affective Domain* (New York: David McKay Co., 1964).

Mager, Robert F., *Goal Analysis* (Belmont, Calif.: Fearon Publishers, Inc., 1972).

——, *Preparing Instructional Objectives*, 2nd ed. (Belmont, Calif.: Fearon Publishers, Inc., 1976).

Popham, W. James, and Eva L. Baker, *Establishing Instructional Goals* (Englewood Cliffs, N.J.: Prentice-Hall, Inc., 1970).

Tanner, Daniel, *Using Behavioral Objectives in the Classroom* (New York: Macmillan Company, Inc., 1972).

Vargas, Julie S., *Writing Worthwhile Behavioral Objectives* (New York: Harper and Row Publishers, 1972).

Planning
for
Teaching

RATIONALE. Planning, like map making, enables one to predict the future course of events. In essence, a plan is a blueprint—a plan of action. As any traveler knows, the best-laid plans sometimes go awry. Occasionally, unforeseen circumstances even prevent one from beginning a well-planned journey; other times conditions while on the trip may cause one to drastically alter plans. More often, however, a well-planned journey is altered in *minor* ways for those unpredictable "side trips" that may seem desirable from close range.

Likewise, teachers must plan classroom experiences—the scope and sequence of courses, the content within courses, the units to be taught, the activities to be employed, and the tests to be given. Though few teachers would deny the necessity of planning, there is some controversy with respect to the scope and nature of planning. Indeed methods specialists themselves differ concerning the essential scope of planning. Some seem to feel that unit planning renders lesson planning almost unnecessary. Others stress the importance of lesson plans while minimizing the value of unit plans. While the planning needs of teachers will vary markedly, there is considerable justification for both unit and lesson planning.

OVERVIEW

Key Concepts

1. A functional unit concept is broader than specific content material; it embodies a current-life application.

2. Although pre-instructional planning is essential, adjustments based upon specific student wants and needs are to be expected.

3. Lesson plans generally are based upon a single unit concept.

4. Behavioral unit outcomes foreshadow instructional methods and techniques of evaluation.

5. A lesson plan, essentially, consists of a proposed analytical development of a selected problem.

New Terms

1. The yearly plan: The overall plan, essentially consisting of unit titles (evolved from general course concepts).

2. The teaching unit: A group of related concepts from which a given set of instructional and evaluational experiences is derived. Units normally range from three to six weeks long.

3. The lesson plan: Those specific learning activities that evolve from a given unit concept. Each lesson plan is structured around a problem specifically designed to guide the processes of reflective thinking.

OBJECTIVES. After this experience you should be able to develop appropriate unit and lesson plans for teaching, as evidenced by your ability to:

1. List eight basic features of unit and lesson planning.

2. Select eight out of nine appropriately formulated lesson plan excerpts from a list of twenty assorted lesson plan samples.

3. Develop, in eight out of ten cases, two key questions (or statements when appropriate) for five selected aspects of a lesson plan.

PRELIMINARY READING. Since the elements of instructional methodology are somewhat variable, the following excerpts are provided to help you develop a frame of reference as a point of departure for this experience. If you prefer, you may proceed directly to the preassessment items.

LEVELS OF PLANNING

The beginning teacher is sometimes confused by the kinds, types, and levels of planning. These levels have been identified as (1) curriculum guides, (2) courses of study, (3) units, both resource and teaching, and (4) lessons. *Curriculum guides* often are worked out in states, counties, or cities by teachers in cooperation with curriculum consultants, administrators, and lay citizens. The guide may cover the whole school experience from kindergarten to twelfth grade. Usually it includes sample units for each grade level. Some school systems develop *courses of study*. These may include many or all of the subjects to be taught at a grade level or in a total school. Courses of study are similar to curriculum guides except that they usually are more comprehensive. Both are useful to the teacher in the overall planning of a year's or a semester's work. *Resource units* can be prepared by one or several persons. They usually are made available to other teachers as resources for planning classroom experiences. The sample units which often are a part of curriculum guides or courses of study are resource units. Resource units are designed to provide a teacher with a variety of *resources* when planning a teaching unit. The *teaching unit* differs from a resource unit in that it contains only those resources which a teacher expects to utilize during the unit. The *lesson plan* contains the specific activities for each day of the time allotted to the unit; it is the means by which the unit is taught.

The classroom teacher, then, is directly responsible for planning courses of study (yearly planning), unit planning, and lesson planning. Each is further clarified.

The Yearly Plan

The process of planning begins when the teacher sets out to determine what major ideas will be emphasized during the year. All available textbooks in the area, curriculum guides, and course-of-study aids should be surveyed for this purpose. Although each teacher often prepares his/her own yearly plan, increased emphasis is being given to joint participation by all members of a department. This promotes appropriate integration of related courses and enables teachers of the same course to develop desirable commonalities. At the same time it leaves each instructor free to develop various aspects of the course in his own way.

Oddly enough, some teachers have limited their preparation for yearly planning to a single selected textbook. Such a practice, in effect, makes both teacher and students slaves to a single frame of reference. Textbook units, chapters, and topics, accordingly, are studied in a chapter-by-chapter and page-by-page manner. It must be emphasized that a textbook, at its best, merely provides all learners with one comprehensive source of information. Since textbooks are designed to fulfill the needs of as many people as possible, they usually contain some materials which will be of marginal value to individual instructors. As each textbook writer tends to emphasize certain aspects over others, it behooves the teacher to survey as many such sources as possible for the purpose of ascertaining what aspects *he or she* will emphasize.

Unit Titles. Major unit titles are developed from broad course ideas or concepts that must be emphasized during the course. Unit titles will reflect basic content, and also the major thrust or focus to be sought. Frequently a need for two or more units may be developed from a single course idea. This suggests the need for more specificity. Eventually there will be a unit for each major course idea. Appropriate unit titles, based upon illustrated concepts in a general business course, follow:

1. The United States: Distribution Center of the World
2. The Consumer Determines the Market
3. Sales Promotion and Advertising

After major unit titles have been tentatively established, an approximate time schedule for each unit is established. This will reflect relative degrees of emphasis to be given to each unit. It may be that time limitations will necessitate basic changes. Sometimes certain proposed units must be deleted. Units are seldom less than three or more than six weeks long.

The Teaching Unit. The teaching unit is designed to center the work of the class around meaningful wholes or patterns, and to make the work of different days focus on a central theme until some degree of unified learning is attained. *The basic elements of a teaching unit consist of a group of related concepts, unified for instructional purposes.*

The process is essentially one of combining related ideas into some intellectual pattern. It provides opportunities for critical thinking, generalization, and application of ideas to many situations. Unit titles, as illustrated in the yearly plan, do not usually correspond to textbook units. In order to make instruction attractive to boys and girls, a teaching unit most appropriately focuses upon a central, practical idea or theme. Although some English teachers would attempt to structure a unit around Julius Caesar, for example, youngsters would likely be more attracted to a unit dealing with "ambition." Such a unit, of course, would focus upon Julius Caesar as an avenue to realizing the major objectives. Instead of studying evolution, a science teacher might construct a unit around the concept of "change." The idea of evolution would become one dimension of a much more comprehensive theme. Such a unit concept approaches what Jerome Bruner has termed the basic structure of knowledge.[1]

The Lesson Plan. A lesson plan is an expanded portion of a unit plan. It represents a more or less detailed analysis of a particular *activity* described in the unit plan. For example, one of the unit activities may be *class discussion*. While the problem title may have been stated in the unit plan, no indication is usually given as to *how* the problem would be developed. In discussing a problem of policy, as described in another LAP, careful planning is essential. The lesson plan serves such a purpose.

The essentials of a lesson plan are somewhat similar to the important elements of a unit plan. Although forms and styles differ markedly from one teacher to another, a lesson plan usually contains a goal, lesson introduction (approach), lesson development, and lesson generalizations. Depending on the nature of the lesson, it also may include a list of materials needed, provision for individual differences, and an assignment.

The common elements of lesson planning erroneously suggest a more or less standard routine. While it is true that most plans will be structured around the common elements described, significant differences will be observed within this framework. Different teaching methods often are designed for different instructional purposes; they involve different sequences.

Instead of a *daily* lesson plan (a different plan for each day), as was common prior to development of the teaching unit, the same plan frequently serves for two or three or more days. For example, a thorough discussion of the problem "What policy should the Western Powers adopt with respect to their dealings with colonial nations?" would in all probability demand two or more class periods. Likewise, a panel discussion and its follow-through discussion usually require at least two class periods. Sometimes, however, the nature of an activity does render a formal lesson plan unnecessary. Usually one does not need to prepare a special plan, for example, when the day's schedule calls for hearing oral reports, studying reference materials, or engaging in collateral reading activities. Here the unit plan may be fully adequate. The type and

---

[1] *Jerome Bruner, The Process of Education (Cambridge, Mass.: Harvard University Press, 1961), pp. 17-18.*

length of a lesson plan will depend on such factors as the particular teacher involved, the nature of the activity, and administrative policy.

A Case for Careful Planning. Planning takes time and is hard work. On the other hand, it is relatively easy to rely upon the textbook as a crutch for teaching. Often student interest and participation may be high. One may even be able to collect evidence of substantial learning if he or she resorts to basically memory-type tests. Although some useful learning *can* accrue from such procedures, it is usually far below what could be accomplished from careful advance planning.

As teachers gain experience, they tend to carry more and more of their plans "in their heads." Thus lesson plans may seem unnecessary, and to some extent this may be so. If carried to excess, however, the teacher may gradually slip back into textbook teaching.

Once appropriate unit and lesson plans have been developed, there is a tendency to rely upon them in subsequent years. Certainly a good unit or lesson is a valuable asset "the next time around." By relying on marginal notes, the same plans may be used more than once. Eventually, however, old plans must be replaced as new data become available. Change may be desirable sometimes merely to revive the teacher's own enthusiasm for the experience.

Occasionally a daily schedule of activities (often required by the school principal) is confused with lesson planning. Brief notes indicating what topics will be covered are no substitute for lesson planning. The difference is between textbook teaching and teaching with carefully planned purposes and activities for reaching desired ends.

PREASSESSMENT ITEMS (answers provided on pp. 59-61)

This experience is designed to help you gain an overall perspective of how teachers plan for teaching. After completing the items, turn to the end of this LAP and check your answers. Note that answers (both correct and incorrect) are provided with supporting reasons to guide your efforts as you work through the LAP.

A. List eight basic features of unit and lesson planning. (To illustrate: A unit plan evolves around a central theme or idea.)

Unit planning

1.

2.

3.

4.

Lesson planning

5.

6.

7.

8.

B. From the assorted lesson plan excerpts, place a check (√) by nine of those most appropriately stated for maximum efficiency. (You are to assume that each excerpt contains all the material in the lesson that is relative to the specific point introduced.)

1. At this time we will show a 10-minute film. Look at the three key questions on the chalkboard. Be prepared to discuss them following the showing of the film.

2. Today we will have a class discussion based upon the topic of drug abuse. The class will be asked to relate this to their own lives.

3. Looking at our problem, "What steps should be taken to minimize the threat of "bush wars?", we have concluded that the U.S. should avoid political entanglements with unsettled countries.

4. Show the film *Less Far Than the Arrow*, and discuss its implications.

5. What is meant by "bush wars"? Give examples. Why has our nation become involved in these?

6. Before we consider possible solutions, the class will be asked to set up criteria for evaluating these.

7. From our lesson today, what big ideas (generalizations) can we evolve? Sample: "Bush wars" represent power plays by the superpowers.

8. Prior to a consideration of possible solutions, we need to establish criteria for evaluating these. What might be one? Sample: Must not result in isolationism.

9. Generalizations to be derived by the students:

    a. "Bush wars" pose a threat to world security.

    b. "Bush wars" have unwritten restrictions imposed in terms of men and materials.

    c. "Bush wars" are usually expensive in terms of men and materials.

    d. "Bush wars" have limited objectives.

10. Following the panel presentation, the class will be led into a brief discussion of the panel process. This will be followed by a discussion of questions raised.

11. As I present each transparency, you are to jot down the major theme of each.

12. We will now go into our selected subgroups. The first thing you are to do is to select a recorder, who will record points and questions raised.

13. Follow-up of panel presentation: What did you like about our panel? What did you dislike? What questions do you have on the panel topic?

14. Students first will be led into an analysis of the problem. Then they will proceed to a consideration of some possible solutions to the problem.

15. Following the demonstration, students will be asked to draw some generalizations.

16. After a brief discussion of the problem of powerless groups, the case will be distributed for study and analysis.

17. Following the resource speaker's presentation, questions will be entertained by the class. Sample: Would you explain why the President is able to commit our nation to a conflict without the prior approval of Congress?

18. The reports will be evaluated on the basis of the following: Clarity, content, delivery, organization.

19. Follow-up discussion of the resource speaker's main points.

20. The basic criteria for evaluating the oral presentations will be listed and explained.

C. Develop two key questions (or statements when appropriate) for each of the five identified aspects of a lesson plan. Use class discussion as a frame of reference and base your responses on the problem, "What steps should be taken to cope with the energy crisis?" (You may find it desirable to refer to the LAP on discussion and debate in this connection.)

1. Lesson Approach

   a.

   b.

2. Lesson Development

   Analysis of the Problem

   a.

   b.

   Establishing Hypotheses

   a.

   b.

   Establishing Criteria

   a.

   b.

3. Deriving Generalizations

   a.

   b.

If you were able to provide twenty-four of the twenty-seven requested responses, your present achievement level is remarkably high. In this case it is quite likely that you already possess the necessary competencies in planning and should proceed directly to another module. Even if you were able to supply few of the requested responses, do not feel too disappointed, for planning is a rather complex and involved aspect of teaching. By first analyzing the reasons for your errors (provided at the end of this LAP), and then by carefully working through each learning activity, you should achieve mastery in one of the most difficult aspects of teaching.

LEARNING ACTIVITIES

Work through each learning activity, complete the self-assessment items, and check your answers before moving to the next one. Note that the last learning activity is optional, depending upon your needs and circumstances at that point. You should be able to complete this LAP in about four hours.

A: *Read.* Re-examine the overview and the preliminary reading sections of this LAP, and of the other LAPs in this module (Concepts and Instructional Objectives). You will broaden your understanding substantially by studying Chap. 3 and Appendix A in the Hoover methods texts, and/or by studying the selected references listed at the end of this LAP. Note specifically the following points:

1. The need for a major "thrust" in each unit title.

2. The major aspects of both a unit plan and a lesson plan.

3. Differences between parallel aspects of unit and lesson plans. (For example: How do unit outcomes differ from lesson outcomes?)

Self-assessment Items (answers provided on pp. 61–62)

(1) What is the purpose of including a major thrust in a unit title?

(2) List six major aspects of a *unit* plan *and* in one sentence indicate the purpose of each.

(3) List six major aspects of a *lesson* plan *and* in one sentence indicate the purpose of each.

(4) Distinguish between unit and lesson introductions.

(5) Distinguish between unit and lesson activities.

(6) Distinguish between the major concept of the lesson and the lesson generalization.

At this point you may select either Option B_1 or Option B_2, depending upon your particular situation. Those who are presently teaching should select Option B_1. Those who are not teaching or who do not have immediate access to students should select Option B_2.

Option B_1: *Examination of model plans.* This experience can be acquired in different ways. It is a relatively simple task for someone to collect a variety of unit and lesson plan samples, provided in various books and manuals. (There is a sample unit plan (Appendix A) and a lesson plan provided for each major instructional method in the Hoover methods texts, for example.)

Another, less desirable, option would involve inspection of especially prepared plans by selected teachers in a selected school. This option is less desirable because it is likely to afford a limited variety of approaches to planning. Moreover, the plans of experienced teachers tend to be somewhat more abbreviated than those needed by beginning teachers.

It is imperative that the observed models meet the basic criteria for planning as nearly as possible. All discrepancies must be clearly identified. Direct your attention to the following:

Unit plans

1. The specific elements included.

2. Differences between the various models.

3. How the different plans foreshadow class activities (including tests, etc.)

4. Various options (if any) provided. (Resource units provide many resources and options, whereas unit plans basically are restricted to what teachers plan to actually accomplish. Usually, however, teachers provide room for some flexibility of instruction.)

Lesson plans

1. The specific elements included.

2. Differences between the various models.

3. Different degrees of specificity among the different models.

4. Differences within given lesson plans relative to different subject areas involved.

5. Differences within given lesson plans relative to different instructional methods to be employed.

6. Provided time allotments relative to different methods to be utilized.

Self-assessment Items (answers provided on p. 62)

(1) How do unit concepts provide basic structure for the unit plan?

(2) Students themselves should become involved in establishing purpose (unit introduction) to the unit. Defend or refute.

(3) It has been said that a resource unit can be developed by a committee of teachers, whereas a teaching unit is the individual teacher's own creation. Explain why.

(4) How may a teacher avoid becoming a "slave" to his or her lesson plan?

(5) For years the assignment has been emphasized and debated as a basic element of lesson planning. Yet you will note that in some lesson plan models it is considered optional. Why?

Option B_2: *Comparing unit and lesson plan samples in different fields.* If you are part of a group, divide into committees of three each, representing different fields of specialization. Each committee should focus on one of the following aspects of unit and lesson planning. Suggest as many ways of developing these as you can. Prepare a brief outline of each technique you suggest.

1. The unit introduction and the lesson approach.

2. The unit content outline and the content of a lesson plan.

3. The unit learning activities and the lesson development.

4. The unit evaluational activities and the lesson generalizations. (If working alone, you might well compare your plan samples with illustrations in different books suggested in the supplementary sources.)

When the committees have completed their respective tasks, reassemble for the purpose of sharing notes. Concentrate on the following:

1. Reflect upon the differences between unit and lesson planning in each of the different dimensions (indicated in the foregoing).

2. Evaluate the different ways of approaching each aspect of the different unit and lesson plans. (For example, one committee may have suggested developing the unit introduction as a "lecture" by the teacher, by a technique of skillful questioning strategy, and so on.)

3. Note different views that seem to reflect the different subject fields represented.

4. Note the variety of learning experiences *and* list others that could be used in each case.

Self-assessment Items (answers provided on p. 62)

(1) Sometimes a beginning teacher will put in his/her lesson plan something like this: "I will discuss _____ and _____ with the class." Other individuals, for the same section of the lesson plan, may list eight or ten questions to be asked. Both are hazardous techniques for effective teaching. Explain why.

(2) In some cases the mere identification of learning activities in the unit plan is sufficient (no lesson plan is needed). Defend or refute.

(3) In some subject fields, lesson plans tend to be more detailed than in other subject fields. Defend or refute.

(4) Occasionally one hears a teacher suggest, "I want to find a method or two that work for me and then stick with them." What are the fallacies of such a position?

C. *Lesson plan analysis.* From the following two lesson plans, select those aspects (sections) which you consider most useful by labeling *A* or *B*, *and then* in one sentence defend each choice. (Since we have developed class discussion method as a frame of reference for this experience, you may want to refer to a sample lesson plan in this area.)*

1. Problem

    Statement:

2. Objectives

    Statement:

3. Lesson Approach

    Statement:

4. Lesson Development

    Analysis of the problem

    Statement:

    Developing hypotheses

    Statement:

*After you complete this task you may check your answers by turning to p. 66.

Developing criteria

Statement:

5. Deriving Generalizations

Statement:

PLAN A

Subject: 10th Grade English

Unit: Adolescent Novel: Search for Understanding

Concept: Communication Is a Two-Way Process

Problem: What steps should be taken to improve adolescent-parent communication?

Goals: After this lesson the student should have furthered his understanding of the factors contributing to good communication, as evidenced by:

1. His understanding of the nature of communication blocks.

2. His feelings on the importance of sharing one's true feelings when communicating.

Lesson Approach:

What are some sources of communication in our everyday world?

What communication problems have you recently encountered?

We have just been reading THE PIGMAN (by Zindel) and TURNED OUT (by Wojciechowska). What factors in THE PIGMAN strained communication between John and his father?

What efforts, if any, were made to correct this problem? (How effective were they?)

In TURNED OUT what factors made it impossible for Kevin to communicate with his family?

What was Kevin's reaction?

This leads us to our problem for today's discussion (on chalkboard). Who will redefine the word "communication" for us?

PLAN B

Subject: 10th Grade English

Unit: Adolescent Novel: Search for Understanding

Concept: Communication Is a Two-Way Process

Problem: What communication blocks do adolescents and parents often encounter?

Goals: After this lesson the student should have furthered his understanding of the factors contributing to good communication, as evidenced by:

1. His contributions during the discussion.

2. His ability to derive generalizations at the culmination of the discussion.

Lesson Approach:

We live in a world of communication.

We receive information from our radios, newspapers, and television daily. We identify with the lyrics of popular songs, and we surround ourselves with constant sound. But for all of our supposed sophistication, we often have trouble communicating with those nearest us.

We have just finished reading THE PIGMAN (by Zindel) and TURNED OUT (by Wojciechowska). As we all realize, literature in the form of prose, poetry, or drama is an author's attempt to communicate with the reader. The two adolescent novels we have just read deal with young people's attempts to communicate with their peers and parents in order to find their identity within their particular world. In both books, the adolescent-parent communication was strained to the point that conflict rather than harmony was the norm within the home. We can laugh when John in THE PIGMAN puts glue in the telephone lock that his father installed to eliminate John's telephone use, but perhaps we need to look at the reasons why an adolescent and his father could reach such a state.

Let us look at the problem I have written on the chalkboard. Here we will redefine the word "communication."

Lesson Development

Analysis of the Problem

Why is adolescent-parent communication important?

What are some common blocks to adolescent-parent communication?

What role do emotions play?

Why do young men and women sometimes avoid major issues or even deliberately mislead their parents in certain areas of communication? Or parents with their teen-age youngsters?

What are some consequences of such behavior?

In families where adolescent-parent communication is good, what general communication techniques seem to stand out?

Establishing Hypotheses

Now in view of our discussion thus far, what steps should be taken to improve adolescent-parent communication?

Possible solutions (suggestive only):

1. Listen to what is being said as well as to what might be the implied meaning.
2. Define your terms and choose words that convey the meaning you want to express.

Establishing Criteria

What are some standards for evaluating the foregoing possible solutions to our problem?

Deriving Generalizations:

From our discussion on communication, let us see if we can evolve some generalizations that might apply (suggestive only).

1. Good communication is a process of give-and-take in an atmosphere of openness.
2. Meaning is communicated in many ways.

Lesson Development

Analysis of the Problem

How does language affect communication?

What type of atmosphere is appropriate for good communication?

If an argument is anticipated, what planning (if any) is necessary in advance?

Does prejudice or bigotry affect communication? How should they be handled?

Can there be anything said that does not carry with it some intended feelings?

Then why (or why not) might tempers and overly emotional reactions be avoided?

What obligation do we have to be honest in our communication?

Is a "white lie" ever appropriate?

What should be done when we know a communicant is not being honest?

When controversy exists, should provision be made for a "cooling-off" period?

Establishing Hypotheses

At this point possible ways to open up communication will be discussed. These will come from students themselves.

Establishing Criteria

Prior to evaluating our possible solutions to the problem, we need to set up some standards that must be met. *Possible standards* (suggestive only):

1. Communication should satisfy both parties.
2. Time should be allowed for thought and consideration.

Deriving Generalizations:

From our discussion today three major ideas seem to have emerged.

1. Good communication is a process of give-and-take in an atmosphere of openness.
2. Meaning is communicated in many ways.
3. Words in a teen-ager's vocabulary sometimes do not mean the same to him as to his parents and other adults.

Self-assessment Items (answers provided on p. 63)

(1) Distinguish between the functions of the lesson approach and the lesson development.

(2) The heart of the reflective process is contained in the lesson development section. Defend or refute.

(3) Why is it important that students (rather than the teacher) evolve lesson generalizations as much as possible?

D: *Instructional application.* By referring to the other LAPs in this module (Formulating Concepts and Developing Instructional Objectives), you will note that you have already developed three unit concepts, instructional objectives, and behavioral outcomes for a selected unit in your field of specialization. Using these as a basis, complete the following as indicated:

Unit planning

1. Develop a unit introduction (of about two pages) in which you attempt to accomplish the following:

   a. Motivation for the unit.

   b. Reasons for studying the unit.

   c. An indication of projected class activities.

2. Develop a brief outline of the major content to be covered.

3. For each of the anticipated unit behavioral outcomes (derived for each of your three instructional objectives), identify learning activities which, in your judgment, will contribute to goal fulfillment.

4. For each of your identified learning activities, develop appropriate problems, techniques, and details necessary for foreshadowing the lessons needed. For example, if class discussion is indicated, you should develop a tentative discussion problem.

Lesson planning

1. Using one of your unit concepts as a basis, develop an instructional objective and two behavioral outcomes for the *lesson*.

2. Develop a brief learning approach in which you attempt to develop interest in the lesson. Limit to two questions or sentences.

3. Using a learning activity as a basis (previously identified in the foregoing under unit planning), construct the lesson development section of your lesson plan. Limit to two questions or sentences for each of the listed phases. Use class discussion as a basic frame of reference. (In preparation for this experience you may want to refer to the lesson plan you analyzed in the preceding learning activity or one of the lesson plans provided in the Hoover texts.)

   a. Analysis of the problem

   (1)

   (2)

  b. Establishing hypotheses

    (1)

    (2)

  c. Establishing criteria

    (1)

    (2)

  d. Deriving generalizations

    (1)

    (2)

After completing the foregoing, discuss your experiences with other new teachers who are working along with you. Attempt to clarify any points of confusion or areas of difficulty or differences encountered. (If working alone, prepare a written critique of your experiences and discuss it with your coordinating teacher or college supervisor.)

Self-assessment Items (answers provided on p. 63)

(1) Distinguish between unit and lesson outcomes.

(2) Why is it desirable to foreshadow learning activities in your unit outcomes?

(3) Why is it desirable to base lesson objectives on a basic unit concept rather than on specific content?

(4) Sometimes teachers hesitate to develop lesson plans when student involvement in planning activities is desired, claiming, "Such plans tend to make the whole experience a sham of merely doing what the teacher wants." Explain how this "trap" can be avoided with skillful planning.

If, after reviewing your learning activities for this LAP, you feel that you can meet the stated objectives, proceed to the posttest. If not, you should complete at least one of the optional activities. Note that each provides for a number of optional situations, depending upon your own individual circumstances.

Optional Activities

E: *Class observation.* In order to fully appreciate the diversity of planning, you should arrange to visit with teachers in various fields of specialization. Working in a committee of three if possible, proceed as indicated. (If working alone, you may be able to achieve the objectives of this experience by visiting the first and third teachers suggested.)

1. Have one member of your committee visit a social science or a literature teacher. Seek the following information:

   a. The major elements of unit and lesson plans used. (Usually you will have to rely upon what the teacher tells you, as some teachers are understandably reluctant to open their lesson plan files for such purposes.)

   b. The general lesson plan format employed. (Considerable variation can be expected.)

   c. Occasions when prepared lesson plans are deemed unnecessary (if any). Determine why.

   d. How often lesson plans are used and how they are altered.

2. Have a second member of your committee visit a math, physics, or chemistry class. Obtain the same information as in the above.

3. Have the third member of your committee visit a mental or motor skills class, such as foreign language, speech, physical education, shop, typing, shorthand. Obtain the same information as in the above.

4. Following the visits, compare notes and discuss your experiences. Use the foregoing visit guide as a basic frame of reference. (If working alone, prepare a written critique, especially noting basic differences from teacher to teacher.)

Self-assessment Items (answers provided on p. 63)

(1) How do you account for the wide diversity of planning activities from one teacher to another?

(2) The assignment is often considered an optional aspect of a lesson plan. Teachers who tend to place least emphasis on lesson planning, however, most often mention the assignment as a major aspect of planning. How do you account for this discrepancy?

(3) Some teachers tend to bypass unit planning, while emphasizing lesson planning. What hazards are associated with such a practice?

F: *Panel discussion.* If working through this LAP along with other new teachers, arrange for a panel discussion of experienced teachers with diverse views as indicated. (If working alone, attempt to confer with such teachers.)
Panel Problem: What factors contribute to divergent views on lesson planning?

1. Arrange to have the following represented on your panel: a principal; a departmental chairman; two teachers who do little formal lesson planning (one in the skills area, another in an academic area); two teachers who do rather extensive planning (one in the skills area, another in an academic area).

2. Make sure that all views are expressed and evaluated by the panel group in a half-hour panel discussion.

3. Provide an opportunity for your own group to ask questions following the discussion. Do *not* in any way challenge members of the panel.

4. *Post-Panel Discussion.* After the panel group has been dismissed, hold a discussion with your own group.

   Problem: How can we plan most effectively?

   Using the facts and opinions from the panel as a basis, concentrate on various possible solutions to planning problems. To illustrate: (1) What impact (if any) does one's field of specialization have upon the nature of planning? (2) What influence (if any) does the particular method have on the nature and extensiveness of planning?

5. Finally, attempt to derive some generalizations from the experience. (If working alone, prepare a written critique of the foregoing and discuss with your supervisor.)

Self-assessment Items (answers provided on pp. 63–64)

(1) Why do school administrators often prefer rather detailed lesson plans for teachers?

(2) The daily lesson plan is a misnomer. Defend or refute.

(3) What potential hazards do you see for the teacher of a mental or motor skill merely directing students to do the job, such as playing a game in Physical Education class?

POSTTEST (answers provided on pp. 64–66)

After you have completed the learning activities, complete the posttest and evaluate by checking your answers with those at the end of this LAP. Note that supporting reasons are provided for both correct and incorrect items.

A. List eight basic features of unit and lesson planning.

   Unit planning

   1.

   2.

   3.

   4.

   Lesson planning

   5.

   6.

   7.

   8.

B. From the assorted lesson plan excerpts, place a check (√) by nine of those most appropriately stated for maximum efficiency. (You are to assume that each excerpt contains all the material in the lesson plan that is relative to the specific point introduced.)

1. Lesson Development: Discuss the political events leading to the outbreak of World War I.

2. Today we have discussed the political, social, and economic events that sparked World War I.

3. The film we have just seen is a narrative account of the events leading up to World War I. What were they? Why did attempts at compromise fail?

4. What political party was in power at the outbreak of the war? What events contributed to Wilson's popularity during the war? In what ways did political events shape the postwar period? What parallels, if any, exist today?

5. Mr. Jones, a political science expert, has agreed to be here tomorrow. What are some questions that might be raised?

6. In weighing alternatives to our problem, be sure to remember that the specter of isolationism must be considered.

7. Our class problem today is "The Events Leading Up to World War I."

8. From our class experience what generalizations stand out in your mind? Example: The scramble for power (e.g., colonialism prior to World War I) leads to political unrest.

9. The attached excerpt from one of Woodrow Wilson's speeches will be read. What is the major issue being discussed? Explain the validity (or invalidity) of Wilson's notion of world involvement as it applies to today's world.

10. Now in view of our analysis of the problem, what steps do you think might be taken to minimize another world conflict such as that of World War I?

11. The debate will be followed by a brief discussion.

12. During World War I the soldier's pay was barely enough to sustain his basic needs. Today's soldier, on the other hand, receives a substantial salary plus numerous fringe benefits. What influence, if any, might this difference have on patriotic feelings? His willingness to go into battle?

13. Today I will present the class with a few slides to stimulate interest in the lesson.

14. What criteria should be considered as we weigh possible solutions to the problem? Be prepared to justify each.

15. Let panel discussion continue without interruption (if possible). Open class to a brief question session immediately following.

16. After the panel discussion a follow-up discussion will be conducted. We will emphasize both panel processes and major points and issues raised.

17. The lesson will be initiated through a series of questions relative to the "Watergate Scandal." This will lead into the major topic for the day.

18. In launching the project, I will ask students to raise questions that interest them.

19. Basic generalizations to be derived from the class experience:

    a. Protective alliances tend to entangle the aims of a nation.

    b. Protective alliances tend to deter aggressors.

    c. A changing political structure tends to lead to world tension.

    d. "Have-not" nations tend to cooperate in order to exert pressure on industrialized nations.

20. We will first go into an analysis of the problems. Emphasis will be placed upon student-initiated questions.

C. Develop two key questions (or sentences when appropriate) for each of the five identified aspects of a lesson plan. Use class discussion as a frame of reference and base your responses on the problem, "What steps should be taken to minimize the expense of political campaigns?"

1. Lesson Approach

    a.

    b.

2. Lesson Development

Analysis of the Problem

    a.

    b.

Establishing Hypotheses

    a.

    b.

Establishing Criteria

    a.

    b.

3. Deriving Generalizations

    a.

    b.

The most frequent complaint against beginning teachers by college supervisors, cooperating teachers, and school administrators alike is their general inability to plan effectively. Thus your successful completion of this LAP deserves definite commendation. Although you still have a lot to learn while on the job, you should find the task relatively easy to achieve. Even if you failed to meet the recommended mastery level, do not be discouraged. By studying the answers to the posttest and the supporting reasons for all items, you should soon reach this level.

ANSWERS TO PREASSESSMENT ITEMS

You can make these items a most valuable learning experience by studying the provided reasons for both correct and incorrect responses. You will note that since Part A has no specific number of correct responses, several additional points (characteristics) are given. Since the last part calls for your constructed answers, they may not be identical to those supplied by the writer. Such feedback, however, can enhance your understanding of the items.

A. 1. A unit plan evolves around a central theme or idea.

2. The unit is supported by a definite body of content.

3. A unit is structured around several related concepts.

4. Each unit concept provides a basis for instructional objectives and behavioral outcomes.

5. Behavioral objectives foreshadow learning and evaluational activities.

6. Identified learning activities set the stage for lesson planning.

7. The lesson plan is based on one (rarely two or three) unit concepts.

8. The lesson plan is organized around an appropriately worded problem.

9. The lesson plan contains objectives and behavioral outcomes (derived from the unit concept [s]).

10. The lesson plan provides *initial* experiences for developing interest in the lesson.

11. The lesson plan contains the framework for *development* of the reflective processes (based upon the particular method(s) to be employed).

12. The lesson plan provides for a lesson *culmination* (usually a synthesis of ideas).

B. 1 (Here the teacher specifies what is to be sought from the film.)

5 (Specific questions which might be asked students are provided.)

7 (Although students themselves evolve lesson generalizations, the lesson plan should provide samples as a possible source of "pump-priming" if needed.)

8 (Students are asked to evolve criteria; a sample is listed in the plan to aid the teacher in getting students started.)

11 (A specific behavior, addressed to students, is defined in the plan.)

12 (Specific directions in the lesson plan provide insurance against forgetting a vital aspect of the activity.)

13 (Here we have specific questions that the teacher might ask.)

17 (The specific question could be used to get the students involved in providing their own questions.)

18. (Specific points are entered in the lesson plan for the activity.)

Reasons for incorrect items

2. (The plan does not indicate how the task is to be accomplished.)

3. (We seldom reach a "conclusion" on the basis of class discussion. Moreover, students themselves would make any such conclusion. Thus one should *not* be entered in a lesson plan.)

4. (Without specific points in the plan, this "discussion of implications" can be only a hit-or-miss affair.)

6. (One should indicate how this "setting up criteria" is to be done.)

9. (This tends to encourage the teacher [rather than students] to draw the generalizations.)

10. (Fails to indicate what this "brief discussion" will entail.)

14. (Although this does involve necessary steps in a class discussion, it fails to provide needed assistance as to how to accomplish the task.)

15. (Again, the lesson plan must depict how the task is to be accomplished.)

16. (Specific points, in preparation of students for the case, are needed.)

19. (No indication is provided as to how this is to be achieved.)

20. (The basic criteria should be listed in the plan to aid the teacher.)

C. 1. Lesson approach

One question should deal with problem clarification, the other with the need for the problem.

Examples:

a. What constitutes the energy crisis?

b. What conditions brought on the problem?

2. Lesson development

Analysis of the problem

Questions should deal with presentation and evaluation of the facts.

Examples

a. What are the various sources of energy?

b. How does a shortage of oil influence industrial output in the various fields?

Establishing hypotheses

Questions must deal with introduction of possible solutions and evaluation of these.

Examples

a. Should the U.S. government retaliate economically against the Arab oil embargo?

b. What might be some advantages and disadvantages of such action?

Establishing criteria

Questions should deal with standards that possible solutions (hypotheses) must meet.

Examples

a. What standards should our proposals meet?

b. How might such standards influence diplomatic relations in the area?

3. Deriving generalizations

These are ideas that result from the discussion.

Examples

a. The U.S. may become economically independent of foreign oil in six to eight years.

b. Substitute energy sources (such as harnessing solar energy) must be preceded by many years of research.

ANSWERS TO SELF-ASSESSMENT ITEMS

Self-assessment items are designed to assist you in gaining depth of understanding as you proceed through the various learning activities. Most of them do not have single correct answers. For feedback, however, you should compare your answers with the samples provided here.

A. (1) This gives focus or direction to the unit activities.

(2) Unit concepts: Provide the basic structure of the unit.

Unit introduction: Provides motivation (reasons for the unit).

Content outline: Provides basic informational pattern from which to develop the unit concepts.

Objectives and outcomes: Set up specific behaviors to guide learning and evaluation.

Learning activities: Offer means of achieving each of the concepts and outcomes.

Evaluation: A means of assessing how well concepts have been internalized.

(3) Problem: Sets up the major problem to be solved.

Concept: Provides a basis for the lesson.

Objectives and outcomes: Set up specific behaviors to guide evaluation of learning.

Lesson approach: Provides motivation for the lesson.

Lesson development: It is here that the major aspects of the particular method or technique are amplified.

Deriving generalizations: Provides for student derivation of major ideals gleaned from the lesson.

(4) A unit introduction is essentially an overview of the lesson, indicating purposes and perhaps some technique.

A lesson introduction foreshadows the specific lesson. It is basically a motivation device.

(5) Unit activities foreshadow specific methods that may be employed. Lesson activities are those of the specific methods of the day.

(6) The major concept of a lesson is simply one of the unit concepts that become a basis for the lesson. A lesson generalization is specific to the unit concept. Several make up a unit concept.

B_1 (1) Unit concepts are the major ideas to be acquired from the unit experience. Thus they set the stage for developing learning activities that will lead to concept attainment.

(2) Defend, within limits. Normally the teacher selects the unit and identifies basic concepts in pre-instructional activities. Then basic ideas may be altered and modified somewhat, depending upon identification of needs and interests of students. Thus student participation in the unit introduction or establishing purpose phase of a unit is desirable.

(3) A resource unit opens the door to the many instructional possibilities available. In a sense it becomes the hypothesis phase of unit planning since the individual teacher selects those particular approaches deemed preferable under existing conditions.

(4) By providing cue words only or merely sample questions or illustrations in the plan.

(5) In some plans the assignment is developed as an integral part of the regular learning activities. This is consistent with today's trend for in-class assignments. As such, they may occur at any point during a lesson.

B_2 (1) To say, "I will discuss. . ." provides no clue as to how. At least a couple of actual questions that might be asked should be developed. To prepare numerous questions tends to limit "discussion" to the teacher's preplanned agenda. This tends to add to teacher talk and to minimize the creative aspects of reflective thinking.

(2) Defend. Although lesson plans are usually necessary, many teachers (who have had considerable experience) effectively bypass lesson plans when such activities as oral reports or collateral readings are planned. In such cases the teacher has a mental picture of how he or she will proceed.

(3) Defend. In the more exact sciences (math and science, for example), there is often less direct student interaction than in the social science fields. When considerable verbal interaction is anticipated, elaborate plans are needed.

(4) Variety is needed for maintaining interest. Moreover, each method is useful in fulfilling different purposes. In most classes purposes vary considerably.

C. (1) The lesson approach is the motivation for the lesson; lesson development embodies the heart of the lesson—the steps of the particular method(s) to be employed.

 (2) Defend. Since this is essentially the method and since methods all embody the reflective processes, this must be true.

 (3) This forces the learner to generalize with understanding. If the teacher "gives" him or her the generalizations, they are likely to be memorized with little basic understanding.

D. (1) Unit activities foreshadow specific methods that may be employed. Lesson activities are those of the specific methods of the day.

 (2) This tends to tie anticipated outcomes to means or ways of achieving them *at the time of the preplanning experience*. The close connection between projected outcomes and learning activities may become obscured if not identified early.

 (3) Basic content merely provides the necessary ingredients for developing an understanding of basic ideas. Basic ideas (content) transfer to related situations readily; specific content does not.

 (4) Focus preplanned materials on techniques of getting students actively involved. Do not anticipate what students will decide, but *do* establish broad limits. Students, for example, seldom, if ever, decide what units will be studied. They may delimit the scope of study within a unit or even have a hand in developing the sequences of units to be studied.

Optional activities

E. (1) There is some need for differences from one subject to another.

 There are many different ways of planning.

 There are differences between new and experienced teachers.

 There are differences between "good" and "poor" teachers.

 (2) In a well-planned lesson the assignment often evolves naturally during the lesson development phase of a lesson. Thus the assignment is integrated into the instructional sequence instead of being added.

 (3) This tends to encourage over-reliance upon a single textbook. Moreover, it tends to segmentize learning. The evidence clearly indicates that unit teaching (emphasizing concepts) results in greater retention and transfer of learning than a mere lesson-by-lesson approach.

F. (1) Aside from the lesson plan's value in effective teaching, the administrator sees value for substitute teachers, who often must come into a situation with little or no advance notice.

 (2) Defend, if daily plan implies a different lesson for each day of class. Many lessons extend well beyond a single 50-minute class period. Some may extend for several such class periods. Usually there is little need to do a new plan for each day of a continuing lesson.

(3) This may result in ill-conceived ideas (generalizations) relative to the experience. Some individuals may become keenly competitive, but fail to gain an acceptable perspective relative to ethical conduct, for example.

ANSWERS TO POSTTEST

For most beneficial results you should work through the entire LAP before you check your answers to the posttest. Failure to meet the provided minimum standards probably suggests certain weaknesses that need to be corrected. As with the Preassessment items, you will find supporting reasons for answers. It is hoped that this will serve as desirable feedback in your quest for mastery.

A. *Unit plan*

1. Evolves around a central idea or theme.

2. Supported by a definite body of organized content.

3. Structured around several related unit concepts.

4. Each concept provides the basis for instructional objectives and behavioral outcomes.

5. Behavioral objectives foreshadow learning and evaluational activities.

6. Identified learning activities set the stage for lesson planning.

Lesson plan

7. Based upon one (rarely two or three) unit concepts.

8. Organized around an appropriately worded problem.

9. Contains lesson objectives and behavioral outcomes (derived from the unit concept).

10. Provides *initial* experiences for developing interest in the lesson.

11. Contains the framework for *development* of reflective processes (based upon the particular method[s] to be employed).

12. Provides for a lesson *culmination* (usually a synthesis of ideas).

B. 3 (Special questions are provided in the plan to guide the film analysis.)

4 (Such questions are useful in guiding the teacher.)

5 (By putting in the question, "What questions might be raised?", the teacher directly involves students.)

8 (Calls directly for students to offer their own ideas; also provides a "pump-priming" point, if needed.)

9 (Denotes specifically what the teacher will do and guides him or her in questions to ask.)

10   (This going into the "hypothesis phase" of a class discussion is marked by the specific question to be asked.)

12   (Spells out specifically how the problem will be approached.)

14   (As opposed to saying what students will be asked, the specific question is asked in the lesson plan.)

15   (Here it is merely necessary to indicate what will be done as there is no basis for projecting what might arise.)

Reasons for incorrect items

1   (This is hardly better than nothing, for it provides no clues relative to how "discussion" is to proceed.)

2   (This point in a lesson plan serves no purpose.)

6   (Here the teacher is throwing in his own biases. In a discussion the students themselves work out the problem.)

7   (This should be stated in question form, as will be used for the lesson.)

11   (Fails to outline how this "discussion" will proceed.)

13   (Notation of slides should be accompanied with actual questions to be asked.)

16   (Would have been desirable to list specific points or questions under each category to guide the teacher.)

17   (Must actually put some sample questions in the plan itself.)

18   (It is desirable to indicate specifically how this will be accomplished.)

19   (This leads to the teacher's doing the task that students should do.)

20   (Should develop sample questions that could be asked.)

C.   1.   Lesson Approach

(One question should deal with problem clarification, the other with the need for the problem.)

Examples:

    a.   What is meant by political campaigns?

    b.   How expensive are political campaigns for national, state, and local offices?

   2.   Lesson Development

    Analysis of the problem

(Questions should deal with presentation and evaluation of the facts.)

Examples:

    a.   Who are the major contributors to political campaigns?

    b.   Why would individuals or businesses want to contribute to an individual's political campaign?

    Establishing hypotheses

(Questions must deal with introduction of possible solutions and evaluation of these.)

Examples:

a. Should political contributions be restricted to the individual involved?

b. What might be some advantages and disadvantages of such action?

Establishing criteria

(Questions should deal with standards that possible solutions must meet.)

Examples:

a. What standards should our proposals meet?

b. How might such standards influence political campaigns?

3. Deriving Generalizations

(These are ideas that evolve from the discussion.)

Examples:

a. Political campaigns are becoming more expensive all the time.

b. Severe restrictions on contributions would eliminate many qualified individuals from seeking elective offices.

Answers to Learning Activity *C*

	Plan A	Plan B
Problem	X (This is an open-ended problem.)	
Objectives		X (Specific behaviors are provided.)
Lesson Approach	X (Relates to immediate interests of students.)	
Lesson Development	X (Specific questions are used; moreover, they deal with consequences of behavior.)	
Developing Hypotheses	X (Actual sample questions to be asked are provided; we also have sample answers which might be expected.)	
Developing Criteria		X (Offers a couple of samples to guide the teacher.)
Deriving Generalizations	X (Students themselves are asked to derive the generalizations; at the same time the teacher has listed samples as a guide in teaching.)	

SUPPLEMENTARY SOURCES

The following sources may be used in lieu of the Hoover texts or, preferably, as supplementary to them. Generally they are consistent with the models provided in the LAPs of this module. As such, the references do not represent all of the most recent references in the area; rather, they constitute selected references designed to broaden or expand needed background information.

Gayles, Anne Richardson, *Instructional Planning in the Secondary School* (New York: David McKay Co., Inc., 1973), Part IX.

Hansen, Kenneth T., *Secondary Teaching: A Personal Approach* (Itasca, Ill.: F. E. Peacock Publishing Co., 1974), Chap. 3.

Hoover, Kenneth H., *The Professional Teacher's Handbook*, 2nd ed. (Boston: Allyn and Bacon, Inc., 1976), Chap. 3.

Hoover, Kenneth H., and Paul M. Hollingsworth, *Learning and Teaching in the Elementary School*, 2nd ed. (Boston: Allyn and Bacon, Inc., 1975), Chap. 7.

Inlow, Gail M., *Maturity in High School Teaching*, 2nd ed. (Englewood Cliffs, N.J.: Prentice-Hall, Inc., 1970), Chaps. 5 and 6.

Kim, Eugene C., and Richard D. Kellough, *A Resource Guide for Secondary School Teaching* (New York: Macmillan Co., Inc., 1974), Parts II and III.

Krueger, M. G., "Putting Social Lightning into Lesson Plans," *Journal of Teacher Education*, 23: 186–188 (Summer, 1972).

Leonard, Joan M., and others, *General Methods of Effective Teaching: A Practical Approach* (New York: Thomas Y. Crowell Co., 1972), Chaps. 3 and 4.

Mosston, Mouska, *Teaching from Common to Discovery* (Belmont, Calif.: Wadsworth Publishing Co., 1972).

module
II

THE
LEARNING
ENVIRONMENT

A proper learning environment is basic to the success of any teaching technique. Management techniques immediately focus attention on the teen-ager. What is he or she like? How are individual needs best met? As an individual in transition from childhood to adult status, the adolescent is caught in a state of ambivalence. Consequently, needs continually vascillate between those of dependency and a desire for almost complete autonomy. The natural outcome of such instability is heavy reliance upon approval of the peer group. Thus any instructional procedure or technique that threatens this relationship is likely to meet with strong resistance.

A symptom of inadequate or misdirected motivation will be reflected in student misbehavior. Discipline has for many years been a major concern for teachers. The problem is even more acute today than it was two or three decades ago. A number of factors have contributed to this state of affairs, among them: (1) greater emphasis on compulsory education, (2) social promotion policies, (3) emphasis on a secondary education for everyone, (4) school integration policies, and (5) larger classes.

Beginning teachers especially are prone to seek quick solutions to discipline problems. They reason that if this one problem—discipline—can be worked out, their chances of survival are assured. While the reasoning process is valid, the problem is considerably more complex. Discipline problems are symptoms of more serious difficulties. They may indicate a lack of student interest, the need for recognition, or problems of group acceptance. Effective corrective action, then, must be directed to the underlying cause(s). Thus motivation and discipline, treated in the first LAP, are viewed as parts of a total complex.

69

Closely associated with the foregoing is the problem of providing for individual differences. It is the rare student indeed who will *not* create disturbances when class expectations are too high or too low for his or her capacities. Yet some teachers typically expect all students to read the same books, to do the same problems, and to keep up with all other members of the class. As might be expected, these teachers often find they are devoting most of their energies to problems of class control.

Students, in whatever manner they may be grouped, will vary widely in any number of ways. With the typical class size of thirty to forty students, individualization of instruction can be most difficult unless some systematized approach is employed. Accordingly, a useful technique for subgrouping within the classroom is emphasized in the second LAP. Subgrouping on the basis of achievement and/or ability, employed widely in the elementary schools, also can be effective at the secondary level. The function of such an approach, of course, is to facilitate individualization of instruction. Individualization techniques feature a variety of self-instructional devices and techniques. Among these is the current prominence of some form of learning programs. In this module focus has been placed upon learning activity packages patterned after the LAPs in this manual.

Motivation-
Discipline
Techniques

RATIONALE. All individuals have a basic motivation to learn. Each of us is continually grappling with difficulties in our daily existence. Motivating students to perform the necessary work in a class, then, is a process of focusing such processes toward the particular subject and lesson involved. Some students enter the situation with a high level of motivation for school work; others tend to possess a relatively low level of such motivation.

Whenever general motivation (reflected in terms of activity) is misdirected, discipline problems tend to emerge. Students learn what they want to learn, behave the way they want to behave. A teacher can establish an environment conducive to learning but cannot force or coerce learning. Many discipline techniques that appear to work are psychologically damaging and self-defeating. Furthermore, appropriate discipline for one student may not be appropriate for another or even for the same person in different situations. Nevertheless, the motivation-discipline complex sets the stage for subsequent learning activities.

OVERVIEW

Key Concepts

1. Motivation is a basic aspect of personality that changes slowly over a period of time.

2. Basic psychological needs, special interests, and incentives are prompters of motivation.

3. Motivational techniques are essential aspects of all instructional activities.

4. Group efforts to activate the desire to learn must be supplemented with attention to the special interests of a few students whose desire to learn is especially low.

5. Misbehavior is often a symptom of motivational difficulties.

6. Student misbehavior must not jeopardize the learning environment of other students.

New Terms

1. Motivation: That part of the self which impels an individual to learn— to work toward a goal. It is thought to represent a basic aspect of personality.

2. Basic psychological needs: Inner forces that drive and direct an individual's behavior. Needs (e.g., success, recognition, acceptance, approval) must be continually fulfilled if adequate self-adjustment is to be realized.

3. Intrinsic motivation: That motivation which originates from within the individual.

4. Extrinsic motivation: Incentives advanced by others to encourage learning.

5. Self-concept: One's assessment of his own capacities and worth.

6. Discipline: A classroom organization conducive to orderly social conduct, leading to a self-disciplined individual.

7. Students with problems: Reasonably normal students who sometimes misbehave. They respond to appropriate instructional direction and guidance.

8. Problem students: Students (relatively few in number) who have problems of psychological adjustment. Misbehavior must be corrected *prior* to introduction of procedures designed to cope with underlying causes.

OBJECTIVES. After this experience you should be able to employ appropriate instructional motivation-discipline procedures, as evidenced by your ability to:

1. List four out of five basic characteristics of an adequately motivated-disciplined individual.

2. Distinguish between "students with problems" and "problem students" in eight out of nine selected illustrations of misbehavior.

3. Distinguish between high, medium, and low instructional priorities in ten of twelve cases from a provided list of motivational techniques.

4. Distinguish between appropriate and inappropriate discipline procedures in ten of twelve instances from a provided list.

5. Employ appropriate motivation-discipline principles and supporting statements in four out of five provided situations.

PRELIMINARY READING. Since the elements of instructional methodology are somewhat variable, the following excerpts are provided to help you develop a frame of reference as a point of departure for this experience. If you prefer, you may proceed directly to the Preassessment items.

PROMPTERS OF HUMAN BEHAVIOR

All individuals have a propensity to act when conditions make them want to act. These prompters of human behavior come from different sources, as indicated.

Personality Determinants. Mounting evidence suggests that motivation is an aspect of personality; motivation is something a student already possesses. It is *not* something that a teacher does to students directly.

Highly motivated students tend to have a positive picture of themselves. They feel competent to handle the problems of their everyday existence. They feel accepted and respected. Being free of their own problems, they tend to have a positive concept of others, as evidenced by a willingness to trust and to rely upon the integrity of others.

On the other hand, students with low motivation tend to have low self-esteem. They feel that they are not liked and respected, that they are not worthy, not important. Accordingly, they feel that other people cannot be trusted, that others will take advantage of them if possible.

Motivation as an aspect of personality changes slowly as personality changes. The teacher's initial task is to understand the fears and frustrations of low-motivated individuals and to help them alter their feelings toward themselves and others. In short, the teacher must develop a mental health approach to learning. Instead of trying to motivate students, the teacher will try to *interest* them. Interests, as opposed to motivation, are immediate and of a relatively short duration. Sustained interest over a period of time, however, can lead to motivational changes.

Basic Psychological Needs. All individuals possess common needs. Their fulfillment, however, is brought about in a variety of ways. Needs common to all individuals include the desire for affection, security, self-esteem, a reasonable degree of success, and the need for activity. In many instances teachers are able to capitalize on these needs. The basic instructional problem is to devise techniques of relating these needs to the values associated with the course involved.

Closely associated with basic needs is the element of curiosity. All individuals are curious. From the small child who asks "Why?" a thousand times a day to the elderly person who rushes to the scene of a fire or accident, individuals display a compelling urge to "know." Miss Webster, a chemistry teacher, capitalized on this natural urge when she set off a hydrogen explosion that literally shook the windows. "What happened?" "Why?" "How?" "What caused it?"—such questions came from all corners of the room. The problem was no longer one of interest, but one of directing the enthusiasm displayed.

Individual Interests.   For many years teachers have attempted to capitalize on the *individual interests* of youngsters as an avenue for developing interest in course instruction. While it is true that interests offer clues to certain needs of the individual, superficial inspection of a special interest may fail to disclose the particular need(s) being met. There is a tendency, however, for an individual to generalize in the area of special interests to *all* aspects of the interest involved. Thus the need fulfillment of satisfaction coming from one aspect of a special interest tends to *predispose* an individual to view other aspects of his special interest in a favorable light. For instance, a girl may have an interest in stamp collecting because it enables her to enjoy many hours of solitude made necessary because of her particular home environment. If the interest is strong enough, she will continue the activity long after the home environment has been altered. In other words, the activity began to fulfill other basic needs, such as gaining prestige from the collection, realizing a certain amount of success in the area, and the like.

The classroom teacher, then, can be reasonably certain that an individual's special interest (especially if it is noticeably high) is intimately associated with the fulfillment of a number of basic needs. His major task is to help the student relate the needs and values associated with his special interest to the needs and values associated with the course values. Almost any special interest *can* be related to course values *provided* the teacher allows himself to think creatively about the issue. The foregoing illustration is designed to suggest ways a special interest can be related to different subject fields.

Incentives or Extrinsic Instructional Devices.   Incentives involve such things as emphasis on marks, demanding certain marks as a basis for competitive sports eligibility, honor roll lists, and scholarship eligibility. Although extrinsic pressure *may* spur some students to greater effort, it is not without serious hazards. Motivation for high grades usually has a favorable impact only on those individuals who have a chance to win! In most class situations this will be a very small percentage of the group. Those most likely to be motivated by competition usually need it least. They are the individuals who are self-motivated to do high-quality work, with or without special motivational activities.

The impact of keen competition for marks on the less able student is likely to be quite unhealthful. Having failed before, the individual tends to be overly anxious at the outset of the learning experience. Added pressure tends to result in *less* effort in academic areas and a turning to other, less desirable, avenues of fulfilling the need for success.

Extrinsic devices *can* be effective if the learner has a fair chance of winning *as he sees it.* Some teachers, for example, have devised ways of permitting a student to compete with *his own past record.* For instance, in typing class a student can attempt to improve speed and accuracy as measured by past performances; in English class one may keep a list of his or her own grammatical errors; the tennis player may keep a record of his or her performance in serving the ball.

Motivational Priorities.   Since all people have certain *basic needs and a basic curiosity*, the teacher might focus attention *first* upon these areas. Thus, if the unit or lesson approach were effectively executed, *most* of the students might respond. One might reasonably expect a *few* students to show relatively little response, however, simply because their most urgent current needs are little affected by the motivational device(s).

The teacher's second line of attack might be in the area of *special interests.* Though this may be just as desirable as the first, it is not likely to be as economical of time and effort. If, however, the desire to learn can be effectively activated in *most* students through basic needs or through the element of curiosity, the teacher can afford the time needed to work through the area of special interests.

As a last resort, the teacher can offer *incentives* and even threaten students who have not yet responded to previous efforts at motivation. For example, it may be necessary to warn one or two students that failure to do the work will most certainly mean failure to receive credit for the course. A great deal of discretion is needed, however, in terms of the individual involved. Sometimes an incentive or threat will provide the stimulus needed for development of interest. In the overwhelming majority of cases, however, incentives and threats can do more harm than good to those students who are in greatest need of motivation. Far too many teachers rely almost exclusively on the use of incentives as an approach to motivation.

THE NATURE OF DISCIPLINE

> *You are working with. . . American children. This is not the same as training animals. . . . Animals are never supposed to rebel, . . . burn the lessons . . . into their brains, and into every pore of their bodies.*
>
> *. . . Only the leaders think in dictator countries. The people obey.*
>
> *Your job is different. Your children must think and obey. They must fit in and break out. They must follow accepted paths and break out on their own.*[1]

The adolescent is tasting independence for the first time. This independence in a democratic society is most important. Yet without some conformity, chaos follows. Hymes makes a most useful distinction between *children with problems* and *problem children.* He contends that the vast majority of youngsters are "well children" who need no more than "straight" teaching. Like all human beings, they have problems from time to time. With these youngsters the teacher discusses, explains, interprets, and talks. This he calls the logical approach. With a few students, however, one must do "remedial teaching." These are the individuals whose past experiences have "hurt" them. They tend to be suspicious, resentful, and overly egocentric. By every act they "cry out" for attention, for success, for love, for security. With these few individuals (the "problem children") the teacher must do "remedial teaching," i.e., he must say "no" and mean it. These are the students who will hurt others and create an undesirable learning situation. Although they need and demand attention, they must be "stopped"—compelled to conform to class rules—and then treated with all manner of kindness possible.

---

[1] *James L. Hymes, Jr.,* Behavior and Misbehavior *(Englewood Cliffs, N.J.: Prentice-Hall, Inc., 1955), p. 8.*

TEACHING DISCIPLINE TO DISTURBED STUDENTS

The thirsty man knows his trouble. He can tell you: "I want water."
The hungry man can verbalize his emptiness: "Food. Give me food."
The sleepy one can say to you: "I'm so tired I cannot keep my eyes
open." These . . . youngsters do not know their trouble. They have no
words to explain how they feel. They cannot say: "This is where it hurts."
. . . They hurt, but they cannot tell you where or why or how.
. . . These psychological hungers are not nicely located—in the belly, in
the throat, in the eyelids. They are all through the body . . . everywhere
. . . in every pore, muscle, and nerve.[2]

A few children—probably not more than three or four in an average classroom—have not had their basic psychological needs adequately fulfilled. The result is a "gnawing emptiness" which tends to dominate their behavior patterns. They are the problem children. They are the ones whose problems seem to obscure the individuals behind them! Identification is easy—just look for the individuals who are always getting into trouble; the ones with school reputations; those who have acquired nicknames: Jughead, Toughie, Weasel, Loudmouth.

Instead of proceeding with a straightforward approach to *teaching*, a reverse order of procedure is in order for these children. They first must be stopped. They will hit others, make wisecracks, talk back, or do anything to attract attention. As a professionally trained person, the teacher knows why. These individuals are trying to satisfy nagging hungers. They seek—they demand—recognition, success, love and affection, a sense of personal worth. These behaviors represent their attempts to adjust. Although they realize that such behaviors often get them into difficulty, they know of no other alternatives. Some recognition, transitory as it is, is better than no recognition.

There is one group of disturbed children that is not easily recognized as needing help. These children are the quiet ones—those who are not causing anyone else trouble but are nevertheless in trouble themselves. They are specialists at covering up. The trouble is there, but is bottled up inside. They are the ones who seek perfection, hide their emotions, or daydream. They are often fearful of social interaction, sometimes refusing to recite in class. "Pushing" is not the answer, nor is exacting high demands upon them a satisfactory approach. They lack confidence in themselves, but clues to the causes are not readily apparent from their behavior. Thus it often becomes necessary to turn to their pasts for answers to the problem. Parents, earlier teachers, and friends can often provide useful sources of data. In the meantime one can establish situations which provide a release for these "tightly sealed" feelings. Opportunities for composing stories, essays, or plays will help. Role playing may also provide the needed release. Although they may cause little or no trouble within the classroom, they are actually in greater trouble than those who overtly misbehave. It is a serious mistake to ignore them. They are the ones who can suddenly explode someday and literally destroy those with thom they associate.

---
[2] *Ibid., pp. 83-84.*

PREASSESSMENT ITEMS (answers provided on pp. 92-94)

This experience is designed to help you gain an overall perspective of the relationship of motivation and discipline to teaching. After completing the items, turn to the end of this LAP and check your answers. Note that answers (both correct and incorrect) are provided with supporting reasons to guide your efforts as you work through the LAP.

    A. List four essentials of an adequately motivated-disciplined student. (To illustrate: The individual possesses a high degree of self-direction and control.)

        1.

        2.

        3.

        4.

    B. Place the following code letters before each of the nine illustrations of misbehavior:

SP—Students with problems

PS—Problem students

    1. Susie seldom interacts with other students or the teacher in class. When called upon, she displays signs of embarrassment; she usually asks that questions be repeated and can seldom provide satisfactory answers.

    2. Tom disturbs frequently. When he is asked to work more quietly, he usually complies. Within a short time, however, he again disturbs the class.

    3. Jill and Mary are the closest of friends, preferring to work together most of the time. The teacher notes that class assignments, for the most part, represent the work of Mary.

    4. Joe is the class comedian. Although his behavior sometimes appropriately relieves class tension, most of the time his behavior diverts attention unnecessarily. Sometimes his jokes embarrass both teacher and students.

    5. Martha is caught cheating on a test. When asked for an explanation of her behavior, she first denies the act; later she admits that she had not properly prepared for the test.

    6. Mark has definite opinions. In class activities he stoutly defends them against all comers, except for his best friend, Joe, and Mr. Tompkins (the teacher).

    7. Nan seldom does her assignments even when pressed by the teacher. Fortunately, her ability is high enough to permit her to pass with minimum effort.

    8. Bill does not abide by the rules. He frequently boasts that he is "not afraid of man or beast." He often confronts the teacher and other students, including his best friends.

9. Hether comes to the teacher and requests that she not be placed on a committee with Ann. By way of explanation she says, "I hate her; she started a rumor about me that is not true."

C. Place one of the following code letters before each of the twelve recorded efforts of instructional motivation below:

H—High motivational priority (preferred efforts)

M—Medium or intermediate motivational priority (when preferred efforts fail)

L—Low motivational priority (when all other efforts fail)

1. Study hard for the test, Joe. If you don't pass, you will not be eligible for football.

2. You are in trouble, Bill. I'll make a deal with you! If you can turn in a good report on this extra project, I'll pass you this time.

3. Each person will display his art work and have five minutes to explain it to the rest of the class.

4. I notice that you have a stamp collection, Sue. Would you care to show and tell the class about it next time?

5. As one of our best basketball players, Tom, it has occurred to me that a report of the history of basketball might be extremely fascinating to our history class.

6. Those students who received an "A" on their work will be excused from the final examination.

7. You've all been asking about this unusual animal. By way of identification, what characteristics can we identify?

8. Those who finish the assignment early can go into any of our "fun-time" activities or do "free-reading," as you prefer.

9. In order to qualify for the club, you must have displayed special interest. Here are some suggested report topics that can satisfy this requirement.

10. As part of the assignment, your completed outer garment might be worn to one of the next two home football games.

11. Bill's father has several hives of bees. Bill has agreed to discuss with us some of the "practical problems of beekeeping."

12. I am arranging a short conference with each student for the purpose of discussing the strong points of each report.

D. Place one of the following code letters before each of the twelve illustrated discipline techniques below:

A—Appropriate

Q—Questionable

I—Inappropriate

1. Hand me your note, Bill. U-m-m-m-m, I see! Now you read it to the class.

2. Since you are unable to keep from talking even after being reminded of the problem, Mary, I think you had better take that empty seat in the back of the room.

3. That was a nasty remark, Joe. Don't you have any better language in your vocabulary?

4. You must realize that our established class rules have been violated. You will have to work alone for the rest of this project as our rules provide.

5. I think you realize that your behavior was not that of a gentleman. Between now and the next class period you must offer your apologies to Sue.

6. You have your choice, Tom. It is either three swats (in private) or an apology before next class period.

7. Since you have refused to leave, Joe, can you offer any suggestions for correcting the situation?

8. (Individually as the teacher passes by his seat) Dick, if you don't keep quiet, I'll have to move you.

9. Which one of you threw that piece of chalk? (Pause) We'll just wait until someone tells me.

10. You say you do not understand the assignment, Tom? Report to class for two fifteen-minute conferences sometime next week.

11. Rewrite your paper, correcting all mistakes. Your mark will be an average between your first and second grades.

12. All misspelled words will be written correctly 100 times and turned in to me by tomorrow.

E. Indicate the basic motivation-discipline principle that applies best in each of the five following situations: *Then*, suggest in not more than two sentences what you would do in each of the five motivation-discipline situations. (To illustrate: You are hired late in the school year. The class in American history is extremely apathetic. They tell you, "This stuff is not the least bit interesting."

Principle: Appeal to basic needs.

Develop an association between American history and the needs of your students.

1. Mary, unlike most of the rest of the class, displays little interest in biology.

2. During a study period Bill dozes in class. He is attracting the attention of other students. This has occurred two or three times within the past week or two.

3. Sam did not do his assignment, claiming he didn't understand how to proceed. You urged individuals to seek help if necessary and provided several days for completion of the task.

4. Bill flunked the test. (You suspect he didn't study.) He comes to you requesting make-up work, in his own words," . . . so that I can stay on the basketball team."

5. Jim's completed paper is almost identical to that of one of his friends. You suspect it was "copied." Both boys have come in for a conference, at your request.

If you were able to complete thirty-eight of the forty-two requested responses, you are to be congratulated. This suggests that you have a firm grasp of troublesome areas for most teachers. Thus you should proceed directly to the next LAP in this module (Providing for Individual Differences). Even if you experienced considerable difficulty with the Preassessment items, do not be distraught, for such was expected. The items not only enable you to visualize the scope of the task, but they also should serve a most useful learning device as you study reasons for correct and incorrect responses at the end of this LAP.

LEARNING ACTIVITIES

Work through each learning activity, complete the self-assessment items, and check your answers before moving to the next one. Note that the last learning activities are optional, depending upon your needs and circumstances at that point. You should be able to complete this LAP in about five hours.

A: *Read.* Re-examine the overview and the preliminary reading sections of this LAP. You will broaden your understanding substantially by studying Chaps. 4 and 5 in the Hoover texts, and/or by studying the selected references at the end of this LAP. You should find the Hymes and Frymier references especially useful. Note specifically the following:

1. Differences between students with high and those with low motivation.

2. Differences between students with problems and "problem students."

3. Personality determinants that influence instructional activities.

Self-assessment Items (answers provided on p. 95)

(1) What is the relationship between highly motivated students and "students with problems"?

(2) What is the relationship between students with low motivation and "problem students"?

(3) Students with high or low motivation in one class will tend to display the same characteristic in all classes. Defend or refute.

(4) Occasionally a "problem student" will exhibit model behavior in at least one of his or her classes. Explain.

(5) Describe how the personality determinants (internal-external; intake-output; approach-avoidance) influence instruction. (See Frymier reference.)

At this point you may select either Option B_1 or Option B_2, depending upon your particular situation. Those who are presently teaching should select Option B_1. Those who are not teaching or who do not have immediate access to students should select Option B_2.

Option B$_1$: *Modeled experience.* This experience can be acquired in different ways. There is an ample supply of films and filmstrips available, especially in the area of discipline.* You will probably find most such media sources fairly consistent with the principles featured in this LAP. Films in the realm of motivation are less likely to provide a complete model of the frame of reference offered here. Thus they should be supplemented accordingly.

Another option is to observe carefully selected teachers. All efforts must be made, however, to have such individuals use as closely as possible the approaches offered in this LAP. *At this point you should avoid visiting* a teacher doing his or her own "thing." Your purpose at this stage is to experience a modeled demonstration.

Make notes on the following points:

1. Motivation
    a. How basic needs provided a focus for developing and maintaining general class interest.
    b. How special interests of individual students were connected with class activities.
    c. How incentives (extrinsic devices) were used.
2. Discipline
    a. How "problem students" were recognized. (You may need to obtain this information directly from the teacher, if one is involved.)
    b. How "problem students" were controlled.
    c. How "students with problems" were handled when disturbing class proceedings.
    d. Differences in conduct standards (if any) tolerated.
    e. How defiant students were handled. (If not in evidence, check with the demonstrator.)

Self-assessment Items (answers provided on p. 95)

(1) List five basic psychological needs of adolescents.
(2) Sometimes a student will repeatedly demonstrate unacceptable classroom behavior, even after the consequences are fully understood. Why?
(3) Why are the problems of withdrawing students (the quiet ones) often considered more serious than the problems of those who frequently disturb the class situation?
(4) Why are incentives (extrinsic motivation) considered the least desirable motives?

---

*One such filmstrip, Motivation in Teaching and Learning, is available from the National Education Association, 1201 Sixteenth St., N.W., Washington, D.C. 20036. Another filmstrip, The Teaching of Discipline, is available from Educational Filmstrips, Box 1401, 1409 19th St., Huntsville, Texas 77340.

Option B$_2$: *Preliminary application and comparison.* Using a unit concept in your field of specialization as a basis, prepare three different lesson motivation experiences (sometimes labeled "lesson approach" in the lesson plan). (You will find it desirable to consult the LAP on Planning for Teaching in the Pre-Instructional Experiences module.) Proceed as follows:

1. Feature a means of capitalizing on the basic needs of students.

2. Feature a means of relating special interests to your lesson. (Special interests here mean those common to a number of students in the class.)

3. Feature a means of using extrinsic rewards (devices) to stimulate performance. *Limit* each "lesson-motivating experience" to one short paragraph. If possible, *discuss* your experiences in a committee. (If working alone, prepare a critique of your "observations.") Focus attention on the following questions:

   1. Which approach seemed to hold the greatest human interest? Why?

   2. Which approach would probably take the most class time to develop? Why?

   3. Which approach seemed to be the most teacher-centered? Why?

   4. Several options are available for presenting a lesson approach, e.g., telling, asking, showing, explaining, demonstrating. Evaluate the relative effectiveness of each.

Self-assessment Items (answers provided on pp. 95–96)

(1) The motivational (approach) aspect of a lesson may be omitted in some cases. Defend or refute.

(2) Under most conditions a lesson approach should not extend for longer than five or ten minutes. Explain.

(3) Structuring a lesson around the intrinsic needs, interests, and curiosities of students sometimes defeats one's purpose. Explain.

C: *Film and/or case analyses.* *

1. View a single-concept film on motivation. (Several such films are available.) Two especially useful ones are:

   a. *I Walk Away in the Rain.* **

   b. *Less Far than the Arrow.* **

   If working in a committee, discuss; if working alone, prepare a critique of the film. If you are able to view the film "*I Walk Away in the Rain,*" focus attention on the following questions:

**The film analysis may be omitted if such films are not readily accessible.*
***Available from Holt, Rinehart and Winston, Inc., 383 Madison Ave., New York, N.Y. 10017.*

a. Would you classify Tom as a highly motivated student or as one with a low level of motivation? Defend your rationale.

b. A student should be expected to achieve up to capacity. Defend or refute.

c. How would you attempt to help Tom reach a higher level of achievement?

2. Study the following case on motivation ("Feelings of Inadequacy") and respond to each of the listed excerpts as indicated.

a. Assign a motivational ranking, using the following code letters:

H—High motivational priority (preferred efforts)

M—Medium or intermediate motivational priority (when preferred efforts fail)

L—Low motivational priority (when all other efforts fail)

b. Defend each of your rankings in one brief sentence in the space provided.*

CASE: "FEELINGS OF INADEQUACY"

Tom Jones was tired of school. Although school work had always been rather difficult, he had managed to get by. For the past several weeks, however, his interest in school and in English in particular had been very low. "If I can just get by for twelve more weeks," he thought, "I think I'll be able to graduate."

As a new senior English teacher, Mr. Jenkins had been appalled at the superficial manner of response that had accompanied class discussion of various social issues. In-depth analysis that seemed essential was frequently completely lacking.

The project that Mr. Jenkins developed was, in a manner of speaking, initiated by students themselves. They had informally expressed concern over "our polluted environment" as a result of a nearby forest fire. Why not let each person select some area of immediate concern and explore it in depth? Mr. Jenkins would guide the students in developing an outline of the essential steps and ask for a written report as a culmination of the experience. The project would continue for about three weeks.

Tom listened to the assignment with a bit more than passing interest. He immediately decided to explore the automobile as a pollutant. For the first couple of days his interest was high. He was able to write out his firsthand experiences with the problem. As he again read over the project outline, however, he began to feel inadequate to the task. He didn't know how to use the library and was reluctant to divulge this inadequacy to the teacher and to his friends. Should he get a friend to help him? Should he turn in what he had and simply explain to the teacher that he could not find needed resources? With each passing day he became more concerned. His preoccupation with his own inadequacies, in fact, soon overshadowed everything else.

*After you have completed this task you may check your answers by turning to p. 99.

a.   . . . he had managed to get by.

b.   . . . his interest in school and English in particular had been very low.

c.   They had expressed concern over "our polluted environment."

d.   Why not let each person select some area of immediate concern and explore it in depth?

e.   . . . ask for a written report as a culmination of the experience.

f.   He (Tom) immediately decided to explore the automobile as a pollutant.

g.   . . . he began to feel inadequate to the task.

h.   . . . was reluctant to divulge his inadequacy. . . .

i.   His preoccupation with his own inadequacies . . . overshadowed everything else.

3.   Study the following case on discipline ("A Defiant Student"). If working in a committee, discuss it; if working alone, prepare a critique of the case. Direct your attention to the following questions:

a.   What facts, feelings, and relationships bear significantly upon the case?

b.   What motivational factors contributed to Bill's "blowup"?

c.   What should Mr. Martin do now?

d.   How might the confrontation have been avoided?

CASE: A DEFIANT STUDENT

Mr. Martin accepted his first teaching assignment on February 10 at Central High School. Having recently completed an extended tour in the armed forces, he felt more than ready to embark on his chosen career. He felt that his considerable teaching experience while in military service should be an asset. Moreover, he received considerable experience in judo tactics in hand-to-hand fighting. Although he aspired to be a biology teacher, he had agreed to take the eighth grade science position for the remainder of the year on the condition that he step into the biology position the following fall.

Students, under Mrs. Jenks's direction, had been given considerable freedom. After the first few weeks she became stricken with internal cancer, resulting in several intermittent absences during the fall semester. As her health continued to deteriorate and various substitute teachers were called in, students became progressively more unruly. By the end of the fall semester, Mrs. Jenks realized that she was no longer able to continue. Her resignation necessitated employment of one substitute teacher after another for a period of six weeks. Most of the substitute teachers reported that the class was unmanageable.

Realizing the situation, Mr. Martin decided to engage the students themselves in formulation of "ground rules" for class behavior. The group seemed enthusiastic and more than willing to cooperate. Minor class disturbances were corrected before they could spread. Such correction usually consisted of verbal reminders, with an occasional change of seats to break up disturbing combinations.

Lacking interest in school, Bill had established a reputation of "giving teachers a hard time." Although he was not accepted by the class group, students seemed to admire his ability to make things tough for the teacher. He liked Mr. Martin, however, and enthusiastically joined in formulation of basic class rules. In fact, he had been appointed to write major points on the chalkboard during the planning sessions on discipline procedures. For several days thereafter, Bill was a model student. (His classmates could hardly believe it!)

The first science test was a crushing disappointment for Bill. For once in his life he had actually tried to pass a test. Although his score was by no means the lowest in class, it was still below passing.

Later, in his own words to the principal, Bill explained his feelings and behavior: "I just had to let off steam, so I started talking to those seated next to me." Mr. Martin first attempted to silence Bill by moving him to another seat. Not only was the technique ineffective, but Bill appeared to be enjoying his success in disrupting class activities. Finally, Mr. Martin asked Bill to report to the principal at once. Bill immediately responded by saying, "I won't go and you can't make me."

Self-assessment Items (answers provided on p. 96)

(1) Competition for grades (extrinsic rewards) should be abandoned. Defend or refute.

(2) What is the relationship between special interests and basic needs?

(3) Under what circumstances may a grade fulfill basic needs?

(4) Why has misbehavior been referred to as basically a symptom rather than a cause?

(5) What is the legal status of corporal punishment in the schools?

(6) Corporal punishment (inflicting pain or suffering) should be avoided at all costs. Defend or refute.

D: *Instructional application.* If working along with other beginning teachers (in different fields of specialization), set up brief instructional or microteaching experiences in one or more of your classes, as indicated.* Each individual should do one of the experiences. (If working alone, try to have your experiences videotaped and replayed for your own analysis.)

1. Motivation. Using a unit concept in one of your classes as a basis, have a different individual prepare *and then do* one of the motivational experiences (sometimes referred to as the "lesson approach"

**If you do not have immediate access to students, you can complete this experience by dividing into subgroups of five each for the purpose of establishing microteaching sessions.*

to the lesson plan). (You will find it desirable to consult the LAP on Planning for Teaching in the Preinstructional Experiences Module.) Proceed as follows:

    a. Feature a means of capitalizing on the basic needs and/or curiosities of students.

    b. Feature a means of relating special interests to your lesson. (Special interests here means those common to a number of students in the class.)

    c. Feature a means of using extrinsic rewards (devices) to stimulate performance.

(*Limit* each "lesson-motivating experience" to one or two short paragraphs in your lesson plan.)

2. Discipline

    d. Have a fourth member of your committee or group hold a short (10-20 minutes) discussion with students on the discipline procedures liked and disliked.

    e. Have a fifth member of your committee or group enlist student assistance in setting up rules of conduct for the class. (Be sure to have someone keep a record of the points made.)

3. If possible, *discuss* your experiences in committee. (If working alone, prepare a critique of your experience.) Focus attention on the following questions:

    a. Which approach seemed to hold the greatest human interest? Why?

    b. Which approach seemed to take most time to develop? Why?

    c. Which approach seemed to be the most teacher-centered? Why?

    d. Several options are available for presenting a lesson approach, e.g., telling, asking, showing, explaining, demonstrating. Evaluate the relative effectiveness of each.

Self-assessment Items (answers provided on p. 96)

(1) The motivational (approach) aspect of a lesson may be omitted in some cases. Defend or refute.

(2) Under most conditions a lesson approach should not extend for longer than five or ten minutes. Explain.

(3) Structuring a lesson around the intrinsic needs, interests, and curiosities of students sometimes defeats one's purposes. Explain.

(4) Active student participation in the lesson approach sets the stage for such participation in the main portion of the lesson. Explain why.

(5) What factors seemed to contribute to a feeling of "warmth" between student and teacher?

(6) What factors block an otherwise effective lesson approach?

If, after reviewing your learning activities for this LAP, you feel that you can meet the stated objectives, proceed to the posttest. If not, you should complete at least one of the optional activities. Note that each provides for a number of optional situations, depending upon your own individual circumstances.

Optional Activities

E: *Class observation.* Working with another beginning teacher if possible, arrange to visit classes in your respective fields of specialization. Each individual should visit one class, as indicated. (If working alone, it is conceivable that both observational experiences can be combined in one visit.)

1. Have one member of the team prepare anecdotes of behavior (with either a teacher or a student focus) in the domain of motivation. (Record what actually happened, including direct quotes of conversation whenever possible.)

2. Have a second member of your team repeat the foregoing, using discipline as a frame of reference.

3. Later, compare your notes and discuss the following questions:

   a. What motivation-discipline priorities seemed to predominate? How do you account for these?

   b. Explain how the behavior of "problem students" seemed to differ from the behavior of "students with problems." What evidence, if any, suggested that the teacher was or was not aware of this distinction?

   c. Note the degree of overlap in the recorded anecdotes of each member of your observation team. How do you account for this overlap? (*Note:* If working in a committee of six, you should be able to obtain a rather broad frame of reference.)

Self-assessment Items (answers provided on pp. 96-97)

(1) How do the pressures of the moment mitigate against application of preferred motivation-discipline procedures? In your judgment how can this be somewhat overcome?

(2) How can inappropriate, hasty decisions in actual situations be minimized?

(3) What are some behavior clues to difficulty that may serve as "signals" to the teacher?

F: *Debate.* Arrange to have two individuals who feel they can support some form of corporal punishment debate two individuals who are opposed to corporal punishment at all costs. (Hopefully you can use instructional and/or administrative personnel from your own school. If not, use members of your committee. In the event you are working alone, confer with teachers in your school who hold such opposing views.)
Problem: Resolved, that corporal punishment in the junior and senior high school should be abolished.

Organize into two-member teams. (Refer to the LAP on Discussion and Debate for additional specifics that may be needed.) Proceed as follows:

1. Constructive speeches (7–8 minutes each)

    a. First affirmative speaker

        (1) Defines terms

        (2) Presents the need (for abolishing corporal punishment)

        (3) Outlines (very briefly) the plan of the affirmative (usually two or three main points)

    b. First negative speaker

        (1) Accepts or rejects definition of the terms

        (2) Refutes the need *and/or*

        (3) Attacks the plan

    c. Second affirmative speaker

        (1) "Patches up" any exploited weaknesses of his or her partner's case

        (2) Expands the plan by offering illustrations and supporting evidence

    d. Second negative speaker

        (1) "Patches up" any exploited weaknesses of his or her partner's case

        (2) Attempts to destroy one or all of the stock issues: the need, the plan, and the desirability of the plan.

2. Rebuttal speeches (4–5 minutes each)

    a. First negative speaker

        Focuses upon the major issue of the debate, quoting evidences of apparent weaknesses and the like

    b. First affirmative speaker

        Does the same for the affirmative case

    c. Second negative speaker

        Sums up the negative case by using opponent's weaknesses to strengthen the negative case

    d. Second affirmative speaker

        Does the same for the affirmative case

3. Hold a follow-through discussion (10–15 minutes) in which major points are summarized. (This is the generalization phase of the experience.)

Self-assessment Items (answers provided on p. 97)

(1) What is the legal status of corporal punishment in the schools?

(2) Corporal punishment (inflicting pain or suffering) should be avoided at all costs. Defend or refute.

(3) It has been observed that students from the lower socioeconomic levels of society tend to come from homes in which corporal

punishment is used as a means of correction. Therefore, for the sake of consistency, corporal punishment should be used with such students. Defend or refute.

POSTTEST (answers provided on pp. 97-99)

After you have completed the learning activities, work through the posttest and evaluate by checking the answers found at the end of this LAP. Note that supporting reasons are provided for both correct and incorrect items to Parts B, C, and D.

A. List four essentials of an adequately motivated-disciplined student.

1.

2.

3.

4.

B. Place the following code letters before each of the nine illustrations of misbehavior:

SP—Students with problems

PS—Problem students

1. Martha prefers to work alone. Her assignments sometimes are not completed adequately. The teacher notes that she daydreams a lot.

2. Jill seldom responds during class discussion; in her own words, "I prefer to let others do the talking." The teacher notes that she does not enter group activities if they can be avoided.

3. Adam and Dick observe another student making a copy of the teacher's test. They decide against reporting the theft, claiming that "it's none of our business."

4. While the teacher's back was turned, Joe hit Tim over the head with a book. When asked if he was responsible for the act, Joe denied it.

5. Tim has been a disturbing element in class for some time now. Mr. Phelps asks him to leave the room but Tim refuses.

6. Each time Molly is to present a speech (in speech class), she misses school, claiming illness. Her illnesses are confirmed by her family doctor.

7. In typing class Tom suddenly throws up his hands, bangs the typewriter, and stalks out of the room, claiming, "The old typewriter keeps making mistakes." This is not the first time that this sort of behavior has been observed.

8. Joe relies heavily upon Tom when doing his math, claiming that "math is just too hard for me."

9. Ann often disturbs the class with her loud talk. Although she readily responds to warnings by the teacher, she soon "forgets" and disturbs again.

C. Place one of the following code letters before each of the twelve recorded anecdotes of teacher efforts to motivate students. Use the following code letters:

H—High motivational priority (preferred efforts)

M—Medium or intermediate motivational priority (when preferred (efforts fail)

L—Low motivational priority (when all other efforts fail)

1. Do you still have your butterfly collection, Mary? We are about to study insects in our biology class now. I thought you might like to report to the class on this collection of yours.

2. All students who do a good job on this assignment may be exempt from our mid-term examination.

3. Several students were complaining of their eyes smarting as a result of our heavy smog condition today. Would you like to find out in our next biology unit how this problem can be alleviated?

4. As a member of our intercollegiate swimming team, Nancy, would you like to do a study of health as it applies to swimming?

5. If you don't produce a higher quality of work over this unit, Betty, I'm going to request a conference with your parents.

6. Everyone can get an "A" on this next project by doing his best. You will not be marked against the progress of others.

7. One who thoroughly learns basic electrical circuits (our next unit) should be able to construct his own radio transmitter. I'll make the necessary implements available if you wish.

8. This box contains an animal you have never seen before. Let's see who can be the first to classify it.

9. To receive an "A", you must complete your projects by tomorrow.

10. This is a contract plan. You decide which grade level to contract for: "A," "B," or "C."

11. Your papers were generally good. I'm going to hold a brief conference with each individual for the purpose of pointing out what I particularly liked about each person's paper.

12. You'll need a solid basic background in math if you enter college this fall.

D. Place one of the following code letters before each of the twelve illustrated discipline techniques below:

A—Appropriate

Q—Questionable

I—Inappropriate

1. Apparently your subject of conversation is more important than mine, Joe. Suppose you just tell all of us about it.

2. (In private) Dick, your gum-chewing seems to be disturbing some of the students. Would you take care of it?

3. (In private) Barton, I'm asking that you move to the back of the room. When you feel that you can follow class rules, let me know.

4. We have experienced considerable disturbance lately. What standards of behavior would you like to suggest for this class?

5. Just for that, Tom, you will have to stay after school. Be sure to bring your history book with you, as I have a special assignment for you.

6. (In private) I'm sure your remarks hurt Sue's feelings, Gilbert. What amends, if any, do you suggest?

7. Unless someone tells me who made this statement on the chalkboard while I was out of the room, we'll just forget about that planned field trip.

8. According to the rules worked out by the class, for each five demerits an individual's grade will be lowered by one-half of a letter grade.

9. Joe refuses to shift seats as requested by Mr. Jones, the teacher. Mr. Jones immediately applies a painful but harmless armhold to force compliance.

10. You should realize why your report card grade was so low, Virnina. You must learn to keep from disturbing in class.

11. Leona, your paper was almost identical to Freda's paper. What would you and Freda recommend that I do about it?

12. You're not going to get by with that sort of behavior, Bart. You either do your work, as I know you can, or you'll flunk.

E. Indicate the basic motivation-discipline principle that applies best in each of the five following situations. *Then* suggest in not more than two sentences what you would do in each of the five motivation-discipline situations. (To illustrate: Ruth dislikes school intensely. She says, "If I didn't like my art class so much, I would quit school." You are a biology teacher.)

Principle: Appeal to special interests.

Try to help Ruth develop art work in connection with biology.

1. Tom continually calls attention to himself. Although the problem is not really serious, he is a disturbing element in class.

    Principle:

    Comments:

2. Mr. Jencks notices that Debbie is extremely listless in class. Her eyes are swollen, suggesting that she has been crying.

    Principle:

    Comments:

3. Bill refuses to do a required oral report. In a conference he says, "I can't stand up before the class; I'll write a paper, however, if you will permit it."

    Principle:

    Comments:

4. Mandy has been absent from your class five times in the past couple of weeks. She is in school. In each case she provides a "legitimate" excuse for missing your class.

    Principle:

    Comments:

5. You note that Jack is doing a sketch of a "hot rod" while he is supposed to be studying English. It has happened before.

    Principle:

    Comments:

To help students want to learn is the earnest desire of every teacher. Although your successful completion of this LAP does not guarantee attainment of such a goal, it does indicate thorough understanding of the rather complex problems of motivation and discipline. If you were not able to attain the recommended mastery level, do not despair. By studying answers to the posttest, along with supporting reasons for correct and incorrect items, you should be able to quickly resolve any remaining difficulties.

ANSWERS TO PREASSESSMENT ITEMS

You can make these items a most valuable learning experience by studying the provided reasons for both correct and incorrect responses. You will note that since Part A has no specific number of correct responses, several additional points (characteristics) have been provided. Since the last part calls for your constructed answers, they may not be identical to those supplied by the writer. Such feedback, however, can enhance your understanding of the items.

A. 1. Possesses a high degree of self-direction and self-control.

    2. Is able to look beyond his or her own needs in perceiving the needs and wants of others.

    3. Has a realistic appraisal of his or her own strengths.

    4. Realistically accepts his or her own limitations and the limitations of others.

    5. Fulfills basic needs in a socially acceptable manner.

    6. Is future oriented, e.g., able to use past experiences in developing goals for himself.

B. 1-PS   (This is evidently withdrawal behavior and is considered most serious as the student is avoiding reality.)

    2-SP   (Although such a student is often a "thorn in the side" of the teacher, Tom's behavior does not suggest a problem out of the ordinary.)

3-PS   (Overdependence upon another is another means of escaping reality and thus needs the teacher's immediate attention.)

4-PS   (Such behavior can only alienate Tom further from his peers. Above all, an individual should learn to cope with his associates.)

5-SP   (Although Mary is resorting to socially unacceptable behavior (cheating), she is attempting to cope with her problem. Helping her prepare for tests will probably cause the behavior to disappear.)

6-SP   (The opinionated student can be readily taught to subject his views to appropriate processes of reflective thinking. Although deference to his friends and the teacher is an undesirable approach, it can probably be corrected in the same way.)

7-SP   (Nan is not avoiding reality because of a fear of the task but because she is insufficiently challenged.)

8-PS   (Such behavior tends to be antisocial. Above all, students must be helped in their quest for social adjustment.)

9-SP   (Assuming Hether's comments were based on fact, this is a rather normal reaction. By "hate," Hether probably means that she is merely upset with Ann.)

C. 1-L   (Such incentives should be used only when other approaches fail.)

2-L   (Again, extrinsic motivation is used.)

3-H   (By explaining their own art productions, students use intrinsic motivation.)

4-M   (Capitalizing on individual interests is desirable, but it is not economically preferable and would bog down if used with all students.)

5-M   (Again, this represents an appeal to an individual's special interest. It is desirable if used only with those who cannot be reached through other intrinsic motivational techniques.)

6-L   (Use of such an incentive tends to penalize those who feel they cannot receive "A"s.)

7-H   (The element of curiosity is intrinsically interesting to all and thus economical of the teacher's time.)

8-L   (Such a reward definitely discriminates against the poor student.)

9-L   (In such a manner the teacher is encouraging students to fake a special interest. This is dishonest.)

10-H   (This encourages use of something that the individual has produced and ties it to an interesting activity of most high school students.)

11-M   (This represents an area of special interest or at least considerable familiarity. As such, it is most effective for those who need a little special attention.)

12-H   (Such feedback is inherently encouraging and enables the individual to compete with his or her own past record.)

D.   1-I   (Humiliating a student before his or her peers is to be avoided at all times.)

     2-Q   (Such corrective action is sometimes necessary, but it does nothing to solve the real problem and may merely spread the disturbance across the room.)

     3-I   (Sarcasm is to be avoided; it can only humiliate and embarrass a student.)

     4-A   (Such corrective action places the peer group behind the action.)

     5-I   (Forced apologies, in effect, compel one to to be dishonest. They also force such students to submit to undue humiliation.)

     6-I   (Although legal in most states, corporal punishment is a questionable procedure at best. Such punishment only tells a student what *not* to do; it does not indicate corrective behavior. Forced apologies encourage one to be dishonest.)

     7-A   (Here the teacher places the decision squarely on the shoulders of the offending person.)

     8-I   (Although the "discipline technique" would have been much less desirable if handled publicly, it is still a threat and should be made only as a last resort.)

     9-I   (To punish a group for the transgression of an individual is to be avoided at all times.)

   10-Q   (This depends upon how the request for private conferences was made. It is likely that Tom recognizes this request as punishment and, as such, establishes a relationship between the punishment and the assignment.)

   11-A   (Marks, which are apparently necessary in the situation, are to reflect individual growth. This also emphasizes remedial teaching through correction of mistakes.)

   12-I   (This is employing punishment for mistakes and thus can only lead to distaste for this sort of schoolwork.)

E.   1.   (Special interests) Find a special interest and connect this to the work in biology.

     2.   (Causes of behavior) Awaken him and get him started on classwork. Set up a conference designed to find out why.

     3.   (Causes of behavior) First, attempt to find out why it was not completed. Then let Sam assist you in setting up rules for future assignments of this kind.

     4.   (Extrinsic to intrinsic motives) Refuse the request. With his help, develop a plan of study for future class experiences.

     5.   (Provide a face-saving out; don't accuse) Show the boys the similarities in the papers; ask for their suggestions in evaluating the papers. Let them know that in the future you will permit them to work together whenever possible.

ANSWERS TO SELF-ASSESSMENT ITEMS

> *Self-assessment items are designed to assist you in gaining depth of understanding as you proceed through the various learning activities. Most of them do not have single correct answers. For feedback, however, you should compare your answers with the samples provided here.*

A. (1) A highly motivated student's intensity and drive will certainly result in temporary behavior problems from time to time.

 (2) Many students with low motivation are preoccupied with their thwarted needs patterns; they become a problem to themselves and to others.

 (3) Defend. Motivation is thought to be a basic aspect of personality.

 (4) He is able to fulfill compelling needs in an acceptable manner under a given set of conditions.

 (5) Internal-external: Some students are "turned on" by the new, the uncertain, the ambiguous. Others are more readily influenced by outside forces such as exciting movies, new methods, vivid illustrations.

 Intake-output: Some students are basically consumers, enjoying such activities as reading, listening, watching. Others prefer to do (to produce) through such activities as writing, talking, performing.

 Approach-avoidance: Some students seek teacher approval, class marks, social approval. Others prefer to work alone; they are not highly impressed by the foregoing.

Option B_1. (1) Success

 Acceptance

 Security

 Affection

 Self-esteem (personal worth)

 (2) Certain basic needs are frustrated. As such, this constitutes a driving force. Peer approval (as tenuous as it may be under the circumstances) is sought at the risk of teacher disapproval.

 (3) They are essentially avoiding reality, even though basic needs are not being met. Such frustrations, if permitted to go unattended, often grow and result in serious personality maladjustments.

 (4) They do not directly cause a student to want to learn. Moreover, relatively few are in a position to excel (make "A"s in class).

Option B_2. (1) Refute. If human interest is already high, it may be shortened considerably, perhaps to one or two key questions or comments. Some minimal readiness activity is essential for every lesson, however.

 (2) The lesson objectives are not achieved through the motivation part of the lesson. It merely prepares students for the basic learning experiences.

(3) Such experiences must be closely associated with the basic purpose of the lesson. Keen interest is no guarantee of achievement of purpose. A short film, for example, may stimulate so many unrelated or remotely related questions that it is difficult to make the transition to the basic learning activities.

C. (1) Refute. Competition with one's own past record or even competition with others of approximately equal ability is a fully acceptable mode of behavior.

   (2) Special interests are avenues to need fulfillment.

   (3) When a high level of success is likely and when the grade has special meaning for the individual involved.

   (4) Misbehavior is usually indicative of frustration of one's efforts to fulfill basic needs.

   (5) In most cases it is presently legal if not administered in anger, if in the presence of a witness (other teacher or administrator), and if the student is not struck about the face or ears.

   (6) Yes, unless in self-defense. Can do irreparable physical and psychological damage. Also makes the teacher vulnerable to damage suits.

D. (1) Refute. If human interest is already high, it may be shortened considerably, perhaps to one or two key questions or comments. Some minimal readiness activity is essential to every lesson, however.

   (2) The lesson objectives are not achieved through the motivation part of the lesson. This phase of the lesson merely prepares students for the basic learning experiences.

   (3) Such experiences must be closely associated with the basic purpose of the lesson. Keen interest is no guarantee of achievement of purpose. A short film, for example, may stimulate so many unrelated or remotely related questions that it is difficult to make the transition to the basic learning activities.

   (4) When activities are intrinsically interesting, students willingly participate. This acts as an "ice-breaker" for participation in other, less intrinsically interesting activities.

   (5) By dwelling upon needs and interests closely associated with their own lives. This is a way of saying, "I understand."

   (6) Talking "down" or patronizing students

   Lack of sincerity

   Excessive teacher talk

   Extending the approach well beyond its usefulness

   Failure to tie the approach solidly to the lesson

Optional Activities

E. (1) The teacher must cope with the immediate problem, often prior to giving the needed time for reflection.

   Anticipate and reflect upon problems before they occur; be prepared to follow a given course of action under such extreme conditions.

(2) Develop contingency plans in advance for anticipated problems.

(3) Disturbing conversation; overdependence; hostility; cheating; refusal to comply with simple requests; withdrawal behavior.

F. (1) In most states it is presently legal if not administered in anger, if in the presence of a witness (other teacher or administrator), and if the student is not struck about the face or ears.

(2) Yes, unless in self-defense. Can do irreparable physical and psychological damage. Also makes the teacher vulnerable to damage suits.

(3) Refute, if the circumstances will permit. The aim of the school is the production of self-directed individuals. Corporal punishment tends to keep such persons dependent upon adult control; it is not very effective in communicating how best to behave.

There are times when some form of physical restraint is necessary if other students are endangered.

ANSWERS TO POSTTEST

For most beneficial results you should work through the entire LAP before you check your answers to the posttest. Failure to meet the provided minimum standards probably suggests certain weaknesses that need to be corrected. As with the Preassessment items, you will find supporting reasons for answers. It is hoped that this will serve as desirable feedback in your quest for mastery.

A. 1. Possesses a high degree of self-direction and self-control.

2. Is able to look beyond his or her own needs in perceiving the needs and wants of others.

3. Has a realistic appraisal of his or her own strengths.

4. Realistically accepts his or her own limitations and the limitations of others.

5. Fulfills basic needs in a socially acceptable manner.

6. Is future oriented, e.g., is able to use past experiences in developing goals for himself.

B. 1-PS (This is a symptom of withdrawal behavior and needs immediate attention.)

2-PS (Any time a student avoids reality consistently there is an indication of serious adjustment problems.)

3-SP (Although undesirable behavior, the students are merely following an unwritten code: "Don't rat on one of your own friends." Some clarification of the issue, of course, is indeed appropriate.)

4-SP (Although dishonest, Joe was forced to choose between two undesirable alternatives of an immediate nature. There is no evidence that such dishonesty is a basic aspect of his personality.)

5-SP (Although a defiant student *may* be a problem student, the problem can probably be worked out through regular value-focusing teaching techniques.)

6-PS (Such avoidance of reality is a definite symptom of a serious problem.)

7-SP (This is a form of adjustment called "displacement." Although it can be serious, the individual is at least bringing strong emotions out into the open. As such, corrective action can be taken.)

8-SP (Apparently Joe is at least making some effort to cope with his problem. Through careful guidance he may be taught to be more self-reliant.)

9-PS (If one assumes that the "loud talk" is deliberate, the behavior probably suggests an unhealthy way of gaining attention.)

C. 1-M (An appeal to special interests, although desirable, is uneconomical of the teacher's time and thus should be reserved for only a few students.)

2-L (Such an extrinsic reward discriminates against those who, from their own point of view, cannot do a "good job.")

3-M (This is a pretty good technique since it capitalizes on an immediate problem of concern to several students. This is placed in the intermediate category only because it falls in the realm of special interests.)

4-M (Again this represents an appeal to special interests. While most desirable for a few students, attempts to apply to all would be prohibitive in terms of time.)

5-L (While this may be a desirable action to take occasionally, it actually represents a form of punishment and is extrinsic in nature.)

6-L (Although the focus is on a criterion-referenced measure [as opposed to a norm-referenced measure], it is doubtful whether "A"s are realistic for all. Moreover, this represents an extrinsic reward [as opposed to an intrinsic one].)

7-H (Capitalizes upon basic needs [success and achievement] and makes the task immediately attainable.)

8-H (Employs the strong motivator—curiosity—and sets up a "game" for the class.)

9-L (Discriminates against slower students and offers an extrinsic reward.)

10-L (One is likely to decide what he or she realistically thinks is possible; the weaker students will probably work for "C"s; thus we have discrimination.)

11-H (Focus is upon the strengths of each person.)

12-L (A form of extrinsic motivation that is remote to a substantial number of students.)

D. 1-I (This is designed to embarrass the student.)

2-A (Provides a rationale that appeals to peer approval.)

3-Q (Although this may be necessary, it may merely spread the disturbance. It offers no permanent solution.)

4-A (Enlists the class in solving its own problems of control.)

5-I (This relegates schoolwork to the level of punishment.)

6-A (Calls attention to the problem, yet leaves solution to the offender.)

7-I (Punishment of the group for the transgressions of one individual is inappropriate.)

8-Q (Although this does capitalize on decisions previously made by the class group, it associates grades with behavior. The two should be kept separate.)

9-I (Although possibly legal, too many things can go awry. Joe could "fight back," resulting in complete disruption of an acceptable class situation.)

10-I (Class behavior must be separated from achievement marks.)

11-A (Calls attention to a fact; places the pressure back on Leona, where it belongs.)

12-I (Uses an extrinsic device as a threat of punishment.)

E. 1. (Appeal to basic needs) Provide a legitimate means of recognition in class.

2. (Determine causes of behavior) Provide an opportunity for her to discuss the problem with you if she wishes.

3. (Feelings of inadequacy) Attempt to provide an alternative close to the reality of his task (problem), e.g., sitting while he presents his report, or perhaps working with a committee on a report.

4. (Determine causes of behavior) Offer assistance if it seems needed.

5. (Appeal to special interests) Try to relate his study in English to this special interest.

Sample Answers to Learning Activity C (b).

a L (Managing to "get by" suggests that he is thinking of barely passing grades. This is extrinsic motivation.)

b M (By appealing to some special interest Tom is likely to find school and English more acceptable.)

c M (This would be classified as a special interest, prompted by local events.)

d M (Again, this point deals with special interests.)

e H (Since the topic deals with a special interest, the report should serve to fulfill one of the basic needs of the individual.)

f M (Tom apparently felt a special interest in the topic.)

g H (A feeling of inadequacy suggests a basic need.)

h H (Again, a basic need—that of acceptance—was at stake.)

i H (When basic needs are frustrated, demoralization soon becomes evident.)

SUPPLEMENTARY SOURCES

The following sources may be used in lieu of the Hoover texts or, preferably, as supplementary to them. Generally they are consistent with the models provided in the LAPs of this module. As such, the references do not represent all of the most recent references in the area; rather, they constitute selected references designed to broaden or expand needed background information.

Batchelder, Henry, "Corrective Measures, Punishment, and Discipline," *Journal of Secondary Education*, 39: 86–93 (Feb., 1964).

Berman, Mark L., ed., *Motivation and Learning* (Englewood Cliffs, N.J.: Educational Technology Publications, 1971).

Carter, Ronald, *Help! These Kids Are Driving Me Crazy* (Oshkosh, Wisc.: Research Press, 1972).

Clarizio, Harvey F., *Toward Positive Classroom Discipline* (New York: John Wiley and Sons, Inc., 1971).

Cofer, Charles S., *Motivation and Emotions* (New York: Scott, Foresman and Co., 1972).

Frymier, Jack R., *The Nature of Educational Method* (Columbus, Ohio: Charles E. Merrill Publishing Co., 1965).

Gnagey, William J., *Controlling Classroom Misbehavior: What Research Says to the Teacher*, No. 32 (Washington, D.C.: National Education Association).

Gray, Jenny, *Teaching Without Tears: Your First Year in the Secondary School* (Palo Alto, Calif.: Fearon Publishers, 1968).

———, *The Teacher's Survival Guide* (Palo Alto, Calif.: Fearon Publishers, 1970).

Hamachek, Don E., *Motivation in Teaching and Learning: What Research Says to the Teacher*, No. 34 (Washington, D.C.: National Education Association.)

Haring, Norris G., and Lakin Phillips, *Analysis and Modification of Classroom Behavior* (Englewood Cliffs, N.J.: Prentice-Hall, Inc., 1973).

Hoover, Kenneth H., *The Professional Teacher's Handbook*, 2nd ed. (Boston: Allyn and Bacon, Inc., 1976).

Hoover, Kenneth H., and Paul M. Hollingsworth, *Learning and Teaching in the Elementary School*, 2nd ed. (Boston: Allyn and Bacon, Inc., 1975).

Hymes, James, Jr., *Behavior and Misbehavior* (Englewood Cliffs, N.J.: Prentice-Hall, Inc., 1955).

Jater, Jan, "Motivational Experiences in Teaching and Learning," *Educational Leadership*, 30: 721–25 (May, 1973).

Steinback, Susan B., and William C. Steinback, *Classroom Discipline: A Positive Approach* (Springfield, Ill.: Charles C. Thomas, 1974).

Williams, Robert L., and Kamala Anandam, *Cooperative Classroom Management* (Columbus, Ohio: Charles E. Merrill Publishing Co., 1973).

lap
5

Providing
for Individual
Differences

RATIONALE. Individuals are not created equal, nor do they become more alike as they grow older. By the time they enter school, physical, intellectual, social, and emotional differences have become very evident. Then, as they move upward through the grades, these differences steadily increase. By the time a student reaches ninth grade, for example, the normal achievement range in all subjects varies from third or fourth grade level up through junior college.

Despite the great variability noted, students are normally taught in groups. Not only may the group itself contribute to learning, but the cost of tutorial instruction is obviously prohibitive. As class size has increased, teachers have sought techniques for personalizing instruction. In the past this has usually involved some type of ability grouping between classes. Even when students are homogeneously grouped (on one or more criteria), individual ability ranges are often exceedingly great. This has led to individualization of instructional patterns, which, in some cases, has resulted in elimination of class lines. Here the focus is upon self-instructional competency-based learning programs. Meanwhile, most teachers still must work within class settings. They see competency-based programs as another option in coping with an increasingly complex problem.

OVERVIEW

Key Concepts

    1.   Students differ in numerous ways relative to the school experience.

101

2. Individual enrichment techniques are ideally suited for individual differences; since they often become unwieldy in large classes, however, some form of subgrouping is often necessary to facilitate such practices.

3. Flexible subgrouping techniques (within classes) can facilitate individualization while maintaining the autonomy of the group.

4. Grouping *between classes* may create or enhance psychological adjustment problems.

5. Excessive retention and acceleration may contribute to social and emotional adjustment problems.

6. Competency-based instructional packages are largely self-directed and permit students to progress at their own rate.

New Terms

1. Academic aptitude: General potential for schoolwork. Traditionally the Intelligence Quotient test (IQ) has been used as an assessment of this potential.

2. Slow students: Those students who are well below the average in academic aptitude.

3. Bright students: Those students who are well above average in academic aptitude.

4. Ability grouping (within given classes): The practice of placing students with others of similar class *achievement* (usually high, average, and low) in separate subgroups, based upon the wishes of the individual and the recommendation of the instructor.

5. Enrichment activities: The provision of different (sometimes additional) materials for learners.

6. Stigma: A feeling of inadequacy, often arising from some sort of unfavorable comparison within the peer group.

7. Competency-based learning: Often a program or package of learning experiences designed to produce a predetermined level of performance, without reference to any other individual.

OBJECTIVES. After this experience you should be able to provide for individual differences within the classroom, as evidenced by your ability to:

1. List six basic essentials of individualized class instruction.

2. Select eight out of nine appropriate individualization techniques from a list of twenty assorted situations.

3. Provide eleven out of twelve applications for selected principles for individualizing instruction.

PRELIMINARY READING. Since the elements of instructional methodology are somewhat variable, the following excerpts are provided to help you develop a frame of

reference as a point of departure for this experience. If you prefer, you may proceed directly to the Preassessment items.

ACADEMIC APTITUDE

Although academic aptitude is still regarded as one of the more important individual differences among students, it is presently conceived as a highly flexible concept that merely provides a useful starting point for instructional diversity. An IQ score is an indirect measure of many attributes including memory, spatial relationships, quantitative and qualitative reasoning, and the like. Many aspects of ability are not tested by most IQ tests (creativity, for example). Other factors such as motivation, reasoning patterns, state of one's health, and cultural determinants influence IQ scores in unknown ways.

Within broad limits IQ scores do enable us to identify students who are likely to experience considerable (or little) difficulty in learning. It is grossly unfair, for example, to expect a slow student to do the same assignments and to otherwise compete with bright students. To illustrate: Slow students tend to

1. have a slow reaction time, needing a lot of practice.
2. be inept at finding new solutions.
3. have a short attention span.
4. be weak in initiative, versatility, and originality.
5. be poor in working with abstractions.
6. be weak in making associations and relationships.
7. be inept in making generalizations.
8. be weak in self-criticism.
9. be weak in detecting absurdities.
10. have a narrow range of interests.
11. be impressed with the physical, the concrete, or the mechanical.

On the other hand, the bright student is usually strong or the opposite in each of these areas. Thus it becomes apparent that instruction most appropriate for the slow is highly inappropriate for the bright, and vice versa. Even though IQ scores do not necessarily identify such students, along with other tools and observational techniques, they serve as useful guides for busy teachers.

CLASSROOM GROUPING

Of all the so-called plans for grouping in an effort to cope with individual differences, classroom grouping has received the greatest attention *at the elementary level*. Oddly enough, such techniques have not been very popular among high school teachers. This may be because the elementary teacher has most often grouped on the basis of reading differences. For many years the typical high school teacher took for granted that all students were effective readers, despite the evidence to the contrary.

Subgrouping plans will vary considerably, depending upon specific class needs. Usually they are not needed unless a class is large (more than about twenty-five students). The need is greatest in so-called academic courses, such as math, science, social studies, English, and the like. Some important criteria for classroom grouping include the following:

1. Subgrouping within the classroom must be flexible. Students must be permitted to shift from one group to another when the need arises. Furthermore, students from each group must have ample opportunity to work with members from other groups.

2. Class groups must be handled in such a manner as to minimize any feelings of stigma or superiority from becoming associated with different groups.

3. Subgroups must *increase* the potential for *individualizing* instruction. As with homogeneously grouped classes, there is danger in the assumption that a subgroup is homogeneous and that instructional materials and procedures can be adjusted to the needs of the group as a whole. Grouping the elementary school student for instruction in reading, for example, has all too often resulted in a new type of "lock-step" teaching, simply because the teacher has tended to treat the *groups* as homogeneous. Giving identical assignments to all students in a group is little better than no grouping at all.

4. Subgroups must provide adequately for the social and emotional needs of youngsters.

5. Group *and* individual cooperation and competition must be provided.

6. Each student must have an opportunity to meet the goals of instruction, commensurate with his capacities.

LEARNING ACTIVITY PACKAGES

Although various techniques for providing for individual differences *within traditional classroom settings* have been proposed, most have been somewhat ineffective in large classes. The most effective techniques (e.g., classroom subgrouping techniques) certainly demand skillful and resourceful teachers.

Perhaps as an outgrowth of the programmed learning movement, there is a decided trend toward the development of various types of individualized learning programs. Every learning program is accompanied by a learning activity package (LAP). Although commercial LAPs are available, many teachers prefer to develop their own, based upon local needs and objectives. A LAP consists of a group of prescribed experiences designed to provide the learner with considerable independence in achieving a limited number of specific objectives. Built into the package are various options that enable the learner to determine for himself his own learning needs and to continually gauge his progress. Although LAPs were originally designed for open schools based entirely on individualized learning programs, they have been adapted to individual class units and even to a given concept(s) within a unit. The latter devices, sometimes referred to as *minipacs,* can be adapted to almost any instructional unit. The essential components are employed in the LAPs you are presently using.

PREASSESSMENT ITEMS (answers provided on pp. 115–17)

This experience is designed to provide an overall perspective of individual differences among students. After completing the items, turn to the end of this LAP and check your answers. Note that answers (both correct and incorrect) are provided with supporting reasons to guide your efforts as you work through this LAP.

A. List six essentials of individualized class instruction. (To illustrate: Each individual, regardless of academic aptitude, should be helped to achieve up to capacity.)

1.

2.

3.

4.

5.

6.

B. Place a check (√) before nine of the individualization techniques you consider appropriate for the situation described.

1. Mr. Bostrom proposes to let Jim skip second-semester American history on the grounds that he has achieved the major objectives, based on a thorough pretest.

2. Mr. Roberds, an American literature teacher, subgroups his class (forty-five students) and then keeps the groups separated for most class activities.

3. Mrs. Mulkey, noting the unusually wide range of typing skill in Typing II class, proposes to group her thirty students for instructional purposes.

4. Different, individualized work is provided for each student in Mr. Masters's algebra class of twenty students.

5. When students finish required assignments in general business class (thirty students), they are provided opportunities to do extra work for credit.

6. In shop class (twenty students) each student is guided in developing his own individual project.

7. Mr. Brown's social studies class (thirty-five students) is broken into subgroups. Each student is recommended for a group based upon past achievement and can shift from one group to another as he or she prefers.

8. Each student is programmed through a learning activity package in a sociology class (thirty-five students). As each individual achieves mastery of one LAP, he or she is guided into the next one, etc., until all class objectives have been met.

9. In employing class subgrouping, Mr. Freeman, the history teacher, prepared an assignment for each subgroup, saying, "I expect each individual to complete his or her assignment with 90-percent accuracy."

10. In using learning activity packages, Ms. Tompkins encourages her business education students to finish as rapidly as possible. She then guides small groups into question-and-answer sessions, based on ideas and problems raised during the experience.

11. Mr. Brown's art students are encouraged to pursue their own ideas for achieving certain objectives. He does request a conference prior to the experience.

12. Some thirty to forty Puerto Ricans have recently been transferred to a suburban high school. As they generally cannot cope with the English language very well, they are placed in certain special classes.

13. The principal of a large high school proposes a system of homogeneous grouping so that "we can narrow the academic aptitude range in our classes." He would not apply this technique to social studies classes.

14. A few very able students are permitted to complete some classes early and bypass others as competence is demonstrated. They are placed in two or three special classes (in high school) that carry college credit.

15. Mr. Butts insists that students in his biology class (thirty students), who have been subgrouped within the class, should work together much of the time.

16. Mary has been absent from school for several days. Ms. Shephard provides her with a learning activity package, asks her to complete it, and suggests that she ask for help as needed.

17. Sue asks to be excused from the frog project in biology because "the odor and sight of the frog make me sick." She offers to do a reading assignment instead.

18. Although Bill doesn't meet the minimum essentials in beginning shorthand, Ms. Debbs passes him anyhow, saying, "I doubt that he would do much better the second time around."

19. Students in Central High are grouped into high, medium, and low classes on the basis of academic aptitude and reading levels.

20. "I don't make any special effort to provide for individual differences," says Mrs. Bagley. "When students want to do extra work, they come to me and I assign it. They are always given extra credit for such work."

C. For each of the listed principles, write out two applications. To illustrate:

Principle: Acceleration and retardation are generally discouraged.

Applications:

1. Acceleration and retardation are carried out only after the social and emotional maturity of the individual involved is carefully examined.

2. College credit is sometimes provided for students prior to graduation from high school.

1. Learning activity packages. (You may use the format of the LAPs in this manual as a frame of reference.)

    a. Feedback is provided

    (1)

    (2)

    b. Assessment procedures are employed

    (1)

    (2)

    c. The total learning experience is competency based

    (1)

    (2)

2. Class grouping techniques (within)

    a. Permit total student interaction

    (1)

    (2)

    b. Minimize stigmas

    (1)

    (2)

    c. Permit individual progress

    (1)

    (2)

If you were able to provide twenty-four of the twenty-seven requested responses, you are doing exceedingly well. In fact, it is quite possible that you already possess the needed competencies in this area and may want to proceed directly to the next module. Even if you were able to provide few of the appropriate responses, do not despair, for individual differences is indeed a complex area. By analyzing the correct answers (end of LAP), and by studying supporting reasons for both correct and incorrect items to Part B of the items, you should be prepared for the learning activities that follow.

LEARNING ACTIVITIES

Work through each learning activity, complete the self-assessment items, and check your answers before moving to the next one. Note that the last learning activity is optional, depending upon your needs and circumstances at that point. You should be able to complete this LAP in about four hours.

A: *Read.* Re-examine the overview and the preliminary reading sections to this LAP and to the preceding one (Motivation-Discipline Techniques). You will broaden your understanding substantially by studying the selected references listed at the end of this LAP. Note specifically the following points:

1. The extent of individual differences and how they influence classroom instruction.

2. Why acceleration and retardation are generally discouraged.

3. Problems associated with enrichment as a means of providing for individual differences.

Self-assessment Items (answers provided on p. 118)

(1) What might be the impact of sex differences on group activities among junior high school students?

(2) A student should not be failed. Defend or refute.

(3) Enrichment generally means providing extra work for the more able. Defend or refute.

(4) Enrichment is highly recommended but not very practical in large classes. Explain why.

At this point you may select either Option B$_1$ or Option B$_2$, depending upon your particular situation. Those who are presently teaching should select Option B$_1$. Those who are not teaching or who do not have immediate access to students should select Option B$_2$.

Option B$_1$: *Modeled experiences.* This experience can be acquired in a number of ways. It may be possible for you to view an especially prepared film or videotaped presentation featuring the use of one or more techniques of providing for individual differences.

Another option is to observe a highly successful approach used in your school system or one in the local area. There are a number of schools that feature different individualized learning programs, for example. They often use *some* form of individualized learning packages. Other programs are associated with some form of flexible scheduling arrangements.

If the foregoing options are unavailable, it may be possible to complete this activity well by visiting a local teacher who has been unusually successful in this respect.

In any event, it is imperative that your observational experiences include a modeled program or at least one in which deficiencies are fully clarified.

If you are working along with other new teachers, a number of different programs may be observed. If working alone, attempt to observe at least two different programs. Direct your attention to the following (this may entail discussing certain points with the teacher[s] involved):

1. General ability and/or achievement levels of the students.

2. Physical conditions of the classroom(s), such as seats, space, facilities, educational media stations, etc.

3. Approximate number of students involved.

4. Content areas.

5. Flexibility of the techniques employed.

6. Provisions for total group interaction (if any).

7. Particular problems (as identified by the teacher [s]).

8. Marking (grading) system employed.

If possible, hold a post-observation discussion in which you share experiences with members of your committee. (If working alone, prepare a written critique of your experiences and share with your supervising teacher or college supervisor.

Self-assessment Items (answers provided on p. 118)

(1) Contrast the merits of establishing subgrouping arrangements (within a class) based upon academic ability (IQ) and achievement.

(2) A class subgrouping arrangement is not needed in small classes (twenty students or less). Defend or refute.

(3) Why are provisions for considerable total-group interaction a necessary condition for providing for individual differences?

(4) Students in an academically weak subgroup should be marked only on their progress relative to the subgroup. Defend or refute.

(5) Some techniques of providing for individual differences (e.g., subgrouping plans) tend to discriminate against minority groups. Defend or refute.

Option B₂: *Developing and comparing LAP models and grouping plans.* Working in pairs in the same field of specialization, complete the following as indicated. (If working alone, you should complete both experiences. In evaluating your prepared LAP, the best procedure would be to go over it with a friend, or perhaps to lay it aside until the following day so that you may view it somewhat "objectively.")*

1. *LAP development.* Using not more than three of your unit concepts as a basis (developed in the module on Pre-Instructional Experiences), each person should prepare portions of a LAP as indicated.

   a. Prepare a rationale (limit to two sentences).

   b. Prepare one minimum essentials–type objective which will involve students in direct application (constructing as opposed to naming or selecting.)

   c. Develop one Preassessment item in which selection is requested.

   d. Develop one learning activity involving student interaction in some way.

You can check your success by inspecting the LAP structure of this book.

e. Construct one self-assessment item in support of your learning activity *and* write an acceptable answer for it.

f. Develop an optional activity *and* indicate in not more than two sentences why it is optional (as opposed to required).

2. *LAP and "plans" assessment.*

a. Critique each part of your LAP and *do* the Preassessment item, the learning activity, and the self-assessment item prepared by the other member of your team. Make a note of points of ambiguity and the like.

b. Assume you have a heterogeneous class of thirty-five students (in your major field). All seats are filled and firmly attached to the floor. There is no extra space in the room. In not more than four sentences, indicate a plan for establishing subgroups within the class.

c. Go over your grouping "plan" with your partner, clarifying points of confusion, ambiguity, and special difficulty. Alter all aspects of the technique accordingly.

Self-assessment Items (answers provided on pp. 118–19)

(1) You will note that the LAPs featured here generally involve pre-assessment items and posttests that call for listing, selecting, and construction, in that order. Evaluate this sequential arrangement.

(2) What basic function do self-assessment items play in LAP development?

(3) Why is the major thrust of the learning activities focused on actual performance?

(4) More optional activities are needed in a heterogeneous class than in a homogeneous class. Defend or refute.

C: *Instructional application.* Using one of your classes in your major subject area as a basis, develop *one* of the individualization plans as indicated.

1. Subgrouping within the class.

a. Set up two or three subgroups (depending on class size and degree of heterogeneity), based upon past achievement in the particular class involved.*

b. In not more than four sentences, introduce the plan to your students.

c. In not more than four sentences, indicate the flexibility of the plan.

d. In not more than four sentences, indicate the differentiated nature of the learning activities.

e. In not more than four sentences, suggest how measurement and evaluation will be handled.

If you are not teaching and are in a class such as a workshop, do this experience by way of a simulation.

2. Learning activity package or learning contract. (In one of your classes make use of *either* a LAP or a learning contract as indicated.*)

    a. Establish basic purposes for students.

    b. Develop differentiated learning activities.

    c. Identify minimum essentials that must be achieved by each student.

    d. In not more than four sentences, indicate how differentiated measurement and evaluation will be handled relative to on-going marks and grades for each unit and the course.

3. Enrichment activities

    a. In not more than two sentences, indicate the purpose of this activity.

    b. In not more than four sentences, indicate how your enrichment activities will differ among bright, average, and slow students.

    c. In not more than four sentences, indicate how evaluation of enrichment activities will be handled.

If working with other new teachers, discuss your experiences, noting practical difficulties and problems. (If working alone, prepare a written critique of your experiences.)

Self-assessment Items (answers provided on p. 119)

(1)   A LAP should be submitted to extensive field testing. Explain.

(2)   Answers to the preassessment items and the posttests should be made available to the teacher only. Defend or refute.

(3)   What factors tend to prevent the "lazy" student from gravitating to the easier groups?

(4)   A plan for subgrouping must be flexible in at least two ways: (a) It should provide for movement from one group to another, and (b) it should provide for interaction of individuals between groups. Explain why.

(5)   Teaching an entire group in the same way has been referred to as "lock-step" teaching. Why then is not the establishment of three or so subgroups not merely another form of "lock-step" teaching?

(6)   Experienced teachers note that able students initially are often reluctant to accept a subgrouping arrangement. After some experience, however, they usually become the most avid supporters of the system. Explain.

(7)   Although usually enthusiastic throughout, weak students often do not make the remarkable improvement anticipated through the use of class grouping techniques. Explain why.

(8)   Indicate how a LAP, subgrouping, and enrichment may be integrated into a single class.

---

*If you are not teaching and are in a class such as a workshop, do this experience by way of a simulation.

If, after reviewing the learning activities for this LAP, you feel that you can meet the stated objectives, proceed to the posttest. If not, you should complete the optional activity.

Optional Activity

D: *Class observation.* Again, working as a team with another person if possible, arrange to visit classes as indicated. (If working alone, you should visit both classes as indicated.)

1. Arrange for one member of your team to visit an "academic class," such as mathematics, science, social studies, or literature. Note and record both organized and unorganized techniques employed for coping with individual differences among students. Focus on the following:

   a. Enrichment activities

   b. Differentiated assignments and study activities

   c. Subgrouping arrangements in evidence

   d. Learning contracts (this involves different activities quantitatively and qualitatively) for different students

   e. Programmed learning or LAPs utilized

   f. Acceleration (often by exempting selected students from certain assignments or activities)

   g. Other techniques employed

2. Arrange for the other member of your team to visit a class in a mental or motor skills area, such as foreign language, some business subjects, industrial arts, physical education, some home economics subjects. Observe and record, as indicated in #1 above.

3. Hold a post-observation conference with the teachers for the purpose of clarifying individualization techniques in evidence.

4. Finally, discuss your experiences with the other member of your team, using your observation guide as a general frame of reference. (If working alone, prepare a written critique of your experiences.) Be sure to note the rationale for any and all techniques utilized.

Self-assessment Items (answers provided on pp. 119–20)

(1) For many years homogeneous grouping (between classes) has been advocated by some practitioners. Generally, however, such a practice is discouraged by professional educators. Explain why.

(2) Contract plans, some enrichment activities, and other techniques are often based upon different grades for different quality (sometimes quantity) of work. Explain why such practices are somewhat questionable. (You may want to refer to the preliminary reading section of the previous LAP (Motivation-Discipline Techniques).

(3) Subgrouping often is not necessary in skills areas **or** in small classes. Defend or refute.

(4) Programmed materials (involving LAPs, programmed texts, teaching machines) are somewhat self-instructional. What is the major **role** of the teacher when using such materials?

POSTTEST (answers provided on pp. 120-22)

After you have completed the learning activities, complete the posttest and evaluate by checking the answers found at the end of this LAP. Note that supporting reasons are provided for both correct and incorrect responses.

A. List six essentials of individualized class instruction. (To illustrate: Each individual, regardless of academic aptitude, should be helped to achieve up to capacity.)

1.

2.

3.

4.

5.

6.

B. Place a check (√) before nine of the individualization techniques **you** consider appropriate for the situation described.

1. Timothy was assigned extra work so that he might develop competence in math. His ability is somewhat limited.

2. Meg has been absent for ten days with the flu. She is asked to work through a LAP to help her "catch up" with the rest of the class.

3. Students in Ms. Roberts's class are subgrouped on the basis of academic aptitude. The subgroups are permitted to work together for certain purposes.

4. Martha asks the teacher for extra work in genetics, claiming **a** special interest.

5. Tom misses a test due to a football game. He asks for permission to take the test or to do some comparable work upon his return.

6. Meg demonstrates her prior understanding of business law on a pretest. She is asked to do an "in-depth" project in the area in lieu of regular class activities.

7. Mrs. Smith has developed a subgrouping arrangement in American literature class. Tom, a member of the top group, desires to move to a lower group in the middle of the unit.

8. In a class in which subgrouping is utilized, Martha asks and is given permission to work with other students on a panel, even though they are in a higher group.

9. Williamena is unusually capable. She is given permission to work through a series of self-instructional materials in lieu of Algebra II so that she can attend an advanced math class for college credit.

10. Bill wants to move to the higher group within his class even though his class marks do not warrant such a move.

11. Mrs. Jones permits students who finish assignments early to do additional work for extra credit.

12. Tom does poorly on a test. He is given permission to do some extra make-up work to compensate for his poor grade.

13. Mr. Dill sets up a contract plan, permitting students to contract for certain grades.

14. A group of Mexican-American students (Chicanos) are placed in a special class since they have difficulty coping with the English language. They attend regular classes in the area of social studies.

15. Mr. Blodke expects all students in each subgroup to complete all assignments with a minimum level of competence.

16. Joe is an extremely weak student who Miss James believes should be placed in a special class. Mr. Tompkins, the principal, asks her to take him and "do what you can." At the end of the term Joe does not come close to meeting the minimum competency level. Miss James "passes" him, saying, "I doubt that he is capable of passing the course."

17. Mr. Blanchard says, "I provide opportunities for students to do extra work as they wish. It is up to them"

18. Mrs. Merritt uses a learning program as a means of permitting students to assess their own competency at the end of a unit.

19. Ms. Works provides special (different) activities for Jo, in recognition of her very limited ability.

20. Bill is exempted from mid-term examination on the basis of his consistent high achievement during the term.

C. For each of the listed principles, write out two applications. To illustrate:

Principle: Acceleration and retardation are generally discouraged.

Applications:

1. Acceleration and retardation are carried out only after the social and emotional maturity of the individual involved are carefully examined.

2. College credit is sometimes provided for students prior to graduation from high school.

1. Learning activity packages

a. Specific requirements are provided

(1)

(2)

b. Source materials are available

(1)

(2)

     c. Group interaction is provided

        (1)

        (2)

  2. Class grouping techniques (within)

     a. Minimum levels of competency are provided

        (1)

        (2)

     b. Instruction is differentiated

        (1)

        (2)

     c. Reinforcement is provided

        (1)

        (2)

If students were all alike and learned in the same way, there would be little need for teachers. Students, however, are *not* alike and learn in many ways, and the teacher must cope with such complexities. Thus mastery in this vital area of teaching deserves a special pat on the back. You are now on your way to becoming a successful teacher! Even if you failed to achieve mastery the first time through, study reasons for preassessment and posttest answers and try again. You'll be surprised how much this will help you clarify misunderstandings.

ANSWERS TO PREASSESSMENT ITEMS

You can make these items a most valuable learning experience by studying the provided reasons for both correct and incorrect responses. You will note that since Part A has no specific number of correct responses, several additional points (characteristics) have been provided. Because the last part calls for your constructed answers, your own answers may not be identical to those supplied by the writer. You should be able to decide whether your answers are reasonably accurate, however.

A. 1. Each individual, regardless of academic aptitude, should be helped to achieve up to capacity.

   2. Student group interaction in the learning process is needed.

   3. Each student is expected to demonstrate a minimum level of competence.

   4. Students of differing levels of academic aptitude should be provided opportunities for working together.

5. Academic aptitude and achievement must be considered as merely a part of the individual difference complex; other important dimensions are social and emotional differences.

6. Although excessive class size often renders some form of grouping necessary, this is merely an expediency measure for meeting individual differences.

7. Academic aptitude is so complex that efforts to narrow the class range on the basis of specific dimensions (e.g., IQ and achievement) are seldom very effective.

8. Although academic aptitude has a general quality, considerable variation must be expected in different classes. (A student who is extremely able in math, for example, may possess no more than average aptitude for American history.)

B. 4 (This is quite possible in small classes.)

6 (Skill development is basically an individualized process.)

7 (Past achievement, not ability, tends to minimize stigmas. Shifting should ultimately be left to the student, but at the end of a unit.)

10 (Group interaction is basic; the packages seldom clarify all questions.)

11 (In the skills area individual work is encouraged. The conference is desirable to make sure that objectives are likely to be achieved.)

12 (Each individual must be helped to achieve necessary entry behaviors for coping with schoolwork. Ideally such a group would be placed in some regular classes also.)

14 (This is a means of keeping students with their age-mates while enabling them to advance academically.)

15 (Total group interaction is essential if stigmas are to be minimized.)

16 (An effective means of using a LAP as an adjunct to regular class activities.)

Reasons for incorrect items

1. (Especially in the social studies class, group interaction is important. Such learnings can hardly be measured on a pretest.)

2 (Group interaction is essential if stigmas are to be avoided.)

3 (Subgrouping is not usually needed in a basic skills area, as this is an individualized process.)

5 (Extra work for credit discriminates against weaker students.)

8 (This eliminates needed student interaction.)

9 (Provisions for individual differences within each subgroup are necessary.)

13 (Such does not appreciably narrow the range as learning is exceedingly complex. Moreover, grouping between classes tends to stigmatize weaker students.)

17 (Assuming the "frog project" involves certain minimum essentials, each student must become involved.)

18 (Each student must meet or achieve certain minimum essentials; if impossible for certain students, they must be placed in special classes.)

19 (Such grouping is undesirable as it paves the way for stigmas. Moreover, learning is much more complex than assumed. Past achievement would be a preferable basis for any subgrouping arrangement.)

20 (Few students will do this. Such "extra credit" discriminates against weaker students.)

C. 1. Learning activity packages

    a. Feedback is provided

        (1) Self-assessment items following each learning activity

        (2) Encouraging comments in different places throughout the LAP

        (3) Provided answers to pre- and posttests

        (4) Reasons for correct (and incorrect) items in pre- and posttests

    b. Assessment procedures are employed

        (1) Pre- and posttests

        (2) Self-assessment items

    c. The total learning experience is competency based

        (1) Minimum essentials–type objectives (specifying specific conditions and minimum level of acceptability)

        (2) Optional activities

  2. Class grouping techniques (within)

    a. Permits total student interaction

        (1) Students from different groups work together frequently (e.g., panel discussion, project work, etc.)

        (2) Teacher-focused instruction, on occasion, will be directed to all students

    b. Minimizes stigmas

        (1) Grouping is originally established on the basis of past achievement in the class, as opposed to ability

        (2) A student can move from one group to another (by unit) upon his or her own request

        (3) Groups are not labeled as fast, slow, and the like

    c. Permits individual progress

        (1) Can move from one group to another

        (2) Provides options for individuals within each group

ANSWERS TO SELF-ASSESSMENT ITEMS

Self-assessment items are designed to help you gain depth of understanding as you proceed through the various learning activities. Most of them do not have single correct answers. For feedback, however, you should compare your answers with the samples provided here.

A. (1) At this age most of the girls are physically mature; they are interested in boys but not those of their own age. Many of the boys at this age have not yet grown out of the "little boy" stage. They are not yet interested in girls. For this reason, class group work frequently is more effective when the sexes are separated.

(2) Generally defend. Theoretically a good teacher can reach every student and has the responsibility for making the student want to learn; the teacher helps him or her achieve up to capacity. Failure not only means repeating the same experiences (which become dull and boring), but also tends to separate the individual from his or her peers.

If a student fails to master an established minimum level of achievement (within the capacity of every student), then failure is unavoidable. Some suggest that under such conditions it is the teacher who actually fails.

(3) Refute. Basically enrichment refers to *different* work for each individual, depending upon needs and interests. It also applies to every student.

(4) Enrichment varies from student to student, depending upon individual needs and interests. In large classes it is practically impossible to cope with such a large quantity and variety of individual differences in the absence of some sort of group arrangement.

Option B_1.(1) One's academic potential does not take into consideration motivation and related factors such as reading level (if the IQ test is, in part, based upon nonverbal elements). Past achievement (especially within the class involved) does reflect (past) motivation. Moreover, it also reflects reading skills since most assessment techniques demand basic reading skills.

(2) Generally defend. Such classes are small enough to permit the teacher to work with each individual as needed. This is the idea behind subgrouping arrangements.

(3) Students at different levels of understanding can learn from each other. More important, however, social interaction of all individuals is a basic function of education in this country.

(4) Generally defend. It is grossly unfair to derive a mark for a weak student on the basis of relative standing with strong students. Usually, however, some indication is expected in this respect when course grades are derived. This may be indicated as a second evaluation.

(5) This can happen, especially if such groups are based upon IQ or even achievement, as most measures currently do not take into account subcultural differences. On the other hand, such plans can be very effective in placing instruction on the level necessary for achievement.

Perhaps the best solution is to provide ample opportunity for all subgroups to work together when differentiated achievement is not a basic factor in the situation.

Option B_2.(1) This takes the learner from the lower to the higher levels of cognition in a hierarchical progression.

(2) As feedback relative to progress. They also serve to broaden understanding.

(3) People tend to remember what they do. Especially in the skills area, a cognitive understanding does not mean that application is automatic.

(4) More optional activities are needed in a heterogeneous class than in a homogeneous class because a wider variety of abilities and interests must be met.

C. (1) Although you probably discovered ambiguities from the critique of a colleague, students not only vary in many ways, but they possess quite a different frame of reference from that of the teacher.

(2) Refute. Pretests and posttests are designed to help the student assess his or her present level of understanding in the area. By checking answers, you will find that the items become valuable learning devices.

(3) Although this occasionally may occur, the system tends to be highly motivating since it places instructional activities on attainable levels for each and every student. Moreover, instruction appropriate for the slow students is usually inappropriate for bright students, and vice versa.

(4) An individual must be permitted to progress at his or her own pace. If one falls behind or advances beyond his own group, frustration and boredom soon become apparent.

(5) Indeed it can be, if this instructor assumes that the individuals within each subgroup are alike. The purpose of such an arrangement is to expedite individualization of instruction by calling attention to broad categories of achievement. Such a plan usually is not needed in small classes (up to twenty to twenty-five students).

(6) In traditional class settings, the able students seldom need to exert much effort since they can often do acceptable work "without cracking a book." As they move into the system, however, they get involved and interested in the activities.

(7) Such individuals often have found successful achievement beyond their reach. Long ago they have despaired of ever competing effectively in the typical high school class. Their study habits, self-concept, and the like need to be altered. Moreover, there is some evidence that most teachers are not fully qualified to work effectively with slow students.

(8) A LAP perhaps finds its greatest utility for students who need special help due to absences, etc. Subgrouping is merely an expediency measure in large classes to facilitate enrichment activities for each individual.

Optional activity

D. (1) The practitioner desires to narrow the academic aptitude range by eliminating the extremes, and the idea seems a logical solution.

   The professional educator has supporting research evidence, however, that such practices seldom reduce this spread substantially, as academic aptitude is extremely complex. Perhaps of even greater importance is the practical difficulty of shifting students from one group (track) to another and the stigma associated with the weaker groups.

(2) Such practices tend to place the major focus of learning on in-centives and thus render them minimally intrinsically rewarding. Moreover, quality, not quantity, is the best gauge of achievement. Quality, however, is relative to the individual.

(3) In a small academic class (no more than twenty students or so) the teacher often has time for providing enrichment activities ac-cording to the needs of each student.

(4) To provide opportunities for student interaction, to combat boredom, and to diagnose learning difficulties. (Successful comple-tion does not always insure mastery as assumed by the program developers.)

ANSWERS TO POSTTEST

For most beneficial results you should work through the entire LAP before you check your answers to the posttest. Failure to meet the provided minimum standards probably suggests certain weaknesses that need to be corrected. As with the Preassessment items, you will find supporting reasons for answers. It is hoped that this will serve as desirable feedback in your quest for mastery.

A. 1. Each individual, regardless of academic aptitude, should be helped to achieve up to capacity.

2. Student group interaction is needed in the learning process.

3. Each student is expected to demonstrate a minimum level of com-petence.

4. Students of differing levels of academic aptitude should be pro-vided opportunities for working together.

5. Academic aptitude and achievement must be considered as merely a part of the individual difference complex; other important dimen-sions are social and emotional differences.

6. Although excessive class size often renders some form of grouping necessary, this is merely an expediency measure for meeting in-dividual differences.

7. Academic aptitude is so complex that efforts to narrow the class range on the basis of specific dimensions (e.g., IQ and achieve-ment) are seldom very effective.

8. Although academic aptitude has a general quality, considerable variation must be expected in different classes. (A student who is extremely able in mathematics, for example, may possess no more than average aptitude for American history.)

B. 2 (An appropriate use for a LAP is to assist those who missed or misunderstood regular class activities.)

   4 (Defensible, so long as extra credit is not extended.)

   5 (Legitimate so long as it is comparable.)

   6 (Different, rather than extra work, is emphasized.)

   8 (Total group interaction is important.)

   9 (This helps the student advance academically while keeping her with her age-mates.)

  10 (Such a decision is left to the student, even though the teacher may not recommend the move. Perhaps the new peer group will stimulate the student to achieve.)

  14 (Such students must cope with the language if any degree of success is to be achieved.)

  19 (Different work, based on student needs, is sound, so long as minimum essentials are achieved.)

Reasons for incorrect items

   1 (This involves heaping additional work on one who is already overloaded due to limited ability.)

   3 (When grouping is based on academic aptitude, weaker students will tend to feel stigmatized. A better basis would be past achievement.)

   7 (Although movement is permissible upon student request, it should be postponed until the new unit is started.)

  11 (Extra work for extra credit discriminates against weaker students.)

  12 (Quantity is no substitute for quality.)

  13 (Utilizes incentives as a basis; intrinsic motivation should be emphasized. This discriminates against weaker students.)

  15 (Providing for individual differences within each subgroup is essential.)

  16 (Such a student should be failed. Each student must achieve a minimum level of performance in order to pass.)

  17 (Few students will so elect. Such a practice permits some students to languish with minimum effort.)

  18 (To work through a learning program following regular class experiences is redundant. Use of a posttest would have been acceptable.)

  20 (Discriminates against weaker students.)

C. 1. Learning activity packages

    a. Specific requirements are provided

      (1) Pre- and posttests specify how many are to be listed, selected, and constructed

      (2) Learning activities designate specifically what to observe, discuss, write

    b. Source materials are available

       (1) Basic preliminary reading provided

       (2) Selected bibliography is offered

       (3) Cross-referenced with other LAPs and modules

    c. Group interaction is provided

       (1) Some activities involve subgroups if possible

       (2) Visits and discussions with experienced teachers are called for, or the equivalent is provided

2. Class grouping techniques (within)

    a. Minimum levels of competency are provided

       (1) Minimum levels (common core) are established for every student

       (2) Provides options for individuals within each group

    b. Instruction is differentiated

       (1) Different degree of depth is provided for each subgroup

       (2) Each person has options within his or her own subgroup

    c. Reinforcement is provided

       (1) Activities are adjusted to each subgroup, and in turn to each individual

       (2) Tests for each subgroup are provided in which each person has a fairly equal chance of success

SUPPLEMENTARY SOURCES

The following sources may be used in lieu of the Hoover texts or, preferably, as supplementary to them. Generally they are consistent with the models provided in the LAPs of this module. As such, the references do not represent all of the most recent references in the area; rather, they constitute selected references designed to broaden or expand needed background information.

Bechtol, William A., *Individualizing Instruction and Keeping Your Sanity* (Chicago: Follett Publishing Co., 1973).

Coppedge, F. L., "Goals of Individualized Instruction," *Educational Technology*, 15: 25–28 (Aug., 1975).

Duane, J. E., "Individualized Instruction: A Symposium," *Educational Technology*, 14: 7–48 (Nov., 1974).

Graff, P., "Some Criticisms of Mastery Learning." *Today's Education*, 63: 88 + (Nov., 1974).

Hoover, Kenneth H., *The Professional Teacher's Handbook*, 2nd ed. (Boston: Allyn and Bacon, Inc., 1976).

Hoover, Kenneth H., and Paul M. Hollingsworth, *Learning and Teaching in the Elementary School*, 2nd ed. (Boston: Allyn and Bacon, Inc., 1975).

Leonard, Joan M., and others, *General Methods of Effective Teaching: A Practical Approach* (New York: Thomas Y. Crowell Co., 1972), Chap. 11.

Model Schools Project, "Individualized Evaluation Is Essential in Individualized Learnings," *Bulletin of the National Association of Secondary School Principals*, 58: 57-72 (May, 1974).

Sherman, T. M., "Individualized Responsive Instruction: An Alternative Approach to Individualizing in Large Group Settings," *Educational Technology*, 15: 56-58 (Oct., 1975).

module
III

DISCUSSION-FOCUSED METHODS AND TECHNIQUES

The aim of every teacher is to somehow get students actively involved in their own learning processes. Broad student participation, however, does not just happen. It is the result of carefully planned experiences. Such is the focus for this module.

Basic to all instructional methods and techniques is the questioning strategy employed (treated in the first LAP). Just as the entire reflective process rests upon an appropriately phrased problem question, so do various aspects of the process depend upon adequate questioning techniques. It has been established that about 90 percent of all classroom questions are at the memory level. Yet, if concepts are to be inductively derived, emphasis should be focused upon the higher levels of cognition. The Bloom taxonomy of educational objectives provides a basis for the questioning strategy developed in this LAP.

The second LAP in this module offers a systematic approach to the two closely related techniques of discussion and debate. Perhaps the most widely used instructional approach today is class discussion in some form. It is known that students will indulge in serious reflection only to the extent that the group setting is conducive to such reflection. Discussion, while designed as a problem-solving process, does not always accomplish this end. In such cases the logical consequence is debate in some form. Debaters utilize all their powers of persuasion in presenting opposing arguments on highly controversial issues. By abiding by the rules of the game, students through the processes of debate can weigh highly emotional matters in an atmosphere conducive to learning.

The ultimate worth of all learning is measured in terms of the student's ability to make applications to life situations and problems. This process is greatly enhanced when students connect class experiences to related problems (review). By taking a *new look* at previous learnings, important associations and insights can be disclosed. This technique differs from traditional review and drill procedures, which too often involve mere repetition of events. Effective drill procedures too must approach a problem from a new angle or from a different context from the previous learning experience. Current misuse of review and practice procedures can serve only to underscore the urgent need for a thorough understanding of these basic instructional tools, treated in the final LAP of this module.

lap
6

Questioning
Strategies

RATIONALE. Questioning strategies are basic to all instruction. They are involved in some way with all methods and techniques of teaching. In fact, in a number of instances they serve as basic instructional techniques by which subject matter is manipulated from moment to moment. They are the "moves" that lead the learner from the general to the specific and back again. Indeed, one might say that the teacher is (or should be) a professional question maker. Yet, in study after study the evidence suggests that more than 90 percent of the questions actually used by teachers are at the memory (lowest) level of learning.[1]

The phraseology of questions has a tremendous influence on the thinking or reflective processes of students. Thus you will recognize a close parallel between the various levels of the cognitive domain (treated in the module on Preinstructional Experiences) and the basic questioning strategy offered here.

OVERVIEW

Key Concepts

1. The questioning level employed, in large measure, determines the level of thinking elicited.

---

[1] *Norris Sanders, "Changing Strategies of Instruction: Three Case Examples,"* *in Dorothy M. Frazier, ed.,* Social Studies Curriculum Development: Problems and Prospects. *National Council for the Social Studies Yearbook, 39: 151, 1968.*

127

2. Appropriately phrased problem questions (e.g., policy questions for class discussion) set the stage for use of higher-order questions.

3. Through appropriate probing techniques, the learner may be encouraged to indulge in the higher process of reflective thought.

4. Higher-order questions necessarily incorporate the lower levels of cognition.

5. Since evaluation questions call for personal reactions, they necessarily overlap with the affective domain.

New Terms

1. Recall questions: Questions that call for the recitation of specific facts, principles, or generalizations. Usually characterized by such words as who, what, when, and where.

2. Comprehension questions: Questions that call for understandings, demanding manipulation of data through interpretation, summarization, example, and definition. Usually characterized by such key words as how or why.

3. Analysis questions: questions that call for taking apart data for the purpose of discovering hidden meaning, relationships, or basic structure. Characterized by using *established criteria* for discovering assumptions, motives, implications, issues, logical fallacies, and so forth.

4. Evaluation questions: Questions calling for judgments, opinions, personal reactions, and criticisms, based upon the *learner's own criteria.* Usually characterized by such key words as should, could, would, in your opinion, and so forth.

5. Probing techniques: Intermediate-questions or clues designed to provide cues, hints, or clarification after the student indicates his inability to respond effectively to an initial question. The technique is designed to lead the learner to the original question by capitalizing upon existing knowledge and understanding.

6. Redirection: Involving more than one student in the answer to a question. Such questions often involve several "reasons" or "factors," differences of opinion, and so forth.

OBJECTIVES. After this experience you should be able to ask appropriate classroom questions, as evidenced by your ability to:

1. List six essentials of basic questioning strategy.

2. Distinguish between recall, comprehension, analysis, and evaluation questions in eighteen out of twenty instances from a provided list of twenty questions.

3. Construct in seven out of eight instances recall comprehension, analysis, and evaluation questions from two provided topics.

PRELIMINARY READING. Since the elements of instructional methodology are somewhat variable, the following excerpts are provided to help you develop a frame of

reference as a point of departure for this experience. If you prefer, you may proceed directly to the Preassessment items.

LEVELS OF QUESTIONS AND COGNITION

Instructional goals, as treated in a previous LAP, are designed to emphasize critical thinking. Consequently, each instructional method is developed within a framework of critical thinking processes. Critical thinking may be conceived as including all thought processes beyond the memory level. Thus it seems appropriate to treat questions from the vantage point of *levels*. The following categories provide such a frame of reference.

Data recall cues the student to respond with a descriptive type of statement. Recalling and reciting previously acquired information are typical tasks at this level.

Data processing involves the student in using data to show cause and effect relationships, to group, classify, synthesize, define, analyze, compare, contrast, and infer from data.

Application cues the student to do some divergent thinking, to make predictions, to develop theories, and to apply principles learned in other contexts.[2]

A number of conceptual schemes have been developed for classifying questions. All provide a systematic approach to questioning at different levels of complexity, progressing from the simple to the complex. Each level builds upon the previous one. Thus, attention to the higher levels or categories of thinking does not imply neglect of those at the lower levels. The scheme used in this LAP is generally patterned after Bloom's *Taxonomy of Educational Objectives*.[3] (See LAP on Instructional Objectives in the module Pre-Instructional Experiences.) The various levels have been identified in the section on new terms and are expanded in the LAP on Instructional Objectives.

Improving Quality of Pupil Responses

Probing for more adequate answers is a well-known but often neglected technique. Probing involves a question or a series of questions addressed to the *same* student. It is used when an initial response is inadequate. There are two principal types of probing: *prompting* and *clarification*.

Prompting involves the use of short hints or clues when the student is unable to give an answer or gives an incorrect answer to a question. Prior to the prompting sequence it may be desirable to rephrase the question to be assured that the student understands what is being sought. Prompting may involve a series of questions designed to elicit those things the student knows relative to the original question. Thus the procedure usually involves a series of *recall* questions, designed to lead the student back to the original question. The procedure is used when the student is suspected of possessing the necessary background knowledge for handling the question. It is designed to guide him in the critical thinking processes. To illustrate:

---

[2] *Kenneth Shrable and Douglas Minnis, "Interacting in the Interrogative,"* Journal of Teacher Education, *20: 201–212 (Summer, 1969).*

[3] *Benjamin Bloom, ed.,* Taxonomy of Educational Objectives, Handbook I: Cognitive Domain *(New York: David McKay Co., Inc., 1956).*

T. How does the principle of immunization work?

S: I don't know.

T: Using a smallpox vaccination as an example, what happens if the vaccination "takes"? (A different question, recall in nature)

S: One usually gets sick. He runs a temperature.

T: Good. Are there any other symptoms? (Recall question)

S: He develops a lesion at the place of the vaccination.

T: Fine. Now what does this suggest to you about smallpox? (Comprehension question)

S: That the individual actually has a mild case of the disease, I guess.

T: Your answer is basically correct. Why is an individual made immune to the disease? (Analysis question)

S: His body would build up defenses against the disease.

Clarification is a probing technique that calls for a restatement or expansion of a response. It is usually sought when the response is not incorrect but still does not measure up to the teacher's expectations. Instead of giving hints, the student is asked to improve his or her response. Such comments as the following are often used: "Explain"; "Would you restate your answer in another way?"; "What else can you add?"; "Are there other reasons?"

Enhancing Questioning Effectiveness

Most teachers and certainly students recognize that the teacher and a few individuals tend to do most of the talking in class. Although there are many psychological forces at work in any given class, there are certain techniques that may greatly reduce teacher talk and expand the number of participating students.

Many students who realize that they are not likely to be called upon unless their hands are raised are likely to keep their hands down. The few students who do raise their hands tend to monopolize the experience. They are usually those who have a good grasp of the problem and who like the reinforcement provided. The teacher, in turn, is reinforced by the apparent group progress suggested by his volunteer respondents. Nonvolunteers, however, most need the experience of active participation. Student participation is enhanced when both volunteers and nonvolunteers are asked to respond.

Another way of enhancing questioning effectiveness is through *redirection*. Teacher talk can be minimized by asking questions which elicit several responses. This may involve a question in which several "reasons" or "factors" may be requested, or it may be one in which differences of opinion exist. Different students are thus expected to offer "reasons" or "opinions." It may be necessary to cue the group to what is expected by saying, "This question has many parts to it. Please give only one when you answer." Redirection has the added advantage of encouraging students to respond to each other. (All too often the pattern is teacher question-pupil response, etc.)

Another rather obvious technique is that of stating a question prior to calling upon the individual who is to respond. The teacher should pause for a few seconds after he asks the question and before he calls upon someone to provide an answer. If the teacher designates a respondent *prior* to the question, the rest of the class will tend to relax and may not even "hear" the question. By pausing, each student is given time to organize his thinking for a thorough answer. It should be pointed out that the higher-level questions usually demand a few seconds for meditation.

Interfering Questioning Practices

Sometimes a teacher falls into the habit of *repeating questions* before a student is asked to respond. The problem seems to be related to a certain lack of security residing within the teacher. Such a person is likely to ask a question and then ask it a second time, using slightly different wording, prior to calling on a student. The practice of calling on nonvolunteers can contribute to the problem. A nonvolunteer may or may not be following the proceedings. By professing not to hear or understand the question, the student "saves face" temporarily. In such instances, the teacher can avoid repeating the question by immediately moving to another student. Thus the behavior of the student is not reinforced; neither is teacher talk increased.

The practice of *answering one's own questions* is a particularly annoying habit that is unfortunately difficult to correct. It too seems to be tied to a basic psychological need of the questioner. By inviting student responses, a discussion, to some extent at least, becomes unpredictable. It is frequently impossible to complete a discussion as planned. Certain unexpected questions and/or responses tend to throw the discussion "off." Nevertheless, the practice tends to be self-defeating since it definitely increases teacher talk and minimizes student volunteering. Moreover, students are likely to expend less effort in preparing for such experiences since the teacher will "answer his own questions anyhow."

Perhaps the most common obstacle to effective questioning technique is the tendency to *repeat student response*. This may be considered appropriate for clarity or for more effective comprehension. If student answers are repeated often enough, however, students will tend to be satisfied with incomplete answers. As indicated in a previous section, incomplete answers usually call for probing techniques. Responses that cannot be heard in all parts of the room should be *repeated by the responding student*. Thus inaudible responses are not reinforced.

The Mechanics of Appropriate Questions

Many leaders encounter difficulty in developing reflective thought because of the way they phrase their questions. A question calling for a "yes" or "no" answer usually discourages discussion. For example, the question "Do you agree with the present United States foreign policy toward Red China?" demands a supplementary "Why?"

Questions that reflect a given point of view or bias of the teacher are all too common. The question, "Why should we withdraw our troops from Indochina?" begs the answer. It merely elicits support for a given point of view. A similar question, "Should we allow this appalling situation to continue?" builds in a bias. Beginning teachers have been observed to ask many "Don't you think. . ." questions.

PREASSESSMENT ITEMS (answers provided on pp. 140-42)

This experience is designed to help you gain an overall perspective of the major aspects of questioning strategy. After completing the preassessment items, turn to the answers found at the end of this LAP and check your answers. Note that reasons for both correct and incorrect items in Part B are provided.

A. List six essential elements of basic questioning strategy. (To illustrate: The question, when initially asked, is not directed to any one individual.)

1.

2.

3.

4.

5.

6.

B. Place the following code letters before each of the questions below:

R—Recall

C—Comprehension

A—Analysis

E—Evaluation

1. What implications does the author list relative to the Watergate issue?

2. What do you think of Langston Hughes's hip language style of poetic expression?

3. How do women's rights in today's society compare with such rights during Civil War days?

4. What prompted the formation of the Ku Klux Klan?

5. What implications can you draw from our nation's attempts to act as a mediator between Israel and Egypt?

6. Explain in your own words why a powerful nation must be constantly prepared for war.

7. What is your judgment concerning mercy killing?

8. Why must a person be reminded of his constitutional rights before being interrogated by authorities?

9. What individual or body possesses the final responsibility for removing an errant president from office?

10. What is your personal reaction to liberalized abortion laws?

11. What logical fallacies are apparent from the speaker's presentation?

12. Would you summarize in your own words the environmentalist's plea for a cleaner atmosphere?

13. What political motive apparently accounted for the candidate's denunciation of a leader of his own party?

14. What motives prompted Benedict Arnold to desert to the British during the Revolutionary War?

15. How would you judge the candidate's motives relative to democratic ideals?

16. How would you define the citizens' opposition to the proposed freeway?

17. What criticisms of the union's stand on the issue of unemployment can you offer?

18. In your judgment who is ultimately responsible for the curtailment of crime in our nation's large cities?

19. Why must an indigent accused citizen be afforded a lawyer at public expense even though he or she may desire to plead guilty?

20. What are the basic issues separating the two candidates?

C. Construct one recall, one comprehension, one analysis, and one evaluation question for *each* of the two listed topics.

   1. Income taxes

     a.

     b.

     c.

     d.

   2. War with Mexico

     a.

     b.

     c.

     d.

If you were able to supply thirty-one of the thirty-four requested responses, you are to be commended. This suggests you are already on the road to becoming an effective question maker and should probably proceed directly to the next LAP in this module (Discussion and Debate). Even if you were able to supply few of the appropriate responses, do not despair, for questioning strategies are much more difficult than is generally assumed. By first studying all answers to the Preassessment items, noting especially supporting reasons for both correct and incorrect items in Part B, and then working through the provided learning activities, you should achieve mastery with little difficulty. Good luck!

LEARNING ACTIVITIES

Work through each learning activity, complete the self-assessment items, and check your answers before moving to the next one. Note that the last learning activities are optional, depending upon your needs and circumstances at that point. You should be able to complete this LAP in about four hours.

A: *Read.* Re-examine the overview and the preliminary reading sections of this LAP and the one on Instructional Objectives (Pre-Instructional Experiences module). You will broaden your understanding substantially by studying Chap. 7 (11) in the Hoover texts and/or by studying the selected references listed at the end of this LAP.* Note specifically the following:

1. The parallel nature of the cognitive domain and questioning levels.

2. The hierarchical nature of questioning levels.

3. How questioning strategy (cognitive in nature) can be used as a vehicle in the achievement of affective and psychomotor objectives. (In this connection you might also want to examine the preliminary reading section of the LAP dealing with value-focusing activities (see module on Personal-Social Instructional Techniques.)

4. The importance of context in determining questioning level.

Self-assessment Items (answers provided on p. 142)

(1) What rationale is offered for combining the six levels of the cognitive domain into four questioning levels?

(2) Why are higher-order questions sometimes no more than recall in practical situations?

(3) Indicate how the following analysis question involves the affective domain: What are your personal reactions concerning the reinstatement of the death penalty (in a number of states) for certain crimes?

At this point you may select either Option B₁ or Option B₂, depending upon your particular situation. Those who are presently teaching should select Option B₁. Those who are not teaching or who do not have immediate access to students should select Option B₂.

Option B₁: *Videotape-modeled analysis.* View prepared videotapes on questioning strategy. (If your school does not have such tapes, appropriate films are available from different commercial suppliers.†) Another option would be a modeled demonstration by your supervising teacher or an "expert" resource person, perhaps from a neighboring university or college. If necessary, optional activity *E* may be substituted for this experience. Working in a committee with other new teachers if possible, discuss the following questions. (If working alone, write out answers to the questions and discuss with your supervising teacher or with a recommended resource person.)

1. What leads teachers into such interfering behaviors as repeating, answering their own questions, and repeating student responses? How can such behaviors be altered?

2. Distinguish between prompting, clarification, and redirection.

Henceforth the chapter number in parentheses refers to the abridged edition of The Professional Teacher's Handbook, *2nd ed.*

†*One such source is "Questioning Skills, Cluster II" (five films on questioning strategy),* The Teaching Skills for Secondary School Teachers *Series, General Learning Corporation, 250 James Street, Morristown, New Jersey 10022.*

3. What are some clues that might help you distinguish between recall, comprehension, analysis, and evaluation questions?

Self-assessment Items (answers provided on pp. 142–43)

(1) Let us suppose that you asked a question and then called upon Mary to respond. Thereupon she asked, "Would you repeat the question?" Assuming that she was not listening when the question was asked, what would probably be the best action to take?

(2) What determines whether a teacher will probe or redirect?

(3) Distinguish between the adequacy of an answer to an analysis question and that to an evaluation question.

Option B₂: *Written exercise.* Using three of your unit concepts as a basis (developed in connection with the LAP on Concept Development), prepare questions as indicated.*

1. Using one of your concepts in the cognitive domain, develop one question for each of the following levels: recall, comprehension, analysis, evaluation.

2. Repeat the above for a concept in the affective domain. (See LAP on Value-Focusing Activities.)

3. Using your third selected unit concept, develop three or four questions illustrating probing techniques.

4. Prepare three questions illustrative of different techniques of redirection. Base upon one of your selected concepts.

Self-assessment Items (answers provided on p. 143)

(1) An evaluation question demands one or more lower-order preparatory questions. Defend or refute.

(2) How do questions in the cognitive domain differ from those in the affective domain?

(3) What determines whether one will probe or redirect?

C: *Instructional application.* Using one of your concepts as a basis (developed in connection with the LAP on gaining the concept), prepare a five- to ten-minute "discussion" session for one of your classes.† Proceed as follows:

1. Write out eight to ten questions featuring no specific level of questioning strategy.

2. Present and record or, if possible, videotape the actual instructional experience. (As an alternative, another teacher or a supervising teacher may be used as an observer.)

As a guide in checking your success on this task, you may want to refer to Part B of the preassessment items.
†*Those who do not have their own classes can complete the experience by organizing into committees of three each in preparation for a simulation.*

3. Replay and critique each presentation, listing at least two or three of your major difficulties. (Concentrate especially on interfering behaviors and prompting techniques.)

4. *Repeat* the experience, concentrating on *specific levels* of questioning strategies (recall; comprehension; analysis; evaluation).

5. Discuss your experience with members of your committee, concentrating upon major problems. (If working alone, prepare a written critique of your experiences and discuss with an experienced teacher if possible.)

Self-assessment Items (answers provided on p. 143)

(1) What hazards are associated with excessive prompting?

(2) What effects did repeating your own questions and repeating student answers have (or what might they have) on subsequent verbal behavior of students?

(3) In your second experience you probably found it necessary to work into evaluation questions gradually. Explain why.

(4) An ill-prepared student is likely to experience his/her greatest difficulty in the early part of a discussion. Defend or refute.

If, after reviewing your learning activities for this LAP, you feel that you can meet the stated objectives, proceed to the posttest. If not, you should complete at least one of the optional activities. (Note that one of these may have been completed in connection with an earlier learning activity.)

Optional Activities

D: *Class observation.* Working in a committee of three if possible, visit "discussion" classes in your field of specialization. (If working alone, you may be able to complete this task in two observations by combining numbers 1 and 2.) Proceed as follows:

1. Have one member record both the questions and the student behaviors associated with the following:

   a. Biased questions

   b. Question phraseology

   c. Attempts to achieve balanced participation

   d. Repeating questions

   e. Answering one's own questions

   f. Repeating student answers

2. Have a second member of your committee make notes of probing and redirection techniques, recording both questions and student responses. These will include:

    a. Prompting techniques

    b. Clarification techniques

    c. Redirection behaviors

3. Have a third member of your committee note the questioning level emphasized, by recording actual questions and responses associated with the following:

    a. Recall questions

    b. Comprehension questions

    c. Analysis questions

    d. Evaluation questions

Also make a note of the problem used as a basis for the lesson. *In addition*, make a tally of the total number of questions asked (both by the teacher and by students) *at each level.*

4. Later, compare notes and discuss the following questions:

    a. What interfering behaviors were noted? How might these have been minimized?

    b. What probing and redirection techniques were employed? How effective were they?

    c. What questioning level(s) was emphasized? How appropriate was this emphasis for the particular problem being developed?

Self-assessment Items (answers provided on p. 143)

(1) In all probability you noted occasions on which the teacher called upon an individual prior to the phrasing of a question. What was (or might be) the impact of such a technique on the rest of the class?

(2) You probably noted a tendency of one or more of the teachers observed to accept an "I don't know" or an inadequate response by passing on to another student. What impact might this technique have on the reflective process?

(3) In all probability at least one of the classes featured a discussion problem of fact or value. What influence did (or would) this situation have on the predominant questioning level employed?

E: *Simulation script.* Write out teacher-student episodes as indicated. Pattern after the illustration offered on p. 130 of the preliminary reading section of this LAP.

1. Prepare at least two of each of the following questioning levels in the order indicated. Make sure that one level logically prepares (or leads) the student for the next level, etc.

    Subject: Film censorship.

    a. Recall

        (1)

        (2)

   b. Comprehension

      (1)

      (2)

   c. Analysis

      (1)

      (2)

   d. Evaluation

      (1)

      (2)

2. First, develop an evaluation question *and then* employ probing techniques as indicated.

    Subject: Blood banks

    a. Evaluation question

    b. Prompting technique (limit to five or six intermediate cues or questions)

    c. Clarification (limit to a couple of questions)

Self-assessment Items (answers provided on p. 143)

   (1) Evaluate the policy of calling on nonvolunteers as a technique to bring the disinterested student into a discussion.

   (2) Under what conditions is probing appropriate?

   (3) An answer to an evaluation question cannot be wrong. Defend or refute.

POSTTEST (answers provided on pp. 144–45)

After you have completed the learning activities, complete the posttest and evaluate by checking your answers with those provided at the end of this LAP. Note that supporting reasons are provided for both correct and incorrect selections for Part B.

   A. List six essential elements of basic questioning strategy.

      1.

      2.

      3.

      4.

      5.

      6.

   B. Place the following code letters before each of the questions below:

      R—Recall

      C—Comprehension

A—Analysis

E—Evaluation

1. How would you evaluate the effectiveness of the "truth-in-packaging" law?

2. What penalty should be levied against Mexican "wetbacks"?

3. What are the implications for stiffer penalties for drug pushers?

4. What law enforcement agency has major responsibility for sky-jacking crimes?

5. How would you sum up the psychological reasons for drug abuse?

6. Why do you believe that smoking advertisements should be banned in public media?

7. What is the relationship between smoking and lung cancer?

8. What implications might be drawn between research findings on the harmful effects of smoking and the recent increase in teenage smokers?

9. What generalizations has the Surgeon General's office drawn relative to the effects of marijuana on health?

10. How does our treatment of the black compare with our treatment of the Chicano?

11. Who is responsible for maintaining an adequate system of integration in the public schools?

12. Why do you consider busing of students a valid means of maintaining integrated schools?

13. What is the relationship between extensive busing of students and race relations in metropolitan area schools?

14. Why do public opinion polls carry so much weight with politicians?

15. How much money is a candidate for national office permitted to spend on his campaign?

16. Would you summarize in your own words the meaning of the "push-pull" type of inflation?

17. What assumptions are behind recent requests for full public financial accounting of all political candidates?

18. Why should a president be permitted to resign for private reasons?

19. What assumptions does the writer state in defense of his position?

20. What does Langston Hughes mean by the expression, "My motto . . . is: Dig and be dug in return"?

C. Construct recall, comprehension, analysis, and evaluation questions for *each* of the two listed topics.

1. World War II

   a.

   b.

       c.

       d.

  2. Diplomatic relations with Cuba

       a.

       b.

       c.

       d.

Mastery of questioning strategies is a difficult and, indeed, a noteworthy achievement. By successfully completing this LAP, you can reduce teacher talk and increase student talk as students indulge in reflective thinking. Even if you failed to attain the recommended mastery level, do not be too discouraged. Study the answers to your posttest, especially noting the reasons for correct and incorrect items in Part B, and then proceed to the next LAP (Discussion and Debate). The close relationship of questioning strategies to these methods should contribute substantially to your understanding of each.

ANSWERS TO PREASSESSMENT ITEMS

You can make these items a most valuable learning experience by studying the provided reasons for both correct and incorrect responses. You will note that since Part A has no specific number of correct answers, several additional points (characteristics) have been provided. Since the last part calls for your constructed responses, your own answers may not be identical with those supplied by the writer. You should be able to decide whether or not your answers are reasonably accurate, however.

A. 1. The question, when initially asked, is not directed to any one individual.

   2. Students are provided time for reflection before a respondent is designated.

   3. Inadequate responses are often probed for greater precision and depth.

   4. Higher-order questions are emphasized.

   5. Involving several students, through processes of redirection, tends to broaden student involvement.

   6. Judicious use of nonvolunteers tends to enhance the processes of group reflection.

   7. Student questions are encouraged.

   8. Student questions frequently are reflected back to the group.

9. Certain level questions predominate at different stages of any given lesson.

10. Questions and student responses are not repeated by the teacher unless absolutely necessary.

11. Questions are asked in an unbiased manner.

B. 1-R (Here we are calling for implications already made by the author; thus the item would be mere recall for the students.)

   2-E (This question demands a judgment by the student. There can be no "right" or "wrong" answer to the question.)

   3-C (A "how" question calling for interpretation, involving relationships.)

   4-R (Since historians have documented this and placed it in history texts, it would be mere recall for the students.)

   5-A (This question calls for a discovery of hidden meaning, deduced from a variety of data.)

   6-C (The student is asked to make his or her own interpretation from existing data.)

   7-E (The student is expected to state his or her views, supported by a defensible rationale.)

   8-C (The question calls for a basic understanding. This, of course, assumes that the "reasons" have not been provided earlier.)

   9-R (This merely demands checking the provisions of the law on this point.)

   10-E (Merely demands one's own views on the issue; the adequacy of the answer is dependent upon the rationale offered by the student.)

   11-A (Calls for discovery of relationships—hidden meaning.)

   12-C (Here the student is asked to manipulate elements of a problem for his or her own use.)

   13-A (The question demands probing for hidden meaning.)

   14-R (The motives have already been divulged by the historians; for the student this is merely recall.)

   15-E (Calls for a personal reaction to motives already apparent.)

   16-C (Student must manipulate existing data by coming up with his or her own definition of the "candidate's opposition.")

   17-E (Here the student is expected to evaluate from the framework of his or her own criteria.)

   18-E (The question assumes that "those responsible for curtailment of crime" is a confusing issue. The student is asked to render his or her own evaluation.)

   19-C (Calls for a relationship to be made; manipulation is involved.)

   20-A (This demands pulling apart certain data for the purpose of reaching a conclusion. The assumption is made that the "issues" have not been previously analyzed for the student. If so, the question would be mere recall in nature.)

C. 1. Income taxes

a. Recall: What was the income tax of the average taxpayer in 1976?

b. Comprehension: How do the taxes of a middle-income single person compare with those of the middle-income married person?

c. Analysis: What basic motives cause some individuals to avoid income taxes whenever possible?

d. Evaluation: In your judgment, how should the poor be taxed, if at all?

2. War with Mexico

a. Recall: What factors led to the war with Mexico?

b. Comprehension: Would you summarize in your own words why Texas thought it must be freed from the rule of Mexico?

c. Analysis: What political motives accounted for the decision of the United States to declare war on Mexico, following the Texas declaration of independence?

d. Evaluation: Why should (or should not) a strong nation have the right to declare war on a weaker nation for the purposes of territorial expansion?

ANSWERS TO SELF-ASSESSMENT ITEMS

Self-assessment items are designed to help you gain depth of understanding as you proceed through the various learning experiences. Most of them do not have single correct answers. For feedback, however, you should compare your answers with the samples provided here.

A. (1) Comprehension-application and synthesis-evaluation questions are so closely related to each other that in a practical situation they are usually incorporated into a single question or question series.

(2) If a response is based upon somebody else's analysis (comprehension or evaluation), it is merely recall to the person who is responding.

(3) Since the question calls for one's personal reactions to an emotional issue, one's values come into play.

Option B_1. (1) Pass on to another student. This encourages all students to be attentive.

(2) If you suspect that an inadequate answer can be improved, probing is in order. If you suspect that the respondent is incapable of an adequate response, redirection is probably best. Questions with many parts (reasons, etc.) are especially appropriate for redirection.

(3) The adequacy of a response to an analysis question is based upon already established criteria. The adequacy of a response to an evaluation question is based upon the criteria (rationale) established by the respondent.

Option B₂. (1) Generally defend. One cannot evaluate unless he/she focuses attention on the necessary background aspects of the problem. Usually this focus is achieved through lower-order questions.

(2) Generally, cognition-type questions are more impersonal in nature, calling for such elements as objective evidence and evaluation. Questions in the affective domain tend to feature the personalized dimension ("you"-type questions).

(3) If you suspect the student possesses the basic background for coping with the question, probing is in order. This leads the student to clarity of understanding and at the same time provides needed reinforcement for the shy student. If, on the other hand, the student is suspected of having little knowledge in the area, it is most economical of class time and less embarrassing to the student to pass on to another student (redirection).

C. (1) It can have the effect of giving the individual the "third degree." This may cause a shy student to withdraw from future discussion.

(2) Probably because less articulate and lethargic. In effect, they probably expected the teacher to come up with clues to "right" responses.

(3) Higher-level questions are built upon information or answers provided through lower-order questions.

(4) Defend. The early part of a discussion emphasizes facts that the ill-prepared student does not possess. After proper foundation has been laid, he can enter into the discussion by providing his own views on the problem (evaluation level).

Optional Activities

D. (1) Students tend to pay less attention to the question or to the answer provided, as this removes the possibility of their being asked to respond.

(2) Tends to limit reflective processes to a relatively few individuals.

(3) Recall level would be emphasized, since the basic facts (or data) would be the chief concern for such a discussion problem.

E. (1) Acceptable if the question is broad and not used to embarrass the student. Usually should be avoided.

(2) When one wants the learner to really think about an issue. When articulation may be difficult.

(3) Refute. It can be considered wrong or inadequate only if the student's rationale is inadequate.

ANSWERS TO POSTTEST

For most beneficial results you should work through the entire LAP before you check your answers to the posttest. Failure to meet the provided minimum standards probably suggests certain weaknesses that need to be corrected. As with the Preassessment items, you will find supporting reasons for answers. It is hoped that this will serve as desirable feedback in your quest for mastery.

A. 1. The question, when initially asked, is not directed to any one individual.

2. Students are provided time for reflection before a respondent is designated.

3. Inadequate responses are often probed for greater precision and depth.

4. Higher-order questions are emphasized.

5. Involving several students, through processes of redirection, tends to broaden student involvement.

6. Judicious use of nonvolunteers tends to enhance the processes of group reflection.

7. Student questions are encouraged.

8. Student questions are frequently reflected back to the group.

9. Certain level questions predominate at different stages of any given lesson.

10. Questions and student responses are not repeated by the teacher unless absolutely necessary.

11. Questions are asked in an unbiased manner.

B. 1-E (Calls for the student's own rationale.)

2-E (Calls for a personal opinion; must be supported by a defensible rationale.)

3-A (Calls for a discovery of hidden relationships, constituting a logic or pattern between variables.)

4-R (Here the student must merely provide the facts.)

5-C (The question implies considerable discussion of the problem. The student, by "summing up," modifies in his or her own way.)

6-E (Calls for the student's own private rationale.)

7-R (This calls for the facts; thus the student makes no relationships of his own.)

8-A (Here the student is asked to "read between the lines" for meaning.)

9-R (As used in this question, the student offers the generalizations of others; thus, for him, they are facts to be recalled.)

10-C (The student is expected to make relationships between ideas.)

11-R (Assuming this has been clearly decided, the student would be merely reciting facts.)

12-E (Calls for the student's own views, which must be supported by a defensible rationale.)

13-A (Here the student is expected to seek out hidden relationships.)

14-C (The student must demonstrate an understanding by making an interpretation.)

15-R (Assumes that facts are known and can be recalled.)

16-C (Student is asked to modify data in his or her own way.)

17-A (Hidden meaning is sought.)

18-E (Calls for the student's own private views. There can be no "right" or "wrong" answer.)

19-R (Since the student is not asked to discover the assumptions, the question is recall.)

20-E (The student's personal interpretation is sought.)

  C. 1. World War II

      a. Recall: Who were the major powers in conflict during World War II?

      b. Comprehension: How were the underlying factors leading up to the two wars different?

      c. Analysis: What basic assumptions probably accounted for our nation's eventual decision that we could not "go it alone"?

      d. Evaluation: In your judgment, why does one nation have a moral responsibility for assisting a weaker nation whose national survival is at stake?

    2. Diplomatic relations with Cuba

      a. Recall: What constitutes diplomatic relations between nations?

      b. Comprehension: Will you summarize in your own words our nation's official diplomatic status with Cuba today?

      c. Analysis: What logical fallacies are associated with withholding diplomatic relations from a nation?

      d. Evaluation: Why should (or should not) a nation maintain diplomatic relations with a nation that launches an active campaign against democratic principles?

SUPPLEMENTARY SOURCES

The following sources may be used in lieu of the Hoover texts or, preferably, as supplementary to them. Generally they are consistent with the models provided in the LAPs of this module. As such, the references do not represent all of the most recent references in the area; rather, they constitute selected references designed to broaden or expand needed background information.

Carin, Arthur A., and Robert B. Sund, *Developing Questioning Strategies* (Columbus, Ohio: Charles E. Merrill, 1971).

Enokson, R., "Simplified Question Classification Model: Bloom and Guilford Systems," *Education*, 94:27-29 (Sept., 1973).

Hoover, Kenneth H., *The Professional Teacher's Handbook*, 2nd ed. (Boston: Allyn and Bacon, Inc., 1976), Chap. 7.

Hoover, Kenneth H., and Paul M. Hollingsworth, *Learning and Teaching in the Elementary School*, 2nd ed. (Boston: Allyn and Bacon, Inc., 1975), Chap. 9.

Hunkins, Francis P., *Questioning Strategies and Techniques* (Boston: Allyn and Bacon, Inc., 1972).

Ladas, H., and L. Osti, "Asking Questions: A Strategy for Teachers," *High School Journal*, 56: 174-189 (Jan., 1973).

Sanders, Norris M., *Classroom Questions: What Kind?* (New York: Harper and Row Publishers, Inc., 1966).

Tinsley, D. C., "Use of Questions," *Educational Leadership*, 30: 710-713 (May, 1973).

Discussion
and
Debate

RATIONALE. When individuals engage in class discussion, they ponder or meditate; they think critically. The discusser reflects upon his ideas along with those of his colleagues. He is a searcher, an inquirer. In effect, he says, "Here are my ideas. How do they relate to your opinions and the facts of the situation?" He is willing to alter views that seem inadequate under the scrutiny of thoughtful group analysis. Indeed the basic attitude is open-mindedness.

Like discussion, debate involves reflective thought. The debater weighs, ponders, thinks carefully. Unlike in discussion, however, the debater has moved from an attitude of searching with others for the best solution to one of conviction that he has found the best solution. Thus his mission is viewed as that of convincing others to accept his point of view. Where discussion is cooperative, debate is competitive. Where the discusser explores and inquires, the debater advocates and persuades.

OVERVIEW

Key Concepts

1. Discussion logically leads to debate.

2. Open-ended (policy) problems are most appropriate for discussion; debate propositions are essentially problems of advocacy.

3. While discussion emphasizes objective, logical reasoning, free from strategic verbal maneuvers, debate makes full use of the persuasive appeal, planned strategy, and the like.

4. Problem analysis, followed by a consideration of alternatives, is a minimum essential of the discussion process.

5. Debate focuses on three stock issues: need, plan, and the desirability of the plan. The affirmative team normally must defend all of these.

6. The negative team supports the status quo (conditions as they are) or (rarely) supports an alternative plan.

New Terms

1. Problem of policy: An open-ended type of question, often preplanned by the teacher, which forms the basis for discussion. Often begins with the word "what," but may sometimes begin with such a key word as "how." The word "should," or "ought," is stated or implied in the question.

2. Problem of advocacy: A proposed solution to a problem, usually beginning with the word "should" or "ought." Such questions enter into discussion especially when hypotheses are being considered. The advocacy problem forms the basis for a debate proposition.

3. Affirmative team: The debate team that supports the debate proposition as stated. Advocates a change from the status quo.

4. Negative team: The debate team that supports the status quo.

5. Burden of proof: Likened to a court of law in which an individual is considered innocent until proven guilty. Assumed by the affirmative team.

6. Rebuttal: Probing weaknesses of opponent's case. Usually involves indirect clash.

OBJECTIVES. After this experience you should be able to effectively utilize the methods of discussion and debate, as evidenced by your ability to:

1. List six of the essential characteristics of discussion and debate problems.

2. Distinguish between a problem of fact or value, a problem of advocacy, and a problem of policy in ten out of twelve instances from a provided list.

3. Select eight out of nine appropriately stated policy problems from a provided list of twenty assorted problems.

4. Formulate appropriate discussion and debate problems in four out of five instances from two provided topics.

5. Develop a key question (or statement when appropriate) for five out of six identified phases of discussion and debate.

PRELIMINARY READING. Since the elements of instructional methodology are somewhat variable, the following excerpts are provided to help you develop a frame of

reference as a point of departure for this experience. If you prefer, you may proceed directly to the preassessment items.

TYPE OF PROBLEMS ESSENTIAL TO DISCUSSION AND DEBATE

Discussion and debate often break down because of the wording of the problem. Four major types of questions have been identified. All are useful in discussion and debate. While debate will focus on a basic problem of advocacy, it also employs all types at some point during the process. The *policy question,* on the other hand, is basic to the type of discussion emphasized in this LAP. It should serve as the major problem for discussion. The four kinds of problems that lend themselves to varying degrees of reflective thinking are described. (The reader should also refer to the preliminary reading section in the LAP dealing with questioning strategies.)

Fact. Problems of fact are concerned with the discovery and evaluation of factual information. They are emphasized during the analysis of the problem when facts are introduced and clarified. For example: "What U.S. goods, if any, are being traded to Communist China?" This corresponds to the recall level of questioning offered in the LAP on questioning strategies.

Value. Problems of value are concerned with matters relative to value judgments. They call for the application of accepted standards in determining the appropriateness, rightness, or effectiveness of an issue. Examples: "How well is our trade policy being administered?" "Is our trade policy interfering with efforts to keep the peace?" Questions of value arise frequently during the early phases of a discussion. They are related to the *evaluation* of facts. Such questions often include comprehension and analysis levels of questioning strategies treated in LAP 6.

Problems of fact and problems of value usually can be identified by the presence of some form of the verb "to be." Indeed they are sometimes referred to as *is* or *are* questions.

Advocacy. Problems of advocacy, as the term implies, focus upon specific solutions. Such a question encourages argument rather than discussion. Advocacy questions most often emerge when hypotheses or tentative solutions to a problem are being evaluated. It is for this reason that establishment of accepted criteria should be developed prior to weighing the alternatives. To illustrate the type of question: "Should trade with Communist China be increased?" This is the kind of problem used as a basis for debate. Such questions usually begin with the word "should" or "ought." Analysis- and evaluation-level questions are employed heavily in this phase (see LAP on questioning strategies).

Policy. Problems of policy deal with matters necessitating decisions or action. Implied in the problem is the importance of exploring all possible solutions. Policy questions often begin with the words "what" or "how." The words "should" or "ought" also are stated or implied in the question. For example: "What should be the U.S. trade policy with Communist China?" Such problems usually reflect the highest level of questioning strategy (evaluation).

In resolving a problem of policy, questions of fact, value, and advocacy will be involved. The reverse does not follow, however. In formulating problems for discussion, teachers often confuse policy with advocacy questions. Advocacy immediately directs attention to concern for one particular solution to a problem. There are four essential phases in resolving an issue through class discussion.

Analysis Phase

As a preliminary step in decision-making, the various components of a problem must be introduced and evaluated. The process leads the learner from definition of important terms to an inspection of important facts and circumstances associated with the problem. In this phase of discussion the cause-and-effect relationships are explored; the overall seriousness of the problem is examined. Analysis questions are offered for the problem: "What steps should be taken to minimize the use of LSD among teen-agers?"

1. What is LSD?
2. How widespread is its use among teen-agers?
3. What are its effects?
4. What evidence indicates the problem is likely to persist? Are there evidences to the contrary?

Hypothesis Phase

After reviewing and evaluating the related facts and ideas relative to the problem, possibilities for solving the problem must be introduced. Sometimes referred to as the "idea generation" phase, this is the very heart of the problem-solving process. It is at this point that the teacher refers the group to the original question and poses the big question, "What should be done?" Students are invited to offer possibilities for solving the problem. Some such possibilities may be entirely new and may seem a bit "wild" when first introduced, as is typical of much creative thinking.

Each proposed solution can be followed by a brief discussion of advantages and disadvantages that seem apparent. An alternative procedure, and one preferred by those who would emphasize creativity in teaching, involves a listing of possible solutions *prior* to any sort of evaluation. Sometimes a fifteen- to twenty-minute brainstorming session may be in order at this point.

Hypothesis-testing Phase

In many relatively simple problems a brief analysis of advantages and disadvantages of the alternatives is all that is needed. Through this process, appropriate action becomes obvious. Other issues are not so easily handled, however. A "best" solution often appears best because of the particular needs or frame of reference of the individual involved.

In such cases the group must develop a set of standards or criteria for evaluating proposals. This may become rather difficult if the problem is close to the lives of students. If the problem is one of national or international policy, the process will be less difficult (for students) but essential if the issue is to be examined from as many angles as possible. To illustrate: "What should be the U.S. trade policy with Communist China?" The problem might be viewed from the standpoint of national security; it may be treated on purely humanitarian grounds; or it may be seen in relation to its effects on the trade balance with other Asiatic nations. Sometimes a priority system must be established.

Generalization-deriving Phase

Sometimes the outcome of a problem-solving discussion is a definite plan of action. Thus, by weighing each of the suggested hypotheses, some decision relative to one or more preferred courses of action may emerge. In most cases, however, the scope of the problem will be too broad to achieve such an end.

Most class discussion experiences culminate with the derivation of generalizations that emerge from the experience. To illustrate:

1. LSD users may incur permanent brain damage.
2. While under the influence of LSD, a person loses his ability to distinguish between reality and fantasy.
3. Use of LSD may render an individual emotionally dependent upon the drug.

THE DEBATE PROBLEM

Once an area of controversy has been identified, a proposed course of action is advanced. This can be reached through preliminary discussion in which division arises on an issue. Sometimes ready-made debate situations are provided through some current issue of controversy at the national, state, local, or school level. In recent years such timely topics as the following have been debated at length in many sections of the country. (Each has been stated in the form of a proposition for action.)

Resolved, That a stronger labor law is essential to the security of the United States.

Resolved, That management-labor differences should be settled by compulsory arbitration.

Resolved, That the local community should assume full financial obligations for private schools.

Resolved, That a course in sex education should be added to the secondary school curriculum.

ORGANIZING THE DEBATE TEAMS

Each team is composed of two individuals. Those on the affirmative side advocate adoption of the proposition, whereas those on the negative side are opposed to such action. For example, the proposition, "*Resolved*, That a stronger labor law is essential to the security of the United States," would be supported by the affirmative team; the negative team, on the other hand, would oppose the proposition.

There are three major issues in a debate. They are usually stated as questions:

1. Is the proposed course of action necessary?
2. Will the proposal remedy the existing state of affairs?
3. Is the proposal feasible or desirable?

The affirmative team must effectively prove all three points. The negative team, however, need only discredit *one* of the major issues, although it *may* concentrate its efforts on all three issues.

In planning overall strategy, members of the affirmative must propose and be prepared to defend a definite and feasible *plan* of action. Generally speaking, two or three main points will suffice, depending on the scope of the topic.

The negative team, being unable to know the exact strategy of the affirmative, must base much of its strategy upon prediction. If possible, it must be prepared for any eventuality. The best debaters often concentrate their efforts on the weakest point(s) of the affirmative case. Such strategy demands thorough preparation, coupled with on-the-spot analysis.

DEBATE TEAM RESPONSIBILITIES

The presentation is divided into two parts: the constructive speeches and the rebuttal presentations. For the most part, the constructive phase emphasizes building of the cases (affirmative and negative). Rebuttal speeches are primarily concerned with attacking weaknesses of opponents' arguments and strengthening one's own case more directly than is usually possible in constructive arguments.

Each person normally speaks twice, alternating between the teams. Constructive speeches are usually about seven minutes long; the rebuttal speeches normally are about four minutes long. The most effective speakers usually follow techniques of effective public address.

Preassessment Items (answers provided on pp. 165–67)

This experience is designed to help you gain an overall perspective of the major elements of discussion and debate. After completing the items, turn to the end of this LAP and check your answers. Note that answers (both correct and incorrect) are provided with supporting reasons to guide your efforts as you work through this LAP.

A. List six basic characteristics of appropriate discussion and debate problems. (To illustrate: A discussion problem is in question form.)

Discussion

1.

2.

3.

Debate

4.

5.

6.

B. Place the following code letters before each of the questions below:

FV—Question of fact or value

A—Question of advocacy

P—Question of policy

1. Should high school dress codes be established?

2. Who should be responsible for enforcing dress codes?

3. What do parents think of the proposed dress code?

4. What steps should be taken to govern the apparel of high school students?

5. Should students be permitted to enforce established dress codes?

6. Who should decide what students will wear to school?

7. What steps might be taken to rescind our existing dress code?

8. Why is a high school dress code an issue?

9. Is it appropriate to send home those who violate the dress code?

10. Why do girls usually have more severe dress code restrictions than boys?

11. How might our dress code be effectively enforced?

12. How can we persuade the administration to abandom our dress code?

C. From the list of problems, place a check (√) by nine of those that meet the criteria for a discussion problem.

1. Should the public support the cost of political campaigns?

2. Does presidential executive privilege pose a threat to our democratic society?

3. How can the national crime rate be minimized?

4. Might students be given the right to have an objectionable teacher replaced?

5. What should be done to reduce the number of teacher strikes in our schools?

6. Why should life be prolonged in cases of teminal illness?

7. What could the superpowers have done to prevent the 1973 Israel-Arab conflict?

8. What steps should be taken to increase economic security for the blacks in Ameria?

9. What steps could have been taken to avoid the energy crisis of the early 1970s?

10. How should the national gasoline shortage be met?

11. What are the merits and problems of a national land use program?

12. What recourse does a person have who has been unjustly accused?

13. How can tooth decay be reduced?

14. What action should have been taken to minimize pollution of our lakes and streams?

15. What might be done to provide students with more responsibility for their own learning?

16. What implications can be drawn from the "Watergate Affair"?

17. Why should an accused indigent be provided a lawyer at the taxpayers' expense?

18. What might be done to improve the health of our nation's teen-agers?

19. What might have been done to prevent the assassination of President Kennedy?

20. Does smoking in public places pose a health hazard to nonsmokers?

D. First, write out a problem for discussion *and then* formulate a debate proposition for each of the two listed topics.

    1. Smog control

       a.

       b.

    2. Gas consumption on the nation's highways

       a.

       b.

E. Prepare one key question (or statement if appropriate) for each of the identified phases of discussion and debate. Use the identified problems as a basis for your answers.

Discussion

Problem: What steps should be taken to preserve the Western deer herds?

    1. Analysis of the problem

    2. Establishing hypotheses

    3. Deriving generalizations

Debate:

Proposition: "*Resolved*, That the Western deer herds should be closed off to all hunting with firearms."

    1. The need

    2. The plan

    3. The desirability and feasibility of the plan

If you were able to provide thirty-four of the thirty-eight requested responses, congratulations are definitely in order. This suggests that you already possess the needed competencies in this area and should, accordingly, proceed to the next LAP in this module (Review and Practice). Even if you were able to provide few of the appropriate responses, do not be depressed, for discussion and debate are much more complex than is generally assumed. By first studying the reasons for correct (and incorrect) answers to the Preassessment items (at end of LAP), and then working through the learning activities, you should soon attain mastery in this vital area of instruction.

LEARNING ACTIVITIES

Work through each learning activity, complete the self-assessment items, and check your answers before moving to the next one. Note that the last learning activities are optional, depending upon your needs and circumstances at that point. You should be able to complete this LAP in about four hours.

A: *Read.* Re-examine the overview and the preliminary reading sections of this LAP and the preceding one in this module (Questioning Strategies). You will broaden your understanding substantially by studying Chaps. 12 (16) and 13 (17) in the Hoover texts and/or by studying the selected references listed at the end of this LAP. Note specifically the following:

1. Key words that often provide clues to the different types of problems.

2. The relationship between problems of advocacy and debate propositions.

3. Present vs. future-time orientation of fact and value problems as opposed to advocacy and policy problems.

Write out a question for each type of problem: fact, value, advocacy, policy. Use "inflation" as the broad topic for these questions.

1.

2.

3.

4.

Self-assessment Items (answers provided on p. 167)

(1) Distinguish between a problem of advocacy and a problem of policy.

(2) Distinguish between a problem of fact and a problem of value.

(3) "*Resolved*, That inflation is a threat to the nation's economy." Explain why this is an inappropriate debate proposition.

At this point you may select either Option B_1 or Option B_2, depending upon your particular situation. Those who are presently teaching should select Option B_1. Those who are not teaching or who do not have immediate access to students should select Option B_2.

Option B₁ : *Modeled demonstration.* This experience can be acquired in different ways, depending upon your particular circumstances. If you are working closely with a supervising teacher or a competent supervisor, such an individual might personally demonstrate both discussion and debate techniques. If this is not possible, another highly qualified teacher may be used for this purpose. Your interscholastic debate team probably provides an ideal demonstration source for debate. (In any event, it is essential that the model offered in this LAP be followed as closely as possible.)

A filmed or videotaped experience can be substituted for the foregoing. There are a number of films available for this purpose.* Any differences between the films and the emphasized structural properties of the methods should be noted.

If working alone, you will probably find it most convenient to visit a highly recommended teacher for this purpose. It is most desirable that such an individual acquaint himself or herself with the techniques as outlined in this LAP and attempt to model the demonstrations accordingly.

Working in a committee(s) of three if possible, arrange for demonstration experiences as indicated below. Make notes on each point and use as a basis for a post-demonstration discussion.

Class discussion

1. How the class was prepared (made ready) for the discussion.

2. How the discussion problem was phrased and introduced.

3. The nature of questions employed in the *analysis phase* of the discussion.

4. Prompting techniques used.

5. How students were guided into the *hypothesis phase* of the discussion.

6. How criteria were developed.

7. How generalizations were derived.

Debate

1. How the class was prepared (made ready) for the debate.

2. How the debate proposition was phrased and introduced.

3. How and when the *need* issue was established (and refuted).

4. How and when the *plan* of the affirmative was introduced and developed (and refuted).

5. How and when the *desirability and feasibility* of the plan were established (and refuted).

6. The specific thrust of the rebuttal speeches.

7. The nature of the follow-through analysis (conducted by the teacher).

Two such films are: Discussion in Democracy, *Indiana University, Audio-Visual Center, Bloomington, Indiana 47401, and* Introduction to Debate, *Central Arizona Film Cooperative, Mathews Hall, Arizona State University, Tempe, Arizona 85281.*

Interscholastic debate (and discussion) (optional)

If your school has an interscholastic debate team that features *university-style* debating, this should provide an ideal demonstration experience. (Sometimes discussion is also featured; discussion, however, is not identical to the *forum*.) Obtain information and discuss with your colleagues as outlined in the foregoing.

Self-assessment Items (answers provided on pp. 167–68)

(1) What is the basic purpose of each of the following phases of class discussion?

Analysis phase

Hypothesis phase

(2) How do the lesson generalizations differ from the hypothesis phase of a class discussion?

(3) Explain why the affirmative debate team normally must assume the burden of proof.

(4) Why must the first affirmative speaker provide a brief outline of the affirmative plan?

(5) How does the rebuttal differ from the constructive portion of a debate?

(6) The negative team need destroy only one of the major (stock) issues. Defend or refute.

Option B$_2$: *Developing preliminary discussion and debate outlines.* For each of the provided debate problems, construct two questions (or sentences as appropriate) for the listed phases.*

1. Discussion. *Problem:* What action (if any) should be taken to minimize traffic fatalities?

   a. Analysis phase

   (1)

   (2)

   b. Hypothesis phase

   (1)

   (2)

2. Debate. *Proposition:* "*Resolved,* That the maximum legal speed on the nation's interstate highways should be limited to 50 miles per hour."

   a. The need

   (1)

   (2)

After you have completed this task, you may want to check the sample responses provided on p. 171.

     b. The plan

       (1)

       (2)

     c. The desirability and feasibility of the plan

       (1)

       (2)

Self-assessment Items (answers provided on p. 168)

(1) What is the basic purpose of each of the following phases of class discussion?

Analysis phase

Hypothesis phase

(2) How do the lesson generalizations differ from the hypothesis phase of a class discussion?

(3) Explain why the affirmative debate team normally must assume the burden of proof.

(4) Why must the first affirmative speaker provide a brief outline of the affirmative plan?

(5) How does the rebuttal differ from the constructive portion of a debate?

(6) The negative team need destroy only one of the major (stock) issues. Defend or refute.

C: *Instructional application.* Using one of your unit concepts as a basis, prepare *both* a class discussion *and* a debate for one or more of your classes. As the teacher, you will lead the class discussion. For the debate your responsibility will entail selecting and preparing students for the experience and then leading a follow-through discussion of the experience.* Proceed as follows:

Class Discussion (Refer to the lesson plan in the Hoover texts on class discussion as a guide, pp. III–18–19 (264–65))

1. Write out a problem of policy and place it on the chalkboard.

2. Prepare three or four key questions for the analysis phase. (These will be essentially fact and value questions.) Let them feature the following:

    a. Definition of terms

    b. Importance of the problem

    c. Cause-and-effect relationships

    d. Aggravating conditions

---

*If you do not presently have access to students and are working in a group situation, divide into a committee(s) of six if possible, and set up simulations, letting your peers play the role of students in your area of specialization. Each individual should develop the experiences indicated. Limit the discussion to twenty to thirty minutes. Have the "teacher" indicate how the rest of the lesson would have been been handled.

3. Write out two possible hypotheses (solutions) as samples. (Remember that these are merely offered as a guide for you to use in eliciting *student* solutions to the problem.)

4. Prepare two possible criteria for evaluating possible solutions. (Again, these are merely illustrative of what students may offer.)

5. Write out two illustrative lesson generalizations that students may be expected to derive from the experience. (These are samples only.)

Debate

1. Prepare a debate proposition appropriate for your class.

2. Select four able students (or four of your committee) for the debate, and divide into affirmative and negative teams. (Do this two or three weeks in advance of the experience so that students can have time for adequate preparation.)

3. Have the debaters read that section on debate planning from the Hoover texts or from some comparable material from the supplementary sources list. Follow with salient points of your own, especially concentrating on points for each of the following:

   a. The need issue

   b. The plan (of the affirmative)

   c. The desirability or feasibility of the plan

   d. The rebuttal emphasis

4. When preparations are complete, hold an actual class debate.* Take notes along with your class or group by dividing a sheet of paper into two parts (for affirmative and negative cases). Enter the three words *need, plan,* and *desirability* on both parts of your paper and make notes of points made and refuted.

5. Evaluate the performance, using the form provided in the Hoover texts or some other comparable form. (Much of this evaluation can be completed during the debate. This is a teacher task.)

6. Lead a follow-through discussion of the facts and issues raised. (Use your notes taken during the debate as a basis for this discussion.)

7. Briefly discuss the merits of the debate presentation. (This provides valuable guidance for future class debates.)

8. Construct illustrative generalizations that the class may derive from the experience. (Limit to two samples.)

If possible, discuss the experiences in a small group with other new teachers. Use the foregoing as points of emphasis.

Self-assessment Items (answers provided on pp. 168–69)

(1) A class discussion does not focus on the resolution of the major discussion problem (usually placed on the chalkboard) for some time after the discussion is launched. Why?

If you do not have immediate access to students, hold a debate simulation. Limit each constructive speech to two minutes and each rebuttal speech to one minute for each individual.

    (2) How should questions or contributions that are "out of sequence" be handled?

    (3) Name some legitimate techniques of strategy.

    (4) When should debate strategy first be employed during a debate presentation?

    (5) It is inappropriate for a debater to bring in new points in the rebuttal portion of a debate. Why?

If, after reviewing your learning activities for this LAP, you feel that you can meet the stated objectives, proceed to the posttest. If not, you should complete at least one of the optional activities.

Optional Activities

D:*Class observation*. Arrange to visit actual classes featuring class discussion and debate.* Attempt to determine how lessons are to be culminated if you see only part of the experiences. (Normally both discussion and debate methods extend for more than one class period.) Obtain the following information:

Class discussion

1. A statement of the problem for discussion

2. Two questions (or statements) that were treated for each of the following discussion phases:

    a.   Analysis phase

    b.   Hypothesis phase

    c.   Generalization phase

Debate

1. A statement of the proposition

2. Two questions (or statements) that were treated for each of the following debate phases:

    a.   The need

    b.   The plan

    c.   The desirability or feasibility of the plan

    d.   The rebuttal

3. How the debate was evaluated

Intercollegiate debate team

Have a third member of your group arrange to visit an intercollegiate debate team in action if possible, obtaining information requested in the foregoing item.

The visits may be divided between different members of a committee.

If working with other new teachers, hold a post-observation conference for the purpose of comparing notes. Use the following questions as a basis for this discussion:

1. If the discussion problem was not one of policy, what problems (if any) seemed evident?

2. If the discussion phases were not clear, what problem (if any) seemed to emerge?

3. If the discussion problem and phases were appropriately followed, what did you note relative to the effectiveness (or ineffectiveness) of the discussion?

4. Evaluate the adequacy of the debate proposition.

5. How effectively did the affirmative team develop the stock (key) issues (need, plan, and desirability of the plan)?

6. Evaluate the effectiveness of the rebuttal phase of the debate.

7. If an alternative debate style was used, what advantages and disadvantages seemed evident?

Self-assessment Items (answers provided on p. 169)

(1) Why is a problem of fact or value generally deemed inappropriate for a class discussion problem?

(2) What were (or might be) some disadvantages associated with moving directly into the solution phase of a class discussion?

(3) Debate has been criticized because it sets up a polarized situation (there is no middle ground). Respond to this criticism.

(4) What were (or might be) the impact of memorized (canned) presentations in a debate?

(5) The objective of each debate team is to persuade the audience to accept given points of view. Why, then, are the debate teams usually evaluated on the merits of their respective cases?

E: *Written exercise.* For each of the provided discussion and debate problems, construct two questions (or statements as appropriate) for the listed phases.*

Class Discussion. Problem: What action (if any) should be taken to minimize traffic fatalities?

1. Analysis phase

   a.

   b.

2. Hypothesis phase

   a.

   b.

For feedback you may want to check sample responses provided for similar problems, pp. 171–72.

Debate. Proposition: Resolved, That the minimum legal speed limit on the nation's highways should be reduced to 50 miles per hour.

1. The need phase

   a.

   b.

2. The plan

   a.

   b.

3. The desirability of the plan

   a.

   b.

Self-assessment Items (answers provided on p. 169)

(1) Why must possible solutions to a discussion problem be withheld until the problem has been thoroughly analyzed?

(2) Why do some teachers prefer to withhold establishing criteria until possible solutions to the discussion problem have been offered?

(3) Why is the negative debate team normally not expected to present a plan?

(4) Explain why strategy is emphasized in debate but not in discussion.

POSTTEST (answers provided on pp. 169-72)

After you have completed the learning activities, complete the posttest and evaluate by checking your answers at the end of this LAP.

A. List six basic characteristics of appropriate discussion and debate problems.

Discussion

1.

2.

3.

Debate

4.

5.

6.

B. Place the following code letters before each of the questions below:

FV—Question of fact or value

A—Question of advocacy

P—Question of policy

1. What steps should be taken to provide an adequate income for welfare recipients?

2. Should each individual be provided a minimum annual wage?

3. Should illegitimate children be a source of additional income for welfare recipients?

4. Who determines those who are eligible for welfare assistance?

5. Why are welfare rolls increasing in size?

6. How do welfare regulations tend to encourage fathers to abandon their families?

7. How can welfare regulations be changed to discourage fathers from abandoning their families?

8. Is the number of black welfare recipients increasing?

9. What steps are being taken to train welfare recipients for self-sustaining employment?

10. Should welfare payments be adjusted automatically for inflation (or deflation)?

11. What action might be taken to minimize the number of welfare violations?

12. Is it likely that the current Congress will correct some of the existing problems associated with welfare?

C. From the list of problems, place a check (√) by nine of those that meet the criteria for class discussion.

1. What steps could have been taken to help the American Indian adjust to the mores of the early settlers?

2. What action should be taken to help the American Indian become economically independent?

3. Should Indian reservations be phased out or should they merely be modernized?

4. How should the American Indian be protected from further exploitation?

5. How might American Indian youth be integrated into the schools?

6. Why do many American Indians resist the "ways of the white man"?

7. What implications does the recent Wounded Knee uprising have for contemporary policy?

8. Is the American public responsible for the welfare of the American Indian who refuses to abandon or modernize reservation living?

9. What action might the schools take to prepare the American Indian for twentieth century living?

10. Who should decide what life pattern is best for the American Indian?

11. What health hazards are most prevalent among the American Indians?

12. Would it be appropriate to provide the American Indian with a guaranteed annual minimum wage?

13. What steps should be taken to reduce the spread of disease on the Indian reservations?

14. How should resentment of the "white community" among reservation Indians be minimized?

15. Must the reservation Indian be governed by the same laws as prevail elsewhere in the nation?

16. What cultural change (if any) should be encouraged in helping the American Indian adjust to a changing society?

17. What action does the Indian Agency take to cope with abuses and misunderstandings of the American Indian?

18. What might an educated Indian do to improve the living standards of his tribe?

19. Is it essential that the Indian preserve his cultural identity?

20. How can communication between the American Indian tribes be improved?

D. First, formulate a problem for discussion *and then* formulate a problem for debate for each of the two listed topics.

1. School integration

   a.

   b.

2. Teachers' right to strike

   a.

   b.

E. Prepare one key question (or statement if appropriate) for each of the identified phases of discussion and debate. Use the identified problems as a basis for your answers.

Discussion. Problem: What steps should be taken to increase the world's food supply?

1. Analysis of the problem

2. Establishing hypotheses

3. Deriving generalizations

Debate. Proposition: Resolved, That agricultural technology should be made available to all nations on an expanded scale.

1. The need

2. The plan

3. The desirability and feasibility of the plan

Mastery of discussion and debate (often considered at the very heart of the democratic process) should enable you to shift your instructional emphasis from teacher-focused to student-focused activities. This is indeed a worthy accomplishment. Even if you failed to attain the recommended mastery level of approximately 90 percent, proceed to the next LAP in this module (Review and Practice). Since review actually is another form of discussion, clarification of one tends to contribute to clarification of the other.

ANSWERS TO PREASSESSMENT ITEMS

> *You can make these items a most valuable learning experience by studying the provided reasons for both correct and incorrect responses. You will note that since Part A has no specific number of correct responses, several additional points (characteristics) have been provided. Since the last part calls for your constructed responses, your own answers may not be identical to those supplied by the writer. You should be able to decide whether or not your answers are reasonably accurate, however.*

A. *Discussion*

1. In question form.
2. Provides for an unlimited number of hypotheses, e.g., open-ended policy question.
3. A broad problem.
4. Based on a current, unsettled issue (assumes dissatisfaction with conditions as they are [the status quo].
5. Usually begins with the word "what" or "how."
6. The word "should" or "ought" is stated or implied in the problem.
7. Is future oriented.

Debate

8. Proposes a change from the status quo.
9. Involves an issue of divided opinion.
10. Is timely, involving a current controversy.
11. Problem begins with the word "should" or "ought" (an advocacy statement).

B. 1-A   (Problem is limited to the merits of one possible solution.)

2-FV (This is a matter of value judgment.)

3-FV (This is a matter of opinion, often based upon very sketchy evidence.)

4-P   (This is an open-ended question; an unlimited number of possible solutions may be considered.)

5-A   (We are limited to the pros and cons of one possible solution.)

6-FV (A matter of judgment or value.)

7-P   (Again, any number of steps might be taken, opening the door to an unlimited number of hypotheses.)

8-FV (There is probably no one factor here making this an issue; answer would vary with each person's view.)

9-A   (Although this is not worded as a "should" question, one and only one possible solution is open for consideration.)

10-FV (There are various opinions for such a restriction.)

11-P (The question opens the door to any number of possible ways of accomplishing this.)

12-P (Again, any number of different ways of "persuading the administration" are open for consideration.)

C. 3, 5, 8, 9, 10, 13, 15, 16, 18. (All are open-ended and deal with action that might be taken.)

Reasons for incorrect items

1   (Limited to one possible solution.)

2   (A value judgment called for only. No problem to be solved.)

4   (Again, this is a matter of value judgment; pros and cons of one possible solution only are to be considered.)

6   (This is a matter of value judgment.)

7   (This question deals with the past, thus a matter of conjecture only.)

11 (Limited to a discussion of facts and values associated with the problem.)

12 (Limited to conditions as they now exist.)

14 (Deals with the past, thus is reduced to a matter of conjecture.)

17 (Clearly a matter of opinion; no problem is being solved.)

19 (In the past, an opinion question only.)

20 (A matter of opinion; no problem is being solved.)

D. 1. Smog control

    a. What steps should be taken to control air pollution in our local area?

    b. Resolved, That all private automobiles should be banned from the inner-city areas.

  2. Gas consumption on the highways

    a. What action should be taken to reduce the gas consumption of our nation's motorists?

    b. Resolved, That businesses should establish incentives for commuter car pools.

E. 1. Discussion (samples)

    a. Analysis of the problem (any factual question pertaining to the status quo)

    Example: What role do our deer herds play?

    b. Establishing hypotheses (repeat the original problem, calling for advantages and disadvantages.)

    Example: What steps should be taken to preserve the Western deer herds?

    c. Deriving generalizations: What big ideas have emerged from our discussion today?

2. Debate

    a. The need: Our deer population has been reduced by 50 percent over the past ten years.

    b. The plan: Open all ranges to bow hunting only.

    c. The desirability and feasibility of the plan: Bow hunting would provide an outlet for hunter pressure and at the same time drastically reduce the deer kill.

ANSWERS TO SELF-ASSESSMENT ITEMS

Self-assessment items are designed to assist you in gaining depth of understanding as you proceed through the various learning activities. Most of them do not have single correct answers. For feedback, however, you should compare your answers with the samples provided here.

A. (1) A problem of advocacy is actually one possible solution to a problem. A problem of policy, on the other hand, opens the door to consideration of an unlimited number of solutions to the problem.

   (2) A problem of fact merely involves recall of available data. A problem of value involves one's opinions about data or ideas.

   (3) Is present oriented with respect to time. Thus the proposition can elicit mere opinion or speculation, based upon certain facts. Any resolution of a problem would necessitate formulation of another debate proposition.

B_1 (1) Analysis phase: To bring to bear in the discussion the critical facts and evaluation of them. (Perhaps a prior task involves clarification of the terms in the problem.)

   Hypothesis phase: Introduction and evaluation of proposed solutions to the problem.

   (2) Lesson generalizations represent a reduction of the discussion to broad ideas relative to the problem. The hypothesis phase involves casting about for possible solutions to the problem.

   (3) Conditions as they are (backed by experience) are usually considered best until proven otherwise. The affirmative team must accept this task.

(4) The negative team has the option of attempting to destroy only one of the three stock issues. It may choose to accept the need developed by the first speaker. The outline of the plan provides the option of attacking elsewhere.

(5) Basically the constructive speeches involve building the cases; the rebuttal speeches involve destroying the cases.

(6) Defend. If one stock issue is destroyed, the other issues are really moot anyway.

Discussion and Debate

Learning Activities

B₂. (1) Analysis phase: To bring to bear on the discussion the critical facts and evaluation of these. (Perhaps a prior task involves clarification of the terms in the problem.)

Hypothesis phase: Introduction and evaluation of proposed solutions to the problem.

(2) Lesson generalizations represent a reduction of the discussion to broad ideas relative to the problem. The hypothesis phase involves casting about for possible solutions to the problem.

(3) Conditions as they are (backed by experience) are usually considered best until proven otherwise. The affirmative team must accept this task.

(4) The negative team has the option of attempting to destroy only one of the three stock issues. It may choose to accept the need developed by the first speaker. The outline of the plan provides the option of attacking elsewhere.

(5) Basically the constructive speeches involve building the cases; the rebuttal speeches involve destroying the cases.

(6) Defend. If one stock issue is destroyed, the other issues are really moot anyhow.

C. (1) A major portion of most class discussions will be devoted to a thorough analysis of the facts as necessary background for grappling with the basic problem.

(2) Usually they should be deferred until ". . . we have developed a more complete understanding of the existing conditions that influence the problem." Attempt to bring such points before the group when they become appropriate, calling upon the original contributor if possible.

(3) Key questions and contradictions

Loaded words

Guilt by association

Emotional appeal

Visual aids

Credibility gaps

(4) From the very first. Naturally it will become more direct and pointed as the debate develops.

(5) Since there is a limited amount of time for analysis, it places an unfair advantage on the initiating team.

Optional Activities

D. (1) It fails to take the class anywhere. Once the facts are presented and evaluated, it is all over.

(2) Evolves into a mere stating of opinion with no basis for due processes of reflection. Ignores the important facts.

(3) Debate appropriately deals with an issue in which polarized views have already emerged. Its function is to assist students at least to hear the side in opposition to their existing points of view.

(4) Not only difficult to maintain contact with the audience but, more importantly, ignores the necessity of dealing with the specific points of the opposition.

(5) The teacher's objective in employing the debate method is to help the class see both sides of a controversial issue. Thus skill in developing the cases is more important than who "wins" or who "loses."

E. (1) It is necessary for establishing a sound foundation for possible action.

(2) Evaluative criteria tend to stifle creativity inherent in the possible solution (hypothesis) phase of a discussion.

(3) It supports the status quo unless a counterplan is offered.

(4) The debater is attempting to "sell" a proposed course of action, while the discusser desires an objective analysis of the available data.

ANSWERS TO POSTTEST

For most beneficial results you should work through the entire LAP before you check your answers to the posttest. Failure to meet the provided minimum standards probably suggests certain weaknesses that need to be corrected. As with the Preassessment items, you will find supporting reasons for answers. It is hoped that this will serve as desirable feedback in your quest for mastery.

Discussion

A. 1. In question form.

2. Provides for an unlimited number of hypotheses, e.g., open-ended policy problem.

3. A broad question.

4. Based on a current, unsettled issue (assumes dissatisfaction with conditions as they are or the status quo.)

5. Usually begins with the word "what" or "how."

6. The word "should" or "ought" is stated or implied in the problem.

7. Is future oriented.

Debate

8. Proposes a change from the status quo.

9. Involves an issue of divided opinion.

10. Is timely, involving a current controversy.

11. Problem begins with the word "should" or "ought" (an advocacy statement).

B. 1-P   (Open-ended, future oriented.)

  2-A   (One possible solution to be weighed.)

  3-A   (Again, one possible solution to be weighed.)

  4-FV (Just a matter of ascertaining the facts, and possibly opinions, of those involved.)

  5-FV (Here we are merely dealing with present situation, no problem is being solved.)

  6-FV (Again, we are merely dealing with the facts and opinions of those involved.)

  7-P   (Opens the door to any number of "changes.")

  8-FV (Answer depends on checking the record only. No problem is being solved.)

  9-FV (Deals with what is now going on. Answer depends on checking the record.)

  10-A   (Only one possible solution is to be weighed.)

  11-P   (Opens the door to a variety of ways of solving the problem.)

  12-FV (A matter of mere speculation; no problem is to be solved.)

C. 2, 4, 5, 9, 13, 14, 16, 18, 20. (All are open-ended and future oriented; they deal with problems to be solved.)

Reasons for rejected items

  1   (Deals with the past; conjecture only, as no problem is being solved.)

  3   (Here we have two possible solutions being offered in one question. Inappropriate, since an unlimited number are not permitted in the problem.)

  6   (Fact or value only; no problem is being solved.)

  7   (Involves value judgment of existing conditions only; no problem is being solved.)

  8   (Again, a judgmental question only.)

  10   (Relegates the "solution" to a matter of opinion; no attention directed to the "best" solution.)

  11   (A matter of checking the records only.)

  12   (Only one possible solution dealt with—an advocacy problem.)

  15   (Deals with existing conditions only.)

17 (Present-oriented question; no problem to be solved.)

19 (Conjecture only; no problem to be solved.)

D. 1. School integration

    a. What steps should be taken to accelerate integration of minority groups into the public schools?

    b. Resolved, That unlimited bussing of students at all grade levels for integration purposes should be initiated.

  2. Teachers' right to strike

    a. What steps should be taken to minimize the harmful effects of teacher strikes on public school students?

    b. Resolved, That teacher strikes should be abolished.

E. 1. Discussion

    a. Analysis of the problem (any question pertaining to the conditions as they are)

    Example: What food supply problems do we have in different nations today?

    b. Establishing hypotheses (repeat the original question)

    Example: What steps should be taken to increase the world's food supply?

    c. Deriving generalizations (would be derived by students)

    Example: What ideas have emerged from our discussion today?

    Food supply is a factor of farm technology.

  2. Debate

    a. The need

    Example: Some nations still rely upon the most primitive agricultural practices.

    b. The plan

    Example: Establish agricultural schools in each nation.

    c. The desirability and feasibility of the plan

    Example: Such schools would bring to backward nations the expertise of the developed nations within existing climatic conditions in each country.

Sample responses for Learning Activity, Option B_2, p. 157.

  1. Discussion

    a. Analysis phase

      (1) How serious is the problem?

      (2) What are some of the major causes of traffic accidents? (This phase of a discussion deals with aggravating conditions of the *status quo*. Here most factual content is sifted and evaluated.)

b. Hypothesis phase

    (1) What action should be taken to minimize traffic fatalities?

    (2) What are some merits and problems associated with your proposal? (The initial question for this phase of a discussion is *always* a repetition of the discussion problem. You will recall that analysis phase merely sets the stage for consideration of hypotheses or possibilities.)

2. Debate

  a. The need

    (1) Slower speeds reduce accidents.

    (2) Slower speeds increase gas mileage.

  b. The plan

    (1) Place governors on all vehicles, which would automatically reduce engine power output when a speed of 55 miles per hour is reached.

    (2) Increase the number of state patrol personnel to enforce highway speed regulations.

  c. The desirability and feasibility of the plan

    (1) Special governors are not only inexpensive, but they would also help the driver remember his responsibility.

    (2) Some individuals can be expected to remove governors for their own selfish desires.

(You will note that each of the above is specific to one of the points of the foregoing plan.)

SUPPLEMENTARY SOURCES

The following sources may be used in lieu of the Hoover texts or, preferably, as supplementary to them. Generally they are consistent with the models provided in the LAPs of this module. As such, the references do not represent all of the most recent references in the area; rather, they constitute selected references designed to broaden or expand needed background information.

Colburn, L. William *Strategies for Educational Debate* (Boston: Boston Press, 1972).

Eisenberg, Abne M., *Argumentation: An Alternative to Violence* (Englewood Cliffs, N.J.: Prentice-Hall, Inc., 1972).

Epstein, Charlotte, *Affective Subjects in the Classroom: Exploring Race, Sex and Drugs* (Scranton, Pa.: Intext Educational Publishers, 1972).

Flynn, Elizabeth, and John F. LaFaso, *Group Discussion as Learning Process: A Source Book* (New York: Paulist Press, 1972).

Gulley, Halbert E., *Discussion, Conference, and Group Process*, 2nd ed. (New York: Holt, Rinehart and Winston, Inc., 1968).

Hoover, Kenneth H., *The Professional Teacher's Handbook*, 2nd ed. (Boston: Allyn and Bacon, Inc., 1976), Chaps. 12 and 13.

Hoover, Kenneth H., and Paul M. Hollingsworth, *Learning and Teaching in the Elementary School*, 2nd ed. (Boston: Allyn and Bacon, Inc., 1975), Chap. 11.

Review
and
Practice

RATIONALE. Review and practice (drill) are two of the oldest, most basic methods of teaching. At the same time, they are probably the most widely misunderstood and misused practices in today's secondary schools. Teachers continually stress the need for frequent reviews in all subject areas. In actual practice, however, their "reviews" are often little more than some version of the outmoded recitation procedure where emphasis was placed upon mere "re-citing" textbook verbalisms.

Practice or drill has even become a "dirty word" to many educators. On the one hand, the technique is associated with rote, passive, or old-fashioned teaching; in actual practice, teachers, parents, coaches, and students implicitly rely on the "practice makes perfect" axiom. The supposed conflict between theory and practice often results in apologetic, half-hearted applications, which are lacking in effectiveness.

Review and practice frequently are employed at timely intervals during a lesson for the purpose of establishing closure on specific points. They are also needed as culminating experiences. Although the latter application is emphasized in this LAP, the principles apply equally to incidental review and practice.

OVERVIEW
Key Concepts

    1. Although recall is a basic aspect of review and practice, it merely sets the stage for further learning.

2. Emphasis in a review lesson focuses upon application of concepts to related problems.

3. Practice is an effective method for polishing mental or motor skills; it is generally ineffective for cognitive and affective learnings.

4. Related problems in a review are merely *identified*; they are not discussed extensively in a review lesson.

5. Review often occurs informally along with other instructional experiences.

6. Practice must be varied constantly if monotony is to be avoided.

New Terms

1. Review: A re-look or new look at previous learnings. Thus the technique, when employed appropriately, may guide the learner in application of original learnings to new situations.

2. Initial learnings: Previously learned concepts (ideas) that form the basis for review.

3. Overlearning: Learning beyond the point of bare mastery.

4. Specific transfer: Application or extension of basic habits and associations to related areas. Mostly limited to skills area.

5. Nonspecific transfer: Application of principles and attitudes to future learning situations.

6. Reminiscence: The tendency of the mind to "continue on" (learn) after a given learning experience has been terminated.

7. Negative transfer: The interference of one learning with another, similar learning. Two words that sound alike (e.g., there and their), for example, may be difficult to master, unless their learning is separated in time and context.

8. Kinesthetic sense: Usually used in connection with motor skill development. Refers to the muscular sensation or "feel" one acquires for a desired movement. Verbal and visual kinesthetic cues are most useful in the early stages of learning, gradually giving way to internal cues as the skill develops.

OBJECTIVES. After this experience you should be able to make effective use of review and practice methods of teaching, as evidenced by your ability to:

1. List three essential features each for review and practice (a total of six).

2. Select eight out of nine appropriately stated occasions for review and practice from a provided list of twenty assorted occasions.

3. Distinguish between appropriate review and class discussion situations in eight out of nine instances.

4. Develop a key question (or statement when appropriate) for five out of six identified phases of review and practice.

PRELIMINARY READING. Since the elements of instructional methodology are somewhat variable, the following excerpts are provided to help you develop a frame of reference as a point of departure for this experience. If you prefer, you may proceed directly to the Preassessment items.

FUNCTIONS OF REVIEW AND PRACTICE

Review and practice are designed to assist the learner to apply original learnings to related life situations. The specifics (facts) of original learning provide a *basis* for this extension process. In the case of practice, the learner recalls what has been learned so that the process can be repeated. While concentrating on the need for making minor adjustments as he or she advances toward greater perfection of the mental or motor skill, the basic framework serves as a constant frame of reference. Re-learning, if it is necessary, is always an extremely difficult task. It seems that the initial learning pattern becomes "imprinted" and thus becomes a basis for a form of inappropriate habitual behavior.

Review, likewise, is facilitated by recall of some of the specifics. In review, however, the specifics consist of the recall of originally derived *concepts*. Instead of recalling these as ends in learning, though, they are merely useful in establishing a departure point for reminiscence. The objective is to "continue on" to the recognition of related applications of the concepts learned. Factual recall plays a negligible role in review techniques.

THE ROLE OF RECALL IN REVIEW

Recall is a fundamental aspect of review. Concepts learned during the unit or module are brought together in one lesson for the first time. As a means of prompting student recall of such concepts, it is often desirable to recall the context from which they were developed. Consequently, the experience may begin with the question, "What have we done during this unit?" When an activity is mentioned (e.g., class discussion), attention will be directed to the major idea(s) that evolved from the experience. In like manner each major concept is identified. (They are usually listed, providing a basis for subsequent review activities.)

It should be noted that major unit concepts, developed by students during a review, will not be identical to individual lesson generalizations. Rather, they will be similar to *unit* concepts developed by the teacher in pre-instructional planning activities. (Each lesson is normally based upon one such concept.) The teacher does *not* provide the learner with his own list of unit concepts, however. Unit concepts, derived by students, are likely to more closely parallel actual learnings than those sought by the teacher.

There is a natural tendency to expand lesson generalizations into broader concepts. This process should be encouraged. To illustrate from an art class concerned with "Color Relationships":

Lesson generalizations:

1. Light, bright colors evoke a happy, gay mood.

2. Dark, somber colors generally evoke a depressing mood.

3. Different colors have different emotional impacts. (Red, for example, is happy, exciting.)

4. Colors symbolize ideas. (Blue, for instance, is associated with loyalty and honesty.)

In recalling these generalizations, students might be guided in evolving the following unit concept: *Color may be used to create mood and symbolize ideas.* The reader will note that mere recall is *not* an essential aspect of review.

DRILL OR PRACTICE AND ITS RELATIONSHIP TO REVIEW

Practice or drill is appropriate whenever a more or less fixed pattern of automatic responses is needed. It is designed to extend or polish skills and generally is restricted to the psychomotor domain (skills area). Motor skills, habits, and mental skills are made more useful and meaningful through appropriate practice procedures. Many courses in today's secondary schools are concerned principally with the acquisition of skills. Such skills as using the typewriter, developing laboratory techniques, driving an automobile, baking a cake, using shop tools, playing a musical instrument, and a host of others make heavy demands on practice or drill procedures.

To facilitate an understanding of the relationship between practice and review, a comparison has been summarized below.

SIMILARITIES BETWEEN PRACTICE AND REVIEW

Practice	*Review*
1. Initial classroom learnings necessary.	1. Initial classroom learnings necessary.
2. An important aspect of review.	2. Uses practice or recall as a vehicle for solving problems.
3. Chief aim is to refine or polish learnings.	3. Chief aim is to extend learnings and associations.

DIFFERENCES BETWEEN PRACTICE AND REVIEW

Practice	*Review*
1. Effective in the teaching of skills and habits.	1. Effective in the teaching of understandings, attitudes, and appreciations.
2. Largely an individualized problem process.	2. Chiefly a group deliberative process.

There are three essential phases of practice or drill.

Developing Initial Learning. Verbal instruction on the essential rudiments of a skill are fully appropriate. In the area of motor skills this verbal instruction may be accompanied by a demonstration. The chief purpose is not to copy the model, but to develop a better comprehension of the purposes of the activity and the general form and sequence of events to be followed.

Detailed explanations or demonstrations should be avoided. If more than the gross aspects of the skill are presented, thinking processes may become confused. A speech teacher, for example, first introduces the art of speechmaking with a brief description of the following points:

1. Introduction—attention getting
2. Body—two or three main points to be developed
3. Conclusion—restatement of the major theme of the presentation.

This can be followed by a five-minute demonstration.

Varied-contact (preliminary-practice) Phase. During preliminary practice the learner must have an opportunity to engage in exploratory trials, ask questions, observe skilled performers, inspect diagrams, and so on. In terms of the problem-solving process, this might be called evaluation of alternative proposals. It is in this phase of development that the student will introduce his own innovations to be tried and tested. This is indeed the *creative* aspect of skill development. Through the individual's own diagnosis, a more complete understanding of the problem is developed. For maximum benefit, conditions should resemble (model) out-of-school situations as closely as possible.

In the early stages of skill development it is desirable to minimize weaknesses. Strengths should be emphasized prior to deficiencies. Some teachers call attention to weaknesses by asking the individual to point out his or her own problem areas.

Repetitive Practice or Polish Phase. A basic skill must be repeated often for the purpose of refining or developing precision. The *situation* within which it is performed, however, should be *varied* as often as possible. This variation not only avoids monotony and thereby facilitates sustained interest, but more importantly, it enhances the likelihood of transfer of the skill to related situations. Let us take an example from the area of mental skills. A group of students in a beginning Spanish class could practice speaking the vocabulary by discussing the topic in class; they might visit the Spanish consul's office; they might take an imaginary trip to some South American country; or they could invite two or three Chicanos to class. The vocabulary drill is similar in all situations, but the situations have been varied.

Self-motivated practice leads to gradual improvement of a skill through *revision of details*. Following a period of accelerated learning resulting from early practice sessions, many learners reach a *plateau* in which relatively little progress is evident. This probably indicates a need for a more thorough understanding of the relationship of certain details to the total skill. At this point added encouragement and direction from the teacher are extremely important. An individual chart showing the student his record of progress tends to contribute to continued interest and improvement.

PREASSESSMENT ITEMS (answers provided on pp. 191–93)

This experience is designed to help you gain an overall perspective of review and practice procedures. After completing the items, turn to the end of this LAP and check your answers. Note that answers (both correct and incorrect) are provided with supporting reasons to guide your efforts as you work through this LAP.

A. List six essential features of review and practice. (To illustrate: Review involves recall of basic concepts as a basis for extension of these to related areas.)

Review

1.

2.

3.

Practice

4.

5.

6.

B. Place a check (√) before each of the nine situations that are appropriately treated, relative to review and practice.

1. Mr. Jones was holding a class drill on the anatomy of the grasshopper.

2. Mrs. Tompkins was going over the facts in history prior to a unit test.

3. Students in Spanish class were using earphones and recorders with individual practice drills.

4. Miss Jones was demonstrating the basic method of serving in tennis.

5. Students in world history class were asked to drill on the causes of World War I.

6. At the beginning of a review Mr. Thomas asked his students to recall basic concepts of the social science unit. They were then written on the chalkboard for a frame of reference.

7. Members of the Spanish class were asked to practice the vocabulary prior to the next class period.

8. The physical education teacher asked students to memorize the rules of tennis.

9. Tom, upon identifying a problem related to forest conservation, was asked to explore it in considerable depth for the class.

10. Mr. Simpson restricted discussion of related problems to two or three comments of both a pro and a con nature.

11. When Tommy insisted that he would like to debate one of Sue's related ideas, Mr. Smith said, "I think this can be arranged within the next week."

12. Joe was dissatisfied with his forehand tennis stroke. The teacher suggested a way of altering it and asked him to practice the new application.

13. The foreign language drill was repeated several times by the class in unison.

14. Students in American literature class were expected to memorize the authors and themes of several selected short stories.

15. In a review for a test the lesson was devoted to a recall of the basic facts studied.

16. Prior to vocabulary drill the students were asked to recall the basic features of the Spanish idioms.

17. When the concept, "Each person must do his own thing," was recalled, Mary said she did not know what it meant. Thereupon Mr. Wilkins asked another student to clarify the concept. Finally, he called for application.

18. The students in a review lesson were asked to go over the parts of the plant cell until they knew them.

19. Mr. Toope asked his students to memorize the causes of the fall of Rome.

20. Shop safety rules were to be memorized by Mr. Doakes's students.

C. Place a check (√) before four appropriate occasions for review (sometimes referred to as review discussion).

1. Mr. Smith announced, "Today we will have a review discussion on the problem, 'Should the President have the right to withhold monies appropriated by Congress?'"

2. As a culminating review, Mr. Jenkins proposed the following question: How can we apply what we have learned about Europe to current related problems?

3. Following a class discussion on: "What action should be taken to minimize our soaring crime rate among teenagers?", the following proposal was offered: We should impose stiffer penalties for youthful offenders. Pros and cons of the idea were limited to one or two brief comments.

4. In a review discussion the major facts were recalled but not evaluated.

5. In a review lesson major unit concepts (generalizations) were recalled and evaluated.

6. In a review of the unit, "Crime in our Cities," the following question was raised: "Should parents be held responsible for criminal acts of minors?" The pros and cons were discussed at length.

7. In a review of the unit, "Inflation in the United States," the following question was raised: "Should the strike be outlawed?" Discussion was restricted to one or two comments on the pros and cons of the issue.

    8. The basic review question was stated as follows: "Should temporary jobs be created for reducing the numbers of the unemployed?"

    9. After a class discussion, the following review question was raised: "Should temporary jobs be created for reducing the numbers of the unemployed?" Pros and cons were discussed briefly.

D. Construct one key question (or statement if appropriate) for each of the six identified phases of review and practice. Use the identified problems as a basis for your answers.

Review. Problem: How can we relate what we have learned about "corruption in government" to other problems in the area?

    1. Recall of basic unit concepts

    2. Recall of how major concepts were developed

    3. Extending unit concepts to related problems

Practice. Problem: How can an individual's tennis serve be perfected?

    4. Developing initial learning

    5. Varied contact (preliminary practice)

    6. Repetitive practice or polish

If you were able to provide twenty-eight of the thirty-one requested responses, you are to be complimented. In fact, you probably have no need for the experiences provided in this LAP and should proceed to the next module. Even if you were able to provide few of the appropriate responses, do not be depressed, for even experienced teachers all too often confuse class discussion, review, and practice procedures. By analyzing the correct answers provided at the end of this LAP, and also by studying the provided reasons for all incorrect items, you should be in an excellent position to proceed to the selected learning activities for this experience.

LEARNING ACTIVITIES

Work through each learning activity, complete the self-assessment items, and check your answers before moving to the next one. Note that the last learning activities are optional, depending upon your needs and circumstances at that point. You should be able to complete this LAP in about four hours.

A: *Read.* Re-examine the overview and preliminary reading sections for this LAP and for the preceding one (Discussion and Debate). You will broaden your understanding substantially by studying Chaps. 19(22) and 20(23) in the Hoover texts and/or by studying the selected references listed at the end of this LAP. Note specifically the following:

    1. The basic function of recall in review and practice.

    2. The instructional domains involved in review and practice.

    3. The group and individual nature of review and practice.

    4. The difference between review and class discussion.

    5. The application and "polish" phases of review and practice.

Self-assessment Items (answers provided on p. 193)

(1) What is the role of recall in review and practice?

(2) To what extent is memorization in the cognitive domain appropriate?

(3) Advocacy questions or statements are used in both class discussion and review but in different ways. Explain.

(4) Distinguish between the application phase of review and the "polish" phases of drill or practice.

At this point you may select either Option B_1 or Option B_2, depending upon your particular situation. Those who are presently teaching should select Option B_1. Those who are not teaching or who do not have immediate access to students should select Option B_2.

Option B_1: *Modeled demonstration.* This experience is designed to help you actually see review and practice methods modeled as accurately as possible. Ideally, a carefully planned demonstration should be made available. This usually can be arranged if you are working with other new teachers under the close supervision of a supervising teacher or administrator.

Another option is a filmed or videotaped experience featuring the basic frame of reference provided in this LAP.* Unless the experience is locally prepared, there are likely to be certain gaps in this respect. (Review and practice, as with most instructional methods, are perceived differently by different "experts." Although not serious, this can be confusing to the beginning teacher.)

If working alone, you will probably want to visit a highly recommended teacher for this experience. Such an individual should thoroughly acquaint himself or herself with the techniques outlined in this LAP and attempt to demonstrate accordingly.

Observe both review *and* practice demonstration lessons, focusing upon the points indicated. After the experience discuss these points with other new teachers.

Review

a. Review problem employed.

b. How recall of basic unit concepts was handled. (Sometimes concepts are placed on the chalkboard for reference.)

c. How the previous unit activities were used (recalled) in setting the stage for the review.

d. How unit concepts were extended to related areas (problems).

Practice

a. Practice problem employed.

b. How basic initial learnings were developed. (Often this involves some type of demonstration.)

One such commercially developed film is Review Lesson (Biology), *featuring an unrehearsed class engaged in a review of a unit of work. Film is available from Pennsylvania State University, Psychological Cinema Register, AV Series, 6 Willard Building, University Park, Pa. 16802.*

c. How preliminary practice (varied contact) was handled.

d. How the basic skill(s) was polished (repetitive practice).

If possible, hold a post-observation conference with a committee of other new teachers who viewed the demonstration. Use the foregoing as a basis for this discussion.

Self-assessment Items (answers provided on pp. 193–94)

(1)   You will note (or might have surmised) that those in the social science areas probably developed "should" type questions in the application phase of review; whereas those in many other subject fields found the "could" type of question best for this aspect of the lessons. Explain.

(2)   Repetitive practice of a motor skill is most efficient in the presence of a qualified observer, permitting a quick diagnosis of difficulties. How can a mental skill be diagnosed?

(3)   What is the role of content (basic facts) in review?

(4)   Why must a near perfect model be provided in a demonstration of a skill to be learned?

(5)   Why is the polish phase of skill development sometimes omitted?

Option B₂: *Developing a preliminary structure.* Using some of your unit concepts as a basis (developed in the module on Preinstructional Experiences), prepare portions of lesson plans, as indicated below.

Review

1. Develop a review problem

2. Recall and list the basic concepts for one of your teaching units. (List may be provided from LAP #1 of the module on Preinstructional Experiences.)

3. Recall the methods used to develop major concept. (Speculate a bit here.)

4. Using your list of unit concepts as a basis, develop key questions for expanding thinking to related areas and problems. (These will usually be advocacy-type questions, e.g., "Should. . . ." or sometimes "How could. . . .")

Write out three or four such questions.

Practice (in either a mental or motor skills area)

1. Develop a practice problem.

2. Develop points designed to establish initial understanding (rudiments) of the skill. (Limit to three of these.)

3. Suggest three ways of establishing varied contact in preliminary practice.

4. Suggest three points that you would make for helping the learner develop polish.

When completed to your satisfaction, discuss your experiences with others who are working through this LAP with you (if possible). If working alone, reflect upon and prepare written notes on the activity. Concentrate on the following points:

1. How the application-type review questions varied (or might be varied) in different subject fields.

2. Similarities and differences between mental and motor skill development.

3. Reasons for emphasizing some basic unit concepts more than others in your "review lesson."

Self-assessment Items (answers provided on p. 194)

(1)   Students in a review lesson often desire to explore identified, related problems. Why is this to be discouraged?

(2)   In a review, students (as opposed to the teacher) should be coaxed into identification of related problems. Explain.

(3)   Developing the initial learnings phase of a practice lesson is largely cognitive in nature. Defend or refute.

(4)   Why does demonstration play a prominent role in the early processes of skill development?

(5)   Under what conditions might repetitive practice "stamp in" undesirable habits?

C: *Instructional application.* Using your unit concepts as a basis (developed in an earlier LAP), conduct both a culmination-type review and a practice lesson for one or more of your classes.* In this connection you may want to refer to the illustrated lesson plans for review and practice (Chaps. 19(22) and 20(23) in the Hoover texts). Proceed as follows:

---

*If you do not have immediate access to students, divide into committees of six if possible, in different fields of specialization, and set up the following simulations. (If working alone, arrange to have your performance videotaped and replayed for your own analysis.) Make sure that each individual has an opportunity to "teach" either a review or a practice lesson.

1. Review. *Consider your committee a class in your major field as selected members of your group lead successive 20- to 30-minute review lessons. In preparation for this experience, the "teacher" should place his/her unit concepts on the chalkboard. Have the "teacher" indicate briefly what happened prior to the lesson and what would happen if he/she had been permitted to complete the experience. (Such lessons often extend longer than 20 or 30 minutes.)*
2. Practice. *Have the other members of your group "teach" mental and motor skills lessons. Make sure that at least one mental and one motor skill lesson are offered. Concentrate on the following:*
   a. *The practice problem*
   b. *Developing initial learnings*
   c. *Varied contact (preliminary practice)*
   d. *Repetitive practice (developing polish)*

Review

1. Write out an appropriate problem and place it on the chalkboard.

2. Place your unit concepts on the board. (These will be evolved by students as previous unit activities are recalled. They usually will parallel, but often will not be identical to, your preplanned unit concepts.)

3. Guide students briefly in the recall of basic facts (content) associated with identified concepts.

4. Using your list of unit concepts and content as a basis, formulate key questions for expanding thinking to related areas and problems. (These usually will be advocacy-type questions, e.g., "Should . . . ." or sometimes "How could . . . .") Write out three or four such questions.

Practice

1. Write out an appropriate problem and place it on the chalkboard.

2. Have students read and/or discuss the rudiments of the skill for the purpose of developing a basic cognitive understanding.

3. Prepare a brief demonstration of the skill.

4. Provide opportunities for each student to try out the skill in a variety of contexts.

5. Have students engage in repetitive practice for the purpose of developing "polish."

(Note: In practical class situations, Step No. 5 is sometimes omitted, depending upon the purpose involved.)

Following your experiences, hold a post-application conference with a committee of other beginning teachers if possible. Concentrate on the following points:

1. How the application-type review questions varied with the different subject fields represented.

2. Reasons for emphasizing some basic concepts more than others in your review lessons.

3. The role of basic facts (content) in review.

4. Why the accuracy of the demonstration is so critical in skill development.

5. Reasons for sometimes omitting the "polish" phase of a practice lesson.

Self-assessment Items (answers provided on p. 194)

(1) You will note or surmise that those in the social science areas probably developed "should"-type questions in the application phase of review, whereas those in many other subject fields found the "could" or "how could" type of question best for this aspect of the lessons. Explain.

(2) In all probability, in your review lesson you found it difficult to concentrate equally on those concepts which received a similar amount of instructional emphasis. How do you account for this?

(3) What is the role of content (basic facts) in review?

(4) Why must a near-perfect model be provided in a demonstration of a skill to be learned?

(5) Why is the polish phase of skill development sometimes omitted?

If, after reviewing your learning activities for this LAP, you feel that you can meet the stated objectives, proceed to the posttest. If not, you should complete one or both of the optional activities, depending upon your own needs.

Optional Activities

D: *Class observation.* Arrange to visit review and practice lessons in your school. Since the purpose of these experiences is to help you distinguish between the modeled techniques and practical applications, it is not essential to make special requests of the instructors involved. This experience should help you gain flexibility of application. It also should help you perceive problems associated with common malpractice aspects of the methods. Since review and practice lessons may extend for more than one class period, attempt to determine how the lessons are to be culminated if you see only part of the experiences. Use the following observation guides for your notes.

If you are working with other beginning teachers, formulate a committee of three and arrange for each member to visit one of the three classes, as indicated. (If working alone, you should visit at least one review and one practice lesson.)

1. The committee member who visits a review lesson should obtain the following information:

   a. A statement of the review problem

   b. Two questions (or statements where appropriate) that were treated for each of the following review phases:

      (1) Basic concepts upon which the review rests

      (2) Application to related problems

      (3) Deriving generalizations (if any)

2. The committee member who visits a practice lesson featuring development of a mental skill (e.g., foreign language, math, certain science classes) should obtain the following information:

   a. A statement of the practice problem

   b. Two questions (or statements) that were treated for each of the following practice phases:

      (1) Developing initial learnings

      (2) Varied contact

      (3) Repetitive practice

3. A third committee member should repeat #2 above for a motor skill type of lesson.

Hold a committee conference following class observations for the purpose of comparing notes. Use the following questions as a basis for this:

1. How were the review and practice problems introduced? How effective were they?

2. In all probability at least some recall of basic facts was evidenced in the review lessons. What effect (if any) did this have on the experience?

3. Who took the initiative in making the review applications? (The teachers, one or two students, several students?) How effectively was this task accomplished?

4. How were initial learnings emphasized in the practice lessons?

5. What means were provided for varied contact in preliminary practice of the skills?

6. Describe the settings for repetitive practice (developing polish). How effective were they?

Self-assessment Items (answers provided on pp. 194–95)

(1) What were (or might be) problems associated with omitting a formal statement of the problems for review and practice?

(2) What was (or might be) the effect of using recall of basic facts as an end in a review lesson?

(3) It is acceptable for the teacher to make some applications for students during a review. Defend or refute.

(4) Why are initial learnings limited to a few main points prior to practice?

(5) In all probability you noted (in the motor skills area) that repetitive practice, even in team sports, was individualistic in nature. (For example, a basketball player might be called out to practice free throws.) Explain whether or not the principle holds equally for development of mental skills.

E: *Written exercise.* For each of the provided review and practice problems, construct two questions (or statements as appropriate) for the listed phases.*

Review. Problem: How can we relate public health principles to our own lives?

1. Recall of basic concepts

   a.

   b.

_____
**When you have completed this task you may want to compare your responses
with the samples provided on p. 195.*

    2. Recall of basic facts (in expanding concept understanding)

      a.

      b.

    3. Extending basic concepts (principles) to related areas

      a.

      b.

Drill or practice. Problem: How may a handsaw be used effectively?

    1. Developing initial understanding

      a.

      b.

    2. Demonstration of its use

      a.

      b.

    3. Varied contact (preliminary practice)

      a.

      b.

    4. Repetitive practice (developing polish)

      a.

      b.

Self-assessment Items (answers provided on p. 195)

(1) Although the organized culmination type of review has been emphasized in this LAP, the point has been made that frequent incidental reviews are also recommended. Explain.

(2) What proportion of a culmination-type review lesson would you devote to recall of basic facts, concepts, and methods?

(3) What basic function does varied contact (preliminary practice) serve in a drill or practice lesson?

(4) Too much practice is impossible in developing skill or "polish." Defend or refute.

POSTTEST (answers provided on pp. 196–98)

After you have completed the learning activities, complete the posttest and evaluate by checking your answers at the end of the LAP.

A. List six essential features of review and practice.

Review

1.

2.

3.

Practice

1.

2.

3.

B. Place a check (√) before nine of the situations appropriately treated, relative to review and practice.

1. In an American literature class, Mrs. Brown spent most of the class period helping students recall various literature selections, the authors, and the major themes associated with each.

2. Upon completion of a class discussion, Mr. Bodie wrote the unit concept on the chalkboard and asked students to make applications.

3. Most of the class period in a practice lesson was devoted to an emphasis on initial learnings.

4. Science terms were repeated by the class group several times.

5. Each of the major concepts was redefined at length during a review lesson.

6. Recall of previous unit experiences was used as a vehicle to guide students in recalling unit concepts.

7. Mrs. Feats asked an able student typist to demonstrate use of a typewriter to a group of beginning typing students.

8. "Each of you should practice your vocabulary several times before tomorrow's class," requested the Spanish teacher.

9. During a review considerable interest was displayed in a new problem. Ms. Trump said, "Let's move on now. We'll have a full discussion of the problem later."

10. The mathematics teacher's review lesson consisted essentially of a drill of the rules associated with quadratic equations.

11. The math teacher asked students to attempt new related problems. He passed from one individual to another, offering specific assistance as needed.

12. Mr. Bagley encouraged his history students to memorize the "reasons for the fall of the Ancient Egyptian Empire."

13. Mrs. Mulkey's swimming students were asked to memorize the basic principles of the skill.

14. When Joe mentioned a remote connection with a unit concept (in a review lesson), he was asked to make a ten-minute presentation on his stand.

15. Mr. Hooker showed a short movie depicting the proper tennis serve.

16. Most of a culminating type of review was spent on two of six unit concepts. In defense of the procedure, Mr. Hatter explained, "The others tend to tie in with this one."

17. The typewriting drill was done repeatedly. Mr. Tucker merely asked students to check the number of mistakes made.

18. The words were sounded out repeatedly by the entire class.

19. After spending about ten minutes in a culminating type of review over one concept, Mr. Tackett asked the class to review the other concepts individually.

20. The boxing instructor explained and then immediately demonstrated the "left hook."

C. Place a check (√) before each of the four appropriate occasions for review (sometimes referred to as review discussion).

1. During a review discussion, advocacy questions were briefly identified for several unit concepts.

2. The review problem was, "What steps should be taken to minimize the use of marijuana among teen-agers?"

3. The review began with a brief discussion of the concepts of the lesson.

4. In a review lesson most of the class period was spent on examining the unit concepts.

5. The major portion of a review dealt with the basic facts and an evaluation of them.

6. The review culminated in a few generalizations (broader than the unit concepts) upon which the lesson was based.

7. Advocacy questions in the review were postponed until the latter part of the lesson.

8. The major thrust of a review dealt with advocacy questions.

9. Some applications were discussed at length during a review lesson.

D. Write out one key question (or statement if appropriate) for each of the identified phases of review and practice methods. Use the identified problems as a basis for your responses.

Review. Problem: How can we relate what we have learned about heredity to our own lives?

1. Recall of basic concepts

2. Recall of how major concepts were developed

3. Extending unit concepts to related areas

Practice. Problem: How can the forehand table tennis stroke be perfected?

1. Developing initial learnings

2. Varied contact (preliminary practice)

3. Repetitive practice (developing polish)

Near the end of a long, illustrious career, William Burton stated that while he had seen several hundred reviews in progress, practically none of them amounted to anything more than drill. Thus you can see that your successful completion of this LAP places you in rather exclusive company. Even if you were unable to attain full mastery, do not be discouraged. Study the answers provided for the posttest, especially noting reasons for all incorrect items. Then repeat the posttest until you feel comfortable in the area.

ANSWERS TO PREASSESSMENT ITEMS

You can make these items a most valuable learning experience by studying the provided reasons for both correct and incorrect responses. You will note that since Part A has no specific number of correct responses, several additional points (characteristics) have been provided. Since the last part calls for your constructed responses, your own answers may not be identical with those supplied by the writer. You should be able to decide whether or not your answers are reasonably accurate, however.

A. *Review*

1. Involves recall of basic concepts as a basis for extension of these to related problems.

2. Since association is the basic function, related problems are identified but not analyzed during a review.

3. Although review may occur incidentally along with other methods, the culmination type of review is essential.

4. Review (and practice) increase retention of original learning.

5. Review is essentially a cognitive process.

Practice

6. Practice or drill is restricted to mental and motor skills areas.

7. Practice basically is an individualized process.

8. Skill refinement and polish are dependent upon recall of basic patterns and sequences.

9. Demonstration is basic to development of skills.

B. 3 (Practice is basically an individualized technique.)

4 (Demonstration is basic to developing a skill.)

6 (Recall of basic concepts provides the basis for review.)

7 (Individualized practice is an essential for learning a skill.)

10 (In a review, related problems are identified only.)

11 (Although a student need became apparent, Mr. Smith correctly postponed the debate until later as it would have defeated the purpose of review.)

12 (Repetitive practice is designed to correct "minor details.")

16 (This experience establishes readiness.)

17 (Application is based upon the assumption that the concept is thoroughly understood.)

Reasons for incorrect items

1 (Group drill basically is inappropriate.)

2 (This "traditional" approach to review is a waste of time; it encourages a memoriter type of learning.)

     5 (Drill in the cognitive domain results in merely committing verbalisms to memory.)

     8 (Rules will be learned as they are applied.)

     9 (Review is designed to help students make new connections or associations only.)

    13 (Group drill is basically inappropriate.)

    14 (A waste of time like this adds nothing to useful learnings.)

    15 (Facts lead to generalizations (concepts). These, in turn, become the basis for review.)

    18 (This is confusing drill with review.)

    19 (Drill, basically, is restricted to the psychomotor domain; this is in the cognitive domain.)

    20 (Rules may be studied for added understanding; memorization is not needed.)

C. 2 (The essence of review is application to related problems.)

     3 (The proposal, in this case, amounted to a new application.)

     7 (In a review, related problems are identified only.)

     9 (Entails an advocacy question, useful in bringing in related problems.)

Reasons for incorrect items

     1 (Although most of the applications will stem from advocacy questions, the review problem should be one of policy—an open-ended problem.)

     4 (Concepts, not facts, are recalled during a review.)

     5 (Concepts, previously derived, are not evaluated during a review.)

     6 (Although this is an appropriate review question to raise during the experience, advantages and disadvantages should not be discussed extensively.)

     8 (An advocacy question as opposed to one of policy.)

D. *Review*

    1. Recall of basic unit concepts: (Any idea previously developed during the unit.)

      Example: The cost of elections encourages the acceptance of money in return for political influence.

    2. Recall of how major concepts were developed:

      Example: What were some of our major learning experiences during this unit?

    3. Extending unit concepts to related problems:

      Example: Referring to the illustrated concepts in #1 above, what influence might this practice have on one's standard of honesty?

Practice

    1. Developing initial learning: (Could deal with any question related to the rudiments of the tennis stroke, its function, problems, etc.)

Example: Watch while I demonstrate and explain the serve, then ask any question that may come to mind.

2. Varied contact: (This usually involves exploratory contact in some manner.)

Example: Each practice the serve ten times; be prepared to ask questions that arise.

3. Repetitive practice: (This involves playing the game, concentrating on certain details [weaknesses].)

Example: As you play the game (of tennis), be sure to concentrate on the power of your first serve.

ANSWERS TO SELF-ASSESSMENT ITEMS

Self-assessment items are designed to help you gain depth of understanding as you proceed through the various learning activities. Most of them do not have single correct answers. For feedback, however, you should compare your answers with the samples provided here.

A. (1) Since both methods build upon previous learning experiences, it is desirable to bring to the learner's attention what is already known in the area.

(2) The memorization of patterns or sequences (as opposed to specific facts) may contribute to understanding.

(3) In class discussion the hypothesis phase focuses upon the merits of various possible solutions—actually advocacy statements. In review, advocacy questions are used to help students make connections between previously developed concepts and outside, related learnings.

(4) Review application consists of merely identifying or making connections between previously learned concepts and related areas. Polish in a practice lesson involves altering minor details that are blocking continued skill development. Much repetition is involved.

Option B_1.(1) The social science area tends to be speculative in nature; applications often are based upon social and ethical considerations. Most other areas (e.g., art, math, music) broadly involve some sort of mental or motor skill.

(2) By having the learner verbalize and write out what he or she is practicing, in the presence of a qualified observer.

(3) Content (basic facts) is recalled in setting the stage for application. Unlike the traditional "review," content serves as a means to an end rather than an end in itself.

(4) Although students will develop some understanding from preliminary reading, explanations, etc., it is through actual application that they complete the process. If, for example, an improper tennis stroke, an improper pronunciation of a foreign language expression, and the like are observed during the demonstration, such techniques are easily acquired (stamped in). Later they will be extremely difficult to alter.

(5)   Since polish is a slow process, the learner frequently is expected to proceed independently of an instructor. In physical education, for example, students may learn the game of volleyball, but since it is not usually a school competitive sport, there is little need to develop polish. Likewise, the student in shorthand class may not be expected to develop polish until he or she enrolls in an advanced class in the subject.

Option B$_2$.(1)   The purpose of a review is to facilitate transfer. If the lesson gets bogged down with one related problem, the major function of the lesson is lost.

(2)   Connecting the new with the old is a creative act. As such it tends to enhance meaning and to be remembered if done by the student.

(3)   Defend. The learner must first understand the basic essentials of the skill involved.

(4)   By utilizing the sense of sight, basic comprehension of the task is facilitated.

(5)   When the faults or weaknesses of the skill are inadequately analyzed and accordingly practiced repeatedly.

C. (1)   The social science area tends to be speculative in nature; applications often are based upon social and ethical considerations. Most other areas (e.g., math, art, music) broadly involve some sort of mental or motor skill.

(2)   Review is a generalization process. Some concepts logically merge into larger concepts as the application process receives emphasis. If, after careful analysis, this is borne out, one need not be concerned with dealing with each concept in turn.

(3)   Content (basic facts) is recalled in setting the stage for application. Unlike the traditional "review," content serves as a means to an end rather than an end in itself.

(4)   Although students will develop some understanding from preliminary reading, explanations, etc., it is through actual application that they complete the process. If, for example, an improper tennis stroke, an improper pronunciation of a foreign language expression, and the like are observed during the demonstration, such techniques are easily acquired (stamped in). Later they will be extremely difficult to alter.

(5)   Since polish is a slow process, the learner frequently is expected to proceed independently of an instructor. In physical education, for example, students may learn the game of volleyball, but since it is not usually a school competitive sport, there is little need to develop polish. Likewise, the student in shorthand class may not be expected to develop polish until he or she enrolls in an advanced class in the subject.

Optional Activities

D. (1)   A clear statement of the problem clarifies lesson purpose. Especially in review, students frequently have a stereotyped mental image of the method as merely a time of recalling important facts.

(2) The practice tends to limit learning to the lower levels of cognition—no problem solving is involved. The result is a deadening experience. Students generally merely attempt to coax the teacher into "spotting" them for an upcoming test. Major purpose of the experience, under such conditions, may not be achieved.

(3) Can be defended primarily as a means for starting the chain of events for student initiative in the area.

(4) Too many tend to confuse and thus retard learning progress.

(5) It applies equally to both mental and motor skills since practice is individualistic in nature. Group drill may be used when initially sounding out words or phrases.

E. (1) Such applications enable students to make application connections, thus expanding and fixing learning as it progresses.

(2) Generally about one-fourth to one-third of the review lesson is needed for this purpose. It provides a basis upon which the application phase of the review rests.

(3) It enables the learner to develop a "feel" for the skill to be developed. Each person possesses certain potential assets and liabilities in every skill area; insight into these is thus developed.

(4) One can definitely indulge in practice sessions for an excessive length of time. When one is too tired, there is a tendency to revert to old habits.

Frequent practice sessions are desirable and seldom pose problems unless they become so excessive as to interfere with motivation.

Sample responses for Optional Learning Activity E, pp. 187–88.

Review

1. Recall of basic concepts

   a. What major ideas were developed during our study of public health?

   b. What major methods were used to help us develop these major ideas?

(Students should be expected to recall the major ideas or concepts of the previous unit. A recall of methods employed provides cues for this recall.)

2. Recall of basic facts (in extending concept understanding)

   a. What did we decide were the major causes of accidents in the home?

   b. What aged persons did we decide were most vulnerable?

(Such questions are sometimes useful in helping students recapture the full meaning of a concept.)

3. Extending basic concepts (principles) to related areas

   a. Looking at our concept, "Carelessness is the major cause of home accidents," let us try to think of specific things that each of us can do (or avoid) to make our homes a safer place in which to live.

   b. Suppose a member of the family smokes. What can be done to ensure maximum safety?

Drill or practice

1. Developing initial learning

    a. Why is it recommended that the thumb be placed alongside the handle of a saw when starting a cut?

    b. Where should a cut be made in relation to the line?

(Such questions are designed to clarify confusing points in the cognitive domain.)

2. Demonstration of its use

    a. Watch how I begin the cut to avoid tearing the wood.

    b. Notice how splitting is avoided as the cut is finished.

3. Varied contact (preliminary practice)

    a. Make a simple cut, using a piece of soft wood such as pine.

    b. Make a simple cut, using a piece of hard wood such as oak.

4. Repetitive practice (developing polish)

    a. Make fifteen cuts, using different woods.

    b. Inspect for problems and repeat to correct your mistakes.

ANSWERS TO POSTTEST

For most beneficial results you should work through the entire LAP before you check your answers to the posttest. Failure to meet the provided minimum standards probably suggests certain weaknesses that need to be corrected. As with the Preassessment items, you will find supporting reasons for answers. It is hoped that this will serve as desirable feedback in your quest for mastery.

A. *Review*

1. Involves recall of basic concepts as a basis for extension of these to related problems.

2. Since association is the basic function, related problems are identified but not analyzed during a review.

3. Although review may occur incidentally along with other methods, the culmination type of review is essential.

4. Review (and practice) increase retention of original learning.

5. Review is essentially a cognitive process.

Practice

6. Practice or drill is restricted to mental and motor skills areas.

7. Practice basically is an individualized process.

8. Skill refinement and polish are dependent upon recall of basic patterns and sequences.

9. Demonstration is basic to development of skills.

B. 2 (This is the way an incidental review is handled.)

   6 (This provides a frame of reference that expedites recall of basic concepts.)

7 (Demonstration in the early stages of skill development is most desirable.)

8 (Practice is an individualized process; this is a mental skills area.)

9 (Taking time out for a discussion during a review tends to defeat its purpose.)

11 (This essentially is an extension of previous learnings to related areas.)

15 (This is basically a demonstration and very desirable in the early stages of skill development.)

16 (There will tend to be unequal emphasis, usually for the reasons stated.)

20 (Explanations are more effective when followed immediately by a demonstration.)

Reasons for incorrect items

1 (Such facts are not important; emphasis is more appropriately placed on major concepts, which will be broader than themes for individualized literature selections.)

3 (The rudiments are necessary prior to any skill development. It is unnecessary to go over these later.)

4 (Drill is basically an individualized technique.)

5 (Unnecessary; takes from the major function of a review.)

10 (Unnecessary; the essence of review is application.)

12 (Memorization in the cognitive domain is generally inappropriate.)

13 (No need to memorize basic ideas; they come with understanding.)

14 (In a review connections are merely made; they are not expanded.)

17 (Varied contact is more appropriate; perhaps different typing drills could have been provided.)

18 (Although one might conceivably justify sounding out words (in a group) once or twice for the purpose of pronunciation, "repeatedly" suggests group drill. This is inappropriate.)

19 (Review is tremendously enhanced through the group as a variety of associations are made.)

C. 1 (This is the basic function of review. Advocacy questions predominate.)

3 (As the review is based upon the basic concepts, it is necessary to briefly clarify any gaps in understanding.)

6 (This is sometimes done. It may be omitted, however.)

7 (Such questions should be entertained only after the preliminary groundwork has been laid.)

8 (Such questions are generally used to assist students to make connections to related areas.)

Reasons for incorrect items

2 (This is a discussion problem. A review problem should include the notion of "relating.")

4 (This should be brief; the major thrust is on application.)

5 (Basic concepts (not facts) are recalled for review purposes.)

9 (Applications are merely identified; they are not discussed extensively.)

D. *Review*

1. Recall of basic unit concepts: (Any idea developed previously during the unit.)

   Example: Traits of inheritance (genes) remain independent, e.g., there is no blending.

2. Recall of how major concepts were developed:

   Example: What were some of our major learning experiences during this unit?

3. Extending unit concepts to related problems:

   Example: Referring to the illustrated concept in #1 above, what effect might this have on the practice of preventative medicine?

Practice

1. Developing initial learning: (Could deal with any of the rudiments of the stroke, its function, problems, etc.)

   Example: Watch while I demonstrate the stroke; be prepared to ask questions that arise.

2. Varied contact: (This usually involves exploratory contact in some manner.)

   Example: Each practice the stroke twenty-five times; be prepared to ask questions that arise.

3. Repetitive practice: (This involves playing the game, concentrating on certain details.)

   Example: As you play the game (of table tennis), be sure to concentrate on the arm motion, especially the follow-through part.

SUPPLEMENTARY SOURCES

The following sources may be used in lieu of the Hoover texts or, preferably, as supplementary to them. Generally they are consistent with the models provided in the LAPs of this module. As such, the references do not represent all of the most recent references in the area; rather, they constitute selected references, designed to broaden or expand needed background information.

Bilodeau, Edward A., ed., *Acquisition of Skills* (New York: Academic Press, 1966).

Clark, Leonard H., *Strategies and Tactics in Secondary School Teaching: A Book of Readings* (New York: The Macmillan Co., 1968), Chap. 10.

Grambs, Jean D., and others, *Modern Methods in Secondary Schools*, 3rd ed. (New York: Holt, Rinehart and Winston, Inc., 1970), Chap. 11.

Hoover, Kenneth H., *The Professional Teacher's Handbook*, 2nd ed. (Boston: Allyn and Bacon, Inc., 1976).

Hoover, Kenneth H., and Paul M. Hollingsworth, *Learning and Teaching in the Elementary School,* 2nd ed. (Boston: Allyn and Bacon, Inc., 1975).

Inlow, Gail M., *Maturity in High School Teaching,* 2nd ed. (Englewood Cliffs, N.J.: Prentice-Hall, Inc., 1970), Chap. 9.

Moynihan, W. J., and R. J. Carroll, "Review Class," *Today's Education,* 63: 78-79 (Nov., 1974).

Nation, S. P., "Motivation, Repetition, and Language-Teaching Techniques," *English Language Teaching Journal,* 29: 115-120 (Jan., 1975).

module
IV

PERSONAL-SOCIAL INSTRUCTIONAL TECHNIQUES

Education at its best must help the individual cope with affairs of everyday life. Achievement in the various content fields is of secondary importance to the social and emotional development of the adolescent boy or girl. Whatever one does, wherever one goes, the complexities of modern-day living must be met. It is not enough to expect that all young people will somehow make the necessary adjustments as they interact in the school society. The accelerated pace of school integration, the mobility of the population, and the sheer weight of increased enrollments are but a few of the factors that have accentuated the problem during the last decade. Systematic instructional strategies are essential to the growth and development of healthy emotions and values. Such is the focus of the LAPs in this module.

Sociometry, a technique for improving the social situation of the existing class setting, is closely allied with sociodrama and simulation games that are designed to portray reality. Sociodrama involves role-playing as a vehicle for simulating an actual event involving social issues. Simulation games go one step further by providing a complex situation in which several vital decisions must be made. Closely allied to these processes is the case method, which serves a similar purpose by capturing significant details, along with important affective considerations, in a more-or-less detailed description of an actual problem situation. All are treated in the first LAP of this module.

Closely associated with the problem of social and emotional interaction are the values an individual holds. Indeed, most unhappy people are made so by their own unique pattern of values. Nevertheless, one tends to cling to his/her values tenaciously since they represent basic dimensions of the personality. The second LAP offers techniques for personalizing learning experience in various contexts. Slowly but surely values can be altered; some of this responsibility falls squarely on the shoulders of the classroom teacher. Values will be acquired and altered during the school experience. The issue is whether they will be "caught" in a haphazard manner or acquired through systematic instructional processes. Most thinking people take the latter position so long as the techniques of coercion are not employed.

Also treated in the second LAP are techniques of creativity. It is a known fact that relatively few individuals have been responsible for the vast majority of the nation's significant inventions and discoveries. Yet such processes too have been neglected and even stifled in the typical classroom. In both value-focusing and creative activities, emphasis is upon learner independence, free from teacher domination and evaluation.

lap
9

Simulation and Related Techniques

sociometry, sociodrama,
simulation games,
and case techniques

RATIONALE. One of the most basic tasks of the school is to assist youngsters to develop satisfactory social competence. It is a well-established fact that most job failures can be traced to deficiencies in human relationships. Moreover, as populations grow and as societies become increasingly complex, the problem takes on increased proportions.

Fortunately, techniques are now available for helping young people develop competence in social relationships. Sociometry is an extremely simple but useful technique for determining an individual's social status within a given group. As techniques for guiding young people in developing empathy in various social situations and in recognizing the complexities of social interaction, sociodrama, simulation games, and case techniques can be especially useful. All these techniques project the individual into simulated situations for study and analysis.

OVERVIEW

Key Concepts

  1. A simulation of reality may be superior to reality itself for instructional
     purposes.

203

2. Through appropriate simulation techniques, social problems may be subjected to analysis.

3. Sociometric grouping is based upon the assumption that one works most effectively with his or her preferred associates.

4. An isolate or neglectee usually chooses one of the most popular individuals; such selections are usually most powerful (psychologically) in coping with the adjustment problems of such persons and should be honored.

5. Role-playing is merely a vehicle for portraying a selected sociodramatic or gaming situation.

6. Sociodramatic problems must be immediate to the lives of those involved; one does not play his or her own identifiable life role, however.

7. Simulation games involve a complex of interacting problems; a number of decisions must be reached.

8. A simulation game has its own payoff or reward system.

9. By emphasizing feeling reactions in the situation, the case analysis closely parallels reality.

10. The short, incident case (structured around a simple conflict) is most effective for secondary school use.

New Terms

1. Simulation: A condensed representation of reality.

2. Sociometry (Sociometrics): Those techniques designed specifically for identifying and improving existing social relations.

3. Isolate and neglectee: An individual not chosen by any other class member (isolate) or one who has only one or two choices.

4. Star: An individual chosen by a substantial number of persons in response to a given sociometric criterion question.

5. Criterion question: The specific question upon which teachers base sociometric techniques. Such questions should refer to specific class situations that are to be used as starting points, such as seating or grouping arrangements.

6. Sociodrama: A spontaneously enacted situation (usually five to ten minutes long), depicting an actual life problem used for study and analysis.

7. Scenario: A relatively complex representation of reality, used in a simulation game, usually involving several problems. Contains necessary background information, objectives, resources, and rules governing the game.

OBJECTIVES. After this experience you should be able to make full use of simulation and related techniques in teaching, as evidenced by your ability to:

1. List twelve characteristic features of sociometry, sociodrama, simulation games, and the case method.

2. Select eleven out of twelve appropriate problems for simulation and related activities from a provided list of twenty-four assorted problems.

3. Develop six out of seven requested responses to key phases of simulation and related techniques.

PRELIMINARY READING. Since the elements of instructional methodology are somewhat variable, the following excerpts are provided to help you develop a frame of reference as a point of departure for this experience. If you prefer, you may proceed directly to the preassessment items.

THE SOCIOMETRIC TEST OR INVENTORY

The sociometric test (inventory) is a flexible procedure that can be administered in a matter of minutes. Directions may be oral, or a sociometric form may be constructed. Such directions should meet the following criteria:

1. The nature of the activity or situation must be clearly delineated.

2. Research indicates that five choices provide the most stable or reliable sociometric results.

3. The use of negative choices (rejections) is usually avoided, as this may make individuals more conscious of their feelings of rejection. In cases of extreme rejection, the chooser is likely to reveal his feelings anyhow. Whenever such a rejection is indicated, the person's wishes should be respected.

4. A definite commitment to honor indicated preferences should be made.

5. Students are asked to accept sociometric grouping as a privilege entailing definite responsibilities.

6. The confidential nature of the responses must be stressed.

7. Students must have had ample opportunity to become acquainted with each other before the test or technique is administered. This may take four to six weeks.

ANALYZING SOCIOMETRIC DATA

Sociometric data may be analyzed by constructing a matrix table and a sociogram (see illustrations on pp. 218 and 219 of this LAP).

The Matrix Table. Proceed as follows:

1. List names of students in alphabetical order on the matrix table. Then number consecutively from top to bottom.

2. Number consecutively across the top of the page.

3. Draw a diagonal line from the upper left to lower right corner of the paper. This serves as a focal point for identifying mutual choices. It bisects the squares not used.

4. Provide for a "total" column at bottom of table.

After all choices are recorded, it becomes apparent that choices given go across the table, whereas choices received go down the table. Mutual choices may be identified and circled. This can be readily accomplished by using the diagonal as a focal point to find the vertical column indicating those who chose a given individual.

Finally, the choices received are totaled at the bottom of the page. The teacher is now able to determine the sociometric status of individuals, but before arranging appropriate groups he or she must make use of a sociogram.

The Sociogram. The sociogram is designed to portray the indicated group social structure. It is often described as a blank target (see illustration on p. 219). Each circle except the outer one is equal distance apart. The vertical line through the center of the diagram is to separate the sexes, as there tends to be a sex cleavage at all ages. The numbers along the line below each circle indicate the choice levels for each of the circles.

Pupils receiving one or no choice would be placed in the outer ring of the diagram; those receiving between 1 and 5 would be placed in the next ring and so forth. The sociogram may be plotted easily by beginning with the least chosen students and moving toward the most chosen students.

It will be noted that only mutual choices have been indicated. This provides a clear picture of the indicated group social structure with a minimum of effort. When it is desirable to ascertain one-way choices, the matrix table may be reviewed. The resourceful teacher usually has a number of blank sociogram "targets" duplicated and ready for use.

SOCIOMETRIC GROUPING

The following steps are recommended for sociometric grouping:

1. Decide the size of the groups to be formed. Work groups of five are often satisfactory.

2. Give unchosen pupils (isolates) their highest choices. Honor their first two choices if possible, but avoid placing two isolates in the same group whenever possible. Never place more than two isolates in a single group.

3. Consider those who received only one choice (neglectee). If the choice should be reciprocated, put him or her with the other person involved, regardless of level of choice.

4. Continue to work from the least chosen to the most chosen individuals. In each case attempt to satisfy mutual choices first.

A number of other considerations should be taken into account when groups are being formed:

1. When more than two choices are possible, attempt to give them to isolates and neglectees.

2. When group cleavages exist, it is often desirable to formulate groups with a view to minimizing them. Some such cleavages may be socio-economic, sexual, racial, rural-urban, and the like. There should be a minimum of two from such subgroups to provide additional security to those involved.

3. Sometimes it is desirable to break up tight cliques. A typical work group, thus formulated, may have one or two isolates or neglectees, one highly chosen individual, and about two pupils of average choice status. Variations can be expected, of course.

THE SOCIODRAMATIC METHOD

Like many other methods of teaching, sociodrama is another approach to problem solving. As such, it involves a series of steps stemming from cognitive processes. It is basically a group-oriented approach concerned with *feeling reactions* as individuals interact with one another. Consequently, two conditions are necessary for implementation: (1) The simulation must be representative of the problems felt by members of the class; (2) most of the group must want or feel the need for exploring the situation.

For purposes of expediency of time, the teacher often identifies the broad situation and then encourages students to develop supporting details. A volunteer cast is selected, the situation is enacted, and then analyzed, based upon the feeling reactions of the participants. Focus is placed upon the person(s) being helped. Role names are used throughout.

The rest of the class is instructed to make notes of verbal and nonverbal clues to feeling reactions. For avoiding a suggestion of criticizing the role-playing techniques, specific key questions might be asked by the teacher in initiating discussion.

1. (To the person who is being helped) How did you feel, Joe (role name), as the situation developed?

2. (To the "leader" of the situation) Do you feel you were making any real progress as the situation developed?

3. (To the class) What specific clues did we note that may have accounted for these feeling reactions?

The analysis is concluded with student derivation of general principles for the enacted (and related) situations.

SIMULATION GAMES

A simulation game is a simplified representation of reality, reduced to manageable proportions. It attempts to include those elements of reality that are essential to the processes under investigation. Like sociodrama (and indeed most methods of teaching), the simulation game is another approach to problem solving. Unlike most other methods, however, the method usually involves a complex situation necessitating *resolution of several problems* as the situation develops.

Although a simulation game may vary in length from one to five or six class periods, it usually embodies at least two or three closely related unit concepts. Basic to the development of a simulation game is conflict or the clash of opposing forces or desires. Using the identified basic concepts as a guide, the teacher must develop a rough outline of the game to be portrayed. It may be hypothetical or a replication of an actual process. In any event, it must be a selective representation of those elements necessary to achieve objectives. If it is too complex, students will become frustrated and may lose sight of the purposes entirely. If overly simple, the game may have little motivational value and may result in basic misconceptions concerning the complexities of actual events.

Identification of roles to be played can be inferred from the model to be portrayed. They are built around the basic concepts previously identified for the situation. Class size, of course, is a practical consideration that will influence role assignments.

Especially in the area of social or political relations, decision-making is usually an outgrowth of group effort. It has been found that subgroups of five are ideally suited for such purposes. Thus, if five political or social groups are involved, five teams of five each can be established. Since decisions of such groups often influence the public, the need for two or three reporters is implied. In a business simulation game, the model office will be organized along the lines of an office staff. This may include company officers and a pool of secretarial staff. Such classes are usually smaller than in the social studies area.

Some teachers prefer to assign subgroups and roles sociometrically. This has the distinct advantage of promoting optimum interaction. Sometimes, of course, the success of a simulation is largely dependent upon the success of one or more key roles to be portrayed. Thus, student assignment on the basis of ability may be desirable. Perhaps a combination of all the foregoing should be considered, dependent upon the nature of the group and simulation involved.

The relationships of the elements in a simulation game are made realistic through resources (troops, money, votes, etc.) to exchange in competition with other players. Although a precise quantification of power is not always evident in real life, most educational simulations attempt to assess precise values of resources exchanged.

A game is played in well-defined cycles, each structured around a crisis. Students must know the precise goals to be achieved in each session and fully understand the rules of procedure to be followed. Rules limit the range and define the legitimate actions of the players. Action begins with a "crisis" of some kind such as a state of war between two nations. Then negotiations are carried out by sending representatives to confer secretly with other representatives. It is here that the spirit of compromise and strategy develop. "My group will support your group if . . . ."

The third phase usually involves group action of some kind. In effect, the strategy, planned and developed in the previous phases, is now put into action.

A final phase focuses upon consequences of action taken in the preceding phase. A peace conference is held to establish realignments and power, which is a logical consequence of war, for example.

Other cycles can be planned that logically follow Cycle I as the occasion demands. Some games may consist of one cycle, others may incorporate three or more such cycles. The nature of the phases within a cycle depends somewhat upon the nature of the game. They usually will involve a sequence of planning, negotiation, action, and consequences.

THE CASE METHOD

A case is an account of an actual problem or situation that has been experienced by an individual or a group. It includes facts available to those facing the problem, along with a description of perceptions and attitudes of those who are faced with the problem. Case problems are often accounts of actual situations encountered by people similar to those engaged in the case analysis. They may be representative problems faced by people already in the field which the learner is about to enter. While fictional cases may be used effectively, the readily available supply of real-life problems favors the recording of actual events.

The case method is characterized by its usefulness in teaching students to think in the presence of new situation. Case problems, taken from real-life experiences, are probably as close to reality as possible in the absence of the experience itself. The learner, placed in the role of a major participant, is able to visualize concrete, specific, personal contact afforded through the situation. Thus a great deal of interest is developed.

Use of cases puts the student in the habit of making decisions. He must think analytically and decisively within specified time limitations. Rather than receiving the solution from his instructor, he himself contributes to the solution through group analysis.

The method emphasizes acquisition of interrelated factual knowledge. In grappling with the case problem, the student often realizes a need for specific information germane to the situation. Thus he tends to develop a functional understanding of facts.

A characteristic feature of the case method is its emphasis on the feeling dimension of decision-making. In a sense, the feelings and purposes of every person portrayed in a given case are "facts" that must be considered.

Case Presentation. The case is usually reproduced for students. (Occasionally a short case may be read to students.) It may be presented to students as an assignment for the next class period, or it may be presented for immediate reading and reaction. This will depend somewhat upon the basic purpose to be served and, accordingly, upon the length and complexity of the case.

While cases *may* be detailed and complex, short incident cases are usually preferred for junior and senior high school use. These will consist of four to five paragraphs.

Case Analysis. Problem solving is indicative of the case method at its best. Case analysis then involves the essential phases of the problem-solving process.

Stage I in the discussion analysis is initiated when the teacher asks, in some manner,

"What is the issue or problem in this case?" It is essential that students know precisely what the difficulty is. In complex cases, there may be three or four minor "problems," but usually it is relatively easy to identify the basic issue upon which the other difficulties rest.

Stage II consists of an analysis of the facts of the situation. *Here the emphasis is upon what actually happened rather than personal opinion of the facts.* The purpose of this phase of the discussion is to get the case facts into the open, making sure that insignificant, but sometimes important, bits of information are not disregarded. Indications of the *why* of behavior can be gained by quoting from what case participants actually said. Key phrases also may be jotted down for future reference.

After looking briefly at the objective facts, the discussion might then turn to the *relations* between the people involved. To whom is the party responsible? Is there evidence of a hidden allegiance? What are the established channels of communication?

The third aspect of factual analysis may be conceived as *sentiments and beliefs.* Here expressed feelings or attitudes are considered. A word of caution is in order, however. It is important to distinguish between attitudes and feelings expressed in the case and those inferred by students who are participating in the case analysis.

Stage III is the hypothesis phase. After case *activities*, *relations*, and *sentiments and beliefs* have been thoroughly explored and evaluated, attention is turned to decision-making. "What needs to be decided, and done, right now?" It is helpful to consider decision or action in terms of *each party* to the conflict.

Stage IV involves the formulation of generalizations and principles. As Pigors and Pigors[1] so aptly express the process, it involves *looking back, looking up, looking about*, and finally *looking ahead.*

Reflecting on the case as a whole (along with other cases previously studied), the student once again assumes a position from "outside" of the case. He examines the fundamental issue explored, reflecting upon those behaviors which appeared to be highly effective (or ineffective) in the situation. For example, the teacher might ask, "How might this conflict have been prevented?" "How might more have been accomplished?" This process naturally leads to *looking up* to the level of general ideas and principles. Thus the teacher might ask, "What guiding concepts can be distilled from our case analysis?" This, in turn, leads to *looking about* for other situations which contain commonalities with the present one. "How well do the general ideas that stand out in this case also apply to other cases?" Finally, the basic concepts are *thrust forward* to problems which might be reasonably anticipated. It must be emphasized that the basic assumption underlying use of the case method is that the fundamental concepts derived from particular cases are applicable to a variety of other, similar situations. The teacher must assist the learner in this knowledge expansion process. In psychological terminology, "Transfer of learning is enhanced when the student is taught to transfer."

PREASSESSMENT ITEMS (answers provided on pp. 229–32)

This experience is designed to help you gain an overall perspective of how simulation techniques are used in teaching. After completing these items, turn to the end of

---

[1] *Paul Pigors and Faith Pigors*, Case Method in Human Relations: The Incident Process *(New York: McGraw-Hill Book Co., Inc., 1961), p. 145.*

this LAP and check your answers. Note that answers (both correct and incorrect) are provided with supporting reasons to guide your efforts as you work through the LAP.

A. List twelve characteristic features of the following simulation techniques as indicated. (*To illustrate:* Sociometry is based on the premise that a young person works most effectively with his/her friendship preferences.)

Sociometry

1.

2.

3.

Sociodrama

4.

5.

6.

7.

Simulation games

8.

9.

Case method

10.

11.

12.

B. From the list of situations and problems, place a check (√) by twelve of those that meet the criteria for the designated methods involved.

Sociometry (Criterion questions)

1. Indicate the five people you would prefer to work with on a committee.

2. List your five best friends in this class.

3. Name the five individuals that you would prefer to be with at a party.

4. Identify the five persons that you would like to work with on our school exhibit.

5. By listing five choices for seating companions, you can help me reorganize our seating arrangements in this room.

6. Suggest five people you would like to take with you on a trip to the moon.

Sociodrama (Broad situation)

7. The junior-senior prom traditionally has been a formal occasion. The expense of formal attire has, in the past, prevented some students from attending this memorable event. A committee of students, representative of different economic levels, has been

appointed to develop a plan so that all may attend. (The desirability of holding this as a formal event is not under consideration.)

8. A high school student who has recently emigrated from Vietnam is attempting to explain to a couple of her American friends why U.S. economic assistance should be continued indefinitely.

9. The Secretary of State is attempting to persuade the U.S. President to extend diplomatic relations to a foreign nation that is in a conciliatory mood.

10. Two Cuban nationals are discussing the pros and cons of the Castro regime.

11. Joe (a black in real life) is discussing with two of his friends (white in real life) the merits of a local busing plan.

12. Two seventeen-year-old girls meet at a local soda fountain. Both have about the same amount of income—approximately seventeen dollars per week. Betty wants to know why the other (Kathy) always has money and if Kathy could help her.

Simulation games (Subject for a scenario)

13. Impeachment of a U.S. President is under consideration. Several committees, representing various vested interest groups, are formed.

14. A local congressman is apprehended by local authorities for drunk and disorderly conduct. Several forces are represented relative to action by the authorities.

15. Two local businessmen are discussing the demands of the union local in their places of business.

16. A busing plan for school integration has been proposed by the local school board. Several community groups have been formed relative to the issue.

17. The parents of a large family are threatening divorce. Various affected parties are represented as groups in resolving the matter.

18. Mr. Johns, the chemistry teacher, is trying to convince the superintendent and the principal that he should have some new laboratory equipment.

Case method (Problems for)

19. Petty cash has recently been missing from an office. Mary, a young secretary, sees a more experienced secretary take the cash.

20. In foods class two students are selected to demonstrate the right etiquette for a simulated formal dinner.

21. In the case, Tom was apprehended for using illegal drugs. After making a plea to the student council and to school authorities, he was dismissed from school.

22. Joe and Tom are the best of friends. The case is structured around their plans for a forthcoming school dance.

23. The boss's son is getting too familiar with his father's receptionist. The case is structured around the aggravating conditions of the situation.

24. Mary likes to draw. Sue, on the other hand, has very little talent. She takes one of Mary's partially completed sketches, completes it, and submits it to the art teacher as a required project.

C. Develop responses to the following as indicated:

   1. Sociometry (Criterion question for committee work)

   2. Sociodrama. *Concept:* Picketing as a means of public expression can influence public policy.

       a. Broad situation

       b. Analysis of the enacted situation (Two key questions)

   3. Simulation games. *Concept:* Same as above.

       Scenario outline

   4. Case method

       Analyzing the problem (Two key questions)

If you were able to provide twenty-eight of the thirty-one requested responses, you are to be congratulated. In this case you probably already possess the needed competencies in the realm of simulation techniques and should proceed directly to the next LAP in the module (Value-Focusing and Creative Activities). Even if you were able to supply few of the requested responses, do not be discouraged, for sometimes simulation techniques consistently elude experienced teachers. By analyzing the correct answers, and then studying the supporting reasons for all correct and incorrect items in Part B of the items, you should soon reach the expected competency level.

LEARNING ACTIVITIES

Work through each learning activity, complete the self-assessment items, and check your answers before moving to the next one. Note that the last learning activities are optional, depending upon your needs and circumstances at that point. You should be able to complete this LAP in about five or six hours.

A: *Read.* Re-examine the overview and the preliminary reading sections to this LAP. You will broaden your understanding by studying Chaps. 8(12), 9(13), and 10(14) in the Hoover texts and/or by studying the selected references.* Note especially the following points:

   1. Why sociometry is needed.

   2. Basic rules of sociometric grouping.

   3. How the sociodramatic situation ties in with the concept to be taught.

   4. Why one party to the sociodramatic situation is asked to leave the room briefly prior to the enactment.

   5. How generalizations are evolved from the sociodramatic enactment.

   6. The power or point system of a simulation game.

   7. How feelings are incorporated into case materials.

The chapters in parentheses refer to chapters in the abridged edition of the Hoover text.

Self-assessment Items (answers provided on p. 232)

(1) Some teachers are reluctant to conduct sociometric studies in their classes, claiming that as much can be accomplished by letting students informally arrange their own seating or grouping patterns. Refute this contention.

(2) Provide a rationale for the three basic rules of sociometric regrouping.

(3) The concept for the lesson is broad, whereas the sociodramatic situation is very specific and immediate to the lives of students. How is the transition from the general to the specific effected?

(4) What determines which party of a sociodramatic situation will leave the room briefly?

(5) The sociodramatic situation is but one of any number of possible life situations. How, then, can generalizations be developed?

(6) Why are tokens (points) awarded for relative power status of the parties in a simulation game?

(7) How are feelings introduced into a case?

At this point you may select either Option B_1 or Option B_2, depending upon your particular situation. Those who are presently teaching should select Option B_1. Those who are not teaching or who do not have immediate access to students should select Option B_2.

Option B_1: *Modeled demonstration.* This experience is designed to help you acquire a full perception of how simulation techniques ideally should be applied. If possible, a carefully planned demonstration should be given. This can usually be arranged if you are working with other new teachers under the careful guidance of a local teacher director or instructor.

Another option would be filmed or videotaped presentations featuring the basic frame of reference offered in the preliminary reading section of this LAP.*

If working alone, you may arrange to visit a highly recommended teacher(s) for this purpose. In order to emulate the basic model, however, such an individual(s) should thoroughly acquaint himself/herself with the techniques outlined in this LAP and attempt to demonstrate accordingly. Observe and discuss each technique, making notes on the following points as indicated:

1. Sociometric study

    a. The criterion question used.

    b. Instructions accompanying the experience.

    c. Have the teacher show or explain how the data are used most efficiently in construction of the matrix table and the sociogram.

    d. Have the teacher show or explain how the students are grouped sociometrically. (Since sociometric data are confidential, some teachers may prefer to discuss this point in general terms.)

One such film is Case Method of Instruction, *Parts I, II, and III, U.S. National Audiovisual Center, National Archives and Records Service, Washington, D.C. 20408.*

    e.   Have the teacher point out hazards and practical problems associated with the experience and how such problems are handled.

2. Sociodrama

    a.   How students were prepared for the sociodrama.

    b.   How the sociodrama was connected with a basic unit concept(s) and course content.

    c.   How the broad situation and specific details were derived.

    d.   The selection of sociodrama participants and how they were prepared for the experience.

    e.   How the audience was prepared.

    f.   Follow-up questions (to avoid placing role players on the defensive).

    g.   How the situation was expanded to related situations.

    h.   How generalizations were derived.

3. Simulation games

    a.   How the simulation game was introduced.

    b.   How the game was connected with basic unit concepts and course content.

    c.   The selection of subgroups for the different roles to be played.

    d.   The teacher's role during the game.

    e.   How the game was culminated.

    f.   How generalizations were derived.

4. Case study

    a.   The case problem

    b.   How the case was introduced.

    c.   How the case materials were made available and used by students.

    d.   The case analysis, noting especially the use of facts, feelings, and relationships.

    e.   How alternatives (hypotheses) were evoked and evaluated.

    f.   How generalizations were derived.

Self-assessment Items (answers provided on pp. 232–33)

(1) Why is the sociometric criterion question specific rather than general?

(2) List three psychological hazards associated with sociometric grouping.

(3) How does one keep the actors from becoming defensive of the manner in which roles were played?

(4) Degree of progress in an enacted situation is not germane to the success of a sociodrama. Defend or refute.

(5) Why are volunteers considered essential to sociodrama and simulation games?

(6) In all probability the case study group got bogged down in discussion of facts, feelings, and relationships. How can this problem be minimized?

Option B$_2$: *Developing preliminary sociodramatic and simulation game situations.* Using one or more of your unit concepts as a basis (developed in the module on Pre-instructional Experiences), prepare a broad situation for a sociodrama and a simulation game scenario, as indicated.

1. Sociodramatic situation

   a. Select a concept that contains a direct or an indirect affective (feeling) element.

   b. Think of an incident that has happened (or could easily happen) to high school students, based upon a conflict of values. (This must relate, in a general way, to your identified concept.)

   c. Prepare three or four sentences that depict the incident. (Be sure to leave the situation open enough for students to later fill in supporting details.)

2. Simulation game scenario (You may want to refer to one or more commercially developed scenarios.)

   a. Select two or three closely related concepts that have social and emotional overtones.

   b. Think of a situation involving a number of interrelated problems. (For example, in a business office we often have receptionists, secretaries, business executives, and perhaps an auditor or two.)

   c. Outline brief problems for each major party involved, depicting interrelationships as well.

   d. Develop game cycles or sequences with accompanying rules of procedure.

3. If working in a committee group, evaluate each of the foregoing situations in terms of:

   a. Practicality

   b. Clarity

   c. Length

   d. Usefulness in terms of the concept(s) involved.

   (If working alone, attempt to have an experienced teacher examine your products and offer suggestions.)

Self-assessment Items (answers provided on p. 233)

(1) Why is the playing of one's own life role in a sociodrama to be discouraged?

(2) Degree of progress in an enacted situation is not germane to the success of a sociodrama. Defend or refute.

(3) Why are volunteers considered essential to sociodrama and simulation games?

(4) Why is a payoff (power tokens, etc.) often used in a simulation game as opposed to actual reality?

Again you have an option, depending upon your access to students. Those who do have students should select Option C_1; those who do not should select Option C_2 (A, B, C, D).

Option C_1: *Instructional application.* Using one or more of your unit concepts as a basis (developed in an earlier LAP), *do* (in one of your classes) a sociometric study *and* at least one of the different simulation methods (sociodrama, simulation games, case study). You will want to refer to the Hoover texts or one or more of the selected references. Proceed as follows:

1. Sociometric study

   a. Prepare a criterion question. (Make sure that the question is specific and realistic to your class situation.)

   b. Ask students to indicate their five preferences. (Note the confidential nature of the data.)

   c. Complete the matrix table on the form provided.

   d. Complete the sociogram on the form provided.

   e. Group students into committees of four or five each, based upon your sociometric data.

   f. Identify problems you encountered in deriving the subgroups.

2. Sociodrama

   a. Prepare a broad situation for enactment. (Make sure it is based upon one or more of your unit concepts.)

   b. Prepare students for the enactment by connecting with content material.

   c. Guide students in developing details of the situation.

   d. Select a volunteer cast.

   e. Have the individual(s) who is leading the situation leave the room while additional details are supplied by the class. (The individual leading the situation leaves so that certain information can be supplied that he/she ordinarily would not know about.)

   f. Prepare students for picking up cues that influence the enactment as it progresses.

   g. Permit the "drama" to proceed for five to ten minutes. (Stop when purposes are achieved or when students start repeating themselves.)

   h. Lead a follow-through discussion of the enactment. (Emphasize clues to feeling reactions.)

   i. (Optional) Replay, by reversing the roles for the enactment, using the members of the original enactment team.

3. Simulation games

   a. Select a simulation game appropriate for three to five of your unit concepts. (Many games are commercially produced; some are produced by teachers themselves.)

PUPILS CHOSEN

Chooser	1	2	3	4	5	6	7	8	9	10	11	12	13	14	15	16	17	18	19	20	21	22	23	24	25	26	27	28
1																												
2																												
3																												
4																												
5																												
6																												
7																												
8																												
9																												
10																												
11																												
12																												
13																												
14																												
15																												
16																												
17																												
18																												
19																												
20																												
21																												
22																												
23																												
24																												
25																												
26																												
27																												
28																												
TOTALS																												

FIGURE 9–1. Matrix Table

     b.   Introduce the game to the students.

     c.   Select subgroups (or individuals) to play the identified roles, explaining the sequence of events and the like.

     d.   Conduct a simulation game, moving from group to group as needed.

     e.   Culminate the game by guiding students in the derivation of generalizations.

   4.   Case study

     a.   Prepare (or find) an incident case appropriate to one or more of your unit concepts. (Reproduce enough copies for all students.)

     b.   Introduce the case to your students, allowing adequate time for them to read and study the case.

     c.   Conduct a case analysis, emphasizing pertinent facts, feelings, and relationships.

     d.   Guide students in proposal and evaluation of various hypotheses (possible solutions).

     e.   Culminate the case experience by guiding students in the derivation of generalizations.

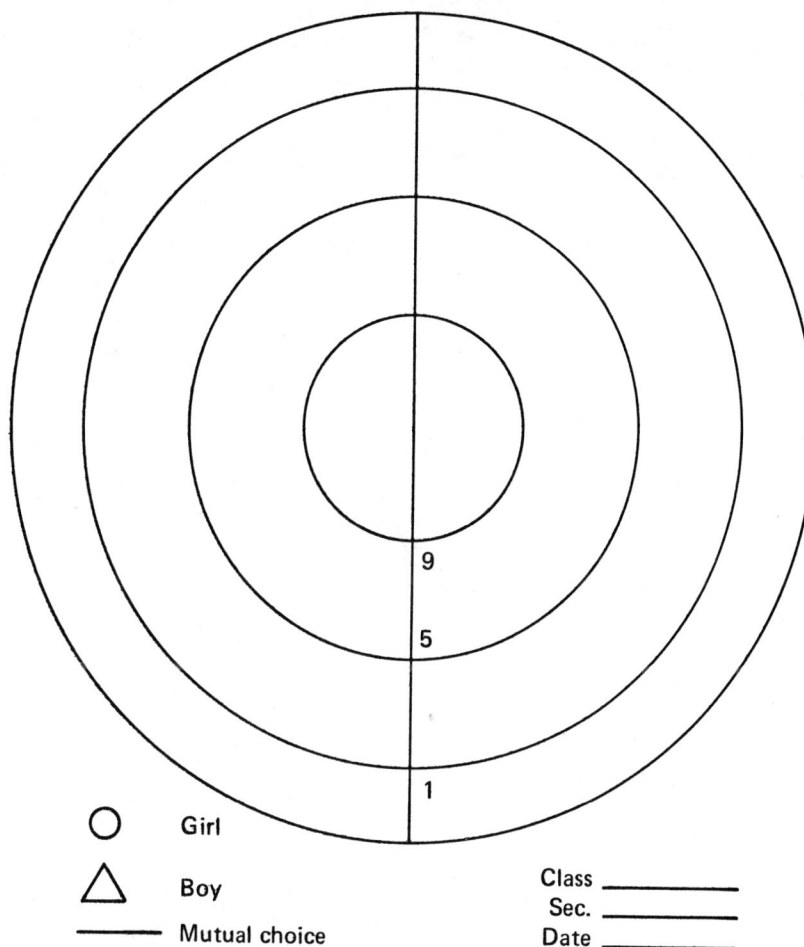

FIGURE 9-2. Sociogram—Mutual Choices

5. If working along with other new teachers, discuss your experiences. Use the foregoing outlines as a guide for this discussion. (If working alone, prepare a written critique of your experiences, especially noting points of confusion and times when interest tended to lag.)

Self-assessment Items (answers provided on p. 233)

(1) The isolate's first choice tends to be one "high" in popularity. Why do we run little risk of rejection by placing him or her with such a chosen person?

(2) Isolates and neglectees are experiencing social and emotional adjustment problems. Defend or refute.

(3) How does one know when to stop the sociodrama enactment?

(4) Why is re-enactment often encouraged?

(5) Why is a payoff (power tokens, etc.) often used in a simulation game as opposed to actual reality?

(6) What advantages does the case method have over the sociodramatic method?

Option $C_2(A)$: *Sociometric study.* From the provided sociometric data, complete a sociometric study, as indicated.

1. Complete the matrix table on the form provided (see C_1).
2. Complete the sociogram on the form provided (see C_1).
3. Group students into committees of four or five each, based upon your data.
4. Identify problems you encountered in deriving the subgroups.
5. If working in a committee, discuss your experience, using the foregoing as a frame of reference. (If working alone, prepare a written critique of your experience.)

Sociometric Data. Criterion Question: With whom would you prefer to work when we move into group activities for our next project?

Chooser	Chosen, *in preference from one to five*
Cecilia	Nancy, Martha, Val, Cathie, Rouse
Tom	Randy, Will, Calvin, Harry, Cliff
Bill	Bob, Will, Danny, Ken, Randy
Buddy	Rouse, Nancy, Danny, David, Patty
Addie	Martha, Nancy, Ann, Val, Rouse
Cathie	Martha, Val, Patty, Rouse, Danny
Rouse	Nancy, Sally, Martha, Cathie, Val
Ann	Martha, Addie, Danny, ? , David
Helene	Martha, Nancy, Addie, Rouse, Danny
Don	Danny, David, Bob, Nancy, Sally
David	Randy, Danny, Bob, Rouse, Cathie
Calvin	Harry, David, Buddy, Danny, Bob
Sally	Rouse, Nancy, Addie, Martha, Cathie
Letha	Val, Danny, Harry, Addie, Martha
Val	Nancy, Rouse, Sally, Helene, Martha
Nancy	Rouse, Sally, Val, Cathie, Martha
Martha	Sally, Cathie, Val, Nancy, Rouse
Randy	Danny, Bill, Tom, Bob,?
Danny	Rouse, Martha, Val, Nancy, Cathie
Kent	Danny, David, Will, Cliff, Randy
Bob	Danny, Ken, Will, Buddy, Cecilia
Ken	Bob, David, Danny, Buddy, Bill
Will	Danny, Bill, Don, Randy, Cliff
Patty	Cathie, Addie, Rouse, Martha, Marie
Marie	Val, Martha, Nancy, Helene, Ann
Cliff	Ken, David, Danny, Harry, Don
Harry	Val, David, Danny, Ann, Rouse

Self-assessment Items (answers provided on pp. 233–34)

(1) Why is the sociometric criterion question specific rather than general?

(2) The isolate's first choice tends to be one "high" in popularity. Why do we run little risk of rejection by placing him or her with such a chosen person?

(3) Isolates and neglectees are experiencing social and emotional adjustment problems. Defend or refute.

(4) List three psychological hazards associated with sociometric grouping.

Option C_2(B): *Sociodrama enactment.* Working in a committee of six if possible, enact the provided sociodramatic situation, as indicated. (If working alone, you should substitute for this experience a single-concept film in the social science area. Prepare a written critique of your experience.)

Sociodramatic Situation

Concept: When individuals (or nations) have basic rights violated, they can be expected to rebel.

Broad situation: A committee of students attempts to impose formal attire upon those who attend the junior-senior banquet. Two representatives of the committee are discussing the matter with an individual who represents students opposing the idea.

Proceed as follows:

1. Have one member of your group act as the leader (teacher); select two for the enactment; let the other members be the class or audience.

2. Supply additional details to the situation. (E.g., the general socio-economic level of the students, cost to those involved, etc.)

3. Have the individual who is to *lead* the situation leave the room while additional details are supplied by the class. (The leader leaves so that certain information can be supplied that he ordinarily would not know about.)

4. Conduct a follow-through discussion of the enactment. (Emphasize clues to feeling reactions.)

5. Derive generalizations from the experience.

6. Replay, by reversing the roles for the enactment, using the other members of your group.

7. Using the foregoing points as a basis, discuss the effectiveness of your experiences with those in the subgroup.

Self-assessment Items (answers provided on p. 234)

(1) How does one know when to stop the enactment?

(2) How does one keep the actors from becoming defensive of the manner in which roles were played?

(3) Why is re-enactment often encouraged?

Option $C_2(C)$: *Case analysis.* Working in a committee of six if possible, conduct a case analysis based upon the provided case materials. Have one member of your committee serve as the leader or teacher. (If working alone, provide a written analysis of the case, as indicated.) Proceed as follows:

1. Each take a few minutes to read and underline key facts, feelings, and relationships.

2. Discuss the above for clarification and priorities.

3. Provide as many alternatives as you can.

4. Evaluate each alternative by looking at advantages and disadvantages relative to the situation.

5. Derive generalizations from the experience.

SAMPLE CASE

Concept: Empathy is essential to a successful marriage.

Jane and her husband, Bill, live in a middle-class suburb. They have three small children, all under school age. Bill is not a college graduate but is capable and ambitious. Jane indicates that she values these traits in her husband. He is a salesman for a large company, but his work is largely confined to his home state. Sometimes he is away for two or three days and he often gets home late at night. Occasionally his work interferes with their weekends.

Lately Jane has been complaining about his being away so much and getting home so late. Bill explained that he had made several contacts that he considered good prospects for a sale and that it was difficult to break up his conferences to come home at a regular hour. Besides, he sometimes had book work to do when he got back to the office. Bill feels that she should appreciate his efforts for the family. Jane said that he was always about to make a sale, which usually fell through, and that he should spend more time with his family. Moreover, financial support, she says, is not the only kind she needs. She would like help with the children.

Questions:

1. What is the problem?

2. What are the incidents that show lack of empathy?

3. What are some understandings about Jane's feelings that Bill needs in order to empathize, and vice versa?

4. What are some specific ways in which Jane and Bill can develop empathy?

5. If the present relationship continues, what type of family life are they likely to have? Give the principles that explain your answer.

6. Using the foregoing as a basis, discuss the effectiveness of the experience with members of your committee.

Self-assessment Items (answers provided on p. 234)

(1) In all probability your group became somewhat "bogged down" in discussion of facts, feelings, and relationships. How can this problem be minimized?

(2) Why are generalizations substituted for a final solution relative to the case problem?

(3) What advantages does the case method have over the sociodramatic method?

Option C_2(D): *Writing a case.* Using the provided photosituation (Figure 9-3) as a basis, prepare an incident case, using the following guide:

1. Case preparation guide

   a. Paragraph I. Background information.

   b. Paragraph II (or more). Bring in one party(ies) to the conflict. (Include a quote or two.)

   c. Paragraph III (or more). Bring in the other party(ies) to the conflict. (Include a quote or two.)

   d. Paragraph IV (or more). Develop an impending decision.

   e. Prepare two or three case questions to stimulate thinking.

2. If working in a committee, go over each individual's case, noting strengths and weaknesses. (If working alone, put your case aside until the next day prior to evaluation, or perhaps find a friend who can look at it somewhat objectively.) Use the following guideline:

   a. Did the case bring in enough of the situation? Too many details?

   b. Were quotes relative to feelings used effectively?

   c. Did important (perhaps hidden) relationships emerge?

   d. Was an impending decision *relative to the basic problem* created?

   e. How effective were the two or three case questions?

Self-assessment Items (answers provided on p. 234)

(1) Why should a teacher usually expect to prepare his or her own cases?

(2) What function do quotes play in a case?

(3) Why is the incident case preferred to the detailed, complex case for high school use?

(4) What function do prepared case questions serve?

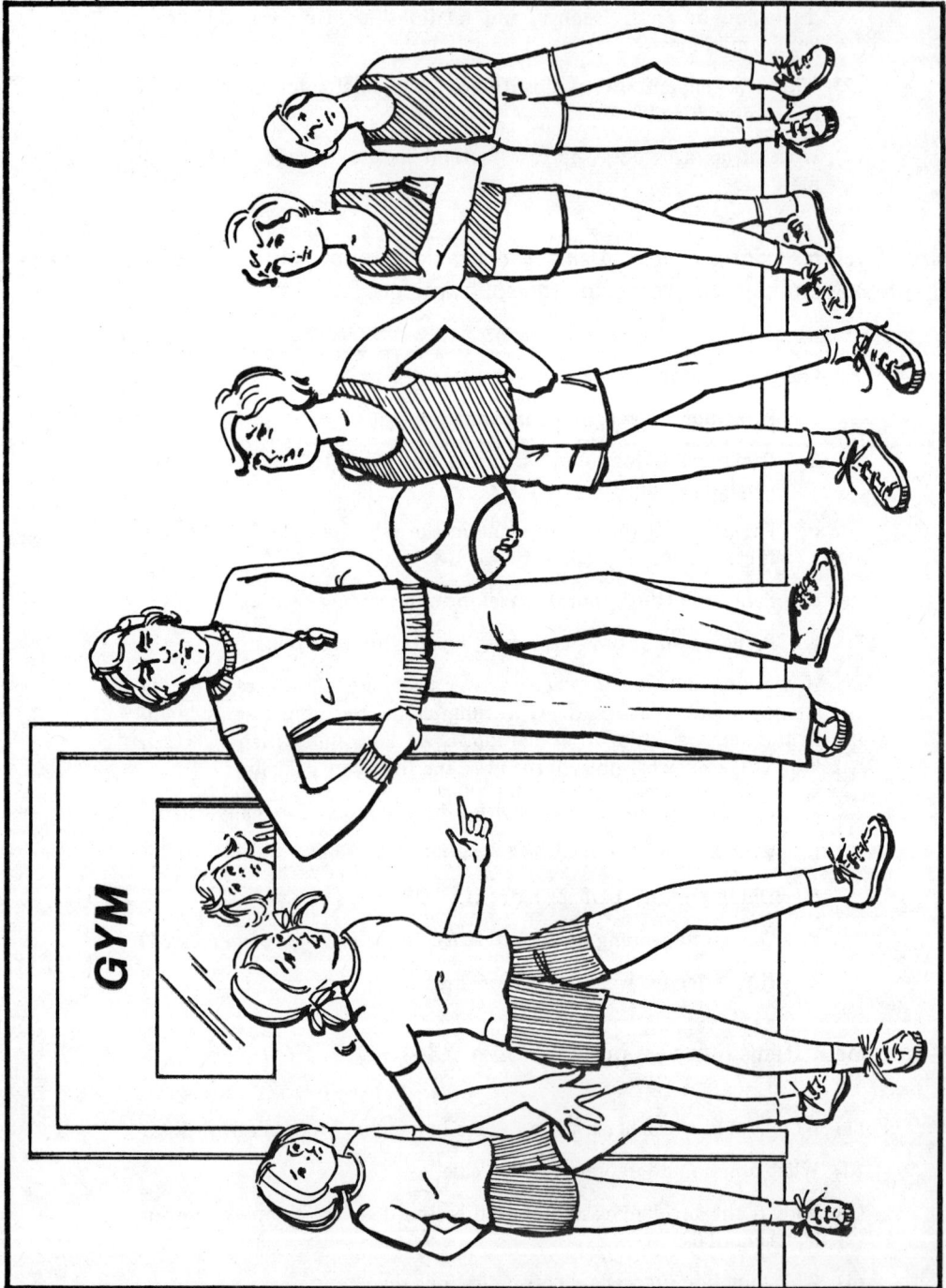

FIGURE 9-3. *The girls want to play on the boys' basketball team.*

If, after reviewing your learning experiences for this LAP, you feel that you can meet the stated objectives, proceed to the posttest. If not, you should complete the optional activity.

Optional Activity

D: *Class observation.* Arrange to visit classes featuring simulation and related techniques. Since the purpose of these experiences is to help you distinguish between the modeled techniques and practical applications, it is not essential to make special requests of the instructors involved. The observations should help you expand your perspective of these methods and techniques. They should also help you detect problems associated with common malpractice aspects of the methods. Since some of these techniques often extend beyond a single class period, you should attempt to ascertain from the teacher how the lessons are to be culminated.

If working with other new teachers, form a committee of four and arrange for each member to visit one of the classes indicated. (If working alone, you should visit at least two of the classes indicated.) Proceed as follows:

1. The individual who visits a class involving sociometry will probably merely glimpse the results of such activity. Most data will be obtained from the teacher in a pre- or post-observation conference. Attempt to obtain the following information:

    a. Criterion question used

    b. Identification of isolates and progress subsequent to regrouping arrangements

    c. Class control problems (if any)

    d. Overall rapport

    e. Plans for a follow-up sociometric analysis

2. The person who visits a lesson featuring sociodrama (often referred to as role-playing) should obtain the following information:

    a. Concept of the lesson

    b. Broad situation and details (developed by the class)

    c. How the actors were selected

    d. How class and players were prepared for the enactment

    e. How the situation was analyzed

    f. How generalizations were derived

    It should be noted that since dramatization or role-playing procedures, in some respects, closely parallel the sociodramatic method, the observer may note considerable difference between the observed experience and that featured in the LAP.

3. A third member of your committee should visit a class featuring the use of a simulation game. Most simulation games in use today are commercially produced. Obtain the following information:

    a. Concepts of the lesson

    b.   How the game is introduced to students

    c.   General rapport during the experience

    d.   The teacher's role

    e.   Follow-through discussion

4. The fourth member of your committee will visit a lesson featuring the case method. Obtain the following information:

    a.   Concept of the lesson

    b.   How the case was introduced

    c.   Case analysis

    d.   How hypotheses were handled

    e.   Derivation of lesson generalizations

5. Hold a post-observation conference for the purpose of comparing notes. Use the following questions as a basis for this conference: (If working alone, prepare a written critique of your experiences.)

    a.   In what ways were the different concepts of the lessons alike? Different?

    b.   How were the different classes prepared for the different simulation experiences?

    c.   What overall class rapport was noted?

    d.   Discuss how the different approaches got "bogged down" (if they did). What commonalities (if any) were noted?

    e.   Compare the analysis and follow-through techniques of the different experiences.

    f.   Compare the nature of lesson generalizations among the different simulation experiences.

Self-assessment Items (answers provided on pp. 234–35)

    (1)   It has been observed that following sociometric grouping, the noise level of a class usually goes up. Normally, after a period of about two weeks, however, the noise level drops, even below that present prior to application of the techniques. Why is this?

    (2)   Contrast the sociodramatic method with dramatization or role-playing procedures.

    (3)   Simulation games have been criticized, since they necessarily represent a reduction of reality to selected factors and forces that influence decisions. Hidden pressures, it is claimed, may be more influential in decision-making than obvious forces. How can this weakness be minimized?

    (4)   Some cases are used for solving problems (illustrated in this LAP); others are used for derivation of principles. How would the construction vary?

POSTTEST (answers provided on pp. 235-37)

After you have completed the learning activities, complete the posttest and evaluate by checking your answers with those found at the end of this LAP. Note that supporting reasons are provided for both correct and incorrect items in Part B.

    A. List twelve characteristic features of the following simulation techniques, as indicated.

    Sociometry

      1.

      2.

      3.

    Sociodrama

      4.

      5.

      6.

      7.

    Simulation games

      8.

      9.

    Case method

   10.

   11.

   12.

    B. From the list of situations and problems, place a check (√) by eleven of those that meet the criteria for the designated methods involved.

    Sociometry

    1. Indicate those five individuals whom you would most like to have on your committee. If there is anybody that you would prefer not be on your committee, indicate that too.

    2. List your five preferences for project work. Since we have a number of blacks in class, put at least one of these on your list.

    3. Indicate your five preferences for a new seating arrangement. Your preferences will be kept strictly confidential.

    4. We'll go in cars on our field trip. Indicate the five people you would most like to accompany you in your car.

    5. Our art exhibit necessitates the use of several committees. Since a committee size of three is needed, would you provide me with your three choices?

    6. Whom would you like to be with on a camping trip? Indicate five choices.)

Sociodrama

7. Thomas Jefferson and Alexander Hamilton are discussing their differences on the Separation of Powers concept of the U.S. Constitution.

8. Two seniors, Mike and Paul, are members of the student senate. Mike is the leader of a small group of students who want to get an unpopular bill through the senate. Mike wants to make sure that Paul is on his side and approaches him for support.

9. Members of the local city council are discussing the merits of annexing a substantial number of acres to the city. The mayor is also present.

10. An exchange student from Mexico is discussing his problems with a class committee. They have been asked to report their findings to the entire class.

11. Ted Smith has spent two days in the hospital. His parents have just brought him home. Ted knows his parents are upset and have been placed in an awkward position. He decides to discuss how he feels about the inconvenience to his parents.

12. Joe, a high school senior, feels he is unable to afford the cost of the formal senior ball. He has announced his intention to stay home. A couple of his friends are trying to convince him to change his mind as he is the class president.

Simulation games

13. A large labor union is engaged in bargaining for higher wages. Three different locals and two large companies are represented.

14. The school principal is meeting with a committee representative of a local club to solve differences of opinion relative to desirable club activities.

15. Mrs. Smith, the school counselor, is conferring with a student who has been sent to her office for misbehaving in class.

16. Several religious groups are meeting for the purpose of developing a united policy for community action relative to pornographic movies. The movie industry, as well as the city council, is represented.

17. Martha and Joe are attempting to resolve perceived role conflicts of husband and wife. They expect to be married soon.

18. Tom is caught cheating on an examination. He is discussing the matter with his teacher after school.

Case (Situation outline)

19. Ted has been asked to report to the principal for misconduct. The discussion ends with two weeks' suspension from school.

20. Miss Jackson, a secretary for four businessmen, gets deadlines which sometimes cannot be met since there apparently is little or no coordination among her four bosses.

21. Mr. Willingham, the local school superintendent, desires to convince the school board of the merits of a bond issue. Members of the board have gone on record opposing such action.

22. Some local high school girls have been denied an opportunity to try out for baseball in the local summer recreation sports program. They have taken their dispute to local authorities.

23. Joe, after having an altercation with his parents, is cited for speeding on the freeway. The judge is about to "pass sentence."

24. Tom Wyatt has been late to class seven times in the past two weeks. It all goes back to a misunderstanding he had with his girlfriend. Mr. Jenkins, his teacher, has heard his story and is about ready to make a decision as to what action should be taken.

C. Formulate responses to the following as indicated:

1. Sociometry (Criterion question)

2. Sociodrama. *Concept:* Propaganda can influence public policy.

    a. Broad situation

    b. Analysis of the enacted situation (Two key questions)

3. Simulation game. *Concept:* Same as the above.

    Scenario outline

4. Case method

    Analysis of the problem (Two key questions)

More important than any body of organized course work is the ability to get along amicably with others. Simulation and related techniques offer opportunities for accomplishing such an end *through the avenue of course work*. Thus your successful completion of this LAP deserves special commendation. Even if you failed to reach the recommended mastery level, do not despair. Study the answers to the posttest, especially noting supporting reasons for both correct and incorrect items in Part B. Then try the test again.

ANSWERS TO PREASSESSMENT ITEMS

You can make these items a most valuable learning experience by studying the provided reasons for both correct and incorrect responses. You will note that since part A has no specific number of correct responses, several additional points (characteristics) have been provided. Because the last part calls for your constructed responses, your own answers may not be identical to those supplied by the writer. You should be able to decide whether your answers are reasonably accurate, however.

A. *Sociometry*

1. Based upon the assumption that a youngster works most effectively with his or her preferred associates.

2.   Is confidential in nature.

3.   Designed primarily to assist those who have "low" sociometric status.

4.   It is presumed that sociometric data will be used along the lines promised.

5.   As friendship patterns do change, new data and new grouping arrangements are effected every six to eight weeks.

Sociodrama

6.   The situation must be immediate to the lives of students.

7.   Spontaneity is essential, i.e., one plays a role according to feelings during the enactment.

8.   Enacted roles are selected from volunteers.

9.   One does not play a specifically identifiable life role.

10.   There is no "right" or "wrong" way of playing the roles.

11.   Analysis of the enactment is based on feeling reactions of the players.

Simulation games

12.   Complex human interaction is emphasized, usually involving some form of group decision.

13.   Wins and losses are determined by some kind of payoff (tokens, points, etc.).

14.   Roles in a simulation game are not necessarily immediate to the lives of students, e.g., a number of games on political relations have been used effectively. The objective is enhanced understanding of such processes.

Case method

15.   Analysis is based on actual case facts; feelings expressed in the case are facts.

16.   Emphasis is placed on relationships of all parties to the conflict.

17   A problem-solving case ends with an impending decision.

18.   Case questions are designed to encourage individual reflection in advance of the actual case analysis.

19.   The case method may be used as a vehicle for solving a problem or for the derivation of principles.

B. 1   (Here we have a realistic criterion question that can be carried out.)

4   (Again the question is specific and a prelude to direct action.)

5   (Dictates the specific action to be taken.)

7   (An immediate situation close to the lives of students.)

12   (The situation is realistic and brings up a definite problem.)

13   (Involves a conflict, with several interacting parties.)

14   (A realistic situation, complex enough to include several related problems.)

16   (Again the situation pinpoints a number of related problems.)

17   (This is a realistic situation that provides the setting for bringing into the picture several interrelated forces.)

19   (A realistic problem, involving a conflict.)

23   (A fairly simple, realistic situation in which important relationships are involved.)

24   (A realistic situation, based on a conflict.)

Reasons for incorrect items

2   ("Best friends" are not always those one would choose for a specific situation.)

3   (Unless a party is planned and some subgrouping is to be arranged, this is not a realistic problem.)

6   (The criterion question must be one that will be acted upon.)

8   (The sociodrama situation must be immediate to the lives of students. Since this is a simulation, it would not involve an actual instance as cited.)

9   (Students cannot realistically project themselves into roles that they have not lived.)

10   (Students have not lived the roles of "two Cuban Nationals.")

11   (Students do not play their identifiable life roles.)

15   (This fails to suggest a variety of interacting elements.)

18   (Not complex enough as stated.)

20   (A case is based upon a conflict; none exists here.)

21   (The decision in a case is left for the student to reach.)

22   (There is no conflict involved.)

C. 1.   Sociometry

Criterion question

(Any situation that is specific enough to be carried out.)

Example: Indicate five choices, in order of preference, for a committee. (Will be forming committees for our next project work.)

2.   Sociodrama

a. Broad situation

(Responses must be immediate to the lives of students and specific in nature.)

Example: As a result of recent student picketing in protest of the exclusion of blacks from an athletic club, the president of the organization is discussing the matter with the school principal.

b. Analysis of the situation

How did you feel (to each of the players)?

What clues did we (the audience) pick up which may have accounted for these feelings?

3. Simulation games

Scenario outline

(Similar to the broad situation for the sociodrama except that a number of groups become involved.)

Example: Blacks and other minorities; the club members; the administration; the community; the school board.

4. Case method

Analyzing the problem

What key facts and feelings have a bearing on the problem?

What important relationships must be considered?

ANSWERS TO SELF-ASSESSMENT ITEMS

Self-assessment items are designed to help you gain depth of understanding as you proceed through the various learning activities. Most of them do not have single correct answers. For feedback, however, you should compare your answers with the samples provided here.

A. (1) Those who need the most help (isolates and neglectees) receive the least help. They usually find themselves off in a corner by themselves or with other "low"-status individuals.

(2) The isolate is of first concern. Each person has one choice as promised. By breaking up tight cliques, expanded interaction is possible.

(3) By thinking of a practical life situation and tying to the concept.

(4) The party being helped will react on the basis of a frame of reference that only he knows—which he lives. Therefore, those who are leading the situation leave, while such elements as the home situation and other out-of-school factors are developed.

(5) By guiding students into identification of related situations and problems. This enables them to see that generalizations of one social situation frequently apply to other situations.

(6) In real life some parties to a dispute enter into the situation with greater strength than others. Thus such points add realism to the game.

(7) By including (often with direct quotes) in the case itself. Expressed feelings in the case become facts to be considered.

Option B₁. (1) Sociometric data are collected with a promise that they will be used within the immediate group. Moreover, specific questions are more likely to reveal the student's true social status.

(2) (a) Three or four members may "gang up" to exclude one member (perhaps the isolate.)

(b) Ethnic minorities may not be accepted by the rest of the group.

(c) Friendship preferences do change (usually slowly but sometimes rather suddenly). Thus an intolerable situation can arise.

(3) By asking each in turn how he or she felt in the situation and then eliciting clues to these feelings from the rest of the class.

(4) Defend. Analysis deals with clues to actual feeling reactions and the derivation of generalizations therefrom. "Rightness" or "wrongness" never enters the analysis.

(5) Such individuals are likely to capture the realism of the assigned roles.

(6) By merely recognizing key points and then shifting back to these during the alternative phase of the discussion.

Option B$_2$. (1) If one is viewed as himself, instead of as a role-player, analysis is severely limited. (This, in effect, changes sociodrama to psychodrama, which must be handled by an expert.)

(2) Defend. Analysis deals with clues to actual feeling reactions and the derivation of generalizations therefrom. "Rightness" or "wrongness" never enters the analysis.

(3) Such individuals are most likely to capture the realism of the assigned roles.

(4) This adds realism by suggesting the notion of "winning" or "losing" as a result of specific actions.

Option C$_1$. (1) An individual "high" in sociometric standing is probably popular simply because he or she does not deliberately hurt the feelings of others unnecessarily.

(2) Although this is usually the case, sometimes an individual is a "loner" by choice. Sociometric analysis merely discloses what exists. It does not indicate why.

(3) When the actors start repeating themselves or (rarely) when one or the other attempts to "analyze" the behavior of another.

(4) Permits application of new insights gained from the original analysis.

(5) This adds realism by suggesting the notion of "winning" or "losing" as a result of specific actions.

(6) Enables the teacher to focus upon specific points in a certain way. Allows for more complexities in the situation. The case materials can be passed out in advance, permitting a longer time for student reflection on the problem.

Option C$_2$ (A).(1) Sociometric data are collected with the promise that they will be used within the immediate group. Moreover, specific questions are more likely to reveal the student's true social status.

(2) An individual "high" in sociometric standing is probably popular simply because he/she does not deliberately hurt the feelings of others unnecessarily.

    (3) Although this is usually the case, sometimes an individual is a "loner" by choice. Sociometric analysis discloses what exists. It does not indicate why.

    (4) (a) Three or four members may "gang up" to exclude one member (perhaps the isolate).

        (b) Ethnic minorities may not be accepted by the rest of the group.

        (c) Friendship preferences do change (usually slowly but sometimes rather suddenly). Thus an intolerable situation can arise.

Option C_2 (B). (1) When the actors start repeating themselves or (rarely) when one or the other attempts to "analyze" the behavior of another.

    (2) By asking each (in turn) how he or she felt in the situation and then eliciting clues to these feelings from the rest of the class.

    (3) Permits application of the new insights gained from the original analysis.

Option C_2 (C). (1) By merely recognizing key points and then shifting back to these during the alternative phase of the discussion.

    (2) Decisions are based on emotional as well as factual analysis. Thus there is no "right" or "wrong" solution.

    (3) Enables the teacher to focus upon specific points in a certain way. Allows for more complexities in the situation. The case materials can be passed out in advance, permitting a longer time for student reflection on the problem.

Option C_2 (D). (1) Prepared cases seldom emphasize the exact concept(s) to be taught. Moreover, most available cases are more complex than necessary for secondary school use.

    (2) They tend to direct attention to feeling reactions and to generally personalize the case situation.

    (3) Students at this age have difficulty coping with too many complexities. If the case if overly complex, there is a tendency to emphasize certain points to the exclusion of others for no valid reason. If the case situation is extended much longer than one or two class periods, students at this age tend to lose interest.

    (4) Merely to start the processes of reflection with students. Frequently they are not specifically discussed in the analysis.

Optional Activity

D. (1) Students must adjust to the added freedom and responsibilities associated with the technique. Friends will talk; if they are placed on opposite sides of the room, the confusion source is merely expanded.

    (2) In a dramatization the role-player is given a part to play. His or her verbal and nonverbal behavior is usually definitely defined. In sociodrama one plays a role he or she feels as the situation develops. Spontaneity is essential.

(3)   By bringing them into a post-game discussion.

(4)   An impending decision is developed in a problem-solving case, whereas the case for derivation of principles would merely represent an account of a broad conflict situation, perhaps with a solution being offered.

ANSWERS TO POSTTEST

For most beneficial results you should work through the entire LAP before you check your answers to the posttest. Failure to meet the provided minimum standards probably suggests certain weaknesses that need to be corrected. As with the Preassessment items, you will find supporting reasons for answers. It is hoped that this will serve as desirable feedback in your quest for mastery.

A.   *Sociometry*

1.   Based upon the assumption that a youngster works most effectively with his or her preferred associates.

2.   Is confidential in nature.

3.   Designed primarily to assist those who have "low" sociometric status.

4.   It is presumed that sociometric data will be used along the lines promised.

5.   As friendship patterns do change, new data and new grouping arrangements are effected every six to eight weeks.

Sociodrama

6.   The situation must be immediate to the lives of students.

7.   Spontaneity is essential, i.e., one plays a role according to feelings during the enactment.

8.   Enacted roles are selected from volunteers.

9.   One does not play a specifically identifiable life role.

10.   There is no "right" or "wrong" way of playing the roles.

11.   Analysis of the enactment is based on feeling reactions of the players.

Simulation games

12.   Complex human interaction is emphasized, usually involving some form of group decision.

13.   Wins and losses are determined by some kind of payoff (tokens, points, etc.).

14.   Roles in a simulation game are not necessarily immediate to the lives of students, e.g., a number of games on political relations have been used effectively. The objective is enhanced understanding of such processes.

Case method

15. Analysis is based on actual case facts; feelings, expressed in the case, are facts.

16. Emphasis is placed on relationships of all parties to the conflict.

17. A problem-solving case ends with an impending decision.

18. Case questions are designed to encourage individual reflection in advance of the actual case analysis.

19. The case method may be used as a vehicle for solving a problem or for the derivation of principles.

B.   3   (A realistic criterion question which, presumably, is to be carried out.)

     4   (Again, this is a realistic problem that can be carried out.)

     8   (Such a role can be played realistically; the situation is specific.)

   12   (Close to the lives of students, and specific.)

   13   (Involves a complex of interrelated problems.)

   16   (The situation features several different parties, which should have an influence on the outcome.)

   20   (Built around a realistic situation.)

   21   (The merits of a school bond issue are usually widely publicized; thus students should be able to cope with such a problem.)

   22   (An impending decision relative to a realistic problem is structured into the situation.)

   23   (Leads up to an impending decision.)

   24   (Again, an impending decision is imminent.)

Reasons for incorrect items

     1   (A pretty good criterion question, but we no longer ask for rejections as this may create more problems than it solves.)

     2   (This is forcing an indication of preferences that may not exist.)

     5   (Today we ask for five choices.)

     6   (Not realistic unless the class is actually planning a camping trip.)

     7   (One cannot be expected to *spontaneously* enact a role completely foreign to him.)

     9   (Too complex for high school use; also somewhat remote to the lives of students.)

   10   (Few students can realistically simulate the role of an exchange student since they have not lived it. If they have lived it, this is not a simulation.)

   11   (This fails to leave us with an impending decision.)

   14   (Not complex enough for a simulation game.)

   15   (Not complex enough for a simulation game.)

17 (Not complex enough; more like a sociodrama situation.)

18 (Again, this is too simplified; more appropriate for a sociodrama situation.)

19 (The problem is "solved." In a problem-solving type of case, the students are expected to solve the problem.)

C. 1. Sociometry

Criterion question. (Any situation that is specific enough to be carried out.)

Example: Indicate five choices, in order of preference, for a committee. (We will be forming committees for our next project work.)

2. Sociodrama

a. Broad situation: (Responses must be immediate to the lives of the students and specific in nature.)

Example: As a result of some unfounded gossip, you (Kathy) have noticed that some of your best friends have suddenly turned "cold" toward you. You are discussing the problem with an individual who reportedly started the whole thing.

b. Analysis of the enacted situation.

How did you feel (to each of the actors)?

What clues did we (the class group) pick up that may have accounted for these feelings?

3. Simulation games

Scenario outline: (Similar to the broad situation for the sociodrama except that a number of groups become involved.)

Examples: Relationships with other students; relationships with parents; with school authorities; with your boyfriend (or girlfriend, as the case may be).

4. Case method

Analyzing the problem: What key facts and feelings have a bearing on the problem? What important relationships must be considered?

SUPPLEMENTARY SOURCES

The following sources may be used in lieu of the Hoover texts or, preferably, as supplementary to them. Generally they are consistent with the models provided in the LAPs of this module. As such, the references do not represent all of the most recent references in the area; rather, they constitute selected references designed to broaden or expand needed background information.

Bennion, John E., "The Case Method in General Business Subjects," *Business Education Forum*, 20, No. 4: 27 (Jan., 1966).

Bonny, Merl E., and Richard S. Hampleman, *Personal-Social Evaluation Techniques* (Washington, D.C.: Center for Applied Research in Education, Inc., 1962).

Boocock, Sarane S., and E. O. Schild, eds., *Simulation Games in Learning* (Beverly Hills, Calif.: Sage Publications, Inc., 1968).

Brennan, William J., Jr., "Teaching the Constitution," *New York State Education*, 52, No. 2: 11-13 (Nov., 1966).

Garvey, Dale M., *Simulation, Role-Playing, and Sociodrama* (Emporia, Kans.: The Emporia State Research Studies, 16, No. 2: Dec., 1967).

Gillion, E. M., "Trends in Simulation," *High School Journal*, 57: 265-272 (April, 1974).

Gronlund, Norman E., *Sociometry in the Classroom* (New York: Harper and Brothers, 1959).

Hoover, Kenneth H., *The Professional Teacher's Handbook*, 2nd ed. (Boston: Allyn and Bacon, Inc., 1976).

Hoover, Kenneth H., and Paul M. Hollingsworth, *Learning and Teaching in the Elementary School*, 2nd ed. (Boston: Allyn and Bacon, Inc., 1975).

Jennings, Helen Hall, *Sociometry in Group Relations*, 2nd ed. (New York: Greenwood Press, 1973).

Rogers, Virginia M., and Andrew H. Goodloe, "Simulation Games as Method," *Educational Leadership*, 30: 729-732 (May, 1973).

Smith, R. M., "Toward Measurement of Human Communication Through Simulations," *Today's Speech*, 22: 17-24 (Fall, 1974).

Worell, Judith, and C. Michael Nelson, *Managing Instructional Problems: A Case Study Workbook* (New York: McGraw-Hill Book Co., 1974).

Value-Focusing and Creative Activities

RATIONALE.   Based upon his own unique experiences, each individual develops guides to human behavior. These are called values. Values accumulate from experience, existing at different levels of commitment from a mere positive feeling to a compelling urge for action. Fortunately the teen-age years are characteristically a time of questing or searching for reliable guides to human behavior. Conventional values are re-examined, often in new or creative ways. An idea is creative when it possesses an element of novelty, often setting the stage for a new approach to a problem, the production of ideas that are both relevant and unusual, advancing beyond the immediate, or merely producing dissatisfaction with conventional assumptions. Various value-focusing and creative class activities can enhance and objectify the value-examination process.

OVERVIEW

Key Concepts

1. Values are acquired in many ways; while some are the products of reflection, many are acquired subconsciously from various social groups such as the family, the church, or the peer group.

2. Values possess both affective and cognitive dimensions.

239

3. Values can be structured and restructured through processes of reflective thinking. Such instruction must be *personalized*, however.

4. The personalized approach to value testing is often characterized by an element of originality.

5. Creative teaching cultivates originality by a process of deferred judgment (evaluation).

6. The outcomes of value-focusing activities are personal and private for each individual.

New Terms

1. Belief: Essentially cognitive in nature, a belief represents one of the early signs of an emerging value.

2. Feeling: The emotional dimension of a value. Not all values are closely associated with feelings, however.

3. Convergent thinking: Emphasizes dependence on reproduction of existing data and the fitting of old responses to new situations in a more or less logical manner.

4. Divergent thinking: Is characterized by flexibility and originality in the production of new ideas. Sometimes such thinking is featured by a sudden "flash" of insight.

5. Value indicators: Expressions of aspirations, purposes, attitudes, interests, beliefs, and the like.

6. The clarifying response: A brief verbal exchange between teacher and student designed to help the learner think about and perhaps clarify his values.

7. Values sheet: A stimulator (e.g., short story, poetry, cartoon, etc.) followed by a few key questions about the values problem raised. Usually designed as a group experience.

8. Value-clarifying discussion: A short, informal discussion designed to raise issues. Often directed informally to a small group of students rather than to the entire class.

9. Brainstorming: A group process designed to amass as many solutions to a problem as possible in the absence of restraints or evaluation.

OBJECTIVES. After this experience you should be able to effectively guide value-focusing and creative class activities, as evidenced by your ability to:

1. List five out of six characteristic features of value-focusing and creative activities.

2. Select eight out of nine comments or situations conducive to value-focusing and creative learning from a provided list of twenty assorted situations.

3. Prepare five out of six questions (or sentences if appropriate) for the three identified aspects of value-focusing and creative teaching.

PRELIMINARY READING. Since the elements of instructional methodology are somewhat variable, the following excerpts are provided to help you develop a frame of reference as a point of departure for this experience. If you prefer, you may proceed directly to the Preassessment items.

THE PLACE FOR VALUE-FOCUSING ACTIVITIES

Some people contend that teachers must indoctrinate students with the basic values of our democracy. Others are convinced that values cannot be taught at all—that they are somehow "caught" in the home, the church, and the school as individuals interact with others and with life in general. As a result, the schools have all too often steered clear of any systematized procedures for teaching values. This seems strangely at odds with the obvious needs of today's youth who must cope with unprecedented value contradictions and complexities.

The teaching of values, like other instructional methods, involves a process of reflective thought. Since values are intimately associated with emotional responses, unusual precautions are necessary. As Raths and his associates[1] point out, ". . . we may raise questions but we cannot 'lay down the law' about what a child's values should be."

Value indicators of the incidental variety are usually statements such as the following:

> Import duties should be enacted to protect our farmers.
>
> The American Indian must be taken off the reservation.
>
> When I'm old enough, I want to join the navy.
>
> I like to read poetry.

As the foregoing suggest, many such statements reveal what one stands for, what he or she prefers to do, what his or her ambitions may be.

The teaching of values is not restricted to any one method. Rather, it may permeate every method if the right type of question is asked. This is not meant to imply that values are easily developed or altered. Indeed the evidence suggests that value teaching has been woefully neglected and mishandled. All too often teachers have held up the "right" values for students to accept, providing few if any alternatives, and almost no opportunity for the weighing and balancing processes that are necessary.

The logical conclusion to a values discussion is some form of action. Values, by definition, are guides to behavior. Sometimes such action is ill advised simply because the learner does not fully understand the legitimate avenues of choice. A student strike, for example, initiated by the acts of a few, can deny education to a majority. Less drastic forms of behavior may involve some reading on the subject, forming

---

[1] *Louis E. Raths, Merrill Harmin, and Sidney B. Simon,* Values and Teaching *(Columbus, Ohio: Charles E. Merrill Publishing Co., 1966), p. 37.*

friendships or organizations designed to nourish the value(s), collecting and spending money for the cause, conducting a letter-writing campaign, floating petitions, and the like. The teacher will want to guide students in recognizing and evaluating possibilities for action relative to values.

VALUE-FOCUSING TECHNIQUES

Although values enter into almost every instructional technique available to the teacher, there are a few techniques designed especially for personalizing the learning experience (value teaching).

The Clarifying Response. The clarifying response represents a way of responding to what a student has chosen, what is prized, and/or what he or she is doing. Its purpose is to encourage the learner to think about and perhaps clarify his own values. The response seeks to raise questions in the mind of the learner by prodding the individual gently into examining his own ideas or activities. It is not designed to lead the student to the "right" answer; rather, it leaves him hanging in the air. The teacher then moves on without moralizing.
    Clarifying responses may take many forms. To illustrate:

> TOM: If the underprivileged are given a guaranteed annual wage, they will lose all initiative.
>
> TEACHER: How might this condition come about, Tom?
>
> TOM: Well, they will not need to work.
>
> TEACHER: Can you give me an example?
>
> JOE: Last night I read a whole book on the life of Napoleon.
>
> TEACHER: Do you enjoy reading about war heroes, Joe?
>
> JOE: Yes, I certainly do.
>
> TEACHER: Do you see war as one acceptable solution to problems?
>
> JOE: Not necessarily. I just enjoy the movement—the courage displayed by some military leaders.

The Values Sheet. Unlike the clarifying response, the values sheet is designed as a group experience. The instrument begins with a stimulator. This can come from novels, essays, short stories, quotations, poetry, cartoons, and the like. This is followed by a few key questions designed to help the student clarify his thinking about the values problem raised by the stimulator. Since valuing is individualistic in nature, each student completes the values sheet on his own. Later, responses from different students may be shared in small- or large-group discussions.
    The illustration was developed for use in a high school English class.[2]

---

[2] *Howard Kershenbaum and Sidney B. Simon, "Teaching English with a Focus on Values,"* English Journal, *58: 1071-1076 (Oct., 1969).*

"In Germany, first they came for the Communists, and I didn't speak up because I wasn't a Communist. Then they came for the Jews, and I didn't speak up because I wasn't a Jew. Then they came for the trade unionists, and I didn't speak up because I wasn't a trade unionist. Then they came for the Catholics, and I didn't speak up because I was a Protestant. Then they came for me—and by that time no one was left to speak up."—
Pastor Martin Niemoller

1. What category are you in? When would they have come for you?

2. Is there something in your school, some "injustice" about which you might well speak out?

3. Why stick *your* neck out? Why not?

4. If you decide to speak up, how do you go about it? What are the best ways?

5. Some people say: "We need to value what we do and do something about what we value." Do you agree? If not, why? If so, what have you done lately?

The Value-clarifying Discussion. A value-clarifying discussion, unlike regular class discussion, is usually informal. It is often initiated by some quotation, picture, scene from a play, provocative questions, etc. Frequently it is used as a follow-up of a values sheet, described in the foregoing.

The value-clarifying discussion does not end with a decision or even with a set of generalizations. Instead, the discussion may lead students to consider the next moves that may be taken. (Value clarification often leads to some form of action or activity.) The whole process usually involves a few thought-provoking, personalized questions, followed with some time for mulling over the ideas and comments. Those who want to further clarify their thinking on the issue will do this in private.

Other Techniques.   All simulation and related techniques treated in the preceding LAP are useful as value-focusing activities. The liberal use of "you" questions can enhance the personalized nature of such techniques.

THE NATURE OF CREATIVITY

An idea is creative when it possesses an element of novelty that can be applied to a given situation. The process includes the ability to change one's approach to a problem, to produce ideas that are both relevant and unusual, to see beyond the immediate situation, and to redefine the problem or some aspect of it.[3]

All individuals are creative to some extent. Some individuals, however, are much more creative than others. While a part of this difference may be of a hereditary nature, much of the difference likely results from the failure of many to express their creative potential. In fact, many essential attributes of creativity are all too often

---

[3] *George F. Kneller,* The Art and Science of Creativity *(New York: Holt, Rinehart and Winston, Inc., 1965), p. 13.*

discouraged in the typical secondary school classroom. Some of these include originality, persistence, independence, involvement and detachment, deferment and immediacy, incubation, illumination, and verification. There is some evidence suggesting
that such attributes in a student tend to pose a threat to the teacher and thus are
often discouraged.

Certainly the processes of creativity include the student's openness to his own
hunches, guesses, emotions, and intuitive feelings about facts that have intrigued him.
These personal motivational factors are crucial, resulting in an individual's operating
on feeling as much as on logic. Such a person is not only adept at dealing with fantasy,
imagination, and emotion, but he has the courage to become a risk-taker by venturing
past the edges of the familiar. He is curious about the possibilities and alternatives
that are generally considered inappropriate by his less creative counterpart.

It is interesting to note that creativity appears rather high in the cognitive domain, predominating at the fifth of the six-level hierarchical structure. (See LAP on
Instructional Objectives.) The hierarchical nature of the domain suggests that the
higher levels build upon the lower ones. Thus instruction designed to achieve objectives at all levels below the *synthesis* level (knowledge, comprehension, application,
and analysis) would offer no guarantee of the achievement of objectives of creativity.
This certainly has a bearing upon instructional experiences to be provided.

Group and Individualized Creative Experiences. Perhaps the most basic feature of
creative endeavor is openness to experience. The tendency to "close" on a problem
shuts off the flow of ideas that might produce unique and often superior solutions to
problems. Thus the principle of "deferred judgment" is basic to both individual and
group creativity.

Many have thought of creative thinking processes as purely individualistic in
nature. Recognizing its inborn, developmental quality, we have placed little emphasis
upon techniques for furthering and enhancing group creativity. Like all attributes
of learning, however, it *can be developed through carefully selected class experiences.*
As with other approaches to problem solving, much individualized instruction is
needed. Creative problem solving in carefully organized group situations is not only
effective but economical of time as well.

Both convergent and divergent thinking are essential to the problem-solving experience. When convergent thinking is applied during a divergent-thinking phase
of the problem-solving process, the latter may be seriously impeded. When students
are casting about for solutions to a problem, for example, an evaluation of each idea
as it is presented tends to minimize the flow of original ideas.

Encouraging Individualized Creativity. Basically creativity is an individualized process.
It involves breaking out of established modes of thought. Each person does this in his
own way.

The natural processes of cognitive thinking involve the creation of patterns that
are used over and over again in critical thinking. New information is admitted until it
is seen to fit one of these patterns. Patterns, of course, can be easily manipulated by
extending or combining related elements. Although useful, the patterns of thought
themselves tend to become restrictive. The creative thinker skips, reverses, and in

many other ways alters established channels of thought. He sees the issue or problem in a new way, for example.

Although there is no established pattern for activating one's imagination, there are a number of guidelines that many creative minds have found effective, some of which follow.[4]

1. *Making a start.* Many individuals feel a vague urge to cope with a problem creatively from time to time. Too often, however, a person defers action until he or she is "in the mood," or until he or she can "find the time." There is no substitute for getting started!

2. *Making notes.* Most really creative individuals carry a pencil and note pad with them at all times. Whenever they attend a lecture or meeting of any kind, they take notes of ideas that are prompted.

3. *Setting deadlines and quotas.* In a sense this is a form of self-discipline. Deadlines and quotas intensify emotional power because we thereby make ourselves vulnerable to the fear of failure to meet our self-concepts. The pressure of deadlines tends to force one to become more efficient in daily routines that take time away from creative effort.

4. *Fixing a time and place.* We should take time for thinking up ideas! It has been suggested that this activity might well precede routines. By setting a time and place for such cognitive thought, one may "lure the muse." Some people allow ideas to *incubate* by napping, listening to soft music, or by just sitting quietly in a dark corner. Of course, sudden illumination can come at *any* time, even in the middle of the night. Here again, a handy pencil and note pad ensures retention of an idea that might not be recalled otherwise.

Although creative imagination is a private, individual virtue, guidance and training *can* substantially increase one's output, as in any other area of education. Too often the able, self-motivated person is permitted to shift for himself while attention is focused on the less able and less motivated student. By setting up intermediate check points for term projects, for example, the teacher can see whether an early start has been made. It should be noted that a sudden flash of insight often comes only after one has been intellectually involved with a problem for some time.

Creativity through the Group. The precise relationship between creative imagination and problem solving is not presently fully understood. Most writers suggest, however, that too much emphasis on the formal structure of analytical thought processes is detrimental to creative thought. Routinized activities of any sort seem to be harmful to the process. Through intuitive (creative) thinking, the individual may arrive at solutions or problems which he or she would not achieve at all, or at best more slowly, through analytical thinking. Ideas reached intuitively, however, must be checked and refined by analytical methods.

Brainstorming is one of the few techniques available for combining individualized and group thinking. In brainstorming by far the greatest percentage of time is spent

---

[4] *Alex F. Osborn,* Applied Imagination, *3rd rev. ed. (New York: Charles F. Scribner's Sons, 1962), Chap. 15.*

in individual ideation and judgment. In effect, the procedure introduces *additional* creative effort into conventional problem-solving procedures. It is a technique by which a group attempts to find a solution to a specific problem by amassing all the ideas spontaneously contributed by its members.

In preparation for a brainstorming session, the leader selects a *specific*, as opposed to a general, problem. The problem, "How can I write a better term paper?" is too broad. To narrow the problem, two or three subproblems might be formulated: "How can I improve my paragraph structure?" "How can I create and hold interest?" "How can I pinpoint major ideas?" Questions of what, why, where, when, who, and how often serve to stimulate ideation on a problem. For example, "Why is it needed?" "Where should it be done?" "Who should do it?" "How should it be done?"

It seems profitable to supply the group with a background memo of not more than one page in length at least two days before the session. The memo serves to orient the participants and to let them ponder the problem in advance of the experience. Contained in the memo is a statement of the question or problem and a few examples of the type of ideas desired. An example follows:

> *Problem:* How can I pinpoint major ideas?
>
> 1. In the classroom
>
>   Write out my thought before expressing it.
>
> 2. In written papers
>
>   Use short subheads.
>
> 3. In conversation with friends
>
>   Enumerate my points with 1, 2, 3, etc., designations.
>
> 4. In my home
>
>   Imagine that I am my own most interested listener.

Participants should not be permitted to read off their lists of ideas, however. Such lists should be handed to the leader in advance of the activity.

In preparation for the actual brainstorming session, the leader explains and writes out four basic rules that must be faithfully followed:

> 1. *Criticism is ruled out.* Adverse judgment of ideas must be withheld until later.
>
> 2. *"Freewheeling" is welcomed.* The wilder the idea the better; it is easier to tame down than to think up.
>
> 3. *Quantity is wanted.* The greater the number of ideas, the more the likelihood of useful ideas.
>
> 4. *Combination and improvement are sought.* In addition to contributing ideas of their own, participants should suggest how ideas of others can be turned into *better* ideas, or how two or more ideas can be joined into still another idea.

Brainstorming must be kept informal, except for a recorder (or two) who keeps a written record of all ideas produced. Its function is idea-finding—not dealing with problems which primarily depend upon judgment.

The utilization of afterthoughts is encouraged when the leader asks the participants to keep the problem on their minds until the next day, at which time they will be requested. This can be made as a definite assignment. Such an *incubation* period sometimes produces some of the most valuable of all the ideas.

How a group uses the ideas generated through brainstorming sessions is largely dependent upon its purpose. In most class settings such experiences are designated to suggest new and novel ideas for some necessary class activity. For example, the task may involve techniques of oral or written expression in art, literature, or music. It may involve novel ways of obtaining proper physical exercise, of memorizing, of doing some chore. It may even deal with certain aspects of human relations, such as how to maintain poise when one is made angry. Whatever the purpose may be, ideas must be implemented. This may be accomplished on an individual basis or in subgroups. Sometimes the fruits of various action programs may be shared with the class. On other occasions they may be of a private nature and may not be shared with anybody else except the instructor.

As a culminating experience, the group eventually may draw generalizations based upon various action programs. This enables all members to profit from the experiences of many. Certain experiences may set the stage for the enactment of one or more selected situations for further study and analysis. Sociodrama has been most useful in this connection. (Refer back to the preceding LAP in this module.)

PREASSESSMENT ITEMS (answers provided on pp. 259-60)

This experience is designed to help you gain an overall perspective of the nature of value-focusing and creative activities. After completing these items, turn to the end of this LAP and check your answers. Note that supporting reasons for both correct and incorrect items in Part B have been provided.

A. List six characteristic features of value-focusing and creative activities.
(To illustrate: Value-focusing activities are of a personalized nature.)

Value-focusing activities

1.

2.

3.

Creativity

4.

5.

6.

B. Place a check (√) before nine of the comments or situations you consider conducive to value-focusing and creative teaching.

Value-focusing activities

1. How would you react to the expression that "might makes right," Bill?

2. Many years ago democracy of the common man was emphasized with the election of Andrew Jackson to the presidency. What parallels do you see in the Women's Liberation movement of today?

3. Your suggestion, Susie, that students should elect their teachers is an interesting one. Suggest for us some consequences of such action.

4. The notion advanced in the short story is that one has the right to use whatever means necessary to circumvent laws that he or she personally opposes. What do you think of this idea, Mark?

5. The thirty-hour work week has been proposed. Let's set up some criteria that must be taken into account before we weigh this proposal.

6. What factors were probably responsible for the recent South Boston race demonstrations?

7. Defacing the walls of our school building is bad business. What suggestions can we offer for correcting the situation?

8. In a recent local election less than 10 percent of the registered voters went to the polls. How do you think the situation might be corrected, Tom?

9. It's true, Joe, that some people believe in the adage, "finders keepers." Suppose you had lost your wallet containing a considerable sum of money. How would you feel in that situation?

10. Today we often hear it expressed that reverse discrimination is as wrong as discrimination itself. How would you feel if caught in such a situation, Jack (a black)?

Creativity

11. Before we entertain your idea, Martha, we had better examine the use of the data.

12. Your idea is interesting, Frank. I'm afraid it doesn't tie in with our problem, however.

13. In the past twenty minutes we have advanced a lot of ideas. I believe we have just about enough time to select those that may be pursued further.

14. That flash of insight, Tom, just might work. Before we try it, however, let's do some more background reading. I think you'll find several possible disadvantages to its implementation.

15. That's a good idea, Sally. It obviously meets our criteria.

16. Your proposal is rather "wild," but indeed interesting. I doubt that it is practical at this time, however.

17. Before we do anything with our ideas, let's "sleep on them." Any additional ideas that come to you in the meantime should be recorded.

18. You've suggested several ways of solving our problem. Let's see if we can't come up with some new, fresh ways of coping with the issue.

19. "Miss Jones, can I solve the problem in my own way? I think I've thought of another way of doing it." "Why don't you do just that, Mike. Later, try our way and decide for yourself which is best."

20. Follow the recommended procedure in our math text. Different ways of attack, short cuts, and the like can only lead to confusion at a later date.

C. Prepare two key questions (or sentences if appropriate) for each of the three identified aspects of value-focusing and creative teaching.

    1. Values-level questions *Subject:* Inadequacy of the world's food supply.

    2. Brainstorming problems *Subject:* Pollution.

    3. Brainstorming memo (to the foregoing problem)

If you were able to provide nineteen of the twenty-one requested responses, you can place yourself in rather exclusive company among teachers everywhere. In this case you are probably ready to advance directly to another module. Even if you were able to supply few of the requested responses, do not be discouraged. The Preassessment experience itself is a valuable learning tool if answers are studied (end of LAP). Then, by working through the varied learning activities, you should be able to achieve mastery with little difficulty.

LEARNING ACTIVITIES

Work through each learning activity, complete the self-assessment items, and check your answers before moving to the next one. Note that the last learning activities are optional, depending upon your needs and circumstances at that point. You should be able to complete this LAP in about five hours.

A: *Read.* Re-examine the overview and the preliminary reading sections to this LAP. You will broaden your understanding substantially by studying Chaps. 28(9) and 29(10) in the Hoover texts and/or by studying the selected references listed at the end of this LAP. Note specifically the following points:

1. How reflective processes are involved.

2. The influence of feelings on such activities.

3. The role of evaluation in the processes. (See also criterion-referenced evaluation, treated in the LAPs of the module on Assessment Techniques.)

4. The individualized nature of the processes.

Self-assessment Items (answers provided on p. 260)

    (1)   Contrast value-focusing and creative reflective processes with normal problem-solving procedures.

(2) How do feelings (the affective domain) enter into value-focusing and creative activities?

(3) How do the procedures of evaluating value-focusing and creative processes differ from conventional problem solving?

(4) The individualized nature of value-focusing and creative processes has been emphasized. How do such group activities as the values sheet and brainstorming cope with this problem?

At this point you may select either Option B_1 or Option B_2, depending upon your particular situation. Those who are presently teaching should select Option B_1. Those who are not teaching or who do not have immediate access to students should select Option B_2.

Option B_1: *Modeled demonstration.* Again, there are certain options available for this task. Perhaps the most effective approach to value-focusing activities would be to bring in resource speakers such as from the *Values Associates* group, who may be contacted at Box 591, North Amherst, Mass. 01002.

A list of materials can be obtained from the same group. This may enable an especially qualified teacher (who has had special training in this area) to demonstrate the use of such approaches to teaching. Similar assistance in the area of creativity is available through *The Creative Educational Foundation, Inc.*, 1614 Rand Building, Buffalo, N.Y. 14203.

There are a number of films and overhead transparencies that focus upon techniques of values and creative teaching.* (Generally, you should avoid commentary films at this point.)

Still another approach might be through resourceful teachers in the area. Extreme caution should be exercised at this point, however, to make certain that the frame of reference developed in this LAP is carefully followed. If working along with a group of beginning teachers, observe and discuss each technique, making notes on the following points as indicated. (If working alone, prepare a written critique of your observations and discuss with your supervisor.)

1. Value-clarifying response

   a. The occasion for the episode.

   b. Who initiated the dialogue.

   c. Note the key question (or response) of the teacher that brought out the value-focused experience.

   d. The way the experience was terminated.

2. Values sheet

   a. How the experience was tied into the major unit concept.

   b. How students were prepared for the experience.

   c. Note one or two key follow-up questions or comments that seemed to contribute to value-focused reflection.

---

*Two such media are: Improving Attitudes *(overhead transparency), University of Iowa, A V Center, Iowa City, Iowa 52240;* and Creative Imagination *(film), Pennsylvania State University, Psychology Cinema Register, A V Series, 6 Willard Building, University Park, Pa. 16802.*

    d. How the teacher handled his or her own private views on the matter.

    e. How the experience was culminated

3. Value-clarifying discussion

    a. How the experience was initiated.

    b. Record one or two samples of personalized questions employed by the teacher.

    c. How some form of action was indicated.

    d. How the experience was culminated.

4. Brainstorming session

    a. The problem.

    b. How rules were introduced.

    c. How contributions were treated.

    d. How the group was pushed for greater quantity of ideas.

    e. How afterthoughts were utilized.

    f. How ideas were processed.

    g. How ideas were implemented.

Self-assessment Items (answers provided on p. 261)

(1) Creativity and value-focusing experiences should receive greater emphasis in some subject fields than in other fields. Defend or refute.

(2) Why do some teachers, when employing class discussion, prefer to defer advantages and disadvantages of proposed solutions (hypotheses) to the problem until all have been offered?

(3) Sometimes, in such classes as math or science, a student will propose a solution that, in effect, represents the "long way around." How might such behavior be handled in the interest of creativity and values?

Option B_2: *Preliminary application.* Working in a committee of three to six if possible, in different fields of specialization, set up the following fifteen-minute simulations. If working alone, arrange to have your experience(s) videotaped and replayed for your own analysis. (Provide every member an opportunity to conduct at least one simulation.)

1. Values sheet. Have one or two members of your committee develop and lead a discussion of a values sheet in his or her field of specialization. Discuss the simulation in terms of the following:

    a. Appropriateness of the content of the values sheet.

    b. Key questions asked.

    c. Role of the "teacher."

2. Value-clarifying discussion. Have a second member of your committee lead a value-clarifying discussion. Base the discussion on the following comments supposedly made by one of the committee members:

I am opposed to the Constitutional Amendment on equal rights for women.

Discuss the simulation in terms of the following:

a. The personalized nature of the "teacher's" questions.

b. How the principle of personal judgment was handled.

3. Have a third member of your committee conduct a brainstorming session based upon a unit concept in his or her field of specialization.

Discuss the experience in terms of the following:

a. Brainstorming problem.

b. How continued ideation was stimulated.

c. How incubation was encouraged.

d. How ideas were implemented.

Self-assessment Items (answers provided on p. 261)

(1) Responses to questions in value-focusing activities must be supported by criteria developed by the learner. Defend or refute.

(2) Suppose a student(s) expresses a value that is inconsistent with democratic ideals. What action would you consider most appropriate?

(3) Why is criticism ruled out during a brainstorming session?

(4) How is the sudden flash of insight handled in a brainstorming session?

(5) What is meant by the incubation phase of creativity?

C: *Instructional application.* You will recall that value-focusing and creative activities often are employed along with other on-going class activities. Using your field of specialization as a frame of reference, complete the following as indicated. (Unlike most such activities, brainstorming is an organized group method based upon a definite unit concept.)

1. Value-clarifying response. (Limit to two or three rounds of dialogue between teacher and student.)

2. Values sheet. (Local newspapers and news magazines provide useful ideas, sometimes depicted in pictures or cartoons. Limit your follow-up questions to four or five.)

3. Value-clarifying discussion. Using the provided photosituation (Figure 10-1) as a basis, prepare four or five key questions designed to clarify values. Be sure to use your own field of specialization as a frame of reference. (This experience demands some *creativity* on your part!)

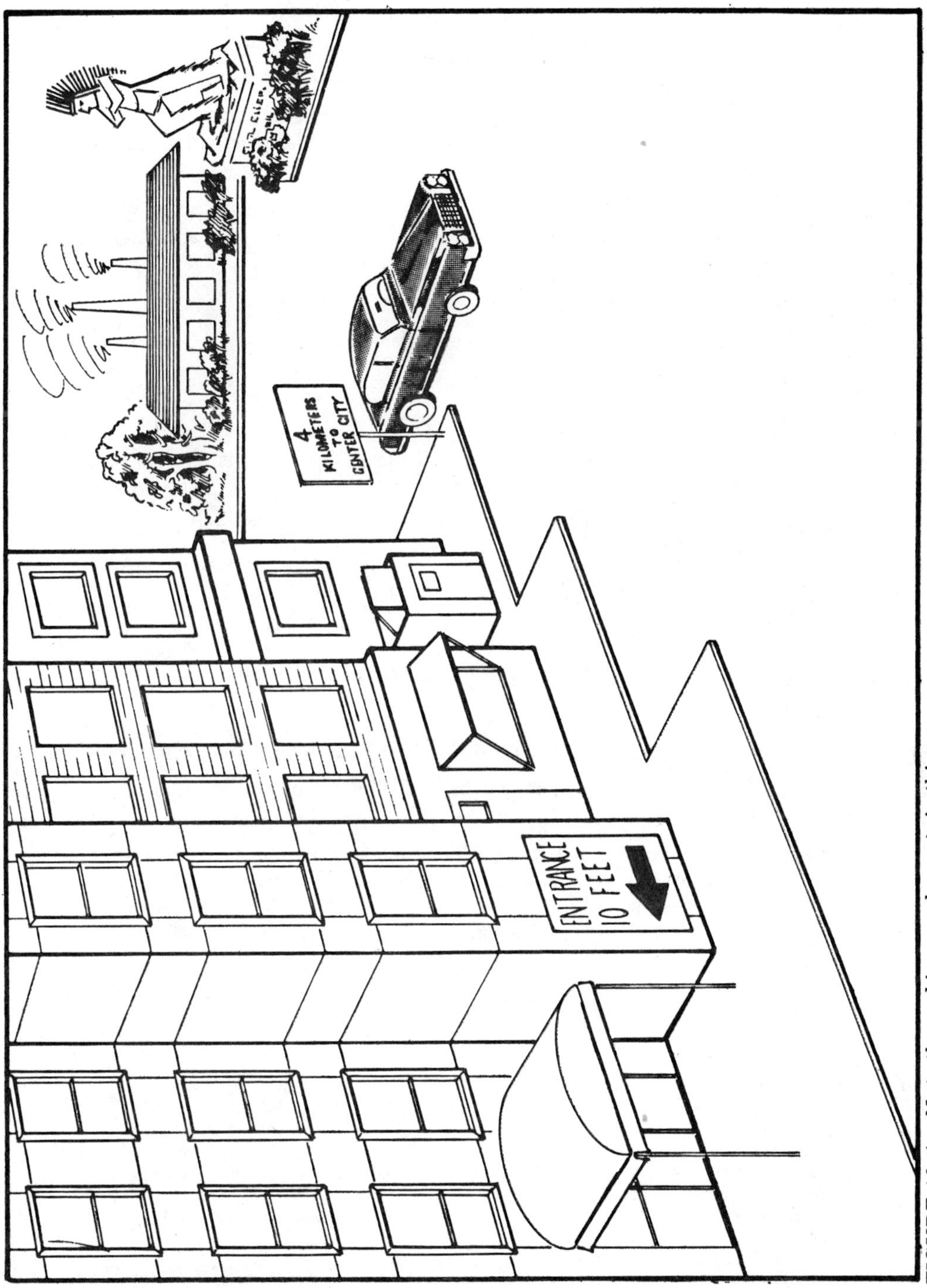

FIGURE 10-1. Note the ambiguous elements in this scene.

4. Brainstorming session. (Base upon a concept in your field of specialization.)

   a. Problem

   b. Memo (categories)

   c. Processing ideas. (Limit your comments to two or three clarifying sentences on how the task would be accomplished.)

   d. Implementing ideas. (Limit your comments to two or three sentences on how this task would be accomplished.)

5. When the above procedures are completed to your satisfaction, *do* (in one of your classes) at least one of the value-focusing activities *and* a brainstorming session.*

6. If working along with other new teachers, hold a post-application discussion of your experiences. (If working alone, prepare a written critique of your experiences.) Focus upon the following:

   a. Major difficulties

   b. General student reaction to the experiences

   c. Time needed for each experience

   d. Value indicators

   e. Ethical limits of value-focusing activities. (The reader is referred to the Fenton reference in this connection.)

   f. Why value-focusing and creative activities tend to culminate in some form of action.

   g. Incidental as opposed to planned instruction in the areas.

Self-assessment Items (answers provided on p. 261)

(1) What value indicators suggest the need for value-focusing activities?

(2) What values (if any) should be "off limits" for classroom instruction?

(3) A value-focusing activity usually culminates with a question such as the following: What will *you do* about . . . (the value)? Brainstorming techniques also culminate with an implementation phase. Why is some form of action thus associated with these techniques?

(4) Since values are personal and private, incidental teaching of values (as opposed to planned lessons) should be emphasized. Defend or refute.

---

*If you do not have immediate access to students, discuss your experiences, if possible, with others who have completed this written exercise. Focus on the following points:

   1. Value indicators.

   2. Ethical limits of value-focusing activities. (The reader is referred to the Fenton reference in this connection.)

   3. Why value-focusing and creative experiences tend to culminate in some form of action.

   4. Incidental as opposed to planned instruction in the area.

If, after reviewing your learning activities for this LAP, you feel that you can meet stated objectives, proceed to the posttest. If not, you should complete at least one of the optional activities.

Optional Activities

D: *Class observation.* Now that you have developed a frame of reference in the realm of value-focusing and creative activities, you will want to see how more experienced teachers apply such techniques. You are likely to note a wide variation between teachers. Since this experience is designed to help you broaden your perspective in this area, no special effort should be made to find "especially creative" teachers. Undoubtedly you will encounter effective techniques other than those emphasized in this LAP. You are also likely to detect certain malpractices.

If working with other new teachers, organize a committee of four if possible, and arrange for each to visit one class as indicated. (If working alone, plan at least two visits, one each dealing with value-focusing and creative activities.)

1. Have one member of your committee visit a class featuring planned value-focusing activities such as the values sheet, value-clarifying discussion, and the like. Make a record of the following:

   a. The value(s) raised.

   b. The personalized nature of the questions asked.

   c. The teacher's role.

   d. How the lesson was culminated.

2. Have a second member of your committee visit any class featuring teacher-student interaction. Make a record of comments as follows:

   a. Value indicators (of students).

   b. Value-clarifying exchanges (between teacher and student and between students).

   c. How the experience was culminated.

3. Have a third member of your committee visit a class featuring brainstorming or related techniques of creativity. Record as follows:

   a. Problem used.

   b. Suggested categories (for "milking the group dry" of ideas).

   c. Requests for afterthoughts (if any).

   d. How ideas were processed.

   e. How ideas were implemented.

   (Note: The last two points of information usually must be obtained directly from the teacher, as they are often emphasized in subsequent lessons.)

4. Have a fourth member of your committee visit any class featuring teacher-student interaction. Prepare brief anecdotes (accounts) of any activity or comments suggesting creative thinking. Indicate how creative episodes were handled.

Attributes of creative thinking:

a. Originality

b. Persistence

c. Independence

d. Involvement and detachment (Able to become detached enough to see the problem in a total perspective)

e. Deferment and immediacy (Tackles a problem but is reluctant to close too soon)

f. Incubation

g. Illumination (Sudden flash of insight)

h. Verification

5. Hold a committee conference following the class observations for the purpose of sharing experiences. Use the recorded data as a basis for this discussion. (If working alone, prepare a written critique of your visits.)

Self-assessment Items (answers provided on pp. 261–62)

(1) In all probability you saw some evidence of the teacher's expression of personal views in at least one of the observed experiences. What is the probable effect of such behavior upon the learner?

(2) It has been observed that creativity has been suppressed in the secondary schools. What evidence, if any, did you gather that would support or reject this contention? Speculate on the reasons for this.

(3) It has been observed that the adolescent, who may consider himself creative in social contexts, is often the least creative of all. Explain.

E: *Values identification.* Every teacher should be keenly aware of the basic values associated with his or her field of specialization. While some of these values may not become the basis for specific lessons, they should each be treated in one way or another. Identify some of these values by proceeding as follows:

1. Write out eight to ten values in your field of specialization which, in your judgment, should be emphasized. (Put in simple, declarative sentences.)

2. Now prepare a list of controversial values related to your field that need attention. Place a check by those (if any) that you consider "off limits" to classroom instruction.

3. For each of your listed controversial values, suggest a value-focusing activity.

4. In one or two sentences, defend your selected activity for each (in number 3 above).

Self-assessment Items (answers provided on p. 262)

(1) Parents and local authorities have a right to ban instruction relative to certain controversial values. Defend or refute.

(2) How can value clarification be assessed or evaluated? (Refer to LAPs on Questioning Strategies and Evaluation Procedures in this connection.)

(3) Value-testing should receive greater emphasis in some classes than in other classes. Defend or refute.

POSTTEST (answers provided on pp. 262-63)

After you have completed the learning activities, complete the posttest and evaluate by checking your answers with those provided at the end of this LAP. Note that supporting reasons are provided for both correct and incorrect selections for Part B.

A. List six characteristic features of value-focusing and creative activities.

Value-focusing activities

1.

2.

3.

Creativity

4.

5.

6.

B. Place a check (√) before nine of the comments or situations which you consider conducive to value-focusing and creative learning.

1. If you caught somebody committing a theft, how would you notify authorities?

2. We have seen how ambition can be the driving force for success. Do you think one can be too ambitious, Nancy?

3. Recognizing that ambition can be misused, let's see if we can establish some criteria for its use.

4. We have seen that an ambitious person can sometimes amass considerable wealth through deceitful means. What might be some consequences of such behavior?

5. What ethical standards will you adopt relative to your desire to succeed?

6. You are too ambitious, Bradley. It's best to patiently wait for the appropriate time for action.

7. What legal safeguards are necessary for re-establishing honesty in government?

8. Must the public continue to bear the cost of shoplifting? What will you do about the problem?

9. Your idea, Bob, is a good one. Why don't you ponder the problem after you leave class?

10. Most would agree with you, Joe, that the poor do need adequate shelter. What would you do to make this possible?

Creativity

11. That's an interesting idea, Pete. Let's weigh the matter for practicality.

12. Before we hear other ideas, let's examine Mike's point in detail.

13. As a result of our recent brainstorming session, we have six new and fresh ideas. Let's now evaluate each of them in terms of the possibility of applying them in our class.

14. You've made a good point, Joe. It meets our criteria quite well, I think.

15. Decide for yourself how you'll complete the task. Let's see if we can't come up with some fresh approaches.

16. You've solved the problem, Dick, but it's the long way around. Let's use the accepted procedure for now.

17. Was your suggestion meant to be a challenge, Bill? You know it would only result in chaos.

18. You've come up with some fascinating ideas. Now let's see how many of them can be implemented:

19. Mary, let's not evaluate Tanaka's proposal just yet. We're not really interested in that, you know.

20. Let's each take today's list of ideas home and decide which of them should probably be applied.

C. Develop two key questions (or sentences if appropriate) for éach of the identified aspects of value-focusing and creative activities.

1. Value-level questions. (Subject: Regulated land use)

2. Brainstorming problems. (Subject: Exclusive clubs)

3. Brainstorming memo. (To your foregoing problem)

One's values largely determine whether one will be happy or sad, law-abiding or outlaw, rich or poor, or any other dimension of living you can imagine. Values and creative expression are very much a part of teaching and learning and should not be left to accident or chance. Your successful completion of this LAP places you in an ideal position to cope with this vexing problem. Even if you failed to reach the recommended competency level of 90 percent, do not be dismayed. Study answers to posttest items, especially noting supporting reasons for both correct and incorrect items in Part B. Then try the test again.

ANSWERS TO PREASSESSMENT ITEMS

You can make these items a most valuable learning experience by studying the provided reasons for both correct and incorrect responses. You will note that since Part A has no specific number of correct responses, several additional points (characteristics) have been provided. Since the last part calls for your constructed responses, your own answers may not be identical to those provided by the writer. You should be able to decide whether or not your own answers are reasonably accurate, however.

A. *Value-focusing activities*

1. They are of a personalized nature.

2. They often occur incidentally during the instructional process.

3. The reflective processes involved are similar to those employed with other instructional approaches to teaching, except that feelings are brought into the open.

4. Since outcomes are individualistic in nature, "rights" and "wrongs" are not emphasized.

5. Emphasis is upon consequences of behavior.

Creativity

6. The method emphasizes the new or the different.

7. Freedom from restraint is stressed.

8. Creative flashes of insight are confirmed through normal processes of reflection.

9. Closure is deferred so that a period of incubation may be encouraged.

10. Although creativity can be sparked at any time, organized group approaches (e.g., brainstorming and related techniques) can greatly facilitate the ideation process.

B. 1 (A personal question directed to one person in class.)

3 (This gently pushes the student into an evaluation of his stand.)

4 (This personalizes instruction.)

9 (This causes the student to project his thinking into his own life.)

10 (This has the advantage of helping the learner project himself into the frame of reference of another.)

13 (All ideas are advanced *prior* to evaluation.)

17 (An incubation period often produces some of the most valuable ideas.)

18 (This is an attempt to stretch students beyond the usual—the conventional.)

19 (Here freedom to pursue one's own ideas is encouraged. At the same time, a later evaluation is to be emphasized.)

Reasons for incorrect items

2 (While this may be a valuable problem to study, it fails to personalize the issue.)

5 (Instruction is not personalized.)

6 (Calls for an evaluation, without personalizing the event.)

7 (Here the teacher passes judgment. No value-focusing activity is involved.)

8 (Same as the above reasons.)

11 (This brings in evaluation and thus stifles the ideation process.)

12 (Here the teacher makes a value judgment; this destroys creativity.)

14 (By the time the background reading is completed, the "flash of insight" will be extinguished.)

15 (Evaluation should be withheld until later.)

16 (This value judgment of the idea's practicality discourages the making of creative or "wild" ideas.)

20 (Such instruction, even if partially true, effectively destroys creativity, which flourishes only in a situation free from restraint.)

C. 1. Values-level questions

(Must be a personalized question—a *you* question.)

What will *you* do to preserve food?

Would *you* limit the size of *your* family if you knew that it would prevent some individual in the world from starving to death?

2. Brainstorming problems

(Must include categories)

a. Air pollution forms in the classroom

Install exhaust fans in the classroom.

b. School ground pollution

Impose a penalty for anyone caught littering our school yard.

ANSWERS TO SELF-ASSESSMENT ITEMS

Self-assessment items are designed to help you gain depth of understanding as you proceed through the various learning activities. Most of them do not have single correct answers. For feedback, however, you should compare your answers with the samples provided here.

A. (1) Value-focusing activities: Encourage the individual to view the value in terms of consequences. "Right" or "wrong" solutions are carefully avoided.

Creative activities: Encourage the new, the different, often characterized by a sudden flash of insight at any point in the process. Evaluation is withheld until later.

(2) Value-focusing activities: The processes are personalized, emphasizing what "you" would do in the situation.

Creative processes: Bold guessing (playing the hunches) is encouraged.

(3) Value-focusing activities: The student is asked to decide what he would do in a specific situation and then to project the consequences of his behavior. "Rights" and "wrongs" are carefully avoided.

Creative processes: Ideas of all kinds and descriptions are encouraged. Evaluation is deferred until later.

(4) Values sheet: Although feeling reactions are stressed in the group, it is expected that the student will mull over the ideas later, on his own. Brainstorming: Definite provision is made for individual ideation in the form of afterthoughts that are later solicited.

Option B₁. (1) Refute, with some qualification. There are values to be considered in every field. They represent an essential part of every course. The scientist must decide the impact of a discovery or technique on mankind just as the physical education major must employ appropriate ethics in competitive sports.

In some classes, however, the major thrust of the entire course may deal with values (e.g., literature classes). Thus greater emphasis can be expected in such classes.

(2) Evaluation is a constant threat to creativity. The usual procedure of evaluating each proposal, in turn, tends to stifle the free flow of ideas.

(3) Entertain the idea with some reinforcement, but then challenge the individual to come up with a more efficient idea (which may still be different from the usual approach).

Option B₂. (1) Defend. All questions at the evaluation level demand this. Adequacy of a response must be assessed in terms of the student's rationale. (Refer to LAP on Questioning Strategies.)

(2) Use personalized questions to probe the consequences of the value. Avoid telling the person how to feel, since feelings are private.

(3) Criticism tends to block creative thinking by setting up barriers.

(4) By giving preference to those who are "bursting to contribute." This encourages "hitchhike" ideas.

(5) Apparently the mind "continues on," subconsciously, after the initial experience has ended.

C. (1) Statements or questions involving aspirations, purposes, attitudes, interests, beliefs, and the like. Example: When I finish school, I want to make a lot of money.

(2) Only those (usually codified into law) of a purely noncontroversial nature. Any value that is controversial for a substantial number of students (even though it may not be for the teacher) is open to examination.

(3) Values and original ideas are springboards for action. Consistency between values and behavior is to be encouraged.

(4) Refute. Both are needed. Since subject areas involve values, planned lessons are essential in some cases.

Optional Activities

D. (1) Occasionally the student may argue his or her views with the teacher. Usually, however, the individual will merely withdraw, keeping his or her values "private." Thus the instructional purpose (of open examination) is defeated.

(2) The creative student tends to pose a threat to the teacher as he or she challenges the prepared order and structure of class activities.

(3) Many adolescents, by mode of dress or speech, seek to be different (from adults) but, in so doing, place themselves into a rigid mold of the adolescent crowd.

The truly creative person is different because of his or her manner of thinking. Thus he or she is likely to differ (at times) from both adults and the peer group.

E. (1) Refute. To the extent that this applies to the values directly associated with the subject matter being taught, it is the teacher's responsibility to dwell upon such values. It should be noted, however, that indoctrination in a prescribed point of view is *not* ordinarily appropriate. Value-focusing activities leave decision making to the student.

(2) Questions at the evaluation level must be supported by the student's own rationale. If the rationale is adequate, then the answer must be accepted.

(3) Some classes (such as those in literature) are primarily concerned with values; others are not. Thus one would expect greater emphasis in some classes than in others. All classes, however, must bring in *some* value-focusing activities.

ANSWERS TO POSTTEST

For most beneficial results you should work through the entire LAP before you check your answers to the posttests. Failure to meet the provided minimum standards probably suggests certain weaknesses that need to be corrected. As with the Preassessment items, you will find supporting reasons for answers. It is hoped that this will serve as desirable feedback in your quest for mastery.

A. *Value-focusing activities*

1. They are of a personalized nature.

2. They often occur incidentally during the instructional process.

3. Emphasis is upon consequences of behavior.

4. The reflective processes are similar to those employed with other instructional approaches to teaching, except that feelings are brought into the open.

5. Since outcomes are individualistic in nature, "rights" or "wrongs" are not emphasized.

Creativity

6. The method emphasizes the new or the different.

7. Freedom from restraint is stressed.

8. Creative flashes of insight are confirmed through normal processes of reflection.

9. Closure is deferred so that a period of incubation may be encouraged.

10. Although creativity can be sparked at any time, organized group approaches (e.g., brainstorming and related techniques) can greatly facilitate the ideation process.

11. Evaluation is withheld until after ideas have been generated.

B. 2 (A value associated with a lesson that is personalized by the teacher.)

  4 (Such a statement, personalized for the individual, encourages the student to think through the problem for himself.)

  5 (A personalized question for the student to ponder.)

  8 (Most value-focusing activities appropriately are culminated in a "call for action" as is done here.)

  10 (Takes the student into the realm of action designed to support his value.)

  13 (Ideas are generated; then they are evaluated.)

  15 (Guides students in breaking away from the usual.)

  19 (By withholding evaluation, the teacher is encouraging the continued free flow of ideas.)

Reasons for incorrect items

  1 (Assumes the "right" action to take.)

  3 (Assumes a certain value as a basis.)

  6 (This is passing judgment; let student make his own evaluation.)

  7 (Assumes a value; students must themselves evolve such a value.)

  9 (By saying "your idea [presumably a value] is a good one," the teacher is evaluating. Rather, the student should be gently guided into reaching the decision for himself if he will.)

  11 (Evaluation is withheld until all ideas have been generated.)

  12 (Same as above.)

  14 (Such an evaluation stifles creativity; withhold until all points have been made.)

  16 (This discourages students from thinking for themselves. Let student himself discover this.)

  20 (Appropriately includes evaluation *after* the generation of ideas, but omits afterthoughts.)

C. 1. Values-level questions

  (Must be a personalized question—a *you* question.)

  What can *you* do to encourage regulated land use?

  Would *you* be willing to have some agency decide whether you could use your own land for a particular purpose or not?

  2. Brainstorming problems

  (Must be specific as opposed to general in nature.)

  How can "exclusive clubs" be prevented from excluding one on the basis of race or sex?

  How can exclusive clubs be made more democratic?

  3. Brainstorming memo

  (Must include categories.)

  a. Exclusive social clubs

   Eliminate them.

  b. Exclusive honor societies

   Make sure that all individuals have an equal opportunity to qualify.

SUPPLEMENTARY SOURCES

The following sources may be used in lieu of the Hoover texts or, preferably, as supplementary to them. Generally they are consistent with the models provided in the LAPs of this module. As such, the references do not represent all of the most recent references in the area; rather, they constitute selected references designed to broaden or expand needed background information.

Barr, Robert D., ed., *Values and Youth* (Washington, D.C.: National Council for the Social Studies, 1971).

deBono, Edward, *Lateral Thinking: Creativity Step by Step* (New York: Harper and Row, Publishers, 1970).

Fenton, Edwin, *Teaching the New Social Studies in Secondary Schools* (New York: Holt, Rinehart and Winston, Inc., 1966), Chap. 3.

Hahn, Robert O., *Creative Teachers: Who Wants Them?* (New York: John Wiley and Sons, 1973).

Harmin, Merrill, Howard Kirschenbaum, and Sidney B. Simon, *Clarifying Values Through Subject Matter* (Minneapolis, Minn.: Winston Press, Inc., 1973).

Hawley, Robert C., and Isabel L. Hawley, *Value Exploration through Role Playing* (New York: Hart Publishing Co., Inc., 1974).

Hoover, Kenneth H., *The Professional Teacher's Handbook*, 2nd ed. (Boston: Allyn and Bacon, Inc., 1976), Chaps. 28 and 29.

Hoover, Kenneth H., and Paul M. Hollingsworth, *Learning and Teaching in the Elementary School*, 2nd ed. (Boston: Allyn and Bacon, Inc., 1975), Chap. 10.

Lewis, H. P., "What Research Says to the Teacher about Developing Creativity," *Art Education*, 24: 32-35 (May, 1971).

Osborn, Alex F., *Applied Imagination*, 3rd rev. ed. (New York: Charles Scribner's Sons, 1963).

Raths, Louis E., Merrill Harmin, and Sidney B. Simon, *Values in Teaching* (Columbus, Ohio: Charles E. Merrill Publishing Co., 1966).

Ringness, Thomas A., *The Affective Domain in Education* (Boston: Little, Brown & Co., 1975).

Simon, Sidney B., "Value-Clarification vs. Indoctrination," in J. Michael Palardy, *Teaching Today: Tasks and Challenges* (New York: Macmillan Publishing Co., Inc., 1975), Chap. 22.

Simon, Sidney B., Leland W. Howe, and Howard Kirschenbaum, *Values Clarification: A Handbook of Practical Strategies for Teachers and Students* (New York: Hart Publishing Co., Inc., 1974).

Torrence, E. Paul, *Encouraging Creativity in the Classroom* (Dubuque, Iowa: William C. Brown Publishers, 1970).

Triadis, Harry C., *Attitude and Attitude Change* (New York: John Wiley and Sons, Inc., 1971).

Worell, Judith, and C. Michael Nelson, *Managing Instructional Problems: A Case Study Workbook* (McGraw-Hill Book Co., 1974).

module
V

FUNDAMENTAL
APPROACHES
TO LEARNING

Teachers have been justifiably criticized for dominating the learning experience. Prescriptions of what and how to think and to behave closely parallel techniques of dictators. Democratic living, on the other hand, demands considerable individual initiative and independence.

Perhaps this "undemocratic" stigma of some of the methods and techniques treated in this module has accounted for their considerable misuse and neglect. The lecture method, for example, has been referred to as an outmoded method by some, despite the fact that some form of informal lecture is needed at frequent intervals in almost every class. Some methods demand considerable teacher domination. If used appropriately, however, the degree of this domination need not be stifling or oppressive, as indicated in the first LAP in this module.

Teachers are discovering that the basic skills are not necessarily mastered in the elementary school. Some secondary students need remedial instruction in reading, for example. *All students* need special instruction in coping with the language of different subject areas. This is the logical task of each classroom teacher. Accordingly, developmental reading techniques are treated in the second LAP of this module. Emphasis is placed upon comprehension and variable reading techniques needed in specialized areas.

Formal and Informal Lecture Procedures

RATIONALE. It has been established that from one-third to one-half of the average teacher's day is devoted to telling, showing, or explaining activities. Ask any student why he or she likes the teacher and he is likely to say, "My teacher can explain things well," or, "I like the way he outlines his points." Even school supervisors often rate teachers on their ability to explain or clarify points.

Strictly speaking, there is no single lecture method. When the teacher (or a student) tells, explains, or shows, he is essentially employing the informal lecture method. Such expository techniques may be used at any point of a lesson when it becomes obvious that outside assistance is needed. They also may be used as the major focus of a lesson if kept short and simple. Frequently the lecture is combined with other methods such as the demonstration.

The formal (large-group) lecture (originally conceived as a technique for resolving issues *for* students) today essentially serves a similar function to the informal lecture or lecturette. Its use in today's middle and seconday schools is (or should be) employed primarily in situations featuring such instructional innovations as open-spaces plans, team-teaching and modular-scheduled classes, often involving large groups (up to 300 or more) and sometimes extending from forty to sixty minutes in length. The formal lecture is often used in such situations as a basic dimension of a planned learning sequence featuring such elements as large- and small-group activities, independent and semi-independent study activities.

OVERVIEW
Key Concepts

1. The informal lecture (lecturette) is a flexible technique often used as a supplement to other methods.

2. The lecture is frequently broken up in various ways to accommodate student feedback.

3. The lecture is usually more effective when hearing is supplemented with visual experiences.

4. The formal lecture usually sets the stage for a structured series of activities.

5. The lecturer establishes set induction by foreshadowing his or her lecture organization.

New Terms

1. Advanced organizer: A technique for developing set induction (intent to remember) for the learner. Sometimes referred to as the initial summary.

2. Closure: Summary. Sometimes referred to as the final summary, the technique involves restating major points as the lecture is culminated.

3. Catch title: A startling or compelling statement used to capture immediate attention at the beginning of the lecture presentation.

4. Attention span: The length of time a fairly mature student can listen effectively. This ranges from three to ten minutes for unmotivated students to about twenty minutes for able, motivated students.

OBJECTIVES. After this experience you should be able to utilize effective lecture procedures in your classes, as evidenced by your ability to:

1. List eight of the basic characteristics of formal and informal lecture.

2. Select eight out of nine appropriate lecture situations from a provided list of twenty assorted situations.

3. Formulate a key statement for each of six identified phases of the lecture method.

PRELIMINARY READING. Since the elements of instructional methodology are somewhat variable, the following excerpts are provided to help you develop a frame of reference as a point of departure for this experience. If you prefer, you may proceed directly to the Preassessment items.

ESTABLISHING INTENT TO REMEMBER (SET)

A lecture (demonstration or report) can be most interesting but quickly forgotten. The lecturer develops *set* to remember by revealing his or her organizational structure in introductory remarks.

In any given learning sequence, the first and the last parts are most readily recalled. Capitalizing upon this basic psychological principle, the lecturer skillfully employs repetition by providing an advanced organizer for the purpose of foreshadowing the main points. He also provides a final summary (closure) in which main points are restated. A speech teacher once expressed the idea in these words, "Tell your listeners what you plan to say, tell them, and then tell them what you have said."

The Role of Nonverbal Feedback. The notion that a lecture represents a form of one-way communication is erroneous. Indeed, nonverbal communication can effectively guide the speaker when used judiciously. It is easy to say through nonverbal language, for example, that "I am not the least bit interested in what you are saying."

By establishing eye contact with his or her listeners, the lecturer learns to read this nonverbal language. A nod of the head, chuckle, facial expressions of understanding or perplexity all serve as useful tools in communication. A general sense of restlessness on the part of several students can serve as a useful cue to change the activity. Perhaps a short question period is in order. Sometimes an entirely different method may be needed.

Attention span for an oral presentation is shorter than generally suspected. Seldom, if ever, should a lecture exceed twenty minutes. Large-group lectures may consist of two modules of about twenty minutes each. Even so, they must be interspersed with periods of activity. In conventional class settings, an extended lecture (rarely used) is usually broken up into two time periods, separated with a lively question-and-answer session.

The Role of Verbal Feedback. Techniques for eliciting student feedback are limited only by the teacher's imagination. One teacher, for example, structured key questions into his lecture presentation at intervals. These were actual questions to which student responses were expected. After a few minutes of this changed activity, the teacher proceeded on until the next planned question session. The effect was a break in the activity in addition to valuable cues for directing the next lecture phase.

Some lecturers encourage students to ask questions as they arise, breaking their presentations to clarify points as needed. Others, feeling that continuity is threatened by this procedure, entertain questions after each main point of the presentation. A few prefer to entertain questions immediately following the presentation. Regardless of how such feedback is handled, it remains an essential aspect of the lecture and related reportorial methods.

THE LECTURE ORGANIZATION

Oral techniques are usually ineffective unless the speaker captures the imagination of the listeners. He can do this by beginning his presentation with an unusual or startling statement. One student, for example, who was reporting the effects of fluoridation on teeth, began his presentation with, "I hate dental appointments."

When the topic is of considerable interest to the group, one may go into it directly. This is usually best accomplished by reference to the main theme or purpose. The teacher, for example, who finds it necessary to interrupt other class activities to give a needed explanation usually will plunge directly into the points to be clarified. Most reports and demonstrations need a catch title designed to arouse curiosity, and also an attention-getting opening. A startling statement, question, or unusual illustration at the very beginning can gain immediate attention. The student who was to present a report on the effects of fluoridation on teeth might open his or her talk with these words:

> *Your teeth are as old as a forty-year-old man. A man who has lived forty years has lived almost two-thirds of his life; a tooth which has lived sixteen years had lived approximately two-thirds of its life. But with the help of fluoridation, the average tooth may chew well for you . . . .*

The *attention* and *need* steps set the stage for that which is to follow. Usually three or four statements will suffice. The speaker must carefully avoid extending this part of his presentation beyond its usefulness.

It is in the *satisfaction* phase of a presentation that one states references and presents the main points of his talk. The individual can greatly increase the effectiveness of this phase of his presentation by adhering to a simple outline.

1. *Advance organizer.* This consists of a brief enumeration of the main points to be made. For adolescents especially, it is desirable to write these points on the chalkboard.

2. *Detailed information.* Here the speaker brings in supporting facts, examples, and illustrations to clarify the issues. Usually it is desirable to show the relationship between the major points.

Some individuals have difficulty in determining what the main points will be. The reporter can consider breaking his topic into such categories as: time sequence (past, present, future); cause-and-effect relationships; interested parties involved; anticipated problems and their solutions; and topical arrangement.

The speaker completes his discussion of a point before proceeding to the next one. By referring to the original points listed on the chalkboard, he is able to move from one area to another without losing his listeners.

3. *Final summary (closure).* The speaker concludes by restating his main points and important generalizations which have been developed.

The writer who reported on the effects of fluoridation on teeth broke his presentation into three parts: causes of tooth decay; effects of fluoridation; permanence of fluoridation treatment. After placing main points on the board for the benefit of the class, he presented facts and examples designed to clarify each of the main points.

PREASSESSMENT ITEMS (answers provided on pp. 279–81)

This experience is designed to help you gain an overall perspective of formal and informal lecture procedures. After completing these items, turn to the end of this LAP and check your answers. Note that supporting reasons for both correct and incorrect items in Part B have been provided.

> A. List eight basic characteristics of formal and informal lecture. (To illustrate: Considerable repetition is needed.)
>
> 1.

2.

3.

4.

5.

6.

7.

8.

B. From the following lecture situations, place a check (√) by nine of those you consider appropriate for either formal or informal lecture.

1. In studying the sources of tooth decay, Mary is asked to present an oral report on the subject based upon a conference with a dental technician friend.

2. Mr. Thompson lectured for twenty minutes on the merits of the United Nations.

3. Mr. Adler, the shop teacher, demonstrated various safety techniques associated with the use of power equipment.

4. Mr. Jones lectured for forty minutes on the role of strikes in our society as a basis for small-group and independent-study activities.

5. Mrs. Wolbert outlined the various conditions leading up to the Civil War.

6. Mrs. Thomas spent most of the class period explaining a difficult trigonometric axiom.

7. Mr. Clausen briefly explained the basic steps in a two-factor genetic cross.

8. After noting a general math deficiency among most of his students, Mr. Doakes briefly illustrated the major sources of common error.

9. Susie was allocated an entire class period for reporting on "sources of pollution in our community." Her report represented the culmination of an intensive survey.

10. Each member of Tom's committee of three was given fifteen minutes last Tuesday for reports on an assigned project.

11. A fifty-minute film was presented, depicting social inequalities among minority groups. Based on the issues raised, small groups were to be organized for in-depth study and analysis.

12. Mr. Smith spent most of the class period lecturing on "little-known aspects of the events leading to the Dred Scott Decision."

13. The provisions of the school integration law (as described in the text) were re-emphasized for a period of approximately fifteen minutes.

14. Martha asked and received permission to invite her brother to speak to the class about his experiences in the latest war (conflict). He was provided "as much time as needed, depending upon student questions."

15. The algebra teacher normally spends one class period lecturing and the next one answering student questions.

16. The resource speaker lectured for forty minutes and then engaged students in a ten-minute question session.

17. Mr. Smith spent most of the class period lecturing on the problems of school integration.

18. The resource speaker needed fifty minutes for his presentation. During that time he held two ten-minute discussion (buzz) sessions.

19. An informative film of approximately forty-five minutes was shown. The following day it was discussed.

20. A videotaped performance of a forthcoming opponent's recent ball game was shown without interruption. The objective was to look for weaknesses in team play.

C. Prepare one key sentence (or question if appropriate) that meets the instructional criteria for each of the six identified phases or aspects of a lecture lesson. Base your responses on the following lecture problem: What are some basic causes of continued inflation?

   1. Catch title

   2. Advanced organizer

   3. Detailed information

   4. Final summary (closure)

   5. Lesson generalizations

   6. Follow-through question session

If you were able to supply twenty-one of the twenty-three requested responses, you are to be complimented. This indicates that you already possess a remarkable understanding of a perennially difficult problem for teachers. In this case you should proceed directly to the next LAP in this module (Developmental Reading Techniques). Even if you were able to supply few of the appropriate responses, do not be discouraged, for lecture techniques are probably among the most misused methods of teaching everywhere. Study all answers and supporting reasons, carefully work through the learning activities and the accompanying self-assessment items, and finally use the post-test as still another learning device. You should find this experience rewarding indeed.

LEARNING ACTIVITIES

Work through each learning activity, complete the self-assessment items, and check your answers before moving to the next one. Note that the last learning activity is optional, depending upon your needs at that point. You should be able to complete this LAP in about four hours.

A: *Read.* Re-examine the overview and the preliminary reading sections to this LAP and the one on Instructional Objectives (module on Preinstructional Experiences). You will broaden your understanding substantially by studying Chap. 17(21) in the Hoover texts and/or by studying the selected references listed at the end of this LAP.* Note specifically the following points:

The number in parentheses refers to the appropriate chapter in the abridged edition of The Professional Teacher's Handbook, *2nd ed.*

1. The relationship of a lecture problem to the hierarchical level of the cognitive domain.

2. How the verb "to be" provides a clue to an appropriate lecture problem.

3. The basic similarities and differences between the formal and the informal lecture.

4. The role of feedback in a lecture.

5. The nature of the lecture follow-through discussion.

Self-assessment Items (answers provided on pp. 281–82)

(1) A problem for a lecture may be at a "low" or at a "high" level of the cognitive domain. Defend or refute.

(2) Why is a problem that is appropriate for a lecture considered inappropriate as a problem for most other instructional methods? (Class discussion, for example.)

(3) Why is the formal (extended) lecture considered more acceptable in the realm of instructional innovations than for conventional class use?

(4) Indicate several ways of providing feedback during a lecture.

(5) How does the follow-through discussion contribute to the problem-solving process?

At this point you may select either Option B_1 or Option B_2, depending upon your particular situation. Those who are presently teaching should select Option B_1. Those who are not teaching or who do not have immediate access to students should select Option B_2.

Option B_1: *Modeled demonstration.* This experience can be achieved in different ways. Perhaps the most practical solution would be to arrange to visit one of your local teachers who is well recognized as an effective lecturer. This approach does possess some hazards, however, as each individual tends to develop his/her own peculiarities relative to such methods. (Sometimes one may be an effective lecturer *despite* certain inherent weaknesses.) If such an approach is used, be sure to have the individual attempt to model the approach offered in this LAP as closely as possible.

Another way of acquiring this experience might involve viewing prepared films or videotaped experiences. Many colleges and universities have their own private collection of such media. Most publishing companies have at least one film dealing with lecture procedures.* Although there may be differences between such media sources and the frame of reference developed in this LAP, these are likely to be minor. The lecture method has probably been studied as thoroughly as any other method.

A third possibility would be a prepared lecture by your supervisor, teacher coordinator, or a visiting lecturer especially picked for the occasion.

One such film is entitled The Lecture and Role-Playing Strategy, *University of Nebraska Television Council for Nursing Education, Inc., University of Nebraska, 1800 N. 33rd, Lincoln, Nebr. 68503.*

Focus attention on the following points:

1. Problem for the lecture.
2. How the lecturer got the immediate attention of his/her listeners.
3. Use of an advanced organizer (if any).
4. Use of instructional media.
5. How each main point was focused and developed.
6. How the lesson was culminated.
7. How student questions were handled.
8. Follow-up lessons planned. (This will come directly from the lecturer.)

If possible, hold a post-observation discussion with other new teachers who completed this experience. Use the foregoing as a basis for this discussion.

Self-assessment Items (answers provided on p. 282)

(1) An important function of the informal lecture is the resolution of issues for students. Defend or refute.

(2) What role does the advanced organizer play in the lecture?

(3) Occasionally a lecturer entertains student questions at any point during the presentation, using them as a general guide for the lecture. Why is such a practice usually discouraged?

Option B$_2$: *Developing a preliminary lecture outline.* Using one of your unit concepts as a basis (developed in the module on Preinstructional Experiences), prepare the outline of a lecture presentation as indicated.*

1. Lecture problem.
2. Attention-getting statement (or question).
3. Advanced organizer (limit to three main points).
4. Detailed information (limit to one illustration or example for each main point).
5. Developing closure (final summary).
6. Deriving generalizations (limit to two examples).

Self-assessment Items (answers provided on p. 282)

(1) Why is an attention-getting statement so important to a lecture presentation?

(2) What role do props (educational media) play in a lecture presentation?

When you have completed this task you may want to compare your responses with samples provided on pp. 285–86.

(3) In what way is repetition structured into a lecture presentation?

(4) Students often inappropriately attempt to take down the lecturer's presentation word for word. Suggest an alternative, using the advanced organizer as a frame of reference.

C: *Instructional application.*

1. Using one of your unit concepts as a basis (developed in the module on Preinstructional Experiences), prepare the outline of a lecture presentation as indicated.

   a. Lecture problem.

   b. Attention-getting statement (or question).

   c. Advanced organizer (limit to three main points).

   d. Detailed information (limit to one illustration for each main point).

   e. Developing closure (final summary).

   f. Deriving generalizations (limit to two examples).

2. Working in a committee of four if possible, in the same field of specialization, have each member *conduct* in one of his/her classes at least *one* of the following experiences as indicated.* (If working alone, videotape or at least record your presentation and replay for later analysis.)

   a. Have one member of your committee *do* a five-minute lecturette based upon a simulated problem that arises out of some on-going class experience. (Here the emphasis will be upon the advanced organizer and detailed information sections of the lecture outline only.)

   b. Have a second member of your committee do a ten-minute presentation of a preplanned informal lecture in which knowledge expansion is the basic function. Base your lecture on the outline provided in the foregoing.

   c. Have a third member of your committee do a formal lecture of about twenty to thirty minutes, designed as a basis for subsequent specifically structured activities. Again use the lecture outline provided.

   d. Have a fourth member of your committee do a twenty-minute lecture-demonstration. In this presentation you should employ props, materials, and equipment as appropriate to your subject field. Follow the same basic outline as in the other types of lecture.

   e. Hold a committee conference on your experiences, based upon the lecture outline provided. Note differences between the experiences and speculate on their impact on students. (If working alone, prepare a written critique of your experiences.)

Self-assessment Items (answers provided on p. 282)

(1) Compile a list of as many functions of a lecture as you can.

If you do not have immediate access to students prepare simulated minilecture presentations with other new teachers. Let members of your group play the role of your students.

(2) A lecture is useful when a teacher is pressed for preparation time. Defend or refute.

(3) By referring to the LAP on Concept Formation, you will note the point that lesson generalizations ordinarily cannot be derived *for* students. How can this statement be reconciled with the lecture method which features lesson generalizations sometimes derived by the lecturer himself?

(4) In what ways is repetition structured into the lecture presentation?

(5) Students often inappropriately attempt to take down the lecturer's presentation word for word. Suggest an alternative, using the advanced organizer as a frame of reference.

If, after reviewing your learning activities for this LAP, you feel that you can meet the stated objectives, proceed to the posttest. If not, you should complete one of the optional activities. Note that they provide for a number of optional situations, depending upon your own individual circumstances.

Optional Activities

D: *Class observation.* Working in a committee of four if possible, arrange to visit middle or secondary school classes featuring a variety of lectures as indicated. (If working alone, one planned [as opposed to an incidental] lecture will probably suffice.) Proceed as follows:

1. Have one committee member visit any class featuring some instructional method *other than the lecture*. Make notes on all incidental lecture situations in evidence (usually ranging from two to five minutes). Note the following:

   a. Occasions for the lecturette.

   b. How student feedback was handled.

   c. How the lecturette(s) tied into the lesson.

   d. Your assessment of the impact of the lecturette(s) upon the ongoing class activities.

2. Have a second member of your committee visit a class featuring a planned informal lecture. Record the following:

   a. The lecture problem. (Sometimes this must be inferred or obtained directly from the teacher.)

   b. How the lecture was initiated. (Often by a "catch" title or question.)

   c. The points of the advanced organizer. (Usually three or four.)

   d. General student behavior during the lecture, such as student inattention or indications of confusion. (Restrict to two or three sentences.)

   e. Instructional media employed, noting effectiveness.

   f. Provisions for feedback. (May be handled in a number of ways.)

   g. Closure techniques. (Often includes a final summary and perhaps lesson generalizations.)

3. Have a third member of your committee visit a class featuring a formal (extended) lecture. (This is often associated with some form of instructional innovation, such as modular scheduling.)

   Record, as outlined in #2 above.

4. Have the fourth member of your committee visit a lecture demonstration class. (The science field often provides an excellent opportunity for such a lesson.)

   Record, as outlined in #2 above.

5. Hold a post-observation committee conference for the purpose of sharing experiences. Concentrate on the following:

   a. Which of the elements of a lecture were omitted (if any) from the lectures? Speculate on the reasons for such omissions and the possible impact on the effectiveness of the lectures.

   b. What additional instructional elements, in addition to those provided in your lecture outline, were employed during the lectures? How effective were they?

   c. Contrast the general behavior of students in the different lecture situations. How do you account for any differences noted?

   d. Discuss the nature and adequacy of student feedback. Can you think of other feedback techniques that might have been employed?

Self-assessment Items (answers provided on pp. 282–83)

(1) It is presumed that discussion in some form logically follows a lecture presentation and its follow-through session. Defend or refute.

(2) The term "lecture-discussion" has been carefully avoided. Offer a brief rationale for keeping the two methods separate with respect to time.

(3) It has been noted that students, when asked to present findings from project work to the class, will always elect to utilize oral reports (lectures) if left on their own. Why is this?

E: *Round table discussion.* Arrange to have two experienced teachers and two high school seniors visit with your group. Make sure that the teachers (from the academic areas) hold different views on the role of lecture procedures. Join them in a round table discussion.

Problem: What role (if any) should the lecture play in teaching?

Focus attention on the following questions:

1. What are some occasions for lecture?

2. What major problems are associated with the method?

3. What common abuses are often associated with lecture procedures?

4. What advantages are seen?

5. How may lectures be improved (from the student's viewpoint)?

6. It has been postulated that while lecture is often useful for the able student, it is often ineffective for the weak student. Reflect upon this statement, offering supporting reasons.

Self-assessment Items (answers provided on p. 283)

(1)   How might one provide for individual differences through a lecture?

(2)   What role do props (educational media) play in a lecture presentation?

(3)   Why are students discouraged from taking down most of what the lecturer says?

POSTTEST (answers provided on pp. 283–86)

After you have finished the learning activities, complete the posttest and evaluate by checking your answers at the end of this LAP. Note that supporting reasons are provided for all answers to item *B*.

A. List eight basic characteristics of formal and informal lecture.

1.

2.

3.

4.

5.

6.

7.

8.

B. From the following lecture situations, place a check (√) by nine **of** those you consider appropriate for formal and informal lecture.

1. Ms. Holt spent fifteen minutes lecturing on the disadvantages **of** student demonstrations.

2. Mr. Bruecker announced, "I know that price controls are a debatable issue. So I've decided to present a twenty-minute lecture in opposition to the problem, and will permit any student an equal amount of time for the other side if he so desires."

3. Bill, who had access to his father's latest chemical equipment, was asked to demonstrate the use **of** the new electron microscope.

4. Several twenty-minute reports were assigned. Each included a brief "discussion" session.

5. Mr. Thorpe announced to his large-group lecture class, "Following this presentation you are expected to develop individual or group problems that you desire to pursue further."

6. The social science teacher spent twenty minutes lecturing on the regular textbook assignment.

7. In order to clarify the new math concept, Mrs. Rassmussen prepared a short lecture involving the use of transparencies and actual objects.

8. Mr. Steele spent the major portion of a class period presenting a lecture on "the merits of a planned economy."

9. "Since none of you were old enough to fight in Vietnam," says Mr. Thompson, "I want to tell you of some of the aspects of fighting that do not get into the history books. My points are based on some of my experiences in the conflict."

10. Since the film was an hour long, Miss Thoreau decided to show approximately half of it today and follow with small-group work. Tomorrow she planned a similar experience for the rest of the film.

11. The resource speaker was instructed to "take as much of the hour as you wish."

12. The science teacher followed his demonstration with a class discussion of the implication.

13. When John raised his hand and was permitted to ask a question, Mr. Thomas suggested that he make a note of the question and bring it up during the follow-through discussion session.

14. Mr. Merkel decided to spend an entire class period on a lecture, saying to himself, "I can't really break the lecture and retain the major theme."

15. Mss. Thames and Thorpe decided to do some "teaming." They agreed to switch classes next Tuesday to lecture on issues of special interest to students.

16. Karen prepared a twenty-minute report, with props and objects. After about thirty minutes Mr. Thorpe asked her to stop so that the class could "discuss" the issues involved.

17. The lecturer's selected problem was, "What action (if any) should be taken to reduce spiraling inflation?"

18. The lecturer introduced his presentation as follows: "Today I'm going to make three main points." He then went into a full analysis of his first point.

19. As a culmination of a series of activities, Miss Mundy presented a brief lecture on the main points that emerged.

20. Mr. Calderwood followed the series of oral reports with a brief lecture in which he derived major generalizations for the class.

C. Prepare one key sentence (or question if appropriate) that meets the instructional criteria for each of the five identified phases or aspects of a lecture lesson. Base your responses on the following lecture problem: Why is early retirement an accelerated trend?

Catch title

Advanced organizer

Detailed information

Final summary (closure)

Follow-through discussion

For your successful completion of the LAP, you deserve hearty congratulations, for lecture procedures are probably the most misused and abused of all instructional methods. Yet they are essential to all instruction. Even if you failed to achieve the recommended mastery level of 90 percent, do not feel too despondent, for the techniques are variable enough to cause confusion. Study the provided answers to the posttest, especially noting supporting reasons for all items in Part B. Then retake the posttest and repeat activities as needed until you do reach competency in the area.

ANSWERS TO PREASSESSMENT ITEMS

You can make these items a most valuable learning experience by studying the provided reasons for both correct and incorrect answers. You will note that since Part A has no specific number of correct responses, several additional points (characteristics) have been provided. Since the last part calls for your constructed responses, your own answers may not be identical to those supplied by the writer. You should be able to decide whether or not your answers are reasonably accurate, however.

A. 1. Considerable repetition is needed.

2. The lecturette is used essentially for clarifying or expanding points that are temporarily blocking the processes of reflective thinking.

3. The lecturette is short, extending for not longer than twenty minutes.

4. The lecturette is often used incidentally as a supplement to other instructional methods. It may be used as a separate lesson, however.

5. The formal lecture is designed to resolve minor problems for students in anticipation of subsequent learning activities.

6. The formal lecture is usually employed in conjunction with instructional innovations as a "launch pad" for other activities.

7. The formal lecture often spans about two time modules, perhaps extending for as long as forty to forty-five minutes.

8. The formal lecture, especially, must be broken into segments involving some form of student interaction (e.g., student questions or comments).

9. The lecture is usually supplemented by a variety of media.

10. Set induction is provided through an advanced organizer and an initial startling or unusual statement.

11. The lecturer must provide adequate time and direction for note-taking.

12. The lecture presentation is culminated with lesson generalizations, derived either by students or by the teacher (depending upon the particular circumstances).

B. 1 (Involves expansion of knowledge not readily available elsewhere.)

   3 (A "lecture-demonstration" in the skills area is basic.)

   4 (Although too long for an informal lecture, the formal lecture is acceptable when used as a basis for other structured activities.)

   7 (Such a lecturette is essential in difficult areas.)

   8 (Again, the lecturette serves one of its most valid functions as clarification necessary for continued progress.)

  10 (This is one valid way of handling committee reports; fifteen minutes is about a maximum time for such presentations.)

  11 (Although normally too long, if used to set the stage for problem solving, it is acceptable.)

  14 (The assumption is that the lecture, possibly an entire class period, will be broken into different activities from time to time as a result of student questions.)

  18 (This is an excellent way of making efficient use of a resource speaker who needs considerable time to get his or her points across. By breaking the presentation with buzz groups, attention is likely to be maintained.)

Reasons for incorrect items

   2 (Although length is within maximum limits, the merits of the United Nations takes students into problem solving. This is an inappropriate function for a lecture.)

   5 (Such information is readily available in any U.S. history text.)

   6 (Most conventional class periods are fifty minutes long; twenty-five minutes is too long for an informal lecture. This is well beyond the attention span of most high school students.)

   9 (Susie's allocation is too long. There is no indication that she will break her presentation into segments.)

  12 (Although Mr. Smith's basic lecture function is acceptable, the time is too long for maintaining student attention.)

  13 (Inappropriate function; content readily available elsewhere.)

  15 (An entire class period is too long for sustained attention.)

  16 (Both purpose and length are unacceptable.)

  19 (Same as in above item.)

  20 (Too long for sustained attention.)

C. Catch title

Any statement or question that catches immediate attention.

Example: Each of us is being robbed every day.

Advanced organizer

A listing of the two or three main points to be covered in the lecture.

Example: Shortages of food and materials; high taxes; power of vested interest groups.

Detailed information

Now for my first point. (The lecturer supplies details, examples, and illustrations as he or she develops each point.)

Final summary (developing closure)

Example: Today we have treated three main points (repeat them.)

Follow-through discussion

Any statement (or question) intended to encourage clarification, *or* a question designed for the use of the lecture as a basis for subsequent problem-solving experiences.

Example: From our lecture let's see if we can develop some ideas for minimizing inflationary pressures. (Of course, the teacher can derive such generalizations if they appear to be rather complex, based on his or her presentation.)

ANSWERS TO SELF-ASSESSMENT ITEMS

> *Self-assessment items are designed to assist you in gaining depth of understanding as you proceed through the various learning activities. Most of them do not have single correct answers. For feedback, however, you should compare your answers with the samples provided here.*

A. (1) Refute. The lecture provides a basis (facts and ideas) for subsequent learning activities. A high-level problem would result in the lecturer's resolving issues for students. This is not an acceptable function of lecture for high school use.

 (2) Almost all other instructional methods feature the entire problem-solving process, necessitating problems of policy. The lecture basically is designed to expand or clarify and to serve as a basis for other activities. Thus it does not encompass the entire problem-solving or reflective process. It should be noted that the traditional college lecture was designed to solve problems for students. Its use in high school, however, is questionable.

 (3) Other activities (e.g., small-group and independent-study) are structured into such programs, thus rendering the lecture a basis for such experiences. While conventional classes, theoretically, could feature this structure, extended lectures in conventional classes are usually inappropriate as ends in themselves.

 (4) Questions at any point during the lecture.

 Questions at intervals, usually following each main point.

 Questions at the end of the lecture.

 Nonverbal expressions, such as inattention, expressions of boredom, and the like.

 Note-taking behaviors, indicating how well the lecture is being followed.

(5) Since the lecture is basically designed to expand and to clarify, the follow-through discussion provides students with the only real opportunity to reflect upon the information or points offered by the lecturer. This, in effect, completes the analysis phase of problem solving and prepares students for the resolution of related problems to come later.

Option B₁.(1) Refute. The informal lecture merely analyzes a problem that, for some reasons, cannot be adequately handled by students themselves.

(2) As the term implies, it provides a much-needed structure for students. The major points are often placed on the chalkboard or reproduced and given to students.

(3) This tends to interfere with the basic organizational structure of the lecture, thus leading to confusion in the minds of some students. It is usually best to provide for student questions at natural breaks or possibly immediately following the lecture.

Option B₂.(1) When not expecting to play an overtly active role, students tend to relax, both mentally and physically. A compelling or startling statement tends to provide a much-needed focus or readiness for those involved.

(2) Introduces the sense of sight to supplement the sense of sound.

(3) Through the introductory and final summaries.

(4) The advanced organizer, consisting of the major points to be made, might be recorded with ample space between points. Then, as the speaker progresses from point to point, an occasional example or illustration, along with basic cue words, completes the student's notes.

C. (1) Inform; expand; clarify; introduce new units or topics; provide illustrations; set the stage for subsequent activities.

(2) Refute. Lecture preparation is probably more time-consuming than most other methods, often involving two or three hours of preparation for each lecture. (This is quite a contrast with an improperly planned lecture.)

(3) Supposedly, the students mentally develop their own generalizations as the lecture progresses. In an informal lecture the students may be asked to derive generalizations as the experience is culminated.

(4) Through the advanced organizer and through the final summary.

(5) The advanced organizer, consisting of the major points to be made, might be recorded with ample space between points. Then as the speaker progresses from point to point, an occasional example or illustration, along with basic cue words, completes the student's notes.

Optional Activities

D. (1) Defend. Small-group activities and the like are generally structured into the learning sequence of such innovation activities as modular-scheduled classes. Likewise, the informal lecture is logically followed by activities essential to the resolution of problems.

(2) Lecture is expository in nature, whereas discussion is a reflective process. By moving from exposition to reflection from one moment to the next, the novice teacher is likely to find himself doing most of the thinking for students.

(3) This seems to the student to be the simplest and least involved method to use. Moreover, students are probably less familiar with other methods; thus instruction is essential. Oddly enough, lecture methods (oral reports) are extremely difficult to do effectively.

E. (1) Since a basic function of a lecture is to set the stage for student involvement, the basic essentials can be offered to all. Then while less able students get actively involved in the learning process, the lecturer can extend his or her presentation to able students, thereby setting the stage for more in-depth analysis.

(2) Introduces the sense of sight to supplement the sense of sound.

(3) In the first place it is unnecessarily time-consuming and laborious. More importantly, however, the lecturer uses many examples and illustrations to add clarity to major points. It helps if the listener merely focuses on main points. Otherwise, there is a tendency to commit every detail to memory, often with little understanding.

ANSWERS TO POSTTEST

For most beneficial results you should work through the entire LAP before you check your answers to the posttests. Failure to meet the provided minimum standards probably suggests certain weaknesses that need to be corrected. As with the Preassessment items, you will find supporting reasons for answers. It is hoped that this will serve as desirable feedback in your quest for mastery.

A. 1. Considerable repetition is needed.

2. The lecturette is used essentially for clarifying or expanding points that are temporarily blocking the processes of reflective thinking.

3. The lecturette is short, extending for not longer than twenty minutes.

4. The lecturette is often used incidentally as a supplement to other instructional methods. It may be used as a separate lesson, however.

5. The formal lecture is designed to resolve minor points for students in anticipation of subsequent learning activities.

6. The formal lecture is usually employed in conjunction with instructional innovations as a "launch pad" for other activities.

7. The formal lecture often spans about two time modules, perhaps extending for as long as forty to forty-five minutes.

8. The formal lecture, especially, must be broken into segments involving some form of student interaction (e.g., student questions or comments).

9. The lecture is usually supplemented by a variety of media.

10. Set induction is provided through an advanced organizer and an initial startling statement or unusual question.

11. The lecturer must provide adequate time and direction for note-taking.

12. The lecture presentation is culminated with lesson generalizations, derived either by students or by the teacher (depending upon the particular circumstances).

B. 3 (Clarification is often done by lecture process.)

    4 (A twenty-minute report, broken up for questions, is one acceptable way of providing information.)

    5 (Lecture in large groups is used today as a basis for direct student involvement in subsequent activities.)

    7 (Clarification of difficult points, supplemented with visual aids, is a fully acceptable procedure.)

    9 (Such expansion of content is desirable, as it probably is not possible in any other way. In this case considerable human interest would likely be in evidence.)

   10 (An innovative way of making use of a needed film that is too long for high school students.)

   12 (A most desirable technique, involving students directly in the reflective processes.)

   13 (This is one acceptable way of getting student feedback during a lecture.)

   18 (Appropriate as an advanced organizer for students.)

Reasons for incorrect items

    1 (Such a problem should be discussed—reflected upon by students. Ms. Holt would likely bias the issue.)

    2 (This is placing the teacher in an unfair advantage; a class debate would be preferable.)

    6 (A three-to-five-minute lecturette on an assignment would be more acceptable. Certainly twenty minutes is too long for such a purpose.)

    8 (Such a problem appropriately involves the processes of student reflection. This is not an appropriate function of the lecture for high school use. Moreover, the lecture is excessively long.)

   11 (Too long, unless the lecture is broken up for questions, etc.)

   14 (Mr. Merkel might better have asked, "Can my students retain the major theme for such a lengthy lecture?" The answer is an emphatic "NO.")

   15 (Presumably they plan lectures that are too long. Of course, if the lectures are broken into "discussion sessions," the procedure would be acceptable.)

   16 (The only problem here is that the lecture was permitted to run excessively long before Mr. Thorpe introduced "discussion.")

17 (The lecturer does not solve problems for students.)

19 (Students should be actively involved in culminating activities of this sort.)

20 (Students themselves should become involved in the derivation of generalizations under such conditions.)

C. Catch title

(Any statement or question that catches immediate attention.)

Example: It's later than you think!

Advanced organizer

(A listing of two or three main points to be covered in the lecture.)

Example: Scarcity of jobs; increased benefits of social security.

Detailed information

Examples: Now for my first point. (The lecturer supplies details, examples, and illustrations as he or she develops each point.)

Final summary (developing closure)

(Treats or goes over again the points in the advanced organizer.)

Examples: Today we have treated two main points (repeat them).

Follow-through discussion

(Any statement or question designed to encourage clarification *or* a question designed for the use of the lecture as a basis for subsequent problem-solving experiences.)

Example (of the latter): From the lecture let's see if we can develop some ideas for helping individuals prepare for early retirement.

Sample responses for Learning Activity B_2, p. 273.

1. Lecture problem

What are the chief contributors to our growing air pollution?

2. Attention-getting statement (or question)

Everyone present was choking, thrashing wildly, gasping for breath. This could be the case for all mankind if our air pollution is permitted to deteriorate unchecked.

3. Advanced organizer (limit to three main points)

   a. Automobile emissions

   b. Industrial wastes

   c. Smoking and related factors

4. Detailed information (limit to one illustration or example for each main point)

   a. Automobile exhaust fumes have been reduced substantially through the introduction of the catalytic converter.

   b. As a result of recent state and federal laws, industrial air pollution has been reduced by more than 50 percent.

   c. More than half the states have recently limited smoking in various places where people congregate.

5. Developing closure (final summary)

Today I have emphasized three main points relative to air pollution:

a. Automobile emissions

b. Industrial wastes

c. Smoking and related factors

(Note that this is a repetition of the advanced organizer.)

6. Deriving generalizations (limit to two examples)

a. Automobile emissions are presently the chief contributor to air pollution in our metropolitan areas.

b. A nonsmoker has the right to clean, fresh air.

SUPPLEMENTARY SOURCES

The following sources may be used in lieu of the Hoover texts or, preferably, as supplementary to them. Generally they are consistent with the models provided in the LAPs of this module. As such, the references do not represent all of the most recent references in the area; rather, they constitute selected references, designed to broaden or expand needed background information.

Clark, Leonard H., *Strategies and Tactics in Secondary School Teaching: A Book of Readings* (New York: The Macmillan Co., 1968), Chap. 10.

Hoover, Kenneth H., *The Professional Teacher's Handbook*, 2nd ed. (Boston: Allyn and Bacon, Inc., 1976).

Hoover, Kenneth H., and Paul M. Hollingsworth, *Learning and Teaching in the Elementary School*, 2nd ed. (Boston: Allyn and Bacon, Inc., 1975).

Leonard, Joan M., and others, *General Methods of Effective Teaching: A Practical Approach* (New York: Thomas Y. Crowell Co., 1972), Chap. 7.

McLeish, John, *The Lecture Method* (Cambridge, England: Institute of Education, 1968).

Risk, Thomas M., *Principles and Practices of Teaching in the Secondary School*, 4th ed. (New York: American Book Co., 1968), pp. 280-285.

Shoen, H. L., "Plan to Combine Individualized Instruction with the Lecture Method," *The Mathematics Teacher*, 67: 647-651 (Nov., 1974).

Titus, C., "Uses of the Lecture," *Clearing House*, 48: 383-384 (Feb., 1974).

Developmental Reading Techniques

RATIONALE. Reading is the basic instructional tool at all grade levels. Traditionally, reading as a secondary school entry skill was assumed. As deficiencies became apparent, however, remedial reading classes were established to help certain individuals cope with the written (and spoken) word. It is only in recent years that secondary school teachers have come to realize that all students need some help in coping with the particular language of different subject fields.

Developmental reading techniques are designed to help *every* student make effective use of basic reading skills in each particular subject area. When developed appropriately, they can drastically reduce study time and generally make learning more permanent. The techniques apply equally to middle and secondary school subject areas.

OVERVIEW

Key Concepts

1. Reading development is a continuous process; most young people need guidance throughout their public school experience.

2. The language of every content area is unique and must be taught.

287

3. Reading rate varies with the purpose. Without assistance, the typical student approaches all reading assignments in a line-by-line and a page-by-page manner.

4. Comprehension is enhanced through a systematized study technique (SQ4R).

5. An individual's reading habits become engrained as he or she matures. Thus a specific program of exercises must be employed if poor reading habits are to be corrected.

6. All assignments that involve reading should call attention to needed reading skills and techniques.

New Terms

1. Readability level: The general reading level of a book or other printed matter. It is based upon sentence length and word syllables and is usually interpreted in terms of grade level.

2. "Stopper" words: Words in an assignment that will tend to stop or block the reader's comprehension or train of thought.

3. Context clues: Clues to word meaning which may be derived from the way a word is used.

4. Indicator or "flag" words: Words, usually italicized or boldfaced, which alert the reader to specific information. Such words are essential to effective scanning.

5. SQ4R: A systematic study technique. It includes the following: survey, question, read, recite, "rite," and review.

6. Skimming: A form of rapid reading useful in gaining a general impression or main ideas.

7. Scanning: A second form of rapid reading that is useful for acquiring specific information such as dates and word definitions.

OBJECTIVES. After this experience you should be able to help students effectively cope with the language of different subject fields, as evidenced by your ability to:

1. List five characteristics of an effective developmental reading program.

2. Select eight out of nine appropriate developmental reading techniques from a list of twenty assorted "assignments."

3. Develop six out of seven requested responses to developmental reading techniques.

PRELIMINARY READING. Since the elements of instructional methodology are somewhat variable, the following excerpts are provided to help you develop a frame of reference as a point of departure for this experience. If you prefer, you may proceed directly to the Preassessment items.

THE ROLE OF COMPREHENSION IN READING

The concept of rate of comprehension is much more useful than the notion of rate of reading. Speed without comprehension is worthless! While it is true that rate of reading and comprehension tend to be closely associated, this does not mean that comprehension will improve by urging one to speed up his reading. Indeed, the evidence indicates that reading-rate adjustments severe enough to disturb one's normal thought processes will result in decreased comprehension.

Comprehension itself is a complex concept. At its lowest level it is a process of *translating* the writer's thought into one's own words. The teacher facilitates this process by calling attention to titles, key words in context, sentence structure, and the like.

From translation, the process of comprehension proceeds to *interpretation* of implied meaning, sometimes referred to as "reading between the lines." Words are mere abstractions of reality; they do not tell all. Instead, the reader is expected to make his own inferences and deductions. For example, such expressions as "buying time," "cold war," "hot dog," cannot be interpreted from the literal meaning of the words but only through their contexts.

Comprehension at its highest level involves "reading beyond the lines" in *making generalizations and drawing conclusions*. Thus the reader must grasp a thought in its totality and reflect upon related possibilities. In essence he goes beyond the lines as he evaluates arguments, deductions, inferences, and so forth. Eventually he draws his own conclusions as he critically evaluates what he reads.

Preliminary Survey of Textbook Aids.   Effective textbook use involves a methodology that bears much resemblance to the various instructional methods of the classroom teacher. Just as the lecturer foreshadows main points in the advanced organizer (initial summary), so does the textbook writer attempt to provide learner readiness through the table of contents, preface, and various chapter headings.

By making the preliminary survey of textbook aids *prior to reading,* the student is able to establish *purpose*. Purpose determines *how* one will read. Finding answers to questions, understanding main ideas, determining the conclusions of the writer, and reading for specific detail are but a few of the many purposes of reading. Each demands a different style of study.

A survey of the preface (introduction or prologue) enables the reader to determine the author's purpose, the limitations of the book, and its intended audience. In addition the writer may indicate his or her points of view toward the subject and suggest how the book may be used.

The preliminary survey, finally, includes a *preview of individual chapters*. This usually involves various chapter instructional aids. Some of these may include the chapter overview or introduction, study questions, chapter headings, summaries, pictures, tables, or charts. When surveying the entire book, the chapter-by-chapter preview will be much more superficial than when one is preparing to study a particular chapter.

Root Words and Origins.   Most polysyllabic words can be broken down into monosyllabic words. The words *polysyllabic* and *monosyllabic* themselves may be sources of difficulty until a few common Latin and Greek word parts are emphasized. *Poly-*, for example, means many, whereas *mono-* denotes one.

Frequently there are easy-to-spot root words within a word, e.g., inter*change*able. By actually "seeing" word parts, aided by context clues, one can often easily master long, imposing words.

Common prefixes and suffixes often provide much-needed clues to meaning. Think of the number of words that begin with the prefix *pre-*, which means before, or *re-*, which stands for again or back.

Many students may simply pass over new words unless word-attack techniques are taught and made a vital part of assignments. By preteaching "stopper" words, one can remove many obstacles to learning. Such preteaching activities eventually may be no more than calling attention to already-familiar techniques of word-attack skills. Learner independence is the ultimate end desired.

The SQ4R Technique. Fortunately a systematic pattern of study has been developed by reading specialists that can reduce study time by as much as 25 percent without reducing comprehension. This technique, sometimes described as the SQ4R method, can be readily employed by the classroom teacher. It involves a sequence of events that include survey, question, read, recite, "rite," and review.

A chapter is *surveyed* for the purpose of determining the author's outline or guideposts. This is the skeleton upon which details and illustrations rest. (Refer back to the preliminary textbook survey technique.) It is also useful to glance at charts, diagrams, and pictures along the way. For those books which do not afford such instructional aids, one should read the first and last paragraphs, followed by reading the first sentence of every third paragraph. A chapter survey can be completed in five or six minutes.

Next, the effective reader develops a series of questions *before he or she reads*. Such a technique arouses a state of curiosity and serves to provide focus to study activities. The author sometimes provides questions in an overview; more often they appear at the end of the chapter as questions for study and discussion. Titles, subheadings, italicized words, and new terms can be easily reworded as questions.

The third step in the SQ4R sequence is *reading*. Rather than reading the chapter line by line and page by page, one reads *selectively*. First skim through the section, reading a few words here and there, attempting to focus upon that material which bears upon your questions. This is accomplished by looking for signal phrases, such as "the first reason," "my next point," and so on.

When one has found the answer to a question, he should *stop* and then *recite* the answer in his/her own words. This thinking-through process results in real learning. It may be necessary to check back until all points are clearly understood.

The reciting process is followed immediately by *writing* key words that serve as cues to answers. One or two words consisting of *cues to one's own recitation* provide the most meaningful connection for later recall of the complete answers. The questions and cue words constitute one's permanent study notes.

The last step in the SQ4R process involves *review*. This consists of concentrating on the questions formulated earlier. For those that cannot be answered, a brief look at one's cue words should be sufficient. This process should immediately follow completion of the assignment. It should be repeated at least once a week to minimize the effects of forgetting.

It is seen from the foregoing that the SQ4R method involves a systematized approach to textbook study. It involves reflective thinking processes just as do all other instructional methods. These are skills that must be taught if effective study is to be assured.

Preparing Students for Reading Assignments. In addition to capturing student interest and providing the learner with valid purpose, the wise teacher preteaches "stopper" words. "Stopper" words should be pulled out of the reading assignment and examined for meaning. Root words, Latin or Greek origins, syllables, appropriate pronunciation guides, etc., should be noted. This tends to remove the fear of the unknown and to reduce obstacles or barriers created by new words.

As the assignment is made, a few minutes can be devoted to the best method of reading it. It may be desirable to provide a few moments of guided practice by way of illustration. This is one reason for beginning most assignments during the class period. If, for example, general background information is all that is needed, the teacher should make this point. He or she might suggest, "Read this section rapidly for a general impression, just to catch the mood without remembering the details." If high-speed scanning is in order, the teacher either includes appropriate questions or guides students in developing such questions. To illustrate: "Scan the material rapidly, looking for flag words, until you think you have found the essential information. Then slow way down to determine whether you have really located the needed information."

Many times close, intensive reading is necessary. The teacher calls attention to this by suggesting that the learner stop and reflect on each sentence and paragraph. The student might be forewarned that the two or three pages of assigned reading are equivalent to fifty or more pages of a novel. Sometimes carefully worded analysis or evaluation questions can be useful in serving such a purpose.

Variable reading rates often are necessary *within* a given assignment. Thus a vital part of every reading assignment involves calling attention to specific parts and how they are to be read. As previously indicated, the SQ4R method is ideal for increasing retention of specific information. Since reading habits are deeply engrained, students need considerable practice under close supervision in adopting more efficient techniques.

Preassessment Items (answers provided on pp. 301–3)

This experience is designed to help you gain an overall perspective of how developmental reading techniques are used in teaching. After completing these items, turn to the end of this LAP and check your answers. Note that answers to Part B (both incorrect and correct) are provided with supporting reasons to guide your efforts as you work through this LAP.

A. List five characteristics of an effective developmental reading program.

1.

2.

3.

4.

5.

B. From the list of "assignments," place a check (√) by nine of those that suggest appropriate developmental reading techniques.

1. Read pages 85 to 96 in the book prior to attempting to answer the provided questions.

2. First scan through the reading assignment, determining meaning for all italicized words.

3. Notice the list of new terms on the hand-out sheet. When you come across these in your reading, attempt to derive meaning *without* consulting your dictionary.

4. As you read, underline key sentences and phrases for later reference.

5. Look up all new words in the dictionary as you study the assignment.

6. First skim the assignment for main ideas; then answer the general questions provided.

7. First read the assignment carefully. Do not get bogged down with the pictures and charts.

8. Here is a list of questions for which you should find answers. The three listed books should be useful sources.

9. There are a number of long words in the assignment that will be new to you. Study prefixes and suffixes as you seek meaning. For example, what does *pre-* mean?

10. Make use of your dictionary after you have obtained the general meaning from the context.

11. You will notice questions at the end of the chapter. Study them after you have read the chapter.

12. Work on your reading speed by reading faster than you normally read. Don't bother too much with comprehension; it will come later.

13. Scan the chapter for main ideas; then skim for specific information.

14. Scan very rapidly until you find your indicator words, then slow way down as you seek meaning.

15. In the SQ4R technique you will want to read over the materials a second time. This is essentially the 4th R.

16. First you will want to survey the materials so you can find answers to your questions.

17. Use the author's subheadings as a basis for questions that you will write out. Then look in the subsequent paragraphs for answers.

18. Although you need not turn in the assignment, be sure to write out complete answers to all of your questions.

19. From the list of provided references, select those useful for your particular questions. First, read through the preface to a book to determine what the author is trying to accomplish.

20. Review your notes (cue words) every few days as we move along through the course.

C. Develop responses to the following as indicated:

  1. Using the following excerpt, provide appropriate answers to portions of the SQ4R technique as requested.

   a. Key question.

   b. Read. List all signal materials.

   c. Recite. Write out the answer you might recite to yourself.

   d. "Rite." Write out what you should enter as written notes.

   e. Review. What is involved?

READING EXCERPT

Short-term Gains Versus Permanent Ones[1]

You have to be always aware too of one real hazard in any quick result. Sometimes the overnight reformation is fine. It can mean that you have done a wonderful job of teaching and have really succeeded. But—it can also mean that the quick change is only skin deep. Youngsters may learn to do what you want them to . . . because you want them to. They do what you want them to . . . because you are there to see that they do it. They do what you want them to . . . because they are afraid of what you will do if they don't.

The result looks all right, but it can be very temporary. Shaky. Very impermanent. The minute your pressure is gone—your presence, your eyes, your threat—the main support for good behavior is gone. Your punishment creates a kind of police state. The motto: Behave . . . as long as the policeman is around.

This danger can be overstated. Even when you talk with children, explain and discuss, your results for a long time are temporary. But you know this and expect it and plan for it when you use a reasoning approach. When you use force this impermanence is apt to surprise you. It can anger you and lead you into more and more force. Once again punishment turns out to be the most intricate and involved approach, the one where ever so carefully you have to watch yourself and what you do.

There is a way to lessen the likelihood of getting only a momentary response as a result of punishment. Use punishment when you seek quick learning and when the learning is a small one: some specific deed, some specific way of acting. "Be quiet in this room" . . . Wait your turn at this machine" . . . "Do not run on this stairway" . . . "Do not touch this apparatus."

General, broader learning—principles, pervasive attitudes—cannot be beaten into people. Kindness, for example, or decency, respect, tolerance, considerateness, cooperativeness, thoughtfulness . . . these can only grow as you help children to think about them and to see the need for them.

---

[1] *James L. Hymes, Jr.,* Behavior and Misbehavior *(Englewood Cliffs, N.J.: Prentice-Hall, Inc., 1955), pp. 70-71.*

2. From the following words pick out a clue to meaning.

reinforce

substratum

If you were able to supply nineteen of the twenty-one requested responses, you are doing exceedingly well. In fact, you probably already possess the necessary developmental reading skills and can skip this LAP entirely. Even if you were able to supply few of the requested responses, do not despair, for this is an area where most experienced teachers are admittedly lacking. By analyzing the correct answers to the pretest and then studying the supporting reasons for all correct and incorrect items in Part B of the pretest, you should find yourself in an ideal position for continuing through the learning activities.

LEARNING ACTIVITIES

A: *Read.* Re-examine the overview and the preliminary reading sections to this LAP. You will broaden your understanding considerably by studying Chap. 11(15) in the Hoover texts and/or by studying the selected references listed at the end of this LAP. Note especially the following points:

1. The difference between developmental and remedial reading techniques.

2. How the readability level of a book is determined.

3. The elements of a textbook survey.

4. The SQ4R technique.

5. Skimming and scanning techniques.

Self-assessment Items (answers provided on pp. 303–4)

(1)   Developmental reading techniques are not necessary when remedial reading instruction is available. Defend or refute.

(2)   What factors enter into the readability level of a book?

(3)   Why is a preliminary textbook (or chapter) survey recommended?

(4)   The SQ4R technique should be useful for all reading assignments. Defend or refute.

(5)   It has been said that when an individual skims, he does not read. Explain.

B: *Assessing readability level.* Using a textbook in your field of specialization, determine its readability level. Proceed as follows[2] :

1. Select three 100-word passages from near the beginning, middle, and end of the book. Skip all numbers and proper nouns.

2. Count the total number of sentences in each 100-word passage (estimating to the nearest sentence). Average these three numbers.

---

[2] Edward B. Fry, "*A Readability Formula That Saves Time,*" Journal of Reading, *11:513-516 (April, 1968).*

3. Count the total number of syllables in each 100-word sample. There is a syllable for each vowel sound. (As a shortcut you may count every syllable over one in each word and add 100.) Average the total number of syllables for the three samples.

4. Plot on the graph the average number of sentences per hundred words and the average number of syllables per hundred words. Most plot points fall near the heavy curved lines. Perpendicular lines mark off approximate grade-level areas.

Self-assessment Items (answers provided on p. 304)

(1)   Under what conditions might three samples (as used above) be inadequate as a basis for assessing readability?

(2)   A student should not be expected to use a book for an assignment if it is well above his or her readability level. Defend or refute.

(3)   Generally, a student should not be expected to use a book that is well below his or her reading level. Why?

C: *Textbook survey.* Using a textbook in your field of specialization, do a textbook survey as indicated. (Make sure that the book is new to you.)

1. Key questions. (Study the preface, table of contents, and each chapter.)

   a. What major purpose is the book designed to serve?

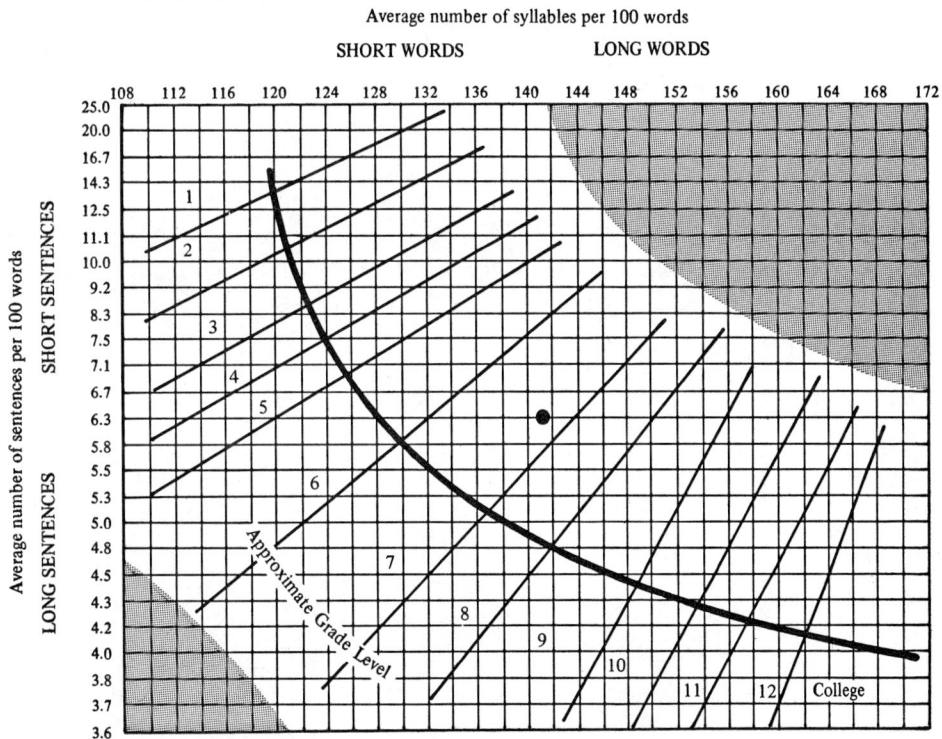

FIGURE 12-1. *Graph for Estimating Readability**

*Edward Fry, Rutgers University Reading Center (Noncopyrighted material).

    b. What limitations, if any, might you expect relative to the scope of the book?

    c. What specific instructional aids are apparent?

    d. How does the author summarize information?

2. When finished, compare notes with other members of your group. (If working alone, prepare a written critique of your experience.)

Self-assessment Items (answers provided on p. 304)

(1) Each student should do his or her own textbook survey as each chapter of a book is studied. Defend or refute.

(2) Some books have few signal words or phrases. Under such conditions how should one best proceed to find needed information?

(3) A textbook survey, including a chapter-by-chapter survey, need not be repeated as each chapter is studied. Defend or refute.

D: *SQ4R technique.* Select a chapter in a book from your field of specialization for the purpose of doing the SQ4R technique. Avoid a chapter that is overly technical. Proceed as follows:

1. Survey the chapter by:

    a. Determining and writing out the author's outline.

    b. Reading the overview or introduction.

    c. Reading the chapter summary.

    d. Glancing at charts, diagrams, and pictures.

    (Limit to five minutes.)

2. Study chapter questions by:

    a. Changing chapter headings into question form (if needed).

    b. Repeating for italicized words and new terms.

3. Read as indicated:

    a. Skim through each section, looking for flag words and phrases as clues to answers to your questions.

    b. Once you have found the answers, read the supporting material carefully.

4. Recite each answer in your own words.

5. Write out key words that will serve as cues to your answers. (Limit to one or two words for each answer.)

6. Review by referring to cue words as needed.

7. Hold a conference with your group for the purpose of clarifying any questions or difficulties. (If working alone, prepare a written critique and discuss with someone knowledgeable in the area.)

Self-assessment Items (answers provided on p. 304)

(1) Why should the chapter survey ordinarily be limited to two to five minutes?

(2) You will notice that, in most textbooks, summaries and questions for study are found at the end of the chapter. Reading specialists, however, insist that they should be at the beginning of the chapter. Why?

(3) List as many flag words and phrases as you can.

(4) Why should one normally avoid writing out complete answers to questions for study notes?

E: *Making use of textbook clues.* Using a textbook in your field of specialization, randomly select a page or two for the purpose of identifying clues to aid students in vocabulary development. (You may want to use your dictionary to assist you in this task.)

1. Identify as many of the following as possible:
   a. Word meaning through direct explanation.
   b. Word meaning through experience or mood.
   c. Word meaning through comparison, contrast, or inference.
   d. Word meaning through prefixes and suffixes.
   e. Word meaning through origin.
   f. Word meaning through root words.

2. Hold a follow-up conference with other members of your group for the purpose of sharing experiences. Make an effort to clarify each of the foregoing through specific examples. (If working alone, discuss with your instructor or supervisor.)

Self-assessment Items (answers provided on p. 304)

(1) Why should a student avoid using the dictionary for word meaning immediately after coming across a new word?

(2) It is the teacher's responsibility to clarify "stopper" words in the assignment. Defend or refute.

If, after reviewing the learning activities for this LAP, you feel that you can meet the stated objectives, proceed to the posttest. If not, you should direct your attention to the optional activities. You may elect to do one or both of the optional activities.

Optional Activities

F: *Class observation and teacher visitation.* Working in a committee of three if possible, arrange for each to visit a different middle or secondary school class or teacher for the purpose of determining how experienced teachers cope with developmental reading problems. (If working alone, visit at least one class and one teacher.) Proceed as follows:

1. Have one member of your committee concentrate on how assignments are handled with respect to developmental reading techniques. Use the following to guide your observation:

   a. How reading materials are to be read.

   b. How new ("stopper") words are handled.

   c. How aspects of the SQ4R technique are handled (e.g., questions to guide study, etc.)

2. Have a second member of your committee attend a class in which study techniques are emphasized directly in class. This may involve any of the aspects introduced in this LAP in addition to others that the teacher may introduce.

3. Have the third member of your committee discuss developmental reading techniques with a teacher who is somewhat skillful in the area. Concentrate on the following:

   a. How differential reading rate is taught.

   b. Study techniques emphasized.

   c. How students are prepared for use of textbooks or related materials.

   d. Note-taking techniques emphasized.

4. Hold a post-observation conference for the purpose of sharing new ideas and techniques. (If working alone, prepare a written critique and discuss with your instructor or supervisor.)

Self-assessment Items (answers provided on p. 304)

(1)   An experienced teacher was quoted as saying, "I can't bother with developmental reading techniques. There is not even enough time now to cover the course adequately." In one short paragraph, refute such a position.

(2)   It has been observed that most students tend to read in a word-by-word and a line-by-line manner. How would you discourage such a procedure?

G: *Skimming and scanning.* Select a book in your field of specialization, other than a textbook. Randomly select a chapter and proceed as follows:

1. Skim the chapter quickly for main ideas. List them on a sheet of paper. (Limit this experience to about one minute for every ten or fifteen pages of printed matter.)

2. Scan parts of the chapter for answers to two or three questions. (Such questions should be derived from topic headings, rephrased in question form if needed.) Be sure to use indicator words and phrases as guides. Time yourself for this experience.

3. If working in a committee, discuss your experiences for the purpose of further clarifying technique. Also compare time requirements, speculating on reasons for the considerable variation usually evidenced. (If working alone, make a note of questions and problems and discuss with your instructor or supervisor.)

Self-assessment Items (answers provided on pp. 304–5)

(1)   A student should skim prior to scanning. Defend or refute.

(2)   Scanning is usually followed by a word-by-word and a line-by-line type of reading. Explain why.

POSTTEST (answers provided on pp. 305–6)

After you have completed the learning activities, complete the posttest and evaluate by checking your answers with those found at the end of this LAP. Note that supporting reasons are provided for both correct and incorrect items in Part B.

A. List five characteristics of an effective developmental reading program.

1.

2.

3.

4.

5.

B. From the list of "assignments," place a check (√) by nine of those that suggest appropriate developmental reading techniques.

1. Skim the material for "flag" words.

2. First read through the assigned reading carefully; then go back and determine the meaning of all "stopper" words.

3. Before you read, formulate key questions to guide you.

4. Don't bother with "stopper" words. Just slide over them. We'll clarify them later.

5. We have several technical terms in this assignment. Study meaning through roots, context clues, prefixes, and the like before you look them up in your dictionary.

6. Underline key sentences in your text; enter marginal notes as needed.

7. First turn to the end of the chapter where you'll find key study questions and a summary. This should guide your study.

8. Don't write out complete thoughts from our oral reports. Merely jot down cue words.

9. Scan for "flag" words, then slow down to make sure of the correctness of your information.

10. Write out answers to your questions and turn them in by tomorrow. I'll give them back to you so you can keep them as notes for review.

11. Study Chapter 4 in this book. If you find it too hard, you can study Chapter 6 of this other book.

12. Before you attempt to answer your questions on the assignment, quickly go through the chapter, noting subheadings, italicized words, tables, and charts.

13. By studying the preface, you will gain a quick summary of main points in the chapter.

14. Don't bother with new words. I think you can get the main ideas needed by quickly skimming through materials.

15. For the long, new words, it will be desirable to look for smaller words that sometimes form the basis for such words.

16. When you come to a new word, don't stop. By the time you finish the reading assignment, you'll probably gain the essence of meaning.

17. When you are unable to find your information from indicator words and phrases, you'll need to go to a careful line-by-line reading of these materials.

18. You may be able to derive meaning from long, difficult words by breaking them down into syllables. There is a syllable for each vowel sound.

19. Keep your dictionary handy. When you come across a new word, look it up.

20. Don't bother with the pictures; they can only slow you down. Direct attention to "flag" words instead.

C. Develop responses to the following as indicated:

1. Using the excerpt below, provide appropriate answers to portions of the SQ4R technique as requested.

a. Key question.

b. Read. List all signal materials.

c. Recite. Write out the answer you might recite to yourself.

d. "Rite." Write out what you should enter as written notes.

e. Review. What is involved?

READING EXCERPT

Assessing Motivation[3]

As it has been described thus far, motivation is something which a student has. It is not something which a teacher does to his students directly. This notion may disturb those who assume it is their responsibility to motivate students toward good work. The basic tenets of this book imply that a teacher should capitalize upon the forces within the individual for maximum learning, but to try to do things which motivate students is ineffective in most cases. Teachers need to arrange their activities and organize their classrooms so that these operations function in harmony with students' motivations rather than against them. This does not mean

---

[3] *Jack R. Frymier,* The Nature of Educational Method *(Columbus, Ohio: Charles E. Merrill Books, Inc., 1965), p. 113.*

that teachers cannot arouse interest in a subject. It does mean, however, that it is generally more effective to design instruction so that the forces in the learner which are seeking expression are tied to the learning process directly rather than indirectly.

A second point about motivation, however, seems pertinent here. Submissiveness expressing itself as motivation to do good work illustrates the thesis that teachers are obliged to encourage children to develop higher levels of motivation. It is not desirable for a child to study because he is afraid of the teacher. But it does happen. Observing this, a teacher must endeavor to help that child move to a higher level of motivation. A good teacher recognizes that he must start with his students where they are, but also that it is imperative to help them move on. The teacher who can assist students to understand their fears and help them feel good about themselves and others may be able to help them move along the continuum toward a higher motivation.

> 2. Pick out a clue to meaning for each of the following words:
>
> interactive
>
> cocography

Your successful completion of this LAP deserves special commendation. Now that you know the needed developmental reading techniques, you must work closely with your students to help them break poor reading habits. This applies to fast as well as slow readers. If you were unable to meet the recommended mastery level, do not be discouraged. By studying the answers to the posttest, especially supporting reasons for items in Part B, you should soon reach this level.

ANSWERS TO PREASSESSMENT ITEMS

> *You can make these items a most valuable learning experience by studying the provided reasons for both correct and incorrect responses. You will note that since Part A has no specific number of correct responses, several additional points (characteristics) have been provided. Since the last part calls for your constructed responses, your own answers may not be identical to those supplied by the writer. You should be able to decide whether your answers are reasonably correct, however.*

A. 1. Guides to using textbooks are provided.

2. Variable reading rate is emphasized.

3. Word meaning, through roots, context clues, and the like is provided.

4. Assignments provide clues for coping with the language involved.

5. Techniques for attaining reading comprehension are emphasized (SQ4R method).

6. Appropriate use of the dictionary is emphasized.

B. Acceptable items, with supporting reasons

  2 (This practice prepares the student for adequate in-depth study.)

  3 ("Stopper" word meaning is best derived from the context.)

  6 (Guides students in an efficient means of completing the assignment.)

  9 (Most long words can be rendered comprehensible through a study of prefixes, word origins, and the like.)

  10 (The dictionary is indeed useful after the general idea of word usage has been attained.)

  14 (This represents a most efficient way of obtaining specific information.)

  17 (The author's subheadings usually foreshadow the essential content.)

  19 (This is the most efficient way of assessing the value of a book for a particular purpose.)

  20 (This sort of review adds immensely to retention; weekly reviews are recommended.)

Unacceptable items, with supporting reasons

  1 (No attempt is made to guide students in how to read the assignment.)

  4 (Usually meaning is best derived from context; a better procedure would be to jot down key words or phrases.)

  5 (Context is best derived from the assignment itself.)

  7 (The first "reading" should focus on charts and diagrams, along with "flag" words, etc., for developing comprehension readiness.)

  8 (Students need guidance on how to find answers.)

  11 (Questions are most useful before any reading is done to guide the student.)

  12 (One must focus on comprehension along with reading rate.)

  13 (The two reading methods have been reversed here.)

  15 (Review merely entails taking another look at cue words at intervals. No reading is done unless the cue words fail to result in recall of ideas.)

  16 (Surveying is done for an overview. It is broader than any specific question.)

  18 (The 3rd R (writing) entails cue words, designed to help one recall a train of thought.)

C.   a. Key question

      Example: What is the difference between short-term and long-term gains in the area of discipline?

      b. Read. List all signal words and materials.

      . . . ; ____;". (This calls attention to the passages.)

      Behave; and. (Italicized words act as flags.)

      Once again . . . ; . . . for example . . . (These are signal phrases.)

   c. Recite. Write out the answer you might recite to yourself.

   (Here refer back to your key question.)

   Short-term discipline gains are quick and temporary and should be used for specific behaviors. Long-term discipline gains are used for general, broad learnings in which students need to know the why of behavior.

   d. "Rite." Write out what you should enter as written notes.

   Examples: Force . . . temporary

            Reason with . . . permanent

   e. Review. What is involved?

   (Look at key words and attempt to answer the question in your own words. If difficulty is encountered, refer to your cue words in your notes.)

2. reinforce

re- is a prefix which means to repeat.

substratum

sub- is a prefix meaning under or below.

strat- is from Latin, meaning to strew or scatter.

-um is a suffix denoting singular.

(Thus a definition can be formed: A part that lies beneath another part.)

ANSWERS TO SELF-ASSESSMENT ITEMS

Self-assessment items are designed to help you gain a depth of understanding as you proceed through the various learning activities. Most of them do not have single correct answers. For feedback, however, you should compare your own answers with the samples provided here.

A. (1)   Refute. Remedial reading is designed to help students develop needed entry reading skills. Developmental reading techniques provide specific assistance in each subject field, needed by all students.

   (2)   Length of sentences and length of words.

   (3)   By perceiving basic author purpose, the learner is able to adjust reading technique accordingly. Moreover, a quick overview of textbook aids renders subsequent study most efficient.

   (4)   Refute. Often mere skimming techniques are all that is needed. The SQ4R technique is useful when careful study of material is in order.

(5) It is quite true that in skimming one does not read line-by-line and word-for-word. Under such conditions the individual is merely seeking the "general drift" of the content material.

B. (1) When parts of the book consist of technical materials. Under such conditions a more thorough sampling is appropriate.

(2) For certain purposes, such a book may be used, i.e., looking up terms or studying diagrams. If used, however, it must always be used selectively and with the help of the teacher.

(3) Such a book may result in loss of interest or motivation to study. If used selectively, however, little difficulty is likely.

C. (1) Defend. The three to five minutes necessary for such a survey can save much needed time later on and renders study much more efficient than would otherwise be possible.

(2) Look for topic sentences, usually found in the first or last sentence of a paragraph.

(3) Refute. The chapter survey is much more specific when accomplished immediately prior to use. Each chapter serves a different purpose.

D. (1) This prevents the student from plunging into the assignment without any plan.

(2) When studied prior to the chapter, such aids alert the reader to what he or she is seeking.

(3) Sentence structure, such as dashes, italics, lists, boldfaced words, Roman numerals, etc.

"In the first place," "Firstly," "My first point," "To summarize,"

"In short," "Briefly," "Thus," etc.

(4) This encourages memorization of "correct" answers. This, in effect, causes one to commit much unnecessary detail to memory.

E. (1) Most words have a variety of meanings. A definition is best obtained from the context if possible.

(2) Defend, if clarify merely means guiding students in deriving meaning. Eventually students should be able to identify and attack "stopper" words on their own. This skill cannot be assumed, however; it must be taught.

Optional activities

F. (1) Developmental reading techniques are not things that are "added." Rather, they represent effective techniques to guide study activities. When applied appropriately, they can save considerable study time

(2) Whenever any reading assignment is made, indicate how it is to be read. To illustrate: "Read this as you would a novel; scan the material quickly, looking for indicator words and phrases; for this, employ the SQ4R method."

G. (1) Not necessarily. If one is generally aware of what the book (or chapter) is about, skimming can be bypassed. If skimming is necessary, however, it usually precedes scanning.

(2)　Once an individual has located the needed information, such reading is often necessary for clarifying the points.

ANSWERS TO POSTTEST

For most beneficial results you should work through the entire LAP before you check your answers to the posttests. Failure to meet the provided minimum standard (of about 90 percent) probably suggests certain weaknesses that need to be corrected. As with the pretests, you will find supporting reasons for answers. It is hoped that this will serve as desirable feedback in your quest for mastery.

A. 1. Guides to using textbooks are provided.

　2. Variable reading rate is emphasized.

　3. Word meaning, through roots, context clues, etc., is provided.

　4. Assignments provide clues for coping with the language involved.

　5. Techniques for attaining reading comprehension are emphasized (SQ4R method).

　6. Appropriate use of the dictionary is emphasized.

B. Acceptable items, with supporting reasons

　3　(Careful reading follows scanning.)

　5　(This is appropriate since the dictionary usually provides many definitions.)

　7　(Students need to have something of this sort to foreshadow important points in their assignments.)

　8　(This makes learning meaningful, as the cue words help the learner remember whole train of thought as opposed to memorized words.)

　9　(This is the recommended technique for obtaining specifics.)

　12　(Such a survey saves time and makes learning most efficient.)

　14　(This is the purpose of skimming techniques. It is best accomplished by reading very rapidly.)

　15　(This is one way of deriving word meaning.)

　18　(This is a fully acceptable technique.)

Unacceptable items, with supporting reasons

　1　(This is a function of scanning, not skimming.)

　2　(Careful reading follows scanning.)

　4　(This is a habit that the teacher should seek to break. "Stopper" words are best understood directly from the context.)

　6　(This is not economical for permanent review notes. It is difficult to obtain full meaning from sentences taken out of context.)

　10　(Cue words only are preferred for review notes; otherwise, the student is likely to memorize words only.)

11 (Students should be told how to study, e.g., purposes must be made clear, as this determines how they will read.)

13 (The preface is designed to establish book purpose, delimitations, and often the author's basic frame of reference.)

16 (This violates good developmental reading techniques. Although this is what many students tend to do, they should stop and derive meaning before progressing further.)

17 (Not so. The next step would be to look for topic sentences for clues.)

19 (Meaning is best derived from context; then you can use the dictionary to extend meaning.)

20 (Since specifics are a part of the assignment, pictures too can act as "flag" words.)

C. 1. a. Key question.

    Example: How is motivation assessed?

  b. Read. List all signal words and materials.

    . . . has; does

    It does mean . . .

    A second point . . .

  c. Recite. Write out the answer you might recite to yourself. Motivation is based on forces that come from within. Arrange to release these forces in class. Aim is a self-motivated, directed individual.

  d. "Rite." Write out what you should enter as written notes.

    Motivation exists; teacher release.

    Aim for self-motivation.

  e. Review. What is involved?

    Look at key question and attempt to answer if possible. If difficulty is encountered, refer to your cue words in your notes.

2. From the following words pick out a clue to meaning:

interactive

    inter—means between or among.

    act—means doing or moving.

cocography

    coco—means bad or evil.

    graphy—means writing.

SUPPLEMENTARY SOURCES

The following sources may be used in lieu of the Hoover texts or, preferably, as supplementary to them. Generally they are consistent with the models provided in the LAPs of this module. As such, the references do not represent all of the most recent references in the area; rather, they constitute selected references designed to broaden or expand needed background information.

Dallman, Martha, and others, *The Teaching of Reading*, 4th ed. (New York: Holt, Rinehart and Winston, Inc., 1974).

Fry, Edward B., "A Readability Formula That Saves Time," *Journal of Reading*, 11: 513-516 (April, 1968).

Hoover, Kenneth H., *The Professional Teacher's Handbook*, 2nd ed. (Boston: Allyn and Bacon, Inc., 1976).

Karlin, Robert, *Teaching Reading in High School*, 2nd ed. (Indianapolis, Ind.: Bobbs-Merrill, 1972).

——, "Developing Comprehension Skills in the High School Student," *International Reading Association Conference Papers*, 18: 108-116 (1973).

Kennedy, Eddie C., *Methods in Teaching Developmental Reading* (Itasca, Ill.: F. E. Peacock Publishers, 1974).

Kennedy, L. D., and R. S. Holinski, "Measuring Attitudes: An Extra Dimension: Attitudes Toward Reading," *Journal of Reading*, 18: 518-522 (April, 1975).

Piercey, Dorothy, *Reading Activities in Content Areas: An Ideabook for Middle and Secondary Schools* (Boston: Allyn and Bacon, Inc., 1976).

Rental, V. M., and F. J. Zidonis, eds., "Reading in the Secondary School: Symposium," *Theory into Practice*, 14: 147-219 (June, 1975).

Shuman, R. B., "Teen-aged Nonreader: Is There a Solution to the Problem?" *Education Digest*, 40: 47-49 (Sept., 1974).

Stauffer, R. G., and M. M. Harrell, "Individualizing Reading-Thinking Activities," *The Reading Teacher*, 28: 765-769 (May, 1975).

The Reading Teacher, International Reading Association, 800 Berkdale Road, Newark, Del., 1971 (Monthly, October through May).

Thomas, Ellen L., and H. A. Robinson, *Improving Reading in Every Class: A Sourcebook for Teachers* (Boston: Allyn and Bacon, Inc., 1972).

module
VI

ASSESSMENT TECHNIQUES

Measurement and evaluation techniques have been recognized as the weakest aspect of the instructional process. Some parents, and indeed a number of educators, recently have made a plea for the abolition of tests and grades. They point to the general poor quality of many teacher-made tests and the all-too-frequent arbitrary, capricious use of grades. Measurement and evaluational techniques and devices, however, need not be of poor quality. When used appropriately, they become an indispensable aspect of the instructional process.

When instruction is based upon basic unit concepts and predicted behavioral outcomes, measurement and evaluation become an integral part of the instructional process. Reflective thinking, then, becomes a basis for assessment experiences. Indeed, multiple-choice and essay test items can be so constructed as to involve the learner in similar processes of reflection.

The two LAPs in this module, although not all-inclusive, provide the necessary components in this vital area. You will recognize that some aspects of measurement and evaluation are difficult to achieve effectively. The writing of appropriate situational test items is not only difficult, but also time-consuming. Nevertheless, it is a task that must be accomplished if the above criticisms are to be negated. Like other instructional skills, such techniques can be mastered with experience. In the final analysis, the quality of measurement and evaluation determines the quality of the learning experience. Students quickly anticipate how they will be evaluated and will react accordingly.

Measurement and Evaluation Devices and Techniques

RATIONALE. The outcomes of learning usually are assessed in terms of some sort of test or observational tool, such as rating scales and checklists. Although widespread misuse of tests has warranted considerable criticism, they remain the most basic instructional and evaluational tools of teachers everywhere. As the LAPs in this manual demonstrate, tests serve many different purposes. Oddly enough, the nature of anticipated measurement and evaluational devices has a tremendous bearing upon a student's responses in different learning situations. A teacher may emphasize concept teaching, for example, but if tests of a factual nature are anticipated, students will concentrate on factual retention so they can pass the tests. The goal, of course, is measurement and evaluation procedures consistent with anticipated pupil outcomes. It has been noted that instructional methods, in some manner, embody reflective processes. Likewise, measurement and evaluation devices can be constructed in such a fashion as to involve students in the processes of reflection.

OVERVIEW

Key Concepts

1. A valid test must be reliable; a reliable test, however, may not be valid.
2. Specified behavioral outcomes, derived from instructional goals and unit concepts, provide the basis for measurement and evaluation.
3. Tests generally should emphasize the higher levels of cognition.

4. Multiple-choice test items tend to be superior to other test items.

5. Through testing, attainment of cognitive and psychomotor objectives can be ascertained; attainment of affective objectives is more readily assessed through the use of observational tools.

New Terms

1. Measurement: A quantitative amount of some experience, such as a test score.

2. Evaluation: The quality of an experience, often based upon some measure.

3. Validity: The trustworthiness of a measure. For example: "Does it measure what it is supposed to measure?"

4. Reliability: The consistency of scores on a given measuring instrument.

5. Situational test item: An item that thrusts the learner into a contrived situation. Designed to determine how well learnings may be applied.

6. Performance test item: An item that requires the learner to actually do (perform) a specified skill.

7. Criterion-referenced measure: Interpreting achievement in terms of a predetermined standard (criterion) of performance, without reference to level of performance of other members of the class.

8. Norm-referenced measure: Interpreting achievement in terms of an individual's position relative to other members of his class.

9. Minimum essentials measure: A criterion-referenced measure used to assess mastery or competence in a specifically defined way. Such a measure is usually most appropriate in the skills area; a minimum passing score of 85 to 90 percent is usually established to allow for sampling and personal errors.

10. Developmental measure: A measure used to assess a class of objectives (often in the cognitive domain) that represents achievement beyond the minimum essentials level. Due to the complexity of such goals, degree of achievement is all that can be expected, often necessitating norm-referenced assessment.

OBJECTIVES. After this experience you should be able to develop and employ measurement and evaluation devices needed in teaching, as evidenced by your ability to:

1. List four essential criteria of measurement and evaluational devices.

2. Distinguish between recall, situational, and performance test items in ten out of twelve instances from a provided list.

3. Select the most appropriate measurement and evaluation devices in eighteen out of twenty instances from a provided list.

4. Formulate sample test items and observational tools in four out of five instances from provided concepts.

PRELIMINARY READING. Since the elements of instructional methodology are somewhat variable, the following excerpts are provided to help you develop a frame of reference as a point of departure for this experience. If you prefer, you may proceed directly to the Preassessment items.

THE DIFFICULTY RANGE OF CRITERION-REFERENCED AND NORM-REFERENCED TEST ITEMS

The difficulty range of criterion-referenced items or tests at the mastery level must be interpreted quite differently from that of norm-referenced items. In the former, student achievement is assessed in terms of performance a student is capable of demonstrating. Level of performance, usually predetermined, is stated as a part of each instructional goal and behavioral outcome. In this manner an absolute standard (criterion) is established for individual achievement. In testing for minimum essentials, complete mastery within reasonable limits is expected. Thus a spread of scores is not expected. The difficulty of a test item (or task) should correspond to the difficulty of the performance task described in the specific learning outcome.

In all norm-referenced measures, difficulty range becomes an important concept. Here one is interested in the student's relative standing in class. Achievement is assessed in terms of how the learner compares in achievement with other students in class. Thus a spread of scores becomes important. Since complete mastery is not expected, a range of item difficulty is needed if one is to assess relative degree of progress toward a given objective.

It has been established that norm-referenced items chosen for maximum discrimination will tend to have a difficulty value of approximately 50 percent, i.e., one out of two students will respond incorrectly to the item. Allowing for chance clues and the like, the point of maximum discrimination usually is placed slightly higher. Although an item ideally will be answered correctly by 50 to 60 percent of the students, it may be desirable to include a few easy items (for encouragement) and a few hard items for the purpose of discriminating among top students. Since a few "easy," along with a few "hard," items are included, the minimum level of about 70 percent is usually considered the "passing" level.

Performance Test Items. In many areas, especially in the area of motor and mental skills, it is relatively easy to provide test situations that demand actual life applications of the concepts involved. The following illustrations suggest the wide applicability of performance test items to different areas of specialization.

> —adds fractions correctly
>
> —prepares and delivers persuasive speeches effectively
>
> —recognizes plant species in the local area
>
> —speaks in a foreign language

—selects art objects that portray a given mood

—analyzes current events in terms of selected concepts gleaned from history

—types thirty-five words per minute with a maximum of two errors

It is evident from the foregoing that performance test items can be employed in most subject fields. Such items are relatively easy to construct once the desired application has been identified. The major task is to establish the conditions and the criteria of acceptable performance. For example, how many plant species in the local area *should* a student be able to identify, and under what conditions? How well *must* he or she speak a foreign language under what circumstances? How many words per minute *should* he or she be able to type?

Situational Test Items.   Unfortunately, it is not always possible to measure behavioral changes directly. The teacher, in an effort to determine degree of understanding, will be obliged to resort to less direct measures. In such instances one can do no better than to *simulate* an experience involving an appropriate application. In other words, a realistic situation is developed that demands an application of what has been learned. For example, in a unit on first aid, one evidence of understanding the principles involved would likely be: ". . . recognizes and administers first aid properly in case of shock." It is impractical to induce a case of shock for test purposes; it is possible, however, to simulate or act out the experience. Since it is not feasible to evaluate thirty-five or forty students on this basis, a written description of a realistic situation may be as close to reality as is possible. Thus one is measured on the basis of what he or she would *plan* to do in the situation rather than on actual actions in the situation. Such a procedure is obviously a compromise with what is desired, because people do not always behave the way they plan to behave.

The Multiple-choice Item.   This item consists of an item stem and four or five responses, one of which is the best answer. The other answers are usually referred to as foils or distracters. The item stem can be in the form of a direct question or an incomplete sentence. In essence, the item stem poses the problem situation and the possible answers represent the alternative solutions. The student "solves" the problem by making a choice. All of the foils should be plausible to those who lack the necessary understanding of the concept application involved. Some teachers include distracters which on the surface are all quite acceptable, i.e., they represent accurate statements. Only one of the five possible answers is best, however, *in terms of the situation posed.* As a general frame of reference, the possible answers should include one *preferred* answer; one distracter will represent a near miss; another will indicate a crude error; while the remaining distracters will tend to fall somewhere between those two extremes.

There are likely to be a number of reasons why a student makes an inappropriate application to a multiple-choice test item. He could misunderstand the item stem or any one of the distracters; he could interpret the question in a unique way; or he simply may not possess an adequate understanding of the concepts necessary. If the first two reasons are involved, the item is not valid *for that particular individual.*

Sometimes the teacher desires to achieve greater validity by giving the student an opportunity to qualify or otherwise justify the answer. This enables the instructor to give credit for a choice that may have been justifiably selected *from the student's point of view*, even though it ordinarily would have been considered incorrect. Ultimately, however, the teacher must decide whether or not the reason given is sufficient to warrant full credit for the response.

Modified, situational forms of the multiple-choice item are illustrated below.

Subject: Art

Concept: Color is derived from light.

Item: A. Suppose you were asked to paint a desert landscape that will convey the impression of intense heat, extreme aridity, and yet contain a "typical" beauty. How would you choose the colors you would use?

    1. Hold your palette up close to the sand and then hold it close to a cactus in order to mix the exact colors of the objects you are painting.

    2. Mix your colors according to directions in a book which gives precise formulae for mixing sky color, a desert color, and a cactus color.

    3. Take a photograph of the desert and match the colors in the photograph.

    4. Study the color of light reflected on the desert at various times of the day before deciding what colors you will use.

    5. Study the color of the sand, the rocks, and several different varieties of cactus before deciding what colors you will use.

    B. Defend your answer.

Subject: American literature

Concept: Realities of life are not always consistent with ideals.

Item: A. Crevecoeur's view of "The American Dream" indicated a concern for the people's ideals. Assuming that ideals can act as a force to help overcome harsh realities, which of the following would be most consistent with Crevecoeur's views?

    1. Setting our goals as high as possible to utilize the greatest force.

    2. Accepting reality as it is, eliminating the stress of striving.

    3. Setting concrete and absolute goals for which to strive.

    4. Setting our goals at the upper limits of what is reasonable and attainable.

    B. Indicate a reason for your choice, consistent with the idea that ideals can be a force.

It should be noted that the second item is to be answered in terms of Crèvecoeur's views. Teachers sometimes err when they merely ask students to respond, with no specific frame of reference indicated. This, in effect, forces the student to "outguess" the teacher. The correct answer, under such conditions, is based upon the opinion of the teacher only.

The Essay Item. Like the multiple-choice item, the essay item is readily adaptable to a specific situation. Unlike other test item types, it may elicit a detailed written response. The item can involve the making of complex relationships, the selection and organization of ideas, formulation of hypotheses, the logical development of arguments, and creative expression.

The essay item can be substantially improved if it is so constructed as to elicit an application of learnings to new or different situations. Test reliability can be improved by giving hints concerning the structure of the answer expected. Sometimes this is called the *qualified* essay question. Illustrations of the *situational* essay, in which the answer is somewhat *qualified*, follow:

Subject: Art

Concept: Color is derived from light.

Item: Every color can be described in terms of three physical properties: hue, value, and intensity. Discuss the color blue in terms of these properties.

Subject: United States history

Concept: Bitter feelings between individuals and nations (e.g., the Allies toward the Central Powers following World War I) make peaceful relationships difficult to establish and maintain.

Item: Wilson urged "peace without victory" at the Versailles Peace Conference. How does this statement reflect upon our relationships in the Middle East today? Be sure to tie in Wilson's statement with the attitudes and feelings of other members of the peace conference and relate your feelings to the situation in the Middle East today.

It should be noted that the second item not only asks the student to draw relationships but relates to current situations as well. This is especially difficult (but essential) in a subject like history or historical units in other subjects.

Recall Test Items. Sometimes teachers assume that if a person can recall important facts in an area, he or she will make actual applications when needed. Using an illustration cited earlier, one could assume that a student who could describe the symptoms and appropriate treatment for shock could reasonably be expected to apply that knowledge. It is assumed that the student will use such information to *plan* his actions and that he will *behave* according to his plans. There is considerable evidence, however, indicating a broad gap between *verbal* understanding and actual behavior experienced in the original learning situation. Nevertheless, there is a place for items at this level.

The True-false Item. It is possible to improve the traditional true-false item substantially so that it can serve a useful function. Even if one desires to emphasize concepts in teaching and selection among alternatives on tests, it is quite likely that he or she will also desire to test for certain specific data. In such cases the true-false item becomes quite useful. It is effective when the teacher desires to have students apply minor concepts or generalizations in some way. To illustrate in the field of art:

> *Concept:*   Color is derived from light.
>
> *Item:*   A red coat will appear red to the eye <u>because it absorbs</u>
>   <u>red color waves and reflects blue color waves.</u>

One of the most important means of improving the item is to use the *modified* form. Such items are designed to permit a student to improve an answer so that it will become a correct answer. The student is asked to correct all incorrect items. In order to guard against the addition or deletion of something like the word "not" as a means of correcting an item, it usually is necessary to underline certain key clauses or phrases. The student is asked to change the underlined portion in such a manner as to make the statement correct. If change is necessary, the student should alter the underlined portion only. Students may be allowed some credit for the mere recognition of a true or false statement and additional credit for their ability to make appropriate corrections.

Rating Scales. Rating scales are used to evaluate situations or characteristics that are present in varying degrees. They seem to work best for judging behavior or products that are easily observable. Due to their subjective nature, they usually are used as supplementary evaluations or in areas where more objective evidence is not available. Each trait or dimension to be evaluated is broken into three or more descriptions, representing qualities of performance. These are usually arranged systematically below a horizontal line. When the scale is completed, the evaluator checks any point along the line from an indication of a very strong to a very weak performance. By writing out somewhat detailed descriptions, greater validity may be assured. The following illustration represents an attempt to evaluate the *approach or beginning* of an oral presentation.

Attention-getting, indicative of general content.	Beginning apparently planned, but effectiveness somewhat lacking.	Beginning poorly given; rambling statements, apologies.

Reliability of a rating scale can be improved if the rater is permitted to disregard any dimension(s) that does not seem to be present in sufficient quantity for an evaluation.

Checklists. A checklist differs from a rating scale in that no effort is made to evaluate the dimensions. It consists of items or dimensions, such as activities or characteristics, which are checked if present. Its chief function is to call attention to the items themselves rather than to their relative importance. The instrument has many uses. It is often employed when some standardized sequence of operation is involved, such as laboratory techniques. Sometimes it is used as an aid in checking off certain characteristics, e.g., the qualities of some finished product. Examples are the completion of some class project in art, industrial arts, or home economics. The dramatics teacher frequently employs a checklist when preparing for stage productions. Likewise, the physical education instructor finds various uses for such an instrument.

PREASSESSMENT ITEMS (answers provided on pp. 327-29)

This experience is designed to help you gain an overall perspective of how measurement and evaluation tools are used in teaching. After completing these items, turn to the end of this LAP and check your answers. Note that answers are provided with supporting reasons to help you further your understanding of the concepts involved.

A. List four essential criteria of measurement and evaluation devices.
   (To illustrate: Items are based upon unit concepts.)

   1.

   2.

   3.

   4.

   5.

B. Place the following code letters before each of the "test item stems" below (recall items embedded in situations or performances should be marked as recall):

R—Recall (memory)

S—Situation (planning level)

P—Performance (new application)

1. In this plot of ground you will find twelve different plants. Identify them.

2. List the characteristics of the spermatophyta plant phylum.

3. You come upon the scene of an accident and find an individual who has a weak pulse, is perspiring profusely, and is experiencing some difficulty breathing. What first aid measure would be most appropriate?

4. We have discovered that ambition is a powerful motive that can be used for good or ill. Identify your fondest ambition and indicate in one paragraph how you hope to realize this goal.

5. Translate the provided Spanish short story into English.

6. Discuss the expression, "Each person must do his own thing," in terms of one of your current activities.

7. What implications does the author draw relative to current race problems in this nation?

8. When you get to item 14, you will have to go to the laboratory and identify the specimen under the microscope.

9. May Jones was preparing an extemporaneous speech for class. What steps are essential in preparing such a presentation?

10. Earthworms normally live in the soil. After a heavy rain, however, they crawl around on top of the soil. Why is this?

11. Frank and Mark were studying for a test. Mark asked Frank to go over the principles of quadratic equations.

12. Prepare a business letter requesting an audit of the AYZ company.

C. Place one of the following code letters before each of the behavioral outcomes listed below. Select the measurement and evaluation tool most appropriate for the provided situation.

OR—Observation, using a rating scale

OC—Observation, using a checklist

TR—Test, at the recall level

TS—Test, at the situational level

TP—Test, at the performance level

1. Asks questions about the variety of art forms in the special school display.

2. Follows established procedures in constructing a garment.

3. Describes how one can be lonely among a group of people.

4. Solves problems involving two unknowns.

5. Measures the height of a tree using trigonometric principles.

6. Voluntarily attends an art exhibit.

7. Names the parts of speech.

8. From a provided manuscript, types forty words per minute with a maximum of two mistakes.

9. Analyzes the fallacies in an argument.

10. Employs appropriate strategy in a debate.

11. Employs proper shop safety rules.

12. Collects six varieties of butterflies.

13. At a prepared meal at school, uses the appropriate rules of etiquette.

14. Delivers an effective impromptu speech when requested.

15. Explains how the local government functions.

16. Selects the most appropriate workshop tool in eight of ten instances from a provided list of twenty-five woodworking tasks.

17. Identifies logical fallacies in the senator's speech on "honesty in politics."

18. Uses analysis-level questions during the discussion.

19. Employs an appropriate genetic cross in eight of ten instances from provided problems.

20. Voluntarily reads several books on poetry.

    D. Construct test items and observational devices from the provided concepts as indicated.

    Test items. CONCEPT: Each marriage partner must be flexible for a satisfying marriage relationship.

        1. Situational multiple-choice item

        2. Situational essay item

        3. Modified true-false item

    Observational devices. CONCEPT: The self-actualizing individual lives by a set of examined values.

        4. One scale of a rating scale

        5. Checklist (one point)

    If you were able to provide thirty-seven of the forty-one requested responses, you have already mastered one of the most difficult areas of teaching and should proceed directly to the LAP on Evaluation Procedures. Although you may have been able to supply few of the appropriate responses, do not be discouraged, for the items themselves have been set up as a learning device. (Note reasons for all correct responses.) Moreover, the learning activities will enable you to become directly involved in the construction of measurement and evaluation devices.

LEARNING ACTIVITIES

Work through each learning activity, complete the self-assessment items, and check your answers before moving to the next one. Note that the last learning activities are optional, depending upon your needs and situation at that point. You should be able to complete this LAP in about three or four hours.

A: *Read.* Re-examine the overview and the preliminary reading sections of this LAP. You will broaden your understanding substantially by studying Chap. 21(24)* in the Hoover texts and/or by studying the selected references listed at the end of this LAP. You should find the Bloom and Krathwohl references especially useful for illustrated test items in various fields at various levels of cognition and affect. Note especially the following:

    1. How reflective processes are involved in multiple-choice and essay test items.

    2. How unit concepts, instructional goals, and behavioral outcomes provide the basis for measurement and evaluation.

    3. Why situational items do not necessarily involve the higher levels of cognition.

    4. The purpose of modified test forms (e.g., multiple-choice, essay, and true-false items).

    5. Why it is difficult to determine progress in the affective domain through class tests.

The number in parentheses refers to the abridged edition of The Professional Teacher's Handbook, *2nd ed.*

6. The difference between formative and summative tests.

Self-assessment Items (answers provided on p. 330)

(1) Describe how reflective processes may be involved in the following test items:

a. Multiple-choice

b. Essay

(2) How are the unit concept and behavioral outcomes used as a basis for test items?

(3) Under what conditions may a situational test item be relegated to the recall level?

(4) Why are modified test forms so highly recommended (but often neglected)?

(5) Why are affective learnings difficult to measure through class tests?

(6) Distinguish between formative and summative tests.

B: *Modeled demonstration.* Before attempting to apply these techniques, you need an opportunity to examine carefully constructed models. Any one of a variety of approaches to this experience may be employed.

If you are working closely with an experienced teacher or supervisor, this individual might make a variety of measurement and evaluation devices available for examination. Such materials may be especially developed for this purpose, or they may be obtained from the files of highly qualified teachers in your school.

Films and filmstrips provide another possible approach to the problem. Such media, available through a number of commercial companies, tend to emphasize test construction techniques.*

A number of books, some of which appear in the list of supplementary sources, provide examples in various fields. Bloom's and Krathwohl's books on the cognitive and the affective domains should be most useful in this respect. The illustrated testing techniques section of Chap. 21(24) in the Hoover texts provides another useful source. See also p. 350 for an illustrated rating scale.

None of the foregoing conditions is ideal in providing a complete model that closely parallels the guidelines outlined in this LAP. By carefully noting discrepancies, however, the experience can be most useful. (It should be noted that some differences will merely reflect different options in accomplishing the tasks involved.) Whatever approach is used, measurement and evaluation devices from *different* fields of specialization should be examined. Note specifically the following:

1. How the concept is embodied in the stem of multiple-choice test items.

2. How items are made situational.

3. The plausibility of the multiple-choice foils.

---

*One such film is Planning Classroom Tests *from the Nursing Effective Evaluation series, University of Nebraska Television Council, University of Nebraska, 1800 N. 33rd, Lincoln, Nebr., 68503.*

4. How items are tied in with objectives and outcomes.

5. Adequacy and variability of the modified portions of test items.

6. Degree of complexity of the essay item.

7. Adequacy of the ordered categories of the rating scale.

Self-assessment Items (answers provided on p. 330)

(1) Many beginners find that the stems of their multiple-choice items become rather complex, thereby opening the door to more than one interpretation or frame of reference desired. How can this problem be minimized?

(2) Explain why minimum essentials test items tend to be in the psychomotor domain.

(3) "If one misses a multiple-choice item, then the individual, of necessity, must miss the qualified (supporting) item." Defend or refute.

(4) A rating scale can be used as a measuring device. More often, however, it is used as an evaluational device. Why?

C: *Instructional application.* Using your unit concepts and selected behavioral outcomes as a basis, prepare measurement and evaluation devices as indicated. Note that your anticipated behavioral outcomes tend to range from "low" to "high" levels of cognition.* Prepare the following:

1. A situational, modified multiple-choice item. (Any cognitive outcome above the memory or translation level can be used as a basis.)

2. A situational, qualified essay item. (Used most often in areas where complex relationships must be made.)

3. A modified true-false item. (Often applies to the lower levels of cognition.)

4. Now construct a performance-level test item in a mental or motor skills area.

5. Finally, take one of your affective concepts and its behavioral outcomes and construct a rating scale or a checklist. (Each behavioral outcome tends to become a separate scale. Several scales usually make up a rating scale.)

Self-assessment Items (answers provided on p. 330)

(1) One approach to constructing the foils of a multiple-choice test item is to ask the student to select the "correct" answers. A better approach, if one wishes to test at the higher levels of cognition, is to ask the student to select the *best* of four or five acceptable foils. Explain.

For feedback you may want to refer to sample items provided for Part D of your Preassessment items, p. 329.

(2) What prevents the "best-answer" approach to multiple-choice testing from becoming an exercise of guessing the teacher's opinions of what is best in the various test situations?

(3) The naive or uninformed student is likely to claim that the "near-miss" foils are unfair, merely amounting to "splitting hairs." Why is this?

(4) What determines whether one will employ a rating scale or a checklist as an observational tool?

(5) What is the purpose of an anchor item scale as part of a rating scale?

If, after reviewing your learning activities for this LAP, you feel that you can meet the stated objectives, proceed to the posttest. If not, you should complete either Option D or Options E and F.

Optional Activities

D: *Visit with experienced teachers.* Working in a committee with other new teachers if possible, arrange to visit experienced teachers who work in areas that tend to emphasize the different domains of instructional objectives. (You may elect to invite such individuals to visit with your committee, displaying samples of measurement and evaluation devices used.) Arrange to inspect tests and observational devices being used, then hold a discussion with the teachers involved. Concentrate on the following:

Tests

1. Relation of concepts and behavioral objectives
2. Cognitive level emphasized
3. Whether situational or not
4. Type of item emphasized
5. Nature of modified or qualified forms (if any)

When discussing a teacher's philosophy relative to testing techniques, you must avoid a judgmental attitude. Some teachers may never have heard of modified forms, for example, or for reasons of their own, elect not to use them. Your objective is that of ascertaining actual practices of a successful teacher in the area.

Observational devices

1. Relation to concepts and behavioral outcomes
2. Rating scale construction
3. Checklist construction
4. How the devices are used (as measuring or as evaluational scales)

In some cases teachers merely evaluate performance on "general impression only." Oral reports, for example, may be handled in such a manner. In other cases, however, scales consisting of five or more categories may be used. Probably observational devices other than those featured in this LAP also may be in evidence. In any event, find out how satisfied the teacher is with the devices being used. Again, your objective is not to pass judgment but to determine the teacher's rationale for current practices in the area.

Hold a postvisit conference with members of your committee for the purpose of sharing experiences. Use the foregoing as a frame of reference.

Self-assessment Items (answers provided on p. 331)

(1) What are the likely consequences of not using concepts, goals, and behavioral outcomes as a basis for testing and observation?

(2) Some teachers permit students to qualify their answers by commenting on the back of their test answer sheet. (Indeed, this is a rather common practice among college professors.) Although it is better than nothing, what major weaknesses do you see in such a practice?

(3) Why is a "general-impression" rating considered inferior to a carefully developed rating scale?

(4) "Every scale of a rating scale must be checked." Defend or refute.

E: *Written exercise.* Prepare measurement and evaluation devices as indicated below. Base each of these on the concept: Standing up for your rights in a hostile group demands courage.*

1. Modified, situational multiple-choice test item.

2. Situational essay item (be sure to qualify the item).

3. Modified true-false item.

4. One scale of a rating scale.

Self-assessment Items (answers provided on p. 331)

(1) Why is "the best answer" preferred to the "correct answer" for multiple-choice test items?

(2) Why are modified or qualified test forms recommended?

(3) What conditions would cause a teacher to employ a situational item instead of a behavioral (performance) item?

F: *Comparing measurement and evaluation devices from different fields.* Working in a committee of three if possible, each in a different field of specialization, evaluate test items, rating scales, and checklists that have been constructed by other new or prospective teachers in connection with learning activity "C." (Your instructor may

*For feedback you may want to re-examine sample answers for preassessment items (Part D), found on p. 329.

desire to modify this experience by providing copies of tests and observational tools from his/her files or from a resource center.) Note specifically the following:

1. How the concept is embodied in the stem of multiple-choice items.
2. How items are made situational.
3. The plausibility of the multiple-choice foils.
4. How items are tied in with objectives and outcomes.
5. Adequacy and variability of the modified portions of the test items.
6. Degree of complexity of the essay item.
7. Adequacy of the ordered categories of the rating scale.

After each individual has completed the task independently of others, use the foregoing as a basis for a small-group discussion (or reflection if working alone).

Self-assessment Items (answers provided on p. 331)

(1) Many beginners find that the stems of their multiple-choice items become rather complex, thereby opening the door for more than one interpretation or frame of reference. How can this problem be minimized?

(2) Explain why minimum essentials test items tend to be in the psychomotor domain?

(3) If one misses a multiple-choice item, then the individual, of necessity, must miss the qualifier (supporting) item. Defend or refute.

(4) A rating scale can be used as a measuring device. More often, however, it is used as an evaluational device. Why?

POSTTEST (answers provided on pp. 332–34)

After you have finished the learning activities, complete the posttest and evaluate by checking your answers at the end of this LAP. Note that supporting reasons are provided for answers when appropriate.

A. List four essential criteria of measurement and evaluation devices.

1.

2.

3.

4.

B. Place the following code letters before each of the "test item stems" below (recall items embedded in situations or performances should be marked as recall):

R—Recall (memory)

S—Situational (planning level)

P—Performance level (new application)

1. Read over your laboratory sheets and then conduct your laboratory work as requested.

2. Fred and Bill are discussing the importance of flexibility in race relations.

3. What implications does the writer draw relative to the impact of the women's liberation movement?

4. What were the causes of the war in Vietnam?

5. Today we'll form a mock court and trial. Each person will be expected to perform as an individual in the real situation.

6. While we are here at this lake, identify the plants in and near the water and then indicate what this means to you in terms of ecological progression.

7. The rattlesnake struck Joe in the upper forearm. He was several miles from the nearest road, but was in contact with his family by way of a walkie-talkie. Briefly outline what action he should take.

8. What is the first thing one should do in case of fire?

9. Make a sketch of the art object that interests you.

10. You are lost and wandering around in the forest without food, water, or compass. Outline what action you should take.

11. Who were the signers of our Constitution?

12. Consider yourself a lobbyist who wants to influence a state congresswoman. What ethical approaches could you use?

C. Place one of the following code letters before each of the behavioral outcomes listed below. Select the measurement and evaluation device most appropriate for the provided situation.

OR—Observation, using a rating scale

OC—Observation, using a checklist

TR—Test, at the recall level

TS—Test, at the situational level

TP—Test, at the performance level

1. Voluntarily examines the various art selections in a local exhibit.

2. Ranks the issues of importance in eight of nine instances from a provided list.

3. Interacts pleasurably with others toward poetry, based on ten chosen poetic selections.

4. Follows prescribed procedures in preparing a project.

5. Is able to identify the fallacies in provided persuasive speech selections.

6. Makes a stage prop from provided materials.

7. Utilizes effective swimming strokes.

8. Performs several responsibilities in connection with preparation for the tumbling event.

9. Names the ten largest cities from a provided list, with a maximum of two errors.

10. Analyzes the fallacies in an argument on a guaranteed annual income.

11. Habitually confers with his neighbor when doing independent study.

12. Takes dictation at normal conversational rate.

13. Selects nutritious foods each day at lunch over a period of two weeks.

14. Names all action verbs in a selected paragraph with 90 percent accuracy.

15. Identifies the parts of a plant stem from a provided sketch.

16. Compares the Tea Pot Dome Scandal with the Watergate Affair.

17. Places a high value on constitutional rights in a contrived situation.

18. Follows appropriate steps in first aid with a simulated drowning victim.

19. Classifies the organisms observed in a drop of water.

20. Habitually takes a negative approach when a certain individual contributes.

C. Develop test items and observational devices from the provided concepts as indicated.

Test items. CONCEPT: Rights of citizenship are accompanied by responsibilities.

1. Situational multiple-choice item

2. Situational essay item

3. Modified true-false item

Observational devices. CONCEPT: The good citizen expresses his preferences at the polls.

4. One scale of a rating scale

5. A checklist (one point)

Congratulations on achieving mastery of a most difficult and confusing aspect of instruction. If you failed to reach the minimum level of acceptability (thirty-six or thirty-seven of the forty-one requested responses), study the supporting reasons for each of the selected items of the posttest and check yourself on areas of weakness. Then proceed to the LAP on Evaluation Procedures, which follows. The close relationship between the two LAPs will probably further clarify any remaining areas of difficulty. You should find this an intriguing experience.

ANSWERS TO PREASSESSMENT ITEMS

You can make these items a most valuable learning experience by studying the provided reasons for both correct and incorrect responses. You will note that since Part A has no specific number of correct responses, several additional points (characteristics) have been provided. Since the last part calls for your constructed responses, your own answers may not be identical with those supplied by the writer. You should be able to decide whether or not your answers are reasonably correct, however.

A. 1. They are valid and trustworthy—consistent with goals and concepts.

2. They are reliable—produce consistent results.

3. They are objective—can be scored objectively. (Although most measurement and evaluation devices do not fully meet this criterion, they can be rendered as objective as possible.)

4. They should emphasize a learning level that is consistent with the outcomes of instruction.

5. Tests emphasize new applications of principles (concepts).

B. 1-P (Involves direct application.)

2-R (A memory item.)

3-S (Sets up a situation similar to the real thing.)

4-S (Calls for expressing one's "hope," a projection of simulation of reality.)

5-R (The lowest level of comprehension, essentially recall.)

6-S (Sets up a situation involving application.)

7-R (Recalls what the "author" does. If the question had been worded to request the test taker's implications, the question would be at a higher cognitive level.)

8-P (Direct interaction with reality is required.)

9-S (Although the first statement sets up a situation, the student needs no more than memory of the essential steps in preparation of an extemporaneous speech for an answer. Sometimes teachers fall into this trap; they set a realistic situation, then make the answers such that mere recall is needed by the respondent.)

10-S (The student must apply knowledge to a specific situation.)

11-R (The situation demands no more than mere memory.)

12-P (Since a student is asked to prepare such a letter, it is a contrived situation. If, however, a student were actually employed by the AYZ company, such a request would render the item performance in nature.)

C. 1-OC   (This suggests interest; at the responding level of the affective domain. As it is not feasible to establish criteria for quality of questions in such a situation, a mere indication of the fact that questions were asked is probably all that can be done.)

2-OC   (In such a situation, each element of the "procedure" is either followed or it is not.)

3-TS   (Student is expected to reflect in a contrived situation.)

4-TS   (Student is expected to reflect in a contrived situation.)

5-TP   (Actually goes out into reality and performs an act that is requested.)

6-OC   (Voluntary behavior can only be observed; in this case it is impossible to gauge quality of this behavior; thus a check of attendance is all that is possible.)

7-TR   (Mere memory is needed for an answer.)

8-TP   (The student actually does the job.)

9-TS   (If the teacher provides a copy or transcription of the argument, it is a contrived situation. If, however, a visiting speaker happened to provide the presentation, and students were asked to analyze, it would then be a performance item.)

10-TP   (If the debate is real, then the student is interacting directly with reality.)

11-OC   (Calls for an indication of whether one does or does not follow the recommended procedure.)

12-TP   (The student actually performs an act in the real world.)

13-OR   (Each rule of etiquette can be performed in degree—from poor to excellent.)

14-OR   (Each aspect of delivery can be assessed in degree.)

15-TS   (Can easily set up a specific, contrived situation for this.)

16-OC   (One either does or does not select the most appropriate tool. This assumes, of course, that there is one best tool for each of the tasks.)

17-TP   (Assuming that this is an actual speech of the senator, the student is asked to interact in actual reality. If the speech were a simulation, the item would be situational in nature.)

18-OC   (If quality of such "questions" was not demanded or feasible to ascertain, the mere presence or absence of the behavior is all that is needed.)

19-TP   (Since the student is unlikely to have an actual laboratory in which to make the genetic cross, a contrived situation offers the best way of coping with the problem.)

20-OC   (It is probably impossible to ascertain how much or how thoroughly the books were read, but it is possible to note that some were read or checked out. Could make this into a rating scale by number of books checked out, but since the act is voluntary in nature, quantity is probably not of basic importance.)

D. 1. Situational multiple-choice item

Example: Because of financial difficulties, Pam has decided to take a job, even though both partners would prefer that she not work. Which of the following adjustments is probably most basic?

a. Changed role patterns for each partner

b. Changed decision-making pattern relative to financial matters

c. Changed attitude toward each other's work

d. A flexible scheduling of meals

e. All of these of equal importance

Defend your answer.

2. Situation essay item

Example: Can use the same stem as above while adding:

Discuss adjustment problems using the following as a frame of reference:

a. New role patterns

b. Financial arrangements

c. Recreational activities

3. Modified true-false item

Example: When a wife accepts a job, new family relations must be established because *equal status is essential.*

4. Observational devices

a. One scale of a rating scale

(Must be at least three categories.)

Defends a specific behavior logically and consistently most of the time.	Defends a specific behavior logically and consistently some of the time.	Is frequently *unable* to justify a given behavior logically and consistently.

b. Checklist

(Involves checking the presence or absence of a given phenomenon.)

Example: In a values conference, the learner justifies his position on at least one issue.

ANSWERS TO SELF-ASSESSMENT ITEMS

The self-assessment items are designed to help you gain depth of understanding as you proceed through the various learning experiences. Most of them do not have single correct answers. For feedback, however, you should compare your answers with the samples provided here.

A. (1) a. The item stem develops the issue; the different foils or distracters can be so constructed as to involve possible solutions. Thus the student must weigh the merits of each as he reaches a decision.

   b. Again, the item develops the situation; the student himself is expected to identify and develop the possible solutions and to evaluate each.

   (2) The item stem embodies the basic concept. Behavioral outcomes indicate levels of cognition to be sought. Generally the higher levels call for situational or performance items.

   (3) When new relationships or associations are needed for the answer, or when the situation has been handled similarly in class activities.

   (4) They probe depth of understanding and permit the learner to provide his frame of reference (which may differ from that of the teacher).

   (5) The ultimate test of the acquisition of a value is what one does on his own—voluntarily.

   (6) Formulative tests are administered at intervals during the learning process for the purpose of helping the learner assess his own progress. Summative tests, on the other hand, are administered for the purpose of assessing final goal achievement.

B. (1) Embody the concept in the item stem or otherwise clearly identify the idea to be used in responding to the item.

   (2) Degree of skill achievement can be readily assessed. In the cognitive domain, we are usually interested in developmental measures; in the affective domain, we are usually not concerned with evaluating one's degree of commitment to a value.

   (3) Refute. The respondent may provide an acceptable rationale while lacking ability to discriminate adequately between the foils.

   (4) Although degree of goal achievement is assessed, there is no guarantee that each scale will carry equal weight or that each scale will be valid for a given observation.

C. (1) Problem solving involves selecting from among a number of possible solutions. Otherwise, the item actually demands no more than mere recall (the lower levels of cognition).

   (2) The concept serves as a basic frame of reference; sometimes it helps by referring to a frame of reference developed in class. For example, "From Milton's point of view . . ."

   (3) The situational multiple-choice item demands considerable discrimination. Superficial understanding does not equip a learner for such items or for immediate posttest clarification.

   (4) If the presence or absence of a factor is all that is needed, a checklist is used. If, however, the quality of such factors is to be assessed, then a rating scale is used.

   (5) Since behavior is extremely complex, it is most difficult to identify all relevant aspects of the situation. The anchor scale is a "catch-all" used to take care of any such neglected areas.

Optional Activities

D. (1) Textbook teaching, usually at the recall level. At best, such tests and devices are likely to have minimum validity.

(2) If a number of large classes are involved, there is a tendency to omit evaluation of such comments.

A student may not realize that his frame of reference differs from that of the teacher. Thus he may not offer comments when they are most needed.

(3) In such situations there is a decided tendency for one to subconsciously focus on one or two criteria (called the "halo effect"). Use of several scales forces the teacher to consider others that may be equally important to the experience.

(4) Refute. Evidence will vary from one setting to another. Sometimes certain scale points will not be in evidence; occasionally the observer may miss a point or two (representing different scales).

E. (1) Selecting the best answer demands careful weighing of selected alternatives. The "correct" answer merely demands ability to distinguish between right and wrong responses. The former demands a higher level of cognition than the latter.

(2) They probe for depth of understanding. They also facilitate communication between teacher and student.

(3) When the conditions for a behavioral item do not exist or are extremely difficult to construct. It would be impractical to deliberately induce shock, for example, for the purpose of testing student reactions.

F. (1) Embody the concept in the item stem or otherwise clearly identify the idea to be used in responding to the item.

(2) Degree of skill achievement can be readily assessed. In the cognitive domain, we are usually interested in developmental measures; in the affective domain, we are usually not concerned with evaluating one's degree of commitment to a value.

(3) Refute. The respondent may provide an acceptable rationale while lacking ability to discriminate adequately between the foils.

(4) Although degree of goal achievement is assessed, there is no guarantee that each scale will carry equal weight or that each scale will be valid for a given observation.

ANSWERS TO POSTTEST

For most beneficial results you should work through the entire LAP before checking your answers to the posttests. Failure to meet the provided minimum standards probably suggests certain weaknesses that need to be corrected. As with the Preassessment items, you will find supporting reasons for answers. It is hoped that this will serve as desirable feedback in your quest for mastery.

A. 1.   They are valid and trustworthy (consistent with goals and concepts).

2.   They are reliable (produce consistent results).

3.   They are objective (can be scored objectively). Although most measurement and evaluation tools do not meet this criterion fully, they can be rendered as objective as possible.

4.   They should emphasize a learning level that is consistent with the outcomes of instruction actually achieved.

5.   Tests emphasize new applications of principles (concepts).

B. 1-P   (Students must interact directly in reality.)

2-S   (For evaluational purposes this would likely be a contrived situation.)

3-R   (Must merely recall what the writer does. The student's implications are *not* requested.)

4-R   (Mere knowledge is needed.)

5-S   (The "trial" is not real; merely a simulation of reality.)

6-P   (The student is asked to interact directly with reality.)

7-S   (A projected situation—not reality itself.)

8-R   (Demands memory only.)

9-P   (Deals with actual objects.)

10-S   (A simulation of reality.)

11-R   (Mere knowledge is demanded.)

12-S   (Projects the student into a contrived situation.)

C. 1-OC   (Does the act occur or does it not? Although it is possible to establish degree of examination, since this is a voluntary act, it would hardly be feasible to assess.)

2-TR   (Student merely recalls, on the basis of past learning experiences.)

3-OR   (The nature of this pleasurable interaction can be measured, e.g., asks questions, chuckles, responds, etc.)

4-OC   (Established procedures are or are not followed; degree of following these is usually not an issue.)

5-TP   (The provided speeches entail a contrived situation.)

6-TP   (Student is expected to perform an actual task in reality.)

7-OR   (Degree of appropriate use is usually important. Consider the LIKERT form: Always uses, sometimes uses, uncertain, seldom uses, never uses.)

8-OC   (In a practical situation, the teacher usually merely checks those who have [or have not] performed such responsibilities.)

9-TR   (Mere knowledge is needed.)

10-TS   (Usually calls for providing the student with such an argument, often developed for this purpose.)

11-OC   (Such a behavior usually is checked merely for trends or patterns.)

12-TP (Best to ask the student to do the actual task.)

13-OC (Under such conditions a mere check is the most practical.)

14-TR (Even though the verbs are placed in a contrived situation (selected paragraphs), all student needs do is employ knowledge.)

15-TS (The sketch makes this a situation in which application is demanded.)

16-TS (Can easily provide a contrived situation for this.)

17-OR (This would seem to lend itself to a simulation involving a complexity of interaction. "High value" suggests relative degrees of application. Could employ a situational test item if *one* specific right were emphasized.)

18-OC (Although this is a simulation, a series of correct steps is expected.)

19-TP (Student is expected to perform the actual task.)

20-OR (Degree of "negative approach" is difficult, if not impossible, to assess. Thus a check of "yes" or "no" is probably preferred.)

D. 1. Situational multiple-choice item (example)

(Concept: Rights of citizenship are accompanied with responsibilities.) Jim has recently reached his eighteenth birthday. It suddenly dawns upon him that he should vote in the forthcoming election (ten days off), for which he is unprepared. Which of the following represents the most appropriate action for a responsible citizen?

a. Bypass the election this time since he is unprepared.

b. Go ahead and vote on the basis of the meager evidence he has.

c. Go to responsible adults for advice on how to vote.

d. Use the next ten days to make himself a qualified voter.

Defend your answer.

2. Situational essay item

Example (can use the same item stem as above, while adding):

Discuss voting responsibilities in terms of:

a. Getting acquainted with the issues

b. Political influence

c. Propaganda appeals

3. Modified true-false item

Example: An individual who feels unprepared for voting wisely *should stay home on election day.*

4. Observation devices

a. One scale of a rating scale

(Must be at least three categories.)

Example: CONCEPT: The good citizen expresses his opinions at the polls.

Votes in most elections for which he is qualified.	Votes in some elections for which he is qualified.	Seldom votes in elections for which he is qualified.

b. Checklist

(Involves checking the presence or absence of a given phenomenon.)

Example: The voter appears at the polls at the ———election.

c. Anecdotal record

(Contains identifiable information, the situation, and an evaluation of the situation (optional).

SUPPLEMENTARY SOURCES

The following sources may be used in lieu of the Hoover texts or, preferably, as supplementary to them. Generally they are consistent with the models provided in the LAPs of this module. As such, the references do not represent all of the most recent references in the area; rather, they constitute selected references designed to broaden or expand needed background information.

Beggs, Donald L., and Ernest L. Lewis, *Measurement and Evaluation in the Schools* (Boston: Houghton Mifflin Co., 1975).

Bloom, Benjamin S., ed., *Taxonomy of Educational Objectives, Handbook I: Cognitive Domain* (New York: David McKay Co., 1956).

Cartwright, Carol A., and Phillip Cartwright, *Developing Observation Skills* (New York: McGraw-Hill Book Co., 1974).

Chase, Clinton I., *Measurement for Educational Evaluation* (Reading, Mass.: Addison-Wesley Publishing Co., 1974).

Englehart, Max D., *Improving Classroom Testing: What Research Says to the Teacher*, No. 31 (Washington, D.C.: National Education Association).

Gorow, Frank F., *Better Classroom Testing* (San Francisco, Calif.: Chandler Publishing Company, 1966).

Gronlund, Norman E., *Preparing Criterion-Referenced Tests for Classroom Instruction* (New York: The Macmillan Co., 1973).

Hoover, Kenneth H., *The Professional Teacher's Handbook*, 2nd ed. (Boston: Allyn and Bacon, Inc., 1976).

Hoover, Kenneth H., and Paul M. Hollingsworth, *Learning and Teaching in the Elementary School*, 2nd ed. (Boston: Allyn and Bacon, Inc., 1975).

Krathwohl, David R., Benjamin S. Bloom, and Bertram S. Masia, *Taxonomy of Educational Objectives, Handbook II: Affective Domain* (New York: David McKay Co., 1964).

Kryspin, William J., and John F. Feldhusen, *Developing Classroom Tests: A Guide for Writing and Evaluating Test Items* (Minneapolis, Minn.: Burgess Publishing Co., 1974).

Mager, Robert, *Measuring Instructional Interest* (Belmont, Calif.: Fearon Publishing Co., 1973).

Marshall, Jon C., and Loyde W. Hales, *Classroom Test Construction* (Reading, Mass.: Addison-Wesley Publishing Co., 1971).

Popham, W. James, *Educational Evaluation* (Englewood Cliffs, N.J.: Prentice-Hall, Inc., 1975).

Rasor, J. E., "Skill Acquisition: A Practical Illustration," *Physical Education*, 28: 155–157 (Oct., 1971).

Thyne, James M., *Principles of Examining* (New York: John Wiley and Sons, 1974).

Wick, John W., *Educational Measurement* (Columbus, Ohio: Charles E. Merrill Publishing Co., 1973).

lap

14

Evaluation Procedures

RATIONALE. Tests and observational devices are merely tools to facilitate evaluation. A superior test is of minimal value in the hands of an incompetent evaluator. Every teacher ultimately must determine the degree of success of each student. In some contexts this task may be accomplished in terms of individual progress toward projected behavioral outcomes, as in the LAPs of this manual. At other times, however, the ends sought are of such a nature and complexity as to necessitate evaluation relative to the progress of other students in the class. Although essentially subjective in nature, evaluation need not be haphazard or nonscientific.

OVERVIEW

Key Concepts

1. Minimum essentials objectives, to be achieved by *all* students, are judged by absolute measures rather than by the scores of other individuals in class.

2. Developmental objectives, to be achieved in varying degrees by different students, may be assessed in terms of the class norm.

3. Evaluational experiences, when interpreted in terms of group performance, are recorded as standard (as opposed to raw) scores.

4. Standard scores (letter grades or stanine marks) are based upon the normal probability curve and thus can be weighted directly and combined for marking purposes. (Raw scores cannot be so combined.)

5. A good test item (when used to measure developmental objectives) has a difficulty value of between 50 and 60 percent.

6. Marks based upon the normal probability curve are based upon the assumption that every individual, regardless of ability, has an equal chance of success.

7. Evaluation is most appropriately based upon actual achievement, rather than ability to achieve.

New Terms

1. Normal probability curve: The expected frequency distribution (bell-shaped) in any unselected group. Scores characteristically cluster near the middle and taper off uniformly toward each extreme.

2. Standard score: Derived from a raw score, a standard score is based on a uniform standard scale (normal probability curve). Its use simplifies comparisons and interpretations of scores on different measures.

3. Item analysis: A technique for assessing the difficulty level and discriminating power of a test item, based on actual student responses. Item difficulty is usually expressed as a percent of those who failed to answer an item correctly. Item discrimination is usually expressed as a ratio between good and poor students who answered an item correctly.

4. Minimum passing score: The lowest score that satisfies a particular requirement. It essentially separates students into pass or fail groups. Determination usually involves a number of somewhat arbitrary decisions.

OBJECTIVES. After this experience you should be able to evaluate students effectively, as evidenced by your ability to:

1. List five essential characteristics of evaluation.

2. Distinguish in eleven out of twelve instances appropriate occasions for criterion-referenced and norm-referenced measures.

3. Select in eight out of nine instances appropriate applications of the normal probability curve from an assorted list of twenty applications.

4. Derive stanines (9-1) and letter grades (A-E) from provided data.

PRELIMINARY READING. Since the elements of instructional methodology are somewhat variable, the following excerpts are provided to help you develop a frame of reference as a point of departure for this experience. If you prefer, you may proceed directly to the Preassessment items.

NORMAL PROBABILITY CURVE

In cases when it is impractical to evaluate progress on the basis of an individual's capacity for progress, one must turn to techniques of assessing progress in terms of that of the *group.* Almost any characteristic or trait is present in varying degrees in any *representative* population. The *pattern* of variation in class groups will always approach a bell-shaped curve so long as the group is *representative* of the entire population. Small groups (fewer than thirty), by chance, usually distribute unevenly along the curve.

Assuming a representative group, in terms of academic aptitude (IQ), we could expect about two-thirds (68.26 percent) of our group to fall within the average category of aptitude, while the remaining third would be evenly distributed between below-average and above-average range of aptitudes. Now if we have a *representative amount of progress,* an application of the normal curve concept would give those students with lowest ability failing marks, and those with highest ability the highest marks. In effect, we are awarding a class mark on the basis of one's ability rather than on the basis of actual achievement. In short, when a teacher uses the normal probability curve as a basis for the distribution of marks, it is presumed that all students have a fairly equal chance. It is only under such conditions that the curve holds validity for the assessment of achievement.

STANINE DISTRIBUTION

The stanine distribution is a simple nine-point scale of standard scores. The word *stanine* is derived from the words *STAndard NINE.* Raw scores are converted to standard scores, ranging from 1 (low) to 9 (high). Thus raw scores can be grouped into intervals or classes. Just as the traditional A, B, C, D, and F scale represented five divisions of a normal distribution curve, so does the stanine represent nine divisions of a normal distribution. The stanine has at least two practical advantages over the five-letter scale distribution system:

1. It enables a teacher to divide class scores directly into nine intervals or classes of whole numbers. In actual practice the use of the traditional five-letter procedure often is somewhat time-consuming. Traditional letter marks, when combined, must be transposed into numbers and then back again into letter marks for student interpretation. Furthermore, if greater accuracy is sought through the use of plus and minus signs, the use of decimals becomes necessary.

2. Stanine scores for one test or project are easily weighted, for the purpose of combining with other stanine scores. For example, if a teacher decides that a given test should count twice as much as another test, he merely multiplies the stanine scores of the more important test by 2 and adds the product to stanine scores of other tests.

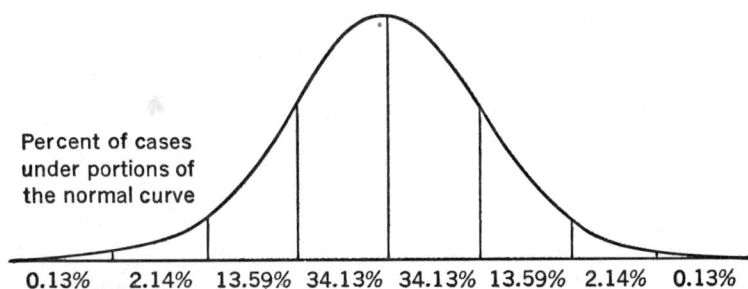

Percent of cases under portions of the normal curve

0.13%   2.14%   13.59%   34.13%   34.13%   13.59%   2.14%   0.13%

FIGURE 14-1. *Normal Probability Curve*

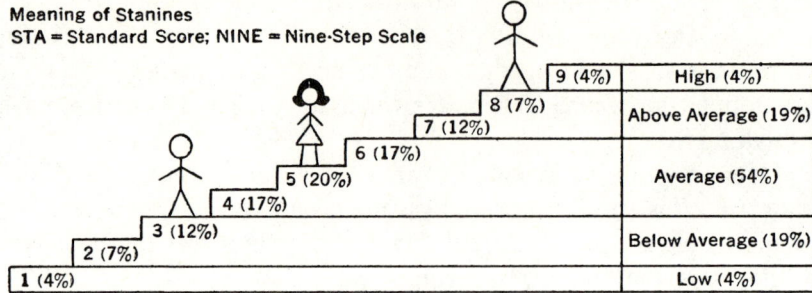

Meaning of Stanines
STA = Standard Score; NINE = Nine-Step Scale

9 (4%)	High (4%)
8 (7%)	Above Average (19%)
7 (12%)	
6 (17%)	Average (54%)
5 (20%)	
4 (17%)	
3 (12%)	Below Average (19%)
2 (7%)	
1 (4%)	Low (4%)

FIGURE 14-2. *Percentage of Cases at Each Stanine Level*

(Reproduced from *Test Service Notebook*, No. 23 [New York: Harcourt, Brace & World, Inc., 1961]. Used by permission of the publisher.)

Stanine scores will conform to the proportions of the *normal curve*. Percentages of the class group(s) which fall within each of the nine stanine classifications for a normal population are shown in Figure 14-2. A useful characteristic of stanines is the equally distanced steps involved.

Stanines can be just as readily applied to written papers, drawings, products, or other exercises as they can to test scores. The only requirement is that the papers or products be serialized or ranked from high to low. For example, individual class projects in industrial arts can be assigned ranks of Excellent, Very Good, Good, Fair, and Poor. Then each project *within each rank* can be serialized from high to low. After serializing or ranking all of the projects in this manner, it is easy to determine the number of cases at each stanine level.

Use of the stanine distribution has been effectively illustrated by Durost, in Table 14-1.[1]

Directions for Table 14-1:

1. Arrange test papers on answer sheets in rank order from high to low. On a separate piece of paper, list every score in a column from the highest obtained score to the lowest (column A). Opposite each score write the number of individuals who obtained that score. This may be done by counting the papers or answer sheets having the same score, or it may be done by tallying the scores in the manner shown in column B.

2. Add the frequencies (C) and write the total at the bottom of the column (D). This is shown to be 90.

3. Beginning at the bottom, count up (cumulate) to one-half the total number of scores, in this case 45 (one-half of 90). This falls opposite the score of 34 (E), which is the median to the nearest whole number.

4. In the column at the extreme right are the theoretical frequencies of cases at each stanine level for 90 cases. Starting with the median, lay off as nearly this number (18) of scores as you can. Here it is 20.

5. Working upward and downward from scores falling in stanine 5, assign scores to stanine levels so as to give the closest approximation possible to the theoretical values. It is helpful to bracket these scores in the manner shown in column A.

---

[1] *Walter N. Durost, "The Characteristics, Use, and Computation of Stanines," Test Service Notebook, No. 23 (New York: Harcourt, Brace & World, Inc., 1961), p. 6.*

TABLE 14-1. *Distribution of Raw Test Scores in a Stanine Distribution*

Stanine	Score Interval	Tallies	Frequencies	Grouping Actual	Theoretical
9	58	/	1	4	4
	57		–		
	56	/	1		
	55	//	2		
8	54		–	7	6
	53		–		
	52		–		
	51	/	1		
	50	/	1		
	49	//	2		
	48		–		
	47	///	3		
7	46	/	1	12	11
	45	///	3		
	44	//	2		
	43		–		
	42	⧸⧸⧸⧸ /	6		
6	41	//	2	12	15
	40	//	2		
	39	//	2		
	38	/	1		
	37	⧸⧸⧸⧸	5		
5	36	⧸⧸⧸⧸	5	20	18
	35	//	2		
	34	⧸⧸⧸⧸ //	7		
	33	///	3		
	32	///	3		
4	31	⧸⧸⧸⧸	5	14	15
	30	/	1		
	29	///	3		
	28	///	3		
	27	//	2		
3	26	////	4	13	11
	25	⧸⧸⧸⧸ /	6		
	24	///	3		
2	23	/	1	4	6
	22	/	1		
	21	//	2		
1	20	/	1	4	4
	19		–		
	18	/	1		
	17	//	2		
			90		

(Circled letters (A) above Score Interval, (B) above Tallies, (C) above Frequencies, (E) pointing to score 34, (D) pointing to total 90.)

After having made a tentative assignment, make any adjustments necessary to bring the actual frequencies at each level into the closest possible agreement with the theoretical values. Remember, however, that all equal scores *must* be assigned the same stanines.

Handling Test Scores. Some teachers reason that the raw scores on each test can be added, with perhaps some additional weight being given to such important measures as the final test. Logically, each test or measure is viewed as part of one big test over the entire course. Although apparently logically defensible, it should be noted that when the raw scores of several measures are combined, those with greater variability (range of scores) have greater weights.

While it is true that a test of greater variability *may* indicate greater reliability, the difference in variability is more likely attributable to the arbitrary nature of different units of measurement in the two cases. In a practical classroom situation it is extremely unlikely that variability of tests of equal importance can be kept equal. The range difference between two tests will differ as much as 30 points for no apparent reason. It is possible to correct for this by adding a constant to the test with least variability, but most students are unlikely to understand the real reason for such a practice.

The most reliable procedure seems to be to convert scores on each test to grade equivalents. While teachers traditionally have favored a five-point scale, many are beginning to make use of the stanine system, described in the previous topic. This has the advantage of units which can readily be added at the end of the course.

There is one hazard, however, that should be taken into account when standard scores are averaged. There is a tendency for marks to *regress toward the mean or average.* Thus actual progress of the weaker students will really be less than indicated. Likewise, actual progress of the better student will be more than is indicated. The problem may be corrected at the end of the course by subjecting the final stanine (or letter mark) to a frequency distribution. Thus a stanine of 7.3 *may* by sufficient for a mark of "A." Such an evaluation would depend on the percent of "A"s deemed appropriate by the instructor.

Deriving Class Marks.   Although not ideal, the following guidelines are offered:

First, at least some marks might be based upon a criterion-referenced measure. This criterion-referenced score is a point along a continuum of subject matter or skill that indicates the degree of proficiency achieved by an individual without reference to anyone else. A minimum proficiency level of 85 or 90 percent is usually established. It is most easily applied in areas where there is some absolute unit of measurement, as in motor or mental skills areas.

A second guideline for the derivation of class marks could be based on some normative procedure involving use of the normal curve of probability. There may be times, for example, when no student can reach the predetermined level of proficiency set for a criterion-referenced measure. If the predetermined proficiency level were realistically determined (based on the *attained* proficiency levels of other students), generally low achievement levels would suggest the presence of a class problem, possibly beyond the control of the student. Thus adjustments could be made on the basis of group progress.

Introduction of the criterion-referenced system can begin in a small way with those skills that are most easily identifiable. During the transition period at least, both criterion-referenced and norm-referenced scores would be essential in the derivation of marks.

In deriving class marks the *first* task is to record the results of *each* measure as a standard score. Raw scores are not usually recorded at all.

Second, the teacher decides the major dimensions which appropriately enter into derivation of a class grade. For example, ten quizzes, four class papers, two oral presentations, and the mid-term test might be judged as of equal importance. The final test might be considered equal to *two* of the foregoing dimensions. Likewise, all criterion-referenced measures are included.

Third, the *standard* scores for each dimension are averaged. For example, the ten quizzes would be averaged, then the four class papers, followed by the two oral presentations.

Fourth, each of the *averaged* marks, in turn, will be averaged. This will provide the teacher with an average standard score. Since averaging of averages tends to produce a regression effect toward the mean (previously explained), the final average standard scores can be evaluated on the basis of a normal curve. From this, class grades may be derived.

It should be noted that such a procedure is considered inappropriate if it is possible to evaluate an individual entirely on his/her own performance, as in skills areas. Until such time as teachers have developed adequate criterion-referenced scales in the academic areas, some such approach may be used.

PREASSESSMENT ITEMS (answers provided on pp. 354–55)

This experience is designed to help you gain an overall perspective of evaluational procedures used in teaching. After completing these items, turn to the end of this LAP and check your answers. Note that answers (both correct and incorrect) are provided with supporting reasons to help you further your understanding of the concepts involved.

A. List five essential characteristics of evaluation. (To illustrate: Evaluation is based upon progress toward projected behavioral outcomes.)

1.

2.

3.

4.

5.

B. Place one of the code letters before each of the occasions for evaluation listed below:

CR—Criterion-referenced measure

NR—Norm-referenced measure

1. Evaluating a term project.

2. Evaluating a speech performance.

3. Evaluating the student's ability to appraise the merits of NATO.

4. Evaluating a shop project.

5. Evaluating a student's paper on "ambition."

6. Evaluating a student's ability to type a business letter.

7. Evaluating a student's ability to contrast the Tea Pot Dome Scandal with the Watergate Affair.

8. Evaluating the student's ability to solve selected thought problems in math.

9. Evaluating the student's ability to analyze the fallacies in an argument.

10. Evaluating the student's ability to demonstrate the strokes in swimming.

11. Evaluating the student's ability to demonstrate various genetic crosses.

12. Evaluating the student's steps in making a garment.

C. From the list of normal probability curve "applications" to evaluation, place a check ($\sqrt{}$) by nine of those that are appropriate.

1. Students should have similar abilities (be homogeneous).

2. Students should possess abilities ranging from one extreme to the other (be heterogeneous).

3. A minimum class size of twenty is needed.

4. A certain percentage must receive an "A," just as a certain percentage must receive an "E."

5. The concept of the curve can be used only when score-type data are available.

6. The curve serves as a guide to distribution of marks.

7. A class size of at least thirty is needed.

8. The curve is useful for norm-referenced measures.

9. Results tell one how much standard error of measurement must be taken into account.

10. Approximately half of the students will fall within the middle (or "C") range.

11. Theoretically the same number who receive the highest mark should receive the lowest mark.

12. For the evaluation to be useful, at least 100 students should be involved.

13. Students with the same score should receive the same evaluation.

14. The curve is useful for criterion-referenced measures.

15. Stanine, letter grades, and percentages are basically norm-referenced concepts.

16. Determining, in advance of a test, what percentages of students will represent certain marks frees one from the disadvantages of the curve.

17. Classes in the same subject (taught by the same teacher) may be combined for evaluation on the basis of the curve.

18. The stanine system of evaluation is superior to letter grades.

19. When a test is unusually hard or easy, use of the curve is inappropriate.

20. The curve cannot be applied in an "honors class," regardless of the number of students who may be present.

D. From the provided test data, derive stanines and then letter grades.

107	70
105	70
104	67
94	67
90	65
89	64
88	63
87	60
87	59
86	59
85	59
84	58
81	58
80	56
79	55
79	54
78	54
77	43
76	39
75	38
75	
72	N = 42

If you were able to provide thirty-six of the forty requested responses, you are well ahead of many experienced teachers and probably do not need the work provided in this LAP. Even if you were able to supply few of the appropriate responses, do not be disheartened, for the provided experiences have been especially designed to help you achieve the necessary competence as expeditiously as possible. Emphasis has been placed upon an activity-oriented program.

LEARNING ACTIVITIES

Work through each learning activity, complete the self-assessment items, and check your answers before moving to the next one. Note that the last learning activity is optional, depending upon your needs and situation at that point. You should be able to complete this LAP in about three or four hours.

A: *Read.* Re-examine the overview and the preliminary reading sections of this LAP and the preceding one in this module. You will broaden your understanding substantially by studying Chap. 22(25) of the Hoover texts and/or by studying the selected references at the end of this LAP. Note specifically the following points:

1. The relationship between minimum essentials and developmental outcomes with criterion-referenced and norm-referenced evaluation.

2. The advantages of stanine scores over letter grades.

3. The effect of combining raw test scores.

4. The limitations of norm-referenced and criterion-referenced measures.

Self-assessment Items (answers provided on p. 356)

(1) Why are developmental outcomes normally evaluated on a norm-referenced scale?

(2) Why is the stanine recommended over use of letter grades through a course?

(3) Some teachers merely develop a point system for all tests and activities to be evaluated. They are recorded and combined for the purpose of arriving at a class grade. Although apparently logically sound, the practice is fallacious. Explain why.

(4) Norm-referenced measures are less valid in required classes today than they were in the early decades of the twentieth century. Defend or refute.

B: *Examination of models.* Now that you have a basic understanding of the techniques of evaluation, you need an opportunity to examine carefully constructed models of these techniques. This step can be accomplished in a number of ways, depending upon prevailing conditions.

If you are working closely with an experienced teacher or supervisor, this individual may want to make a variety of actual evaluation illustrations available for examination. Such materials may be especially developed for this purpose or collected from the files of highly qualified teachers in your school.

A number of books (see list of supplementary sources) provide useful data in the area. In this connection the reader is urged to examine the illustrated evaluation techniques section of Chap. 22(25) in the Hoover texts.

Other options are available, such as films, filmstrips, and videotapes. Most of these, however, tend to emphasize the "why" and the "what" as opposed to the "how."*

With the exception of the provided illustrations in the Hoover texts the suggested alternatives for observation are likely to fall short of providing a complete model. If, however, discrepancies are noted, the experience can be most valuable. Evaluational techniques from different fields can clarify basic differences between norm-referenced and criterion-referenced evaluation. Note specifically the following:

1. How assignments, used in connection with learning activities, are applied in evaluation. (Note specifically quizzes, open-book tests, reports, written papers, and exercises.)

---

*Two such media are: Evaluation of Student Performance *(film), from the Teaching Role Series, Minnesota Video Nursing Education, 801 E. 26th, Minneapolis, Minn. 55404; and* Current Conceptions of Educational Evaluation *(sound filmstrip), Vimcit Associates, P. O. Box 24714, Los Angeles, Calif. 90024.*

2. How observational devices are used in norm-referenced and criterion-referenced assessment.

3. Problems associated with including norm-referenced and criterion-referenced items on the same test.

4. The place for optional (extra) assignments in norm-referenced and criterion-referenced evaluation.

5. How criterion-referenced evaluation is translated into letter grades.

6. Cases when assumption of a normal curve of probability likely would be erroneous.

Use the foregoing points as a basis for small-group discussion if you are working through the LAP with other new teachers.

Self-assessment Items (answers provided on pp. 356–57)

(1) The efforts of students who are completing learning tasks for the first or second time should not be subjected to evaluation for a class mark. Why?

(2) What are the relative merits of using a rating scale as a criterion-referenced measure as opposed to a norm-referenced measure?

(3) A checklist can be readily used as a criterion-referenced measure with a minimum standard of 90 percent. Defend or refute.

(4) Why must minimum essentials items be evaluated separately from norm-referenced items on the same test?

(5) Optional or extra work should have no bearing on either norm-referenced or criterion-referenced assessment. Defend or refute.

(6) Evaluation may be planned so as to pass all students who meet the minimum essentials with the accepted standard of accuracy, and to award "A"s and "B"s to those who go beyond the minimum essentials. Defend or refute.

(7) Indicate three cases in which use of the normal probability curve would not be appropriate for evaluational purposes.

C: *Instructional application.* *

1. From the provided norm-referenced data, derive stanine marks *and* letter grades.

After you have completed the tasks for this learning activity you may want to check your responses with the answers on pp. 359–60.

Test results

177	119	89
170	117	87
157	114	86
156	110	83
156	110	81
148	110	80
145	110	76
142	108	75
140	108	72
134	108	70
134	106	68
130	104	60
129	99	58
126	99	52
126	97	28
122	94	N = 47

2. From the criterion-referenced data, assign stanine marks. Twenty students completed all requirements and all optional activities with a 90-percent accuracy level.

Ten students completed all required activities with a 90-percent accuracy level.

Seven students originally completed all required and all optional activities with a 75-percent accuracy level. After working through the program the second time, three attained a 90-percent accuracy level, while four reached an 80-percent accuracy level.

Three students completed all required activities with a 50-percent accuracy level. They did not bother to work through the materials the second time.

3. From the provided data, derive an average stanine mark for each student.

Course Average (Stanines)

8.3	6.6	6.1	5.5	4.9	4.4
7.9	6.6	6.0	5.5	4.8	4.4
7.8	6.5	6.0	5.5	4.8	4.3
7.7	6.5	6.0	5.4	4.7	4.2
7.3	6.5	6.0	5.4	4.6	4.2
7.2	6.5	5.9	5.4	4.6	4.0
7.2	6.5	5.9	5.3	4.6	3.7
7.1	6.4	5.8	5.3	4.5	3.5
7.0	6.3	5.8	5.3	4.5	3.4
6.9	6.3	5.6	5.3	4.5	3.3
6.9	6.2	5.6	5.2	4.5	3.1
6.8	6.2	5.5	5.2	4.5	2.5
6.8	6.2	5.5	5.1	4.5	2.3
6.8	6.1	5.5	5.0	4.4	N = 83

4. From the provided course average stanines, derive a final course stanine for each student *and* assign letter grades.

Term Averaging

	Seven quizzes	Fifteen periods of class participation	Three reading analysis reports	Mid-term exam*	Term project	Optional work†	Final exam*	Term average
Ellen	4.1	5	8.0	7	9	7.6	6	
Judy	5.0	3	6.7	5	4		6	
Bill	4.1	9	7.0	4	8	9	8	
Bob	4.9	6	6.7	4	7		7	
Pat	6.6	9	7.0	3	7		7	
Yvonne	7.4	7	8.7	9	9		8	
Mary	7.3	6	7.0	7	7		6	
Moya	1.3	6	5.0	2	7		3	
Valiane	3.4	5	5.0	5	5		1	
George	7.0	5	7.3	3	6		4	
Marla	3.0	6	3.7	3	7		4	
Diane	2.3	6	2.0	2	5		4	
Elaine	5.7	2	7.7	8	7		7	
Lynda	4.0	6	4.7	6	7	5.0	3	
Larry	4.9	7	3.0	2	7	8.0	4	
Kathy	6.1	7	8.0	7	6		4	
Mary Lou	4.0	6	8.0	4	8		5	
Nancy	5.3	6	7.7	9	8	8.9	9	
Lindy	1.9	6	5.0	5	6		2	
Johnnie	1.7	5	5.7	5	9		5	
Penny	2.7	2	5.7	6	6		5	
Mary Jo	2.1	4	1.0	4	1		5	
Carol	2.7	7	7.7	4	6		5	
Fred	5.0	7	8.3	7	8		6	
Christine	5.1	7	8.0	8	8		6	
Sandy	2.3	5	4.3	4	4		4	
Charlene	6.3	5	8.0	9	4		8	
Glenna	5.4	5	8.0	5	6		4	
Janie	3.7	5	5.7	5	7	8.6	6	
Maureen	3.9	8	7.7	5	9	8.0	7	
Ruthanne	3.7	4	7.3	7	7	7.3	5	
Marijane	2.4	6	6.3	4	8		2	

*Since the teacher desires that the mid-term and final each count about 25 percent, an extra stanine should be added for each of these. All other activities count equally.

†For students who completed optional work, the term average is derived by dividing by nine instead of eight.

Self-assessment Items (answers provided on p. 357)

(1) In applying the normal probability curve, the lowest class mark can be appropriately evaluated a "C" if the teacher so desires. Defend or refute.

(2) In assessing the quality of a test score for a norm-referenced test (item analysis), why is a success level of 50 to 60 percent considered ideal?

(3) When stanine marks are averaged at the end of the term to derive a final average, there is a tendency for the final average to "regress toward the mean." What implications does this have for deriving class marks?

    (4)   Students who are unable to meet criterion-referenced requirements at the minimum level of acceptability should be failed. Defend or refute.

    (5)   Let us suppose that a term project is being evaluated on a criterion-referenced scale. What would you do if the project failed to meet the established minimum level of requirements?

If, after reviewing your learning activities for this LAP, you feel that you can meet the stated objectives, proceed to the posttest. If not, you should complete at least one of the optional activities. Note that each provides for a number of optional situations, depending upon your own individual circumstances.

Optional Activities

D: *Visit with experienced teachers.* Working in a committee with other new teachers if possible, arrange to visit experienced teachers who work in areas that emphasize the different domains of educational objectives. (You may elect to invite such individuals to visit with your committee and to display samples of evaluational procedures employed.) Arrange to inspect evaluational data (use the previous learning activity as a guide) and then hold a discussion with the teachers involved. (Be careful not to criticize techniques that seem questionable to you.) Concentrate on the following points:

1. Have one member visit a teacher in a basic skills course, such as typing or foreign language, for the purpose of obtaining the following:

    a. Nature of criterion-referenced measures employed.

    b. Standard level of performance expected.

    c. How a student's failure to meet prescribed levels of performance is handled.

    d. How letter grades (if any) are derived.

2. Have a second member of your committee visit a teacher whose classes are essentially divided between skills and other types of learning (e.g., biology, home economics, math). Determine how criterion-referenced measures are integrated with norm-referenced assessment. Seek the following:

    a. What areas are used for each type of measurement.

    b. What standard of performance is expected in each.

    c. How substandard work is handled and marked.

    d. How criterion-referenced and norm-referenced evaluations are combined for final evaluational purposes.

3. Have a third member of your committee visit a teacher of a class that is essentially cognitive and/or affective in nature, such as literature, history, or general business. Determine how norm-referenced measures are employed, seeking the following information:

    a. How tests and observational devices are evaluated (e.g., stanine, letter grades, percentages, etc.).

b. Minimum level of performance (if any) expected.

c. How substandard achievement is handled.

d. Special provisions (if any) for less able students.

e. What criterion-referenced measures (if any) are employed.

Hold a postvisit conference with members of your committee, if possible, for the purpose of sharing experiences. (If you are working alone, you will find it desirable to visit three different teachers.) Use the foregoing as a frame of reference.

Self-assessment Items (answers provided on p. 357)

(1) Some teachers who use various criterion-referenced measures (e.g., for a class project) do not establish a minimum level of performance. What implications does this practice hold for the quality of student work?

(2) An accuracy level of 85 to 90 percent usually is established as a minimum level of performance for criterion-referenced measures. Why not 75 or 80 percent?

(3) The conventional item analysis technique is inappropriate for criterion-referenced measures. Why?

(4) How would you evaluate the traditional practice of establishing a minimum passing score and various grade score ranges (for a norm-referenced measure) prior to the administration of the measure?

(5) Students with widely ranging abilities can be evaluated effectively on a norm-referenced scale. Defend or refute.

E: *Written exercise.*

1. Class participation. Evaluate the following data by deriving a stanine mark for each student.*

27	7
21	6
17	6
13	6
13	6
13	5
12	5
12	5
11	4
9	3
9	3
9	3
8	2
8	0
7	0
7	
7	N = 32

*For feedback, refer to Part D of Preassessment items. See answers on p. 355.

TABLE 14-2. Rating Scale for Oral Presentations

Directions: Student will be marked with a check (√) on a continuum from one end of the line to the other. A check within the broken lines will be roughly equivalent to an average rating.

I.   Delivery

    A.   Lesson Beginning

Attention-getting, indicative of general content.	Beginning apparently planned, but effectiveness somewhat lacking.	Beginning poorly given; rambling statements; apologies.

    B.   Audience Contact

Looks directly at his listeners.	Depends heavily on notes, apparently does not "see" his listeners.	Reads from notes or looks above heads of listeners.

    C.   Enthusiasm

Intensely interested in topic. Stress is "natural" or "spontaneous."	Some interest evident. Occasionally lapses into a monotone.	Lack of interest; just another job to be done.

    D.   Use of Communication Skills

(voice, posture and gestures, grammar, spelling, penmanship)

Communication skills above reproach.	One or two of the communication skills need further development.	Several communication skills need immediate attention.

II. Content

    A.   Major points

Major points stressed and supported with pertinent examples.	Major points not very clearly defined and developed.	Content of the presentation confusing or extremely vague.

    B.   Objectivity

Distinguishes between "facts" and opinion. To-me-ness evident.	Sometimes difficult to distinguish between facts and opinion. Tends to overemphasize own opinions.	Facts and opinions generally indistinguishable. Apparently unaware of projections.

III. Audience Reaction

Students attentive; take notes and ask pertinent questions.	Some audience interest evident. Note-taking and questions are brief.	Little evidence of interest. Only occasionally does a student take notes. Few questions.

IV. General Effectiveness

High overall effectiveness. Appropriate "balance" maintained.	Presentation reasonably effective.	Presentation generally ineffective. Lacks needed "punch."

Scale key

9	8	7	6	5	4	3	2	1

2. Rating scale. Evolve a stanine mark, based on the scale evaluations.*

3. Checklist. Evolve a criterion-referenced assessment (in terms of satisfactory or unsatisfactory) from the following data:

Use of Microscope	*Yes*	*No*
Selects appropriate material for observation		√
Prepares an adequate slide	√	
Initially focuses under low power		√
Later focuses under high power	√	
Keeps both eyes open during observation	√	
Uses light to best advantage	√	
Returns microscope to appropriate place following observation	√	
Returns all materials to appropriate place	√	

Self-assessment Items (answers provided on p. 357)

(1) Lack of class participation (number 1 of the foregoing activity) warrants a zero stanine. Defend or refute.

(2) You have probably noted that some of the individual scales of this rating scale (in the foregoing) were not marked. Why is this?

(3) Why is the foregoing "use of the microscope" unsatisfactory?

(4) What action would you take to make the "microscope use" experience acceptable?

POSTTEST (answers provided on pp. 358–60)

After you have completed the learning activities, complete the posttest and evaluate by checking your answers with those provided at the end of this LAP.

A. List five essential characteristics of evaluation.

1.

2.

3.

4.

5.

B. Place one of the code letters before each of the occasions for evaluation listed below:

CR—Criterion-referenced measure

NR—Norm-referenced measure

1. Evaluating a term paper.

2. Evaluating the student's ability to compare selected documents.

After you have completed this task you may want to check the suggested response, found on p. 360.

3. Evaluating the student's ability to derive implications from a number of selected readings.

4. Evaluating the student's ability to recognize applications of concepts to related areas.

5. Evaluating the student's ability to conduct a selected laboratory experiment using the microscope.

6. Evaluating the student's ability to apply the rules of grammar in a given assignment.

7. Evaluating the student's ability to identify hidden assumptions in an argument.

8. Evaluating the student's ability to apply correct procedures in archery.

9. Evaluating the student's ability to translate a selected passage from Spanish to English.

10. Evaluating the student's ability to contrast conditions leading up to the two world wars.

11. Evaluating the student's ability to show how the theme (responsibility) applies equally to the short story and to each individual today.

12. Evaluating the student's ability to identify selected plants while on a field trip.

C. From the list of normal probability curve "applications," place a check (√) by nine of those that are appropriate.

1. The curve is useful if all students are about average in ability.

2. It is useful when applied to criterion-referenced measures.

3. The curve is based upon the assumption that the scores will pile up in the middle range.

4. If one feels that students should not be failed, then use of the curve is inappropriate.

5. The curve can be applied to any type of data which can be quantified.

6. The curve is a useful tool in deriving relative class standing marks.

7. The curve tells one how valid his test is.

8. The curve indicates the precise number of students who should receive each grade.

9. The curve cannot be employed if some criterion-referenced measures are used.

10. The curve is based upon the assumption that some students will achieve more than others.

11. In order for the curve to be useful, students must possess a wide range of ability.

12. A stanine of 9 always represents an "A."

13. Use of the curve is questionable if fewer than thirty students are involved.

14. Two or three parallel classes may be effectively combined for evaluating on the basis of the curve.

15. Criterion-referenced measures may be assessed on the basis of the curve.

16. The curve is more appropriately applied to the junior high school level than to the high school level.

17. The curve assumes a normal distribution based on a large group.

18. When a substantial number of ethnic minority members are present, the use of the curve may be misleading.

19. Standard scores are based upon the student's relative position on the curve.

20. Use of the curve is inconsistent with today's trend to pass all students if possible.

D. From the provided data derive stanines *and* then letter grades.

Test data

190	119
173	112
165	112
155	112
152	109
150	107
145	102
145	101
139	93
139	92
137	92
136	91
135	90
134	78
129	62
124	54
124	30
123	
120	N = 36

Your successful completion of this LAP indicates competency in one of the most difficult and controversial areas of teaching. Although there is much more to evaluation than is reflected in this experience, you now possess sufficient expertise to cope with the usual problems in the area. If you failed to reach the recommended minimum level of proficiency (about 90 percent), you can profit by reading thoroughly from your related readings and by studying the justification for the answers to both correct and incorrect responses to Parts B and C of the posttest.

ANSWERS TO PREASSESSMENT ITEMS

You can make these items a most valuable learning experience by studying the provided reasons for both correct and incorrect responses. You will note that since Part A has no specific number of correct responses, several additional points (characteristics) have been provided. Since the last part calls for your own constructed responses, your own answers may not be identical to those supplied by the writer. You should be able to decide whether or not your answers are reasonably accurate, however.

A. 1. Evaluation is based upon progress toward projected behavioral outcomes.

2. Evaluation is based upon many sources of data.

3. Evaluation is basically subjective in nature.

4. Statistical tools are useful guides in objectifying normative evaluation.

5. Minimum essentials outcomes are most appropriately evaluated on a criterion-referenced basis; developmental outcomes are most appropriately evaluated on a norm-referenced basis.

6. The learner's ability to achieve must be taken into account.

7. Standard scores add meaning to raw scores in normative evaluation.

8. Evaluation is both formative and summative in nature.

B. 1-CR (It is quite feasible to set up specific criteria for the project; a complex of skills is involved.)

2-CR (Again we are dealing with a set of specific skills that can be observed.)

3-NR (The merits of NATO will vary, depending upon the student's frame of reference.)

4-CR (The quality of a finished project can be evaluated on the basis of specific points or steps in evidence.)

5-NR (Assuming that the evaluation is based upon depth of analysis, it is quite evident that different students might employ different points or combinations thereof. Thus no minimum level of analysis can be readily established.)

6-CR (Here a specific skill [typing] is involved.)

7-NR (In contrasting such complex events, each student is likely to proceed in a different manner. Thus maximum as opposed to minimum progress is sought.)

8-NR (Generally, thought problems can be solved in more than one way and the teacher is usually interested in the processes as well as the final answers. Therefore, different students are likely to proceed in different ways.)

9-NR (Number and kind of "fallacies" in an argument will vary according to individual analysis. No minimum number can be established.)

10-CR   (These are specific, observable skills that have a definite "right" way.)

11-NR   (A demonstration may involve use of a variety of resources and materials; thus no specific criteria can be established in advance.)

12-CR   (Here it is assumed that there are specific, identifiable steps that every student should follow.)

C. 1, 6, 7, 8, 10, 11, 13, 15, 17 (All involve basic concepts associated with the normal curve of probability.)

Reasons for incorrect items

2   (If one desires to assess achievement, it must be presumed that all students have a fairly equal chance at the outset of the learning experience.)

3   (In groups of less than thirty, local distortions in the curve can be expected since, by chance, extremes or unexpected "piling up" of cases are likely to occur.)

4   (Although this is theoretically true, the curve must be applied according to the particular students involved.)

5   (So long as all papers can be serialized from one extreme to the other, the concept of the curve can be applied.)

9   (Standard error of measurement refers to the probable difference between an obtained score and a "true" score. It has been established that the standard error of measurement for a test of up to about forty-nine items is approximately 3, i.e., a score of 45 actually might just as readily have been as low as 43.5 or as high as 46.5. Our use of the curve in evaluation, however, does not provide such information.)

12   (With a group of thirty or more, one can make the reasonable assumption that a bell-shaped curve exists.)

14   (Criterion-referenced measures are in no way influenced by progress of other students.)

16   (Such a procedure itself is based upon a theoretical curve; it does not take into account the relative difficulty of the present test.)

18   (Not superior; merely more economical of the teacher's time.)

19   (Appropriate use of the curve is based upon actual achievement of all students in class. A "hard" or "easy" test would merely influence the size of individual raw scores relative to stanine assessment.)

20   (An "honors class" might be an ideal group for use of the curve if it were of sufficient size (thirty or more). In such a situation all individuals should have a fairly equal chance of success.)

D. 105–107 = 9; 90–104 = 8; 86–89 = 7; 78–85 = 6; 67–77 = 5; 59–66 = 4; 55–58 = 3; 43–54 = 2; 38–39 = 1.

Letter grades for stanines can be adjusted as the teacher judges, on the basis of the situation. The usual grade breakdown, however, follows: 8 and 9 = A; 7 = B; 6, 5, 4 = C; 3 = D; 2 and 1 = E.

ANSWERS TO SELF-ASSESSMENT ITEMS

Self-assessment items are designed to aid you to gain depth of understanding as you proceed through the various learning activities. Most of them do not have single correct answers. For feedback, however, you should compare your own answers with the samples provided here.

A. (1) Such outcomes represent a class of behaviors designed to take the learner as far as he can go toward a destination. Accordingly, class progress will be at many points along the way.

   (2) More economical of one's time. Does not necessitate translating from grades to points when averaging and comparing different test results.

   (3) Measures having the greater variability range actually count more in the evaluation. Thus a result with a range of 30 points, for example, actually counts half as much as one with a range of 60 points.

   (4) Defend. At the turn of the century most of the less able students dropped out before reaching high school. Thus each person had a fairly equal chance of competing with his peers. Today a slow student does not have a chance of success when compared with his more able counterparts.

B. (1) Class marks normally represent goal achievement—not those experiences which lead students toward a goal. Mistakes must be systematically eliminated through formulative evaluation, feedback, and self-assessment.

   (2) Since a rating scale enables the user to assess the qualities of individual performance, it is most readily used as a criterion-referenced scale. Because it may be impossible to establish a minimum level of performance, however, various stanine or grade distributions are often employed. (For example, consider the quality of an oral report.)

   (3) Defend. This is possible since the mere presence or absence (satisfactory or unsatisfactory) of points is assessed.

   (4) Minimum essentials items usually demand an accuracy level of about 90 percent. This level must be reached by all. Norm-referenced items are planned so that a spread of scores will result.

   (5) Norm-referenced assessment: Often an instructor develops certain objectives that only the most industrious and willing students will achieve. When used accordingly, optional work can be used as one dimension of evaluation.

   Criterion-referenced assessment: Option (extra) activities are used to clarify confusing or difficult points for those in need. Thus their completion should play no role in formal evaluation.

   (6) Defend. In classes that include a wide variety of outcomes, representing the different domains, such a system is logically sound.

(7) (a) When dealing with minimum essentials or criterion-referenced measures.

    (b) When the ability range of students is wide.

    (c) When the number of students in the group being evaluated falls well below thirty.

C. (1) Defend. The curve is merely a tool to guide the teacher.

  (2) In norm-referenced measures we desire to distinguish between the weak and the strong students. Ideally, all weak students (lower 27 percent) would provide incorrect answers, while all strong students (top 27 percent) would answer the item correctly.

  (3) "A" students are likely to show up in the "B" category at the end. Likewise, "E" and "D" students may appear in the low "C" category. Thus the final average stanine, in turn, must be subjected to a stanine analysis.

  (4) Not necessarily. If the program is so designed as to permit them to be recycled through the deficiency area(s), this is preferable. Otherwise, they should be failed.

  (5) Ask the student to re-do until it meets the minimum level of expectation.

Optional Activities

D. (1) Almost precludes them from profiting from their own mistakes. In a sense the practice rewards shoddy work.

  (2) The figure is rather arbitrary. Ideally, the standard would be 100 percent. It is recognized, however, that human error must be incorporated into the system.

  (3) Since ideally all learners would answer all criterion-referenced items correctly, the procedure of comparing highs and lows is meaningless.

  (4) This is fallacious, since the test may be harder or easier than expected.

  (5) Refute. Such a system is based upon the assumption that all have a fairly equal opportunity to achieve the objectives of the measure.

E. (1) Refute. The lowest marks fall into the "1" category.

  (2) In individual cases some factors will usually stand out over others. If a particular scale does not seem to apply at the time, it is probably best to leave it blank. In effect, this means that the dimension in question receives an average rating.

  (3) A minimum acceptable level of 85–90 percent is not achieved.

  (4) Teach in the deficient areas and then ask the student to re-do the task.

ANSWERS TO POSTTEST

For most beneficial results you should work through the entire LAP before you check your answers to the posttests. Failure to meet the provided minimum standards probably suggests certain weaknesses that need to be corrected. As with the pretests, you will find supporting reasons for answers. It is hoped that this will serve as desirable feedback in your quest for mastery.

A. 1. Evaluation is based upon progress toward projected behavioral outcomes.

2. Evaluation is based upon many sources of data.

3. Evaluation is basically subjective in nature.

4. Statistical tools are useful guides in objectifying normative evaluation.

5. Minimum essentials outcomes are most appropriately evaluated on a criterion-referenced basis; developmental outcomes are most appropriately evaluated on a norm-referenced basis.

6. The learner's ability to achieve must be taken into account.

7. Standard scores add meaning to raw scores in normative evaluation.

8. Evaluation is both formative and summative in nature.

B. 1-CR (Rather easy to set up specific criteria for such a project.)

2-NR (Such a comparison involves many intangibles which might vary from one student to the next.)

3-NR (Here we are after maximum achievement rather than any readily identifiable minimum number of implications.)

4-NR (The process of making associations or connections to related areas is complex and will vary from one student to another.)

5-CR (There are definite, identifiable steps in conducting an experiment.)

6-CR (The rules of grammar are more or less "cut and dried"; thus a minimum level of achievement can be established.)

7-NR (The identification of "hidden assumptions" will vary, depending upon a student's frame of reference.)

8-CR (When there are identifiable procedures, a criterion-referenced measure can be applied.)

9-CR (There are definite standards for assessing this ability to "translate" one language into another; thus a minimum level of acceptability can be established.)

10-NR (In making such a contrast, a maximum rather than a minimum level of acceptability is sought.)

11-NR (Such a drawing of parallels will vary from student to student; thus no minimum level of acceptability can be established.)

12-CR (Can easily establish a minimum level of acceptability in terms of number of plants identified.)

C. 1, 3, 5, 6, 10, 13, 14, 18, 19 (All represent various applications of the normal curve of probability.)

Reasons for incorrect items

2 (The curve concept is based upon an individual's relative standing in the group. Criterion-referenced measures apply to each student independently of any group.)

4 (The curve does not dictate any particular grade; it is merely a tool, denoting relative class standing.)

7 (The curve is based upon the scores actually made.)

8 (It merely indicates the precise number of students who fall in each category [9 if the stanine system is used or 5 if letter grades are used]. Grades for each category are a matter for the teacher to determine.)

9 (Standard scores, based upon criterion-referenced measures, may be used with standard scores that are norm-referenced-based if desired. All of these can become different dimensions in developing a final average stanine.)

11 (Use of the curve for evaluation purposes is based upon the implicit assumption that each student has a fairly equal chance of achievement.)

12 (If a teacher were to decide that the top scores were not worth more than "B"s or even "C"s, then it would be perfectly acceptable to award such marks for those receiving the "9" stanine.)

15 (The curve applies to relative group progress; criterion-referenced measures apply to individual progress only.)

16 (Age or grade level has no bearing on the use of the curve.)

17 (Assumes each student has a fairly equal chance; the assumption of a normal distribution applies to achievement rather than ability.)

20 (Can still be used to guide the teacher in determining who should pass and who should fail.)

D. 190 = 9; 155-173 = 8; 145-152 = 7; 134-139 = 6; 112-129 = 5; 93-109 = 4; 90-92 = 3; 54-78 = 2; 30 = 1.

Letter grades for stanines can be adjusted as the teacher desires, on the basis of the situation. The usual grade breakdown, however, follows: 8 and 9 = A; 7 = B; 6, 5, 4 = C; 3 = D; 2 and 1 = E.

Sample responses and comments for Learning Activity C, pp. 345-47

1. | 170 - 177 - 9 | |
    | 156 - 157 - 8 | A |

    134 - 148 - 7 - B

    | 114 - 130 - 6 | |
    | 104 - 110 - 5 | C |
    | 83 - 99 - 4 | |

    70 - 81 - 3 - D

    | 58 - 68 - 2 | |
    | 28 - 52 - 1 | E |

2. All student who complete the required activities (90 percent accuracy) should receive a stanine of 9. This includes those who reached the minimum level of acceptability the second time through the program.

Students who do not complete the required activities with 90 percent accuracy should not pass.

3. Final average stanines for a class also must be subjected to a stanine analysis. This is necessary because of statistical regression resulting from averaging of standard scores.*

$$
\left.
\begin{array}{l}
7.8 - 8.3 - 9 \\
7.0 - 7.7 - 8
\end{array}
\right\} \ \text{A}
$$

$$
6.5 - 6.9 - 7 - \quad \text{B}
$$

$$
\left.
\begin{array}{l}
5.9 - 6.4 - 6 \\
5.4 - 5.8 - 5 \\
4.6 - 5.3 - 4
\end{array}
\right\} \ \text{C}
$$

$$
4.3 - 4.5 - 3 - \quad \text{D}
$$

$$
\left.
\begin{array}{l}
3.3 - 4.2 - 2 \\
2.3 - 3.2 - 1
\end{array}
\right\} \ \text{E}
$$

4. This task merely involves supplying extra stanines for the midterm and the final examinations, adding all stanines for each student, and then dividing by the number of scores for each student. Note that stanine averages for those who completed optional work would be calculated by dividing by a different number than for those who did not complete such work.

Sample responses for Learning Activity E, pp. 349–51.

2. Checks on a rating scale are used as a rough guide in assigning an average stanine. A stanine of 6 or 7 seems reasonably accurate. This is derived by considering the left extreme of the continuum as representing a 9 and the right extreme as representing a 1.

3. Answers would depend upon your accuracy level. On the basis of the usual level of 90 percent, the student would fail.

In certain critical areas (such as this one) an accuracy level of 100 percent might be established. Thus failure to meet any one of the established standards (criteria) would make the work unsatisfactory.

SUPPLEMENTARY SOURCES

The following sources may be used in lieu of the Hoover texts or, preferably, as supplementary to them. Generally they are consistent with the models provided in the LAPs of this module. As such, the references do not represent all of the most recent references in the area; rather, they constitute selected references designed to broaden or expand needed background information.

Baker, E. L., "Cooperation and the State of the World in Criterion-Referenced Tests," *Educational Horizons*, 52: 193-196 (Summer, 1974).

Blachford, J. S., "Teacher Views Criterion-Referenced Tests," *Today's Education*, 64: 36 (March, 1975.)

Clark, D. C., "Objectives-based Evaluation: Ending Up Undernourished," *Educational Leadership*, 15: 27-30 (March, 1975).

Collins, Harold W., and others, *Educational Measurement and Evaluation: A Worktext*, 2nd ed. (Glenview, Ill.: Scott, Foresman and Co., 1976).

The effect of statistical regression is a "squeezing toward the mean" of extreme scores.

Ebel, Robert L., *Essentials of Educational Measurement*, rev. ed. (Englewood Cliffs, N.J.: Prentice-Hall, Inc., 1972).

Engelhart, Max D., *Improving Classroom Testing: What Research Says to the Teacher*, No. 31 (Washington, D.C.: National Education Association).

Flynn, J. M., and E. R. Simco, "Individualizing Evaluation and Individualized Learning," *Educational Technology*, 36–38 (Nov., 1974).

Hoover, Kenneth H., *The Professional Teacher's Handbook*, 2nd ed. (Boston: Allyn and Bacon, Inc., 1976).

Hoover, Kenneth H., and Paul M. Hollingsworth, *Learning and Teaching in the Elementary School*, 2nd ed. (Boston: Allyn and Bacon, Inc., 1975).

Humphrey, B. J., and A. McAloon, "New Trends in Evaluation: A Symposium," *Educational Horizons*, 52: 158-201 (Summer, 1974).

Leary, J. L., "Grading Controversy, How Do You Meet It?" *Educational Leadership*, 33: 25-27 (Oct., 1975).

Sax, Gilbert, *Principles of Educational Measurement and Evaluation* (Belmont, Calif.: Wadsworth Publishing Co., 1974).

Terwillinger, James S., *Assigning Grades to Students* (Glenview, Ill.: Scott, Foresman and Co., 1971).

Index